CLOWNING AND AUTHORSHIP IN EARLY MODERN THEATRE

To early modern audiences, the "clown" was much more than a minor play character. A celebrity performer, he was a one-man side-show whose interactive entertainments – face-pulling, farce inter-ludes, jigs, rhyming contests with the crowd – were the main event. Clowning epitomized a theatre that was heterogeneous, improvised, participatory, and irreducible to dramatic texts. How, then, did those texts emerge? Why did playgoers buy books that deleted not only the clown, but them as well? Challenging the narrative that clowns were "banished" by playwrights like Shakespeare and Jonson, Richard Preiss argues that clowns such as Richard Tarlton, Will Kemp, and Robert Armin actually made playwrights possible – bridging, through the publication of their routines, the experience of "live" and scripted performance. *Clowning and Authorship* tells the story of how, as the clown's presence decayed into print, he bequeathed the new categories around which theatre would organize: the author, and the actor.

RICHARD PREISS is Associate Professor of English at the University of Utah, where he teaches undergraduate and graduate courses on Shakespeare, early modern drama, and Renaissance literature. He has edited *The Tempest: Shakespeare in Performance* (2008), and his essays have appeared in publications including *Renaissance Drama*, *Shakespeare Yearbook*, and *From Performance to Print in Shakespeare's England*. He is also a contributor to the forthcoming collections *The Cambridge Guide to the Worlds of Shakespeare* and *Early Modern Theatricality*.

CLOWNING AND AUTHORSHIP IN EARLY MODERN THEATRE

RICHARD PREISS

CAMBRIDGE
UNIVERSITY PRESS

CAMBRIDGE
UNIVERSITY PRESS

University Printing House, Cambridge CB2 8BS, United Kingdom

One Liberty Plaza, 20th Floor, New York, NY 10006, USA

477 Williamstown Road, Port Melbourne, VIC 3207, Australia

314-321, 3rd Floor, Plot 3, Splendor Forum, Jasola District Centre, New Delhi - 110025, India

103 Penang Road, #05-06/07, Visioncrest Commercial, Singapore 238467

Cambridge University Press is part of the University of Cambridge.

It furthers the University's mission by disseminating knowledge in the pursuit of
education, learning and research at the highest international levels of excellence.

www.cambridge.org
Information on this title: www.cambridge.org/9781108438773

First published 2014
First paperback edition 2022

A catalogue record for this publication is available from the British Library

Library of Congress Cataloging in Publication data
Preiss, Richard.
Clowning and Authorship in Early Modern Theatre / Richard Preiss.
pages cm
Includes bibliographical references and index.
ISBN 978-1-107-03657-4 (hardback)
1. English drama–Early modern and Elizabethan, 1500–1600–History and criticism.
2. Fools and jesters in literature. 3. Clowns in literature. I. Title.
PR658.F7P75 2014
822′.309353–dc23
2013033961

ISBN 978-1-107-03657-4 Hardback
ISBN 978-1-108-43877-3 Paperback

For Jessica

what larks

Contents

Figures

Acknowledgments

This book is about how audiences make theatre; here are the audiences that made the book. Stephen Orgel helped me find my way to this book, and to the person I needed to be to write it. Those are debts I can never repay. In a few of these sentences I can hear his voice, and they are my favorite ones. My other teachers at Stanford, Jennifer Summit, David Riggs, Seth Lerer, Patricia Parker, and Martin Evans, were exemplars of learning, generosity, and professionalism. The scholars I met in Stanford's Renaissance Reading Group have become my extended family: David Goldstein, Shawn Kairschner, Elizabeth Pentland, Carolyn Sale, Amy Tigner, and Deanne Williams. Anston Bosman and Bradin Cormack painstakingly read drafts and gave surgical advice. Jim Marino has shared with me more conference panels, hotel rooms, and wisdom, than I can sum.

At the University of Utah, I have been fortunate to find colleagues whose rigor is matched by their conviviality, and who make thanking friends separately redundant. I am especially grateful to Matt Basso, Scott Black, Craig Dworkin, Andy Franta, Lela Graybill, Howard Horwitz, Anne Jamison, Jay Jordan, Dennis Kezar, Stacey Margolis, Susan Miller, Ella Myers, Matt Potolsky, Paisley Rekdal, Angela Smith, Tom Stillinger, Kathryn Stockton, and, most of all, Barry Weller. Vince Pecora, Chair of the Department of English during the writing of this book, and Robert Newman, Dean of the College of Humanities, were steadfast supporters. I hope my efforts vindicate their optimism.

An embryonic version of Chapter 5 appeared in *From Performance to Print in Shakespeare's England* (Palgrave, 2006). I am indebted to audiences at the Shakespeare Association of America, the Modern Language Association, the Group for Early Modern Cultural Studies, the Huntington Library, the University of California Berkeley, the University of Oregon, the University of Western Ontario, and the University of Utah's Tanner Humanities Center for their responses. I have profited from the attentive reading, mentorship, and research suggestions of too many colleagues to list, including Douglas Brooks, Brooke Conti, Bill Germano, Barbara Hodgdon, Peter Holland, Zack Lesser, Jeremy Lopez, James Mardock, Jeffrey Masten, Paul Menzer, Tiffany Stern, Holger Syme, Henry Turner, Sarah Wall-Randell, and Will West. I received generous funding from the Stanford English Department, the Mabelle McLeod Lewis Memorial Fund, and the University of Utah English Department.

Sarah Stanton believed in this book when it was still rough, and gave me time to polish it; she knows where I would be without her. My anonymous readers at Cambridge University Press told me things I needed to hear, and saw what I could not see for myself. This book is immeasurably better for their judgment. Rebecca Taylor, Anna Lowe, and Jenny Slater were excellent production coordinators, and Wendy Toole performed first-rate copy-editing. Whatever errors remain are my own.

My parents, George and Jolan Preiss, have suffered patiently my reluctance to talk about how this book was going; I am now ready to talk about it. I thank them, along with Tina Straley, Wilt Straley, and Meg Cole, for their trust. David Preiss offered perspective and comic relief. Better than anyone, Jessica Straley knows how little like a clown I am, and how much. Her wit, brilliance, and strength allowed me to finish this book, and are the reason I want to. Thanks to her – and to the two beautiful sons we will share by the time it appears – I know that it can never be the best thing I have made.

Introduction
The play is not the thing

This is only accidentally a book about clowns. It began as an investigation of the history of early modern dramatic authorship, and an attempt at the prehistory of this category we need in order to make our current histories more coherent. Such a prehistory, I claim, involves not just changing patterns of dramatic publication, but underlying changes in the nature and meaning of theatrical performance itself. And if that prehistory involves performance, as we will see, then it passes pivotally through the figure of the stage clown. What makes this book challenging to write, however, is the fact that hardly anyone today – scholars of early English drama included – quite understands any longer what the term "clown" means, or what it meant to playhouse audiences in the period. This is not a fault; it is a legacy.

When we hear the word "clown" – if it does not immediately evoke the painted face, frizz wig, red nose, floppy shoes, and tattered hat of the half-hobo, half-circus-freak Victorian pantomime descended from Grimaldi, Pierrot, Punchinello, and Harlequin – we usually think, in the Renaissance theatrical context eclipsed by this lineage, of specific dramatic characters.[1] Asked to list some of them, a student of Shakespeare might name Bottom, Dogberry, Launce, Speed, Gobbo, Costard, Grumio, Dromio, Touchstone, Feste, Lavatch, Cloten, Thersites, Autolycus, perhaps (daringly) Falstaff, *Hamlet's* Gravedigger, *Lear's* Fool; there is a sometimes troubling distinction in here between "clown" and "fool," but we will come to that in due course. If they were versed in Shakespeare's contemporaries, they might also mention Robin and Rafe from *Doctor Faustus*, Miles from *Friar Bacon and Friar Bungay*, Cob from *Every Man In His Humour* and Buffone from *Every Man Out*, Passarello from *The Malcontent*. Beaumont's *Knight of the Burning Pestle* is a trickier case, because here the most readily identifiable clowns, George and Nell, are – tellingly – members of the audience.

Nevertheless, such experimental deviations from type serve only to confirm the type's basic traits. Clowns are, in accordance with our present-day usage, essentially comic; clowns are, in accordance with the strict early modern sense of the term, generally rustic. They have names like Hob, Nobs, Strumbo, Booby, Derick, Curtis, Peter, Slipper, Mouse, Much, Jenkin, Simkin, Sim, Swash, Elbow, Clem, Crotchet, Hodge, Fiddle, Frisco, Jeer, Simpleton, Bottle, Bubble – a representative but fractional list[2] – and they personify this largely monosyllabic crudity in more or less the same way. They are clods, dolts, wags, oafs, bumpkins, shepherds, villagers, drunks, hired hands, tinkers, tradesmen, servants, porters, pages, occasionally constables or criminals, the people who fill the gaps of a society and who sometimes are those gaps themselves: strangers to metropolitan life and its manners, but wise enough to critique them; strangers to the nuances of language, but witty enough to manipulate them; strangers to the duplicity of human desire and the intricacy of social relations, but clever enough to survive them; strangers to the world of the play in which they find themselves, and happy enough to remark on that fact. If their names are a vision of life reduced to atomic simplicity, an encyclopedia of household objects, body parts, noises, instruments, and foodstuffs, by the same token they each attain a stubborn uniqueness, unwilling or unable to surrender their quirky individualism to the forces of social pretense. And the astonishing frequency with which their name is given simply as "Clown" or "the Clown," not just in speech prefixes but in *dramatis personae*, tells us we are looking at a fixture of early modern dramaturgy. We know we are looking at a clown when he is speaking prose – and an intensely colloquial, carnal, oath-laced prose at that; when he is lower in rank than his interlocutors; when his name is English rather than the Greek, Latin, or Italian of his superiors; when he is tripping over his words, tripping over his feet, tripping over someone else's feet, eating, expressing a desire to eat, being called "honest fellow" by someone about to give him instructions, miscarrying the most rudimentary of those instructions, being beaten or chased for his stupidity and impertinence, complaining of his abuse, or issuing a verbal stream of self-reference whose incomprehensibility might be alleviated if we could see the physical antics that accompanied it. We know we are looking at a clown when he considers himself the hero of his own story, yet is all too aware that it is not his own; we may find that story a refreshment from the main plot, or even surprisingly relevant to it, but it is never the main plot itself. His marginality amuses us, and we marginalize that amusement.

Above all, we know we are looking at a clown when what we are doing is reading, and when what we are reading is a play. Playbooks make up the overwhelming majority of our archive of early modern theatre: texts were the medium by which theatre preserved itself, and whenever we recon-struct it, we do so through their logic. Nowhere has this been truer than in critical accounts of the clown, which until well past the mid-twentieth century – when interest in this sort of study waned, and for better or worse became amalgamated with the more politicized field of "popular culture" – formed an extension of arguments for the "aesthetic unity" of English Renaissance drama.[3] Taking their cue from Sidney's *Defence of Poesie*, which condemned the tendency of the public playhouse to con-fuse the refined comedy of "delight" with the vulgar comedy of "laugh-ter," critics have spent much of the past two centuries trying to vindicate canonical poets from the equally canonical charge of "mingling Kings & Clownes, not because the matter so carrieth it: but thrust[ing] in Clownes by head & shoulders to play a part in maiesticall matters, with neither decencie, nor discretion."[4] This – along with Hamlet's advice to the play-ers to "let those that play your clownes speake no more than is set down for them," advocating instead a "purpose of playing" that "was and is, to holde as twere the Mirrour up to nature" – is the derogatory state-ment around which post-Romantic discussions of the clown crystallized, and the response was to argue that "the matter" did indeed "carry it," or more accurately that clowns carried the whole matter.[5] Since Thomas de Quincey first articulated it, there have been various elaborations of the "comic relief" hypothesis – still the reflex answer of college undergradu-ates today – according to which, in its most robust version, the presence of low comedy in tragedy worked to mitigate (or amplify) the intensity of audience emotion, whose exact humoral balance was necessary to achieve Aristotelian *catharsis*. This notion of clowns as physiological pres-sure valves, of course, does nothing to explain their ubiquity in comedy as well, thereby leaving arbitrary their relation to the *mimesis* whose affective force they supposedly helped to calibrate.[6] If it did not especially matter what genre of play clowns were in, it becomes harder to argue, from this functional perspective, that clowns especially mattered – and that they were not, as Pope and Johnson had (with Sidney) snobbishly maintained, simply an excrescence, the playwright's regrettable capitulation to the demands of a boorish public.[7]

The New Criticism, in turn, sought to integrate clowns into those *mimeses*, positing tiered networks of signification through which plays conveyed their meaning. Seminally established in essays like Jonas Barish's "The Double

Plot in *Volpone*" (1953) and Richard Levin's "Elizabethan 'Clown' Subplots" (1966), this effort consisted of structural analyses of how plays employ resonant exchanges between seemingly segregated tragic, historic, or romantic "main plots" and low-comic "subplots" – linked by motif, wordplay, situational parallel, parodic inversion – to achieve the grander, socially inclusive expression of a single thematic architecture.[8] Far from introducing a note of discord, the clown refuted Sidney's castigation by being the active principle of drama's didactics: he was the play's moral made accessible, reduced from esoteric verse to the hard-headed vocabulary of prose, dumbshow, and common experience. He was not an anomaly to be dismissed or apologized; rather, like his classical antecedent in the *servus* type of Greek New Comedy and Roman drama, he was precisely what defined a nascent cultural institution trying to bridge diverse audiences, and what had enabled its greatest triumph – a unified vision of both art and nation.

Several other, more sophisticated critical schools have since arisen that use clown characters variously to elaborate or complicate this synthesis: Robert Weimann's studies of how the purely "presentational" performance traditions on which they drew helped to reinforce the Shakespearean drama's increasingly complex representational systems, for instance, making the play an organic collaboration between author and actor; Richard Helgerson's more pessimistic view of those same plays as staging the breakdown of that collaboration; the complementary readings of Marxist critics, finally, for whom the clowns' roles give voice to genuinely plebeian desires subversive of the plays' dominant ideologies.[9] We shall have occasion to revisit each of these perspectives in greater detail. For now, however, we must begin by recognizing the anachronistic assumption under which all of these approaches continue to labor, which renders them – however disparate their conclusions – methodologically equivalent. From the Romantics onward, every theory of the clown has taken at face value his status as a character, seeking to reconcile his meaning with that of the overarching aesthetic structure in which we find him, "the play." This is an understandable assumption: playbooks are what we have, and plays, along with everything in them, have meanings.

Thanks to the New Historicism, Cultural Materialism, and allied poststructural movements, we have replaced the formalist fantasy that every play possesses only one meaning with an attention to the ideological frictions that texts, as culturally embedded productions, continuously negotiate and perform. But the autonomy of dramatic texts – and how we can speak of their ability to "perform" things, as if they perform themselves – remains nevertheless uninterrogated, the invisible lens through which all the foregoing accounts of the clown are focused. As a result, we have merely replaced one mode of reading with several, when if clowning ultimately suggests a tension between text and performance, it should prompt us to ask why we "read" theatre at all, and whether playbooks are really the place to look for theatre. The clown, in other words, is the stray thread that potentially unravels the whole fabric, by revealing the successive interpretive fictions our dependence on playbooks has dictated. By subordinating the clown to the play, we presuppose a superstructure of representation to which he exists in a necessarily supportive relation: because plays have meanings, the clown – whether therapeutically, thematically, or oppositionally – must have one too. Whatever that meaning, furthermore, we presuppose its fixity: because the clown is so stable a type, there must be a single theory to explain how plays use him, as surely as there is a single theory to explain how plays work. We presuppose that plays were established communication technologies whose dominant language was always mimesis, a hierarchy to which the non-mimetic was merely an adjunct and never a rival. We presuppose that *plays* were the dominant commodity of theatre to begin with, that a play inherently possessed a commercial legibility and experiential integrity sufficient to be perceived as, and afterward rendered as, a text. We presuppose that what audiences paid to see were, thus, essentially *texts*, and that they paid to be moved, diverted, dazzled, pained, surprised, edified, humbled, ennobled, transported, and transformed by them. We presuppose that the texts we have today reflect what audiences wanted; we presuppose that they reflect – indeed, could ever reflect – what audiences actually got.

In doing these things, we are perpetuating a project begun four hundred years ago by – and in – the early modern playhouse itself, for institutional reasons borne out by the very survival, study, and pedagogy of the texts we unthinkingly treat today as complete, transparent records of its production. Those texts were not the first fruits of that project: early modern playgoers themselves were, insofar as it plotted an eventual convergence between the phenomenology of performance and the phenomenology of reading, the mutual interchangeability of live and textual events. That is why, for most of those past four hundred years, our theories of "the clown" have devolved onto theories of the play. Regardless of whether we choose to view plays as the willed creation of an individual mind or as the spontaneous emanation of a cultural moment, we still conflate them with the textual deposits they left behind, and conflate that residue in turn with the first half of the word "play-house" – as the sum total of what theatres were about, as if such discrete aesthetic objects as "plays" were the base unit of theatrical experience, and the theatrical transaction as clearly defined then as it is for us now. We do so because those texts have predisposed all of us to be, as suggested at the outset, students of "Shakespeare," or Marlowe, or Jonson, rather than of the early modern theatrical landscape in its fullest and thickest sense. As a result, a stage figure whom Elizabethan and Jacobean audiences would have associated far more intimately with the organizing agency of the theatrical event has become for us reducible merely to a minor species of dramatic character, his theatrical role coterminous with his fictional one, evacuated of any historical specificity or function beyond the words accorded him on a printed page.

This is a remarkable outcome, since the historical reality was the reverse. As we all know, it was dramatic authors who began as anonyms, their identity the most obscured from audiences' apprehensions. And, as we are often told – usually without connecting the two – it was the comedians, like Richard Tarlton and Will Kemp, who were the first celebrities of the early modern stage. If it is not to be found in their limited duties in plays, what were clowns doing to earn such renown, and how did they and authors come to trade places? What must have been the real shape of early modern performance, and what was at stake in clowning that demanded – and at the same time enabled – this transposition? And yet, if the problem clowning poses is the degree to which it exceeded the written, where do we look for evidence of a process whose constraints place it beyond the reach of those texts – playbooks – that, despite being the readiest sources we might consult, were also its end products? How helpful is the information plays give us, after all, when the two most basic facts about the clown that we glean from them are contradictory: that what was seemingly always getting him into trouble was doing precisely what he was supposed to do – talking to the audience?

If plays tell us anything about this shift, indeed, they tell us that it was a far more complex negotiation than they alone can, or perhaps wish to, record. A playbook is not a performance: it is the retrospective fantasy of one, abstracted from the play's synchronic and diachronic stage lives, privileging certain voices over others, retroactively framing playgoing as a continuous, monological, readerly experience. When we do theatre history through playbooks, we are looking through an artifact *of* theatre history, a filter biased toward the values that constructed it – and designed to make that bias undetectable, to naturalize its representation. In the case of clowning, they invariably turn theatre history into literary criticism, insofar as playbooks represent plays as books, and theatre as plays, autotelic verbal systems into whose matrix the clown can be assimilated. In so doing, of course, they also obscure what conditioned their own existence: how playing came to be equated with writing in the first place, its integrity stabilized and its agency fixable, such that dramatic authorship could be foregrounded and performance excluded.

The evidentiary obstacles to a study of stage clowning thus become part of its object. To recover clowning from beyond the margins of printed plays is inescapably to *account* for that marginalization – and with it, the origin of those margins themselves, the constructedness of print as a medium of theatrical preservation and consumption. If early modern theatre starts with clowns and ends with (or at least ends gesturing toward) authors, the middle term that bridges them is textuality. Ironically, because it can make only limited use of playbooks, a history of the stage clown *becomes* a history of the playbook: the former entails the latter, because it entails discovering just how *unlike* our playbooks early modern theatre really was – and hence just how unlikely its subsequent translation into them was, and what discursive work it took to make the two conversible.

This book has two axes of inquiry, then, an archival and a theoretical one, which, while split more or less across its midpoint, remain organically interlocked. Since its theoretical concern is the emergence of dramatic textuality itself, furthermore – not the dramatic authorship on playbook title pages, but the genesis of those playbooks – its archival excavations are correspondingly deep. Chapters 1 and 2 attempt to recover the conventions of clown stage practice, which requires recovering the elements of early modern performance – and in the process, revising its fundamental dynamics. In Chapter 1, "What audiences did," I begin by observing that early modern audiences did not passively consume drama as we now do. They demanded to participate, registering their pleasure and displeasure alike with violent, disruptive intensity. Hardly a utopian space of authorlessness either, the playhouse environment was one of authorial competition, wherein spectators vied aggressively with both the players and each other for possession of the stage. Surveying the extant evidence of audience behavior, it becomes possible to see the underlying content of "theatre" as precisely the struggle to determine the content of theatre. In their compulsive invasions of the stage – invasions physical as well as vocal, as uniformly distributed across the geography and socioeconomic spectra of early modern London as they were ubiquitous throughout the period – playgoers behaved not as consumers, but as collaborative producers. To them, "the play" was not a static, self-contained verbal artifact, but an occasion for spontaneous social exchange. "Plays" were merely a subset of "playing": far from commodities capable of being concretized in a fixed form or of ascription to any single creative agency, they were scenes of contest over that very form, and over that very agency.

And yet, as the remainder of the chapter illustrates, this immediately confronts us with a problem. Play*books* represent those contests as if their agency were pre-decided – indeed, as if those contests had never taken place. Printed playbooks were a relatively late institutional innovation: they began to proliferate only in the mid-1590s, nearly twenty years after the inception of dedicated playhouses. And viewed in relation to the theatrical performances that preceded them, they are incipiently authorial productions. Collapsing the plurality and multiplicity of theatrical events into monological, atemporal objects – now containing only what the players said and did (or perhaps merely intended to do), as if in a vacuum – playbooks silently reconfigured their material into literary property. And people – largely the *same* people who had exercised their agency so strenuously at the playhouse – bought them. How did they recognize these two phenomena – "the play" as both live, malleable social event and as ahistorical, impermeable text – to be related? Why did they purchase representations of theatrical experience that erased them? Before they could even acquire authors, how did plays become capable of existing on paper? In their increasing consumption of such texts, playgoers seemed to understand that theatre existed *before* performance, and thus could survive beyond it – that performance was not its originary moment, and that plays possessed their own independent, textual authority. The sheer fact of a playbook cannot retroactively teach this. Such a discursive remapping, rather, could only occur in the contact zone *between* performance and print, where each domain might gradually take on the character of the other. If playgoers were learning that plays could also be books, I argue, the place they were learning it had to be at the playhouse – where plays were emphatically *not* books.

What begins as the motivating question of this study, then, by the end of Chapter 1 becomes its core paradox. If the problem with dramatic textuality was its disjunction with the reception conventions of performance, the solution likewise lay in performance – amid those very same conventions, as resistant to textual authority as they were constant. For most of Chapter 2 it will seem as though clowning, in its response to these audience pressures, merely widened the gap between text and theatrical event. Indeed, this tendency conforms to our traditional view of clowning: namely, that clowns were transgressive, anti-textual agents, in league with the audience against the rule of the author. Yet this impression again derives anachronistically from their appearances *in* plays, where such rebellion is foreclosed: whatever the clown says or does there has, of course, already been absorbed into a text. The clown's *theatrical* function, on the other hand, vastly exceeded his token role in the play – unsettling, in fact, the centrality of the play itself – and was fundamentally disciplinary in its conception. Unlike the flattened, uniform textual landscapes of playbooks, the theatrical program consisted of a medley of interstitial, interactive entertainments, whose goal was to check the agonistic energies of the audience by giving them an individual opponent. The stage clown, whose origins are here traced not to the "Vice" character of Tudor morality (as has long been supposed) but to the sacrificial folk-motif of the Jack-a-Lent, developed a repertoire of sadomasochistic performance genres – face-pulling preludes, slapstick interludes, jig postludes, rhyming contests with the crowd – suited to this task. In "Send in the clown," I systematically reassemble that repertoire, incorporating along the way the exploits of lesser-known comedians such as John Singer, Thomas Greene, John Shanke, Timothy Reed, William Kendall, and others, but primarily through the career of Richard Tarlton (*c.* 1553–88), its undisputed pioneer. In the facial contortions with which he began the show, for instance, the clown made himself a grotesque extension of the audience's will, only to convert that collectivity into a sudden statement of defiance; in the custom of "themes" with which the show ended, playgoers bombarded him with versified prompts, with spontaneous barbs volleyed back and forth until the loser was shamed into departure; still other evanescent ludic forms – the "merriment," the jig – interrupted, and defined, the day's offerings. For many playgoers, indeed, the play was what interrupted *them*: it was an afterthought, and the clown, the ringmaster who transcended it, was the main attraction.

   Clowning thus met short-term institutional needs while exacerbating longer-term ones. He embodied the authority of the playing company, ritually negotiating their right to the stage, but at the expense of the integrity of performance; he became the "protoauthor" of the Elizabethan stage, his name motivating and governing its earliest textual documentation, but such documentation merely reinforced the paradigm of theatre as instantaneous, polyvocal event. Rendering every performance particulate, dialogic, and unique, the clown personified the heterogeneous, improvisatory dimension of theatre that playgoers craved – everything, in other words, inimical to its perception as literary commodity. In that protoauthorship and its radical concentration, however, lay enormous potential. If the clown was the epicenter of theatre's "liveness," only he could deactivate it – and he could do so only from within his own performance, by merging it with writing. As we might expect – only more so – the clown was the most un-booklike thing about theatre. So what happened if the clown became a book?

That is the fulcrum of this study's thesis. The way around the paradox is through it: if the clown necessitates a history of dramatic textuality, that history in turn requires him. Challenging the received narrative in which theatre "banished" its clowns in favor of more stable, iterable dramatic products – somehow transforming itself, unilaterally and overnight, from a performance-centered experience to a textual one – I argue that clowns *created* those very products, installing a hierarchy of text over performance at precisely the site of their maximum dislocation. Before theatre could have individual authors, it had to claim institutional ownership of itself, from its audience; in order to become a book, theatre had to unfold as if it were *already* a book, making visible in performance its prior origin in writing. Our word for this immanent, phantom book is "the script," and our tacit consciousness of it during a performance accounts for nearly every major difference between early modern reception habits and our own. The missing link between a theatre whose audience instinctively participates and one whose audience instinctively consumes is that theatre's legibility as pre-produced, as something purely recititative and rehearsed. Today, we expect performers to mask such "scriptedness," because we are all too aware of it; Elizabethans needed it revealed, because to them it was a new idea.

The remainder of this study tells the story of that idea – the idea that theatre was scripted, its textuality always present in its performance, and its performance, as a result, capable of being absented from those texts – from, I argue, its inception. Certainly I do not pretend that plays were hitherto unscripted, though the degree to which even late sixteenth-century drama seems to have called for improvisation is often overlooked.[10] Rather, at stake here was the *awareness* of that scriptedness, the audience's ability to *distinguish* the play from its own contributions – a distinction the expressly improvised occasions which surrounded and pervaded the play made difficult to draw. In the extradramatic games, the audience participated; in the drama proper, the audience also participated. What was the difference? Why was one an open text and the other closed, one porous and the other permanent? Eradicating improvisation from the play – much less the clown from it – was thus never the point, because the clown was more than the play. His own man, his potential to generate theatre was founded elsewhere, and he carried it with him. Because he already embodied "unscriptedness," no one could script him. And for this reason, a universal condition of scriptedness needed the clown to install it – by scripting himself.

To be sure, the particular clowns I examine did so not out of altruistic loyalty to institutional imperatives. As we will see, the solitary nature of their stage practice often made for uneasy relations with their companies – and also, crucially, with the audiences on whom their stage practice too much depended. Because he worked directly with the crowd, the clown felt earlier and more acutely than any other theatre professional the pressure to delineate that work. Ironically, the same autonomy that in performance made him "his own man," above the prescriptions of poets, subjected him before anyone else to the anxieties of authorship. The impetus for theatrical authorship thus began not with playwrights but with players themselves, those whose labor was most proximal to the audience, and who most urgently needed texts to materialize, theorize, and individuate it.

That moment can be traced to the growing entanglement of clown stage practice and print publication during the late 1580s, 1590s, and early 1600s – not coincidentally, the same moment (or even just before) printed playbooks began to appear in significant numbers. As clowns began to compile and publish (or have published for them) their stage routines, the interplay of media sparked discursive conflict. How can a book purport to capture and reproduce authentic personalities and "live" events? Once the book exists, how do those personalities and events avoid reproducing it? Which was real, and which the simulation? If the clown could be scripted, what did his performance mean, or his audience's relation to it? And if he could be scripted, what wasn't? In an early modern precursor of what Jean Baudrillard calls "mediatization," theatre came to be experienced dissociatively and self-referentially – a process that attacked it at its most basic circuit, progressively complicating and diffracting the subject positions needed to comprehend it.[11] Was the clown a writer who also performed what he wrote? Or was he a performer who merely spoke what he had written? He could not be both performer and writer at once, simultaneously present and absent, simultaneously an embodied agent and merely the bodily extension of textual agency: the clown, I show, did not so much disappear as theoretically disintegrate. In the fragmentation of the multiple identities he had hitherto sustained, he seeded the new, more sharply defined production categories around which modern theatre would coalesce: the author, and the actor.

In each of the subsequent three case-study chapters, the clown's migration into a textual space is seen to alter the meaning of

performance – retroactively, concurrently, or prospectively – furthering
the conceptual breakdown of improvisation, immediacy, and presence as
coherent possibilities of theatrical experience. Chapter 3, "Wiring Richard
Tarlton," studies the series of pamphlets that posthumously appropriated
Tarlton's stage persona upon his death in 1588, and that adapted it to the
marketing needs of popular prose. Tarlton's "ghost," irrepressibly returned
from the afterlife, returned not to the stage but expressly to the arena of
print, becoming a narratorial device for collections of Continental *fabliaux* and a mouthpiece for contemporary social critique. Yet in importing
that persona across media, these spinoffs profoundly revised its relation
to representation. Offering nostalgic playgoers continued access to the
clown's wit, books like *Tarltons Newes out of Purgatorie* (1590) and *Kind-
Harts Dreame* (1592) ostensibly aim to naturalize the alienated experience of reading by packaging it in the spontaneous intimacy of theatre.
When this pseudo-Tarlton's canned ventriloquizations are inevitably, and
increasingly pointedly, unable to deliver on that promise, however – at
one point his ghost announces he will improvise a song, then claims to
have laryngitis – they reveal an altogether contradictory motive: to materialize a theatre just like print, no less dependent on textual transmission
and recirculated agency, in which even Tarlton had always merely recited
someone else's lines. As his failed authorship gradually reassigned him to
the category it was itself creating – the "actor" – the clown's verbal generativity could now also be expropriated as a purely literary operation.
The figure who would succeed him as a posthumous author function was
not another player, but the playwright Robert Greene. Foregrounding the
question of whether theatre had a soul, and of where it resided, Tarlton's
ghost dislodged that soul from the performer, making it possible for the
first time to theorize the clown as just another actor, and the actor as just
an empty body.

Chapter 4, "Nobody's business," goes on to consider more deliberate,
in vivo acts of self-textualization – meant, initially, to affirm the clown's
relation to performance rather than rupture it. Will Kemp, the principal comedian of the Chamberlain's Men, is usually thought of as the stalwart defender of folk theatre who abandoned the new Globe to protest
its intolerance of improvised forms; so, at least, he seems to have thought
of himself. The extensive written record of his celebrity, however, much
of it by him, tells a different tale. Kemp's repertoire centered on the jig,
a postlude of dance and farce which he developed into its own elaborate, narrative form – and which he began serially to publish, in the early
1590s, under his own name. This self-capitalizing impulse, not clowning

in general, was the motive for the company's abolition of the jig, and with it Kemp. As *Hamlet* both analyzes and elegizes his departure, I argue, he could not see in his resistance to one kind of script his adherence to another. And when he forfeited the shelter of the stage, that domineering, possessive sensibility was set to collide with his participatory performance practice. The rest of the chapter reads *Kemps Nine Daies Wonder* (1600), Kemp's documentary of an entrepreneurial morris dance from London to Norwich, as the real-time drama of that collision. As Kemp struggles to reconcile the event's incompatible identities – both private venture and public festival, both labor and holiday – he progressively recoils from the very carnival he describes, withdrawing into a textual solitude from which he can commodify "his" entertainment only by imagining it free of community. He thus emerges as a tragic figure, his career bisected by the moment when the choice between clowning and authorship finally became irrevocable – a choice that Kemp, Hamlet-like, came to under-stand only after he had already made it.

In addition to miscoloring the tensions behind Kemp's exit, the cessa-tion of jigs at the Globe in 1599 has led us to believe that early modern stage clowning as a whole came to an end with it. This has given rise to the theory that, in one swoop, playwrights somehow displaced clowns by symbolically repudiating them (Hal's banishment of Falstaff in *2 Henry IV* being the paradigmatic example), heralding the actual banishment of clowns themselves. Nothing could be further from the truth: not only did clowning continue to flourish at other playhouses, but even at the Globe jigs eventually returned. The clown was not the play's to banish; he was not just a dramatic character, and in the satellite entertainments with which the play was still ringed, his incitement of audience intercourse remained in perpetual demand. Robert Armin, Kemp's successor, seems to have internalized more than any clown of his age the encroachment of the audience upon performance, and more than any resorted to text-uality to dissever them. The first clown to view his stage practice as part of a cohesive authorial strategy, he used it to banish not just himself, but that very audience. Chapter 5, "Private practice," focuses on Armin's *Quips Upon Questions* (1600), a compilation of his "themes." How are "themes," the most distributive, cacophonous genre in the clowning canon, to be rendered textually? Armin chose to preserve precisely this illegibility, in order to reflect – or perhaps, in a feedback loop of print and perform-ance, to *effect* – a stage routine in which he performed all the audience's voices himself, speaking as no one and everyone, turning participation into a discipline of alienated passivity. In contrast to a critical tradition that sees Armin's literate, anonymous "fool" characters as Shakespeare's domestication of the clown to the dramatic script, I identify such roles as actually outgrowths of Armin's *extra*dramatic persona – a persona he continued to develop in tandem on page and stage, in works like his idiot anthology *Foole Upon Foole* (1600) and in his own full-length play, *The History of the Two Maids of More-clacke* (1613). Disappeared into textuality, if Armin finally became a playwright, that is in a sense where he began, and where the real work of "scriptedness" was being done – not in the play, but around it, in the extraneous material that playbooks would in turn subsequently disappear.

And yet clowning seeded dramatic authorship in less nuanced, more direct ways as well. In my epilogue, "The principal verb," I broaden my thesis to suggest that even as clowns were evolving into authors, authors were regressing into clowns – imitating the very figures whose necessity they had deplored, for the same reasons they had proven necessary. At the indoor halls like the Blackfriars and Paul's, poets such as Ben Jonson hoped that a more patrician mode of reception would take root, based on individual rather than collective self-performance. Jonson was right. Here, I look at the intensely revealing moment when early modern theatre first tried to jettison the support system with which it had grown up. Specifically, I link the rise of city comedy at these venues – with its poetics of disidentification and self-surveillance – to the inherent deficiencies of the boy companies there, who, because they were boys, could not offer clowning. The byproduct of both factors, in turn, was the nearly instantaneous fashion of gallants who sat on the stage, belittled the players, and did whatever possible to annoy and incite the audience. Clowning harnessed the antagonistic social dimension of theatre by engaging it; now that function had reverted, in shockingly plain terms, to the audience. Dramatists responded, in kind, by restoring that function themselves. In a carnivalesque subversion of their didactic programs, poets (chief among them Jonson) began to depict themselves as "live" and present in the playhouse, as comic figures of arrogance and humiliation, perpetually sulking, skulking, and peeping behind the curtain. In this way, they sought to train the audience's destructive energy on a new organizing agent; and in this way, I argue, the clown's authority began to pass to them. Stage-sitting thus returns us to the foundations of my argument, merely a more sophisticated version of the primal battle for the stage. And it illustrates how, though the combatants might have changed, authorship of theatre ultimately involved authorship *in* the theatre: it ended on paper, but it – and the paper too – always began in performance.

It will doubtless seem by now that this is an unwieldy book, spanning a range of topics that might separately fill (and have filled) entire books in themselves. But each of those topics – the behavior of audiences; the nature and structure of performance; the idea of "the play," and of the playbook; dramatic authorship; its corollary, the actor; how such factors influenced specific dramatic genres at specific playhouses – is interconnected, because early modern theatre was interconnected. No single aspect of it can be segmented and treated in isolation, without reference to or revision of the whole. This turns out to be truest of clowning, because clowning was the nexus where all these forces converged: where the institutional identity of theatre – who made it, who owned it – was explicitly being debated, in the elemental clash of performer and spectator. Clowning was, so to speak, where the rubber met the road, the point of contact between all the amorphous, hitherto undefined economic relations theatre subtended, and where new models could be – indeed, had to be – both invented and put into practice.

This makes stage clowning also where the rubber left the road: where the identity of early modern theatre began to uncouple from the immediate scene of its performance, and became fixed dually in texts as well – and where, now collated and repackaged as a series of freestanding, self-contained dramatic fictions, it could cultivate a more mimetic, fantastical, and powerful relationship to the culture that surrounded it. This, of course, is the preternaturally omnipresent, disembodied early modern theatre that historical distance and textual mediation have long led us to take for granted. Here is a familiar formulation, from Jean-Christophe Agnew:

> The professional theater of the English Renaissance became in effect a "physiognomic metaphor" for the mobile and polymorphous features of the market. But it did not merely represent those features ... by confronting the conditions of its own performance, it invoked the same problematic of exchange ... between the practical liquidity of the commodity form and the imaginative liquidity of the theatrical form.[12]

"The imaginative liquidity of the theatrical form": this is the philosopher's stone of New Historicism, underpinning the privileged relation it accords theatre to nearly every aspect of early modern culture. As the discourses constitutive of early modern subjectivity grew ever more fluid, attenuated, and unmanageable – not just capitalist accumulation, but religion, education, class, politics, nationalism, race, sexuality, science, globalization – selfhood became, increasingly, dreamwork. Theatre, already a space of dreamwork, its productions already labile and diaphanous, offered itself as a kind of fictive laboratory in which competing configurations of selfhood could be staged, in which what Katharine Eisaman Maus calls "the new complexities of intersubjective comprehension" could be prismatic-ally visualized, analyzed, and negotiated.[13] But "the imaginative liquidity of the theatrical form" on which the theatre's cultural relevance rested was itself not a given: it too had to be negotiated – *against* "the conditions of its own performance," which were anything but liquid. How, against a backdrop of performance whose participants strove constantly to punc-ture it, did theatre secure its virtuality?

Despite our profound intellectual investment in that virtuality, we tend to treat it as more or less baked-in, neglecting the audience performativ-ity that counteracted it. For Agnew, as for Steven Mullaney, the special liminality of theatre was a result of the playhouses' extraterritorial orien-tation to the city; for Anne Barton, a generation earlier, it was the orien-tation of plays toward themselves, their self-referential vocabularies and the newfound sophistication of their dramatic illusions, such that "in the Elizabethan theatre, the line dividing a world of shadows from reality came to separate the actors from their audience."[14] Yet there was in Elizabethan theatre as yet little break from the reception conventions of medieval thea-tre – if anything, indeed, an intensification of them – where "audiences and actors shared the same ritual world": audiences regarded themselves no less as "actors" in the performance, which was assuredly as real as they.[15] Rather, what intervenes between Barton's incorporated, active medieval spectators and her excluded early modern ones is the very textual medium that *makes* the latter appear excluded – and which, I argue, altered the meaning of performance in turn.

That is where I locate the nascent hybridity of theatre: not in its intrinsic identity – its urban geography, its technical achievement – but precisely in its *dis*identity, in the fact that, unique among forms of mass entertainment in early modern London, theatre came to be experienced in two parallel media. Those media, the stage and the page, were starkly different and at first not simultaneous, but over time they grew together, each taking on properties of the other. What enabled that intergrowth is the subject of this study.[16] And again, it begins with clowning. In the increasingly textu-alized clown, audiences saw both his practice and their participation in it reproduced, and produced *as* reproduced – caught in suspended anima-tion, between then and now, between body and book, existing wholly in neither. In due course, that sense of timelessness, of being nowhere, would be codified in printed playbooks, and in the textual culture that ideal-ized their reading over their enactment. So it is not that audiences were always "real," and plays purely "imaginary." As plays *became* imaginary, so the audience became imaginary as well, made negligible and transitory;

the ultimate "illusion," "the imaginative liquidity of the theatrical form," became not the play but performance itself, rendering its ownership as textual commodity available to monopolistic, authorial claim. Though they would take centuries to look the same, this is the first chapter of the story that ends with how, in our playhouses and cinemas, we consume performance today, as a reciprocal performance of self-dissolution – in short, as a fantasy of Romantic reading: silent, meditative, alone, and in the dark.

This is on some level inevitably a teleological study, then, but one that at least complicates previous teleologies, from an unlikely direction. It is comforting to think of clowns as committed to the value of perform-ance, no less than it is to conflate them with their dramatic characters, and to think of their performance as confined to the play. If our whig-gish histories have done the latter, offering purgation narratives that fail to account for the clown's persistence, our revisionist histories have done the former, refusing narrative altogether. For Nora Johnson, the only recent scholar to take up these issues, the texts produced by clowns – like their performance – constitute "alternatives" to the modern equation of authorship and ownership, artifacts of theatrical collectivity which "reg-ister the power of playing to construct forms of authorship that cannot be explained by later notions of literary property."[17] Yet this leaves those later notions still unexplained, marginalizing clowning once again as anomalous and retrograde to the direction cultural history would take. If early modern authorship and performance defy easy reconciliation, we need to be less rigid in our conceptions of each. Following Johnson's trail, this book strives to go further: to see clowning not as a mere "alternative" authorship, but as its progenitor, part of an ongoing, dialectical exchange in which clowns and authors traded positions, gradually disembodying the one and solidifying the other.

Attending to that process changes how we read much of early modern theatre. But this book's larger objective is to ask how we came to "read" theatre in the first place, and how what we do *not* read in it forms part of the answer. If clowns were banished, it was from the very theatrical texts whose visibility they enhanced, yet from whose final shape – plays – they were cut. I thus reinscribe them into the narrative of their own exci-sion, making them its agents and victims at once. To rematerialize them is only to watch them dematerialize themselves. There can be no recovery of clowning, ultimately, except of its loss; whenever a clown began to exist on paper, he began to exist onstage a little less. Theirs is a history of eras-ure, and every trace it leaves us is of that erasure underway.

CHAPTER I

What audiences did

SLIE. Come *Sim*, where be the plaiers? *Sim* stand by Me and weele flout the plaiers out of their cotes.

– *The Taming of a Shrew* (1594), A4v

Authorship and the axis of reception

How does a play get an author? Despite our tendency today to use authors as rubrics for localizing, organizing, and interpreting cultural production, this was hardly a procedure intuitive to the early modern theatre, especially if we consider its textual output as an extension of the conditions of its performance. Theatre was – as it still remains – a collaborative activity. Playing companies, joint-stock corporations composed of sharers and occasionally led by manager-impresarios like the Admiral's Men's Philip Henslowe or the Queen Anne's Christopher Beeston, were the base economic units of the nascent industry. They installed themselves at particular playhouses, and developed repertories that matched the innovations of their competitors and established a market niche with their audiences. To meet the insatiable demand for novelty, and to maintain a near-daily performance schedule during peak months, those repertories could include as many as two dozen different plays, with some eighteen new ones rotated in for trial over the course of a season.[1] Playwrights, freshly minted from the universities or grammar schools and with financial hardships that impelled them into the players' employ, were in ready supply. Companies commissioned work from them, prescribed its content and supervised its progress, and paid them in advance, in installments, or upon completion. What the company commissioned it also owned: unless (as in rare cases like Shakespeare's) they were also sharers, poets retained no necessary rights in a manuscript, even if it were later retired. Few companies – the Lord Chamberlain's/King's Men from the 1590s onward, Queen Anne's Men from the 1610s onward, and the boys' troupes of the 1580s and 1600s being the prominent exceptions – kept individual playwrights on permanent retainer, as "poets-in-ordinary." Writers were hired men, disposable and replaceable; assignments were parceled out piecemeal to syndicates that recognized talent only at an efficient distance.[2] From Henslowe's accounts, as well as from the relative lateness of playbook title pages to acknowledge co-authorship, we know that collaboration was the standard mode of composition, the unmarked case that more often than not remained unmarked.[3] Poets relentlessly recycled subject matter from classical literature, chronicle histories, topical news pamphlets, and popular Continental narratives; they imitated each other and, if a play did well enough to justify a sequel, they imitated themselves.

When a manuscript was finished, moreover, its utility instantly became a function of its disintegration. It was copied out into parts for the actors to study separately, each of whom was presumably free to add, delete, forget, or rearrange material so long as their cues stayed intact, and each of whom would have had little sense of the play's shape as a whole until rehearsal – of which there was perhaps only one, and in which playwrights probably enjoyed minimal involvement.[4] Despite evidence (mostly later in the period) of a custom whereby poets took a cut of the gate receipts from a play's second performance, they were not required to attend their own plays – some made a point of avoiding them – and the first extant instance of a playbill advertising an author's name dates from 1698.[5] Whatever singular creative labor still inhered (if it ever did) in their work, finally, now diffused itself among the players, prompters, scribes, stagehands, tailors, cosmeticians, carpenters, and musicians who coordinated its enactment on the stage. Buried beneath so many layers of physical realization and interpretation, nearly all of them more costly than the acquisition of a manuscript, it is hardly surprising that the writer of a play occasioned almost no comment from early modern playgoers compared to its performers, plot devices, *sententiae*, songs, dances, costumes, music, affect, effects, pyrotechnics, swordfights, and props. In most cases, they would have no way of knowing, and no reason to know, the writer's name. Theatre, as the term's wider sense in the period denoted, was the domain of the visible, the audible, the sensory: it rendered the abstract tangible, the distant present, the medial immediate, collapsing depth into alluring, overwhelming surface.[6] Except for scattered allusions to it in prologues too stylized to be meaningful, theatre was a technology fundamentally engineered to *conceal* authorship, if not utterly to foreclose it.

This litany of obstacles to authorial attribution on playbook title pages should by now be familiar. It serves as a preamble to the counterpart credo

of the New Textualism, listing the levels of intercession in a manuscript's
transition from performance to print – unknown source copy, adaptation
for staging, sharers, scribes, state censors, publishers, printers, composi-
tors, booksellers – that for us, as for early modern readers, render inaccess-
ible any final, "authorial" intention. My purpose in rehearsing them here
is not to dispute them, but actually to point out their incompleteness.
This inventory of factors inhibiting the recognition of a play's "author,"
that is, spans only the *vertical* axis of production, the collaborations atten-
dant upon a play's composition, formal realization, and commercial publication: in other words, the proprietary dilations and contractions of its
life as a text.[7] It dichotomizes a play's staging and printing, in order to cast
into relief the relative constructedness of print and its discursive codes –
such as, most saliently, the fiction of authorial bylines. In so doing, however, it also constructs *staging* as a play's ontologically ideal state, the
moment when its identity is most "natural" because it is maximally distributed among all agents of production. At this moment of performance,
we imagine, the play properly "belongs" to its native and largest possible
constituency of owners: the playing company, even the institution of theatre as a whole.[8]

Such theoretical back-formations of a dramatic ownership anterior to
print – still modeled on linear, textual development – are too narrow,
because they entirely neglect the multidimensional reality of that "purely"
theatrical, performative moment: what might be termed the horizontal
axis of reception. Performance does not take place in a vacuum, a clinical exercise impervious to its audience. And yet our narratives about the
emergence of singular authorship are calibrated to a maximal, collective
authorship that ignores this fact. Johannes de Witt's drawing of the Swan
Theatre *circa* 1595, our only illustration of the interior of an Elizabethan
amphitheatre, may in a small way be responsible for this oversight – since
it curiously omits any spectators, depicting only the players onstage,
seemingly performing for an empty ground and galleries. (See Figure 1.)
What was in turn responsible for de Witt's drawing itself, for the discursive realignment that made this schematization thinkable, is in a sense the
whole object of this study.[9]

Performance was, to begin with, inherently multiple, never identical
from day to day. This had little to do with the obvious fact that players
are human, fallible, sometimes ill-studied, and sometimes make spontaneous decisions, or the fact that technical effects do not always come
off as planned. Everyone who has seen a play takes this for granted as a
reality of theatre, though today we tend to suppress our appraisal of such

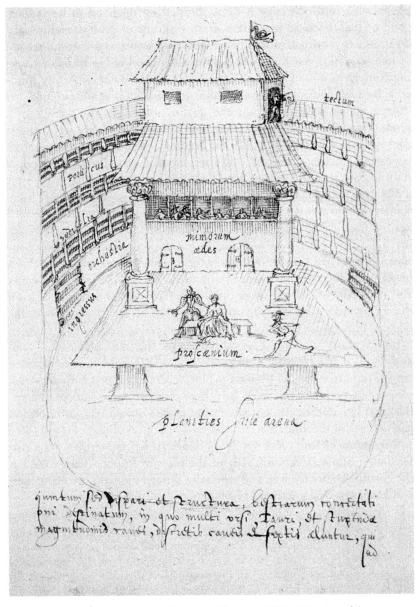

Figure 1 Aernout van Buchel, after Johannes de Witt. Drawing of the
Swan Theatre, *c.* 1595.

phenomena until the play is done, bracketing them off as deviations, good or bad, from an imaginary norm – norms of professionalism and decorum, or norms enshrined in a text that serves as a communal site of reference. ("It was a shame the Nurse flubbed her big speech"; "playing Romeo as nervous was an interesting choice.") For the early moderns, however, no such reference point (other than previous attendance) existed against which to assess the quality, much less the fidelity, of a production. Performance preceded text: as far as we know, not a single commercial play was ever published before it premiered onstage – often appearing years later if at all.[10] It also outpaced text: playhouse receipts dwarfed the standard size of playbook print runs, such that even after a play was published, one was still far more likely to encounter it live.[11] Rather than in print, a play inhered primarily in its performance, judged against itself or its predecessors, according to the instantaneous pleasure it gave. Its "text" was not fixed but memorial, and thus highly contingent. Even by the Restoration, when Shakespeare's plays had been in print for forty years, Samuel Pepys could see *The Tempest* eight times and maintain wildly divergent opinions of it – dependent not just on the acting but on his companionship that day, his health, his mood, the degree of his fellow spectators, and on one occasion his harassment by an orange vendor.[12] To him, it was simply never the same play twice – and as a result, it was barely the same play once. Each performance afforded regular opportunities for pleasure – plots, characters, speeches, costumes, songs, dances, jokes, mistakes. But those elements were subject to amplification by another element which was always unique: the composition and activity of the audience.

Take John Tatham's *Knavery In All Trades* (1664), in which several coffeehouse gentlemen reminisce about the plays of Prince Charles' Men at the Fortune before the war, and especially about a moment involving their bombastic tragedian, Richard Fowler:

> *Fowler* you know was appointed for the Conquering parts, and it being given out he was to play the Part of a great Captain and mighty Warriour, drew much Company; the Play began, and ended with his Valour; but at the end of the Fourth Act he laid so heavily about him, that some Mutes who stood for Souldiers, fell down as they were dead e're he had toucht their trembling Targets; so he brandisht his Sword & made his *Exit*; ne're minding to bring off his dead men; which they perceiving, crauld into the Tyreing house, at which, *Fowler* grew angry, and told 'em, Dogs you should have lain there till you had been fetcht off; and so they crauld out again, which gave the People such an occasion of Laughter, they cry'd that again, that again, that again. (D4v–E1r, emphasis in original)

The anecdote's historical veracity does not finally matter as much as its narrative form. What starts as the fond recollection of an actor by the end becomes something else: as a sort of punchline – past the point where, if we have been imagining this sorry scene, any punchline is necessary – the gentleman makes sure to incorporate the audience's gleeful response. It becomes, in other words, not so much the memory of a play as a memory of the experience of watching it with others, an experience here recapitulated to include the audience's very desire for recapitulation – "that again, that again, that again." Clearly, they did not feel that this collapse of the play's fictional integrity in any way diminished its function. If anything, by collapsing it further – calling, impossibly, for the mistake to be repeated – they were actively *collaborating* in that function. Their participation is not the point of the story, but it is the precondition of the gentleman's remembering it: the players provided a stimulus, but the audience made it an event. That event here eclipses the identity of the play itself, for the gentleman never once bothers to mention its title. If it fell to him to prepare the playbook, what would it look like? Would it look like this?

Against meaning

To think of theatre in this way – as governed by the logic of social events, rather than by dramatic texts – may sound like a fairly banal claim, familiar to us since the advent of Performance Studies in the 1970s. But I want to pressure this banality as far as possible, in order to expose the critical paradox it serves to conceal. We tend only to pay lip service to the role of the audience, sprinkled anecdotally into introductory lectures to give our students a sense of the vitality of the books they are about to read. We invoke the boisterousness of early modern playgoers, their physical proximity to the stage, their intimate knowledge of the performers, their multiple registers of perception, their level of vocal involvement, and their appetite for self-conscious display. Yet seldom do we dwell on this range and intensity of affect long enough to ask how, in the same breath, we can also speak of plays as "commodities" in an early modern cultural marketplace, as self-contained aesthetic and ideological experiences available for purchase, as unilateral causes of predictable, replicable effects – as stable, discrete texts, in other words, capable of resolution into those very books our students are about to read. As charming as we find the idea of theatre-as-event, that is, we make little effort to reconcile it with our idea of theatre-as-text. Because if we did, we would discover them fundamentally incompatible.

Recent treatments of early modern audiences have cut a wide path around this problem, preferring (when not confined to demography) to recover theatrical response *via* the very dramatic texts by which it is assumed to be already controlled.[13] "The plays contain within themselves," argues Jeremy Lopez in *Theatrical Convention and Audience Response in Early Modern Drama* (2003), "most of the evidence needed to understand what audiences expected, enjoyed and experienced."[14] Yet that will hold true only of an audience exactly like the text through which it is being strained. While Lopez recognizes that "above all they enjoyed … *responding*, visibly, audibly, and physically," the kinds of "response" a play encodes are invariably limited to its own field of possibilities.[15] Every play assumes, for instance, that it is being watched intently from start to finish – that an audience's "response" is a response to *it*. Under these conditions, "response" starts to look more like "cognition," and, though multivalent, invitingly governed and predictable. It starts to look, in other words, like an expression of the "correct" way to watch the play. Thus, for Anthony Dawson, in his and Paul Yachnin's *The Culture of Playgoing in Shakespeare's England* (2001), "participation" becomes the apotheosis of dramatic absorption, a eucharistic transport into the body of the actor; any resulting cries of ecstasy from the audience, rather than being disruptions, are effects the play has calculated.[16] Likewise, though Dawson acknowledges the cluttered visual field of the Elizabethan playhouse and its competition for playgoers' attentions – often generated by those playgoers themselves – the distractions he considers occur only on the stage itself, part of a complex "scopic management" by which spectatorial gaze is strategically redirected and heightened.[17]

The playgoer has a funny way of disappearing from these accounts: what is really being studied are *plays*, and their techniques for structuring the experience of an audience that, to them as for us, remain hypothetical and homogenized. From the perspective of the play, the most basic impediment to playing – the playgoer's cooperation – seems already overcome, and theatre can be depicted in a state of perfect equilibrium, finely calibrated to the instincts of its audiences. Extraordinarily supple though these reader-response analyses are, they reduce early modern playgoers to just that – *readers*, engaged merely in a more immersive version of the same process as the literary critic: the construction of meaning. Thus, for Dawson, plays stage "a contest … between alternative ways of turning theatrical experience into meaning," only when "theatrical experience" means dramatic experience, and when that contest unfolds solely onstage, in "the actor's body in concert with the poet's text."[18] Similarly, for Lopez, a play's intricate orchestration of audience affect reveals "how Elizabethan and Jacobean drama works" only if we presuppose *that* it worked, as well as an audience inclined to be so orchestrated – exactly the blank audience playbooks allow us to theorize.[19]

More recently, Jennifer A. Low and Nova Myhill have challenged this view of early modern audiences as mere extensions of dramatic effects, noting that it adopts the model of the antitheatrical writers of the 1570s and 1580s. Stephen Gosson, for example, describes plays as exerting a kind of hypnotic grip on the minds of audiences:

> When *Bacchus* beheld her [Ariadne] … and embraced her … At this the beholders beganne to shoute … when *Bacchus* rose vp … the beholders rose vp … when they sware, the company sware … when they departed to bedde; the company presently was set on fire, they that were married posted home to their wiues; they that were single vowed very solemnly to be wedded.[20]

No less simplistically, they argue, New Historicist critics tend to treat as absolute "the power of spectacle" to fashion early modern playgoers as political and aesthetic subjects, to shape "not merely the audience's interpretation but the audience itself."[21] In place of this "one-sided vision," they call for a less idealized approach to "audience," alive to the fact that "what a spectacle was intended to show and what its spectators made of it do not coincide with any great regularity."[22] They turn in particular to the work of Keir Elam, whose definition of theatre as "a set of competencies shared between the playwrights, actors, and audiences" – most basically, the agreement to "recognize the performance as such" – allows us "to consider the audience's role as active rather than passive."[23]

Yet as the phrase "made of it" suggests, there are still strict limits on this activity. As before, it is *interpretation*. Taking prologues and epilogues as the sites where these "competencies" were articulated, for Elam "[i]t is the spectator who must make sense of the performance for himself … However judicious or aberrant his decodification, the final responsibility for the meaning and coherence of what he constructs is his."[24] Spectators may no longer be passive or perfect, but they seem already party to the prior condition – to "recognize the performance" – that stipulates their job as "making sense," "decoding," as the "construction" of "meaning" and "coherence" from a representation that remains the center of their attention.[25] Low and Myhill, though aware that "the theater audience is ultimately free … to bring whatever expectations and spectatorial practices it pleases to bear," nevertheless conclude that "the theatrical spectacle … constitutes the audience and provides the object of interpretation";

the terms on which they would recuperate that audience, then, like the very New Historicism they critique, are "as a vital partner in the production of meaning."[26] Yet to reduce theatre to a producer of meanings is again to take such "partnership" for granted, and not to alter its juniority. Their paradigmatic early modern playgoer might be someone like Simon Forman, whose idiosyncratic records of playgoing may bizarrely omit from *The Winter's Tale* Hermione's resurrection, but are nonetheless records of *plays*, single-mindedly focused on extracting prudential wisdom therefrom.[27] Meaning is variable, but its *construction* remains normative, and the target of this effort – the play – unquestioned. Audiences may be individuals, "interpreting" drama with different degrees of "competence," but in their *core* competence – accepting their role as such – they remain uniformly receivers, more or less malleable surfaces onto which authorial intention is inscribed.

Why do we assume early modern theatre understood itself to be about producing meanings? Were those two categories, "theatre" and "meaning," completely synonymous, or even always compatible? The answer depends on whom we listen to. Plays certainly suggest so, in the cerebral ministrations of their prologues and epilogues to "piece out our imperfections" or to "think but this, and all is mended." But we must remember that technically these passages speak to no one: talking to the audience is not the same as the audience talking, which playbooks seldom give us. Gosson's description of overheated playgoers, on the other hand, is worth a closer look, because it illustrates something more than mind control. Ostensibly, it shows the audience's enthrallment to representation, the direct transfer of *eros* from the stage into them. But that process is neither quiet nor passive. Even as they are compelled by the play, they compel it in turn, "shout[ing]" when the lovers embrace, which the lovers themselves do not. When they rise up at the lovers' rising, and "sware" in answer to the lovers' oaths, they physically impose themselves on the performance, creating visual distractions and auditory delays the actors must navigate. When the lovers depart, finally, they too depart – despite no indication that the play has ended. Unable to contain their arousal, they simply stampede for the exit. Gosson's account serves as an instance of hypernormative theatricality, yet the crowd's behavior is transgressive at the same time: their "recognition of the performance as such" seems to vary inversely with their enjoyment of it, such that, in a single, remarkable sequence, they disrupt it, overtake it, exceed it, and abandon it. Paradoxically, at the very moment that theatre transmits its meaning perfectly, "theatre" begins to break down – which may prompt us to reconsider just what the meaning of theatre was, and whether it inhered solely in the reception of representations. If Gosson's spectators are overpowered by the play, they overpower it in kind; the more yielding they are to its impressions, the more they impress themselves upon it in return. Perhaps they suggest – like the audience in the Fowler story – that what appears to us theatrical incompetence may simply be a different "competence," consisting not in constructivity but in destructivity. Perhaps, unfiltered through the evidence of plays, what better describes the relation between theatre and audience is not "partnership," but competition.

Theatrical success: or, audiences behaving badly

The bulk of this chapter advances a radically simple, radically counter-intuitive hypothesis: that early modern theatre was not about watching plays. Or at least, it was not about *watching* plays, insofar as by "watching" we tend to mean versions of "reading"; neither, as later chapters will argue, was it about watching *plays*, insofar as by "plays" we mean self-contained *mimeses* running uninterrupted from start to finish, and the totality of theatrical events. It looks that way to us, because playbooks are most of what survive, and the form in which they do so – as pre-packaged, integrated, delivered experiences – retroactively frames playgoing in its own image. Once we move beyond their internal evidence, however, we quickly begin to destabilize the hierarchy they seem designed to promote, discovering in the reception practices of the period, as Charles Whitney puts it, that "the emphasis … is as much on consumption as on production, on appropriation as on contemplation, and on creative re-performance as on creative performance."[28] Despite these claims, and its methodological value to this study, Whitney's *Early Responses to Renaissance Drama* (2006) is still largely concerned with "response" as a belated and secondary phenomenon, exploring how commonplace books, memoirs, and popular allusions attest to the "commodiousness" of dramatic material, in the variegated uses playgoers made of it after they left the playhouse.[29] Those claims can be pushed a great deal further if we attend to descriptions of what playgoers did *in* the playhouse itself, in the moment of performance: there, we will see, their far more literal "responses" suggest a basic inaccuracy to calling early modern theatre a "commodity" at all.

Plays almost never incorporate their real-time audiences, and more seldom still do they admit why they cannot. Early in *The Roaring Girl* (1611), Sir Alexander Wengrave takes his guests into his parlor, and unfurls an

extended analogy between the tapestries in his "galleries" and the playhouse around them:

> Stories of men and women (mixt together
> Faire ones with foule, like sun-shine in wet wether)
> Within one square a thousand heads are laid
> So close, that all of heads, the roome seemes made,
> As many faces there (fil'd with blith lookes)
> Shew like the promising titles of new bookes,
> (Writ merily) the Readers being their owne eyes,
> Which seeme to moue and to giue plaudities ...
> The very flowre (as twere) waues to and fro,
> And like a floating Iland, seemes to moue,
> Vpon a sea bound in with shores aboue. (B3r)

This is an idealized portrait: it captures not what Sir Alexander sees, but
what he wishes to see. Had it really been this pacific, the Fortune audience
would probably not need to be addressed in such mollifying terms, or at
all. It is not even being addressed, indeed, since Sir Alexander describes it
only obliquely, by means of metaphors that enclose what they describe.
Middleton and Dekker here conjure the audience onstage in order to negate its real presence in the theatre, framing and binding it within static,
two-dimensional media ("stories," paintings, "bookes") that isolate each
spectator and displace them from the scene of production, rendering them
solipsisms who "Read" only their own faces and applaud only with their
eyes. By the end, where we expect "the very flowre ... wau[ing] to and fro"
to be the sea, it suddenly becomes "a floating Iland," land hemmed in by
land, "bound in with shores aboue," with no real fluidity in sight.

The Roaring Girl is hardly unique for talking to (or at least about) its
spectators. Yet the exceptional pressures of this play suggest why it works
so hard to quarantine the audience: it is the only Tudor or Stuart play to
star an audience member, depicting a real-life local celebrity and a patron
of that very theatre. The audience, in other words, must be brought
onstage because it is *already* onstage, and that incursion delicately handled. From its prologue, indeed, The Roaring Girl has been defusing that
explosive potential:

> A Play (expected long) makes the Audience looke
> For wonders: – that each Scœne should be a booke,
> Compos'd to all perfection; each one comes
> And brings a play in's head with him: up he summes,
> What he would of a Roaring Girle haue writ;
> If that he findes not here, he mewes at it ...

I see attention sets wide ope her gates
Of hearing, and with couetous listning waites,
To know what Girle, this Roaring Girl should be …
None of these Roaring Girles is ours …
But would you know who 'tis? would you heare her name?
Shee is cal'd madde Moll; *her life, our acts proclaime.* (A4r)

The *first* time the play imagines its audience, they are not "Readers," but writers, each adamant that theatre realize their desires, and poised to do so themselves if it refuses. Here again the specter of mass authorship is raised only to dissolve into auditory. "Each" playgoer is tempted with a fantasy of totalized articulation with the stage, of "a play in's head" that might perfectly embody both the roaring girl and, by extension, him – and whose inevitable failure to appear, to let him "find" himself there, will elicit "mewes" instead. Dividing the audience against itself, however, the Prologue implies not just the mutual incompatibility of these fantasies but their individual error. He enumerates several permutations of "roaring girl" – "Suburbe roarers" who brawl in taverns, "civill Citty" ones who flout their husbands – as if they reflected the audience's fractious imaginings; he then affirms that "None of these Roaring Girles is ours." There is of course no doubt in anyone's mind about which Roaring Girl they expect to see; they know perfectly well this is a play about Moll Cutpurse. But that collectivity is here broken down and alienated from the object of its desire, and that object then reclaimed as the company's to perform. The authority of the stage, of "*our* acts" as a privileged site of representation, is ironically constructed in opposition to "bookes," which become instead figures for the audience. As silently as they "compos'd" before coming to the theatre, each playgoer must now "with couetous listning wait" for a play that will give everyone what they want only by giving no one in particular what they want.

Had Middleton and Dekker expected this shell game to trick a crowd into docility, however, they would likely not have replayed it just 130 lines later. Such metadramatic manipulations did not, as we will see, form a system of audience management. But *The Roaring Girl* at least pinpoints the nature of the problem: namely, why for early modern playgoers (as Sir Richard Baker explains in *Theatrum Redivivum* (c. 1634)), "a play *read*, hath not half the pleasure of a play *Acted*," and why we cannot easily reduce to "reading" the affective horizon they brought to the playhouse, no matter how capacious we make that term.[30] If this is what *The Roaring Girl* seems to ask for, it does so because what it truly fears is *writing*: the audience's belief that its *own* "stories … mixt together" should dictate the content of theatre, that its own reactions constitute an independent dramatic action, a play inclusive of yet greater than the play they are watching. The Prologue takes for granted their participation, just not their consensus about what they are participating in; that must be manufactured, here by invoking their differences to reunify them behind, if not in deference to, a single dramatic presentation.

The reverse – a crowd unified only by the individuality of its members – renders participation not passive but aggressive, and poses an intimidating prospect even in its most academic description. "Sit in a full Theater," writes an anonymous essayist in *New and Choyce Characters* (1615), "and you will thinke you see so many lines drawne from the circumference of so many eares, whiles the *Actor* is the *Center*."[31] Not normally organs of transmission, the gathering of "so many eares" here enacts a spatial violence on its object, radiating almost palpable lines of force that converge on a solitary body at the center of massive atmospheric pressure; theatre is depicted not just as a bodily system but as a writing system, a "drawing" that originates *from* its audience instead of terminating there. That audiences did not "read" performances as we read texts does not mean they did less, just that the forms of attention they brought could be *too* abundant, too intense, too diverse, to guarantee a clear division of producer and consumer – what *The Roaring Girl* called "*couetous* listning," an "ope[n] gate" that swings both ways. Every "eare" probes the stage for what it wants, and ("If that he findes not here") is ready to become – in this passage, is on the verge of becoming – a mouth, capable of generating its own satisfaction. Even the playgoer who writes this description, indeed, has already turned his ear away from the play in order to do so.

The evidence of early modern playgoing lies littered throughout the archive in miscellaneous sources like these: not just in dramatic paratexts (prologues, epilogues, inductions, dedications, commendatory verse, marginalia), but extradramatic documents as well (legal briefs, Revels accounts, civic and university regulations, essays, pamphlets, antitheatrical tracts, sermons, poetry, letters, diaries, ballads, jestbooks). Much of it has been compiled by the scholars already mentioned – most copiously in Andrew Gurr's *Playgoing in Shakespeare's London* (1987) – but its cumulative interpretation remains open.[32] Each datum carries a bias, to be sure, its own interests through which playgoing is viewed; naturally, they tend toward hyperbole, because their rhetorical investments are often extreme. "Everyone applauded politely and left" does not make for much of a story. But for every well-mannered audience that went unrecorded, the frequency and sweep of these references suggest, there must have been unruly ones whose misconducts also went unrecorded – which argues the surviving data a fairly representative sample. No one ever made a clinical study of theatrical behavior, chronicling a day at the playhouse from the audience's perspective. Yet that fact is in itself revealing. It tells us that an audience's experience was not especially felt to need preserving – not just because its principles were widely shared, but because on some level an audience's activity may have already constituted its own self-documentation, a spontaneous, evanescent, collective inscription on the face of the theatrical event.[33] It tells us, in other words, that what evidence we have may be closer to the rule than to the exception: that this volatile combustibility was the default condition of early modern theatre.

This is the common theme of theatre's promoters and detractors, its practitioners and regulators, its successes and failures alike. The conception of theatre as, in Whitney's phrase, "a participatory activity integrated into social occasions in which the distinction between stage and world was often moot," does not imply solely the distinction between mimetic and non-mimetic performance.[34] Regardless of the degree to which spectators might apprehend drama in either mode, what concerns us here is how they understood the parameters of their own *response* to exceed mere "apprehension" – even (and especially) in cases where illusionistic spectacle ought to have overpowered it. Such outbursts and ejaculations were, after all, predicted by Aristotelian *catharsis*, whose truth was never questioned by either the antitheatrical polemicists or their opponents. Gosson charged that players "studie to make our affections overflow, whereby they draw the bridle from that parte of the mind that should euer be curbed," and Heywood's *Apologie for Actors* (1616) only reinforces this by citing several instances of spontaneous criminal confession at the playhouse.[35] Less often noticed, perhaps, is the fact that when his woman from Lynn "suddenly skritched and cryed out Oh my husband, my husband! I see the ghost of my husband," it not only halts but in effect becomes the play itself: "at which shrill and unexpected out-cry, the people about her, moou'd to a strange amazement, inquired the reason of her clamour, when presently un-urged, she told them …"[36] The aftermath of the disruption proceeds to occupy the rest of Heywood's narrative, as it likewise does in his account of Spanish raiders in Cornwall who are surprised into discovering themselves by the alarms of a stage battle, and subsequently chased back to sea by the townspeople. In both cases, the play moves the audience to displace, and replace, the play.

While the spectators in these sensational examples may be forgiven for forgetting the performance at hand, such emotional excess features as a *topos* in far more mundane assessments of dramatic effect. Nashe reports that Talbot's death in *1 Henry VI* elicited "the teares of ten thousand spectators at least ... who in the Tragedian that represents his person, imagine they behold him fresh bleeding"; in Chapman's *The Widowes Teares*, Lycus confesses of Cynthia's grief that "I was so transported with the spectacle ... I was forc't to turne woman, and bear a part with her," to which Tharsalio replies: "So haue I seen many a moist Auditor doe at a play; when the story was but a meere fiction."[37] The satirical sense here, both qualitatively and quantitatively, is of mass psychic identification so disproportionate to its object that audience display threatens to join, or undermine, the play that provoked it; the convulsive weeping of even one spectator, let alone hundreds, can be a loud and distracting business. Curiously, only from the safe distance of print does the arousal of such empathy become a standard of literary praise in the 1630s, and only then does the counter-drama it formed in the playhouse start to become evident as well. For R. Gostelow, commending Thomas Randolph's *Poems* in 1638, it spanned both tragedy and comedy: "If sad, the mourners knew no thrifty size / In teares, but still cri'd out, oh lend more eyes. / If merry, then the juyce of *Comedy* / Soe sweetned every word, that we might see / Each stander by having enough to doe / To temper mirth."[38] Unlike Heywood's subjects, these are playgoers not suddenly called back to reality but, in Chapman's words, wholly "transported" out of it – a rapture they experience corporeally, as an inability to contain the speech and motion of their bodies. They become, in other words, players in their own right: "transported *with*" the fiction rather than by it, their participation in it becomes inevitable. So Thomas Palmer, in a verse for Beaumont and Fletcher's *Works* in 1647, describes how in their plays *"Like Scenes, we shifted Passions, and that so / Who only came to see, turn'd Actors too."*[39]

These examples, of course, are rather soft-focus accounts derived from the indoor halls of Jacobean and Caroline London – whose audience culture, as we will see, was not always so credulous – and from a belletristic culture perhaps attempting retroactively to spin vulgarity as refinement.[40] The critical vocabulary being invented here for proper dramatic reception, indeed, does not stray very far from its pejorative counterpart. Across the wider geographic and economic spectrum of early modern London, audiences showed their approval for a play most basically by making *noise*. And despite the conventional request for (or, perhaps, the disciplinary allowance of) "plaudities" at the end, this noise seems to have been almost continuous. Bylaws issued at Cambridge prior to a royal visit in 1632 give us a sense of what the professional players must have had to cope with:

nor before the comedy begin, nor all the time there, any rude or immodest exclamations be made; nor any humming, hawking, whistling, hissing or laughing be used, or any stamping or knocking … nor that any clapping of hands be had until the Plaudite at the end of the Comedy, except his Majesty, the Queen, or others of the best quality there, do apparently begin the same.[41]

Such behavior can hardly have been exceptional, or there would be no need for rules to prohibit it. And if a command performance by amateur players in a socially homogeneous setting required these strictures, then an urban, commercial playhouse, gathering a nearly comprehensive array of social strata under no official supervision, must have been a sound-scape of brutal cacophony. The author of the utopian travelogue *Pimlyco, or Runne Red-Cap* (1609), describing the unruliness of the inhabitants as "a most strange confused noyse, / That sounded nothing but meere voice," is even in this exotic situation reminded of the London theatres: "Amazde I stood to see a Crowd / Of *Ciuill Throats* stretch'd out so lowd: / (As at a *New-play*) all the Roomes / Did swarme with *Gentiles* mix'd with *Groomes*. / So that I truly thought, all These / Came to see *Shore*, or *Pericles*."[42] Sir John Davies, in the crush of "A thousand townsmen, gentlemen, and whores, / Porters and servingmen" that made up a typical amphitheatre audience of the 1590s, singles out Inns of Court men as particularly "clamorous frye."[43] *The Faerie Queene* describes a chariot's thunderous wheels as "a troublous noyes, / That seemd some perilous tumult to desine, / Confusd with womens cries, and shouts of boyes, / Such as the troubled Theaters oftimes annoyes."[44] Drayton imagines an Olympian revelry "the thick-brayn'd Audience liuely to awake, / Till with shrill Claps the Theater doe shake"; elsewhere, more haughtily, he dismisses "those the thronged Theaters that presse … With showts and claps at euery little pawse."[45] Dekker's acid Prologue to *If It Be Not Good the Diuel Is In It* (1612) detests precisely this constant, unthinking approbation, reviling any play that, "Ift fill a house with Fish wiues, *Rare, They All Roare*"; it can only pray for at least a moment of "rare Silence" before they "clap their *Brawny hands*, / T'applaud, what their *charmd* soule scarce understands."[46] Nearly twenty years on, the din of Dekker's Red Bull remained unchanged. According to Thomas Carew in 1630, there *"noyse preuayles, and he is taxd for drowth / Of wit, that with the crie, spends not his mouth"*; *"These are the men in crowded heapes that throng / To that adulterate stage, where not a tong / Of the untun'd Kennell, can a line repeat / Of serious sense: but like lips, meet like meat."*[47] It is unclear whether the "untun'd Kennel" who senselessly "repeat" are the actors delivering their lines, or the spectators repeating aloud lines they

found impressive – which makes one wonder, as it does Carew, how anyone heard much of anything at all.

Similar challenges of audibility were encountered by London's outdoor
preachers – congregants relaying lines to latecomers and to those on the
fringes of the assembly, or echoing in appreciation, or enthusiastically
answering the preacher himself – and recent reconstructions of sermonic
performance shed indirect light on playhouse realities. John Donne, a
convert from one venue to the other, routinely anticipated such feedback,
and built his sermons around soliciting them.[48] He speaks of his congrega-
tions, indeed, as having imported to their churchgoing precisely the disruptive habits of their playgoing:

> all that had been formerly used in Theaters, *Acclamations* and *Plaudites*,
> was brought into the *Church*, and not onely the vulgar people, but learned
> hearers were as loud, and as profuse in those declarations, those vocall
> acclamations, and those plaudites in the passages, and transitions, in
> Sermons, as ever they had been at the Stage ... if you do not joyne with
> the Congregation in those *Plaudites*, the whole Congregation will thinke
> you the onely ignorant person, in the Congregation ... the people doe yet
> answer the Preacher, if his questions be Applyable to them, and may induce
> an answer, with these vocall acclamations, *Sir, we will, Sir, we will not.*[49]

Discussing this passage, John N. Wall concludes that, rather than mere rec-
itations of text, sermons were "conversations ... interactive performance[s]
in which the congregation and preacher collaborated in the creation of
the occasion," usefully suggesting that "theatrical performance" be viewed
in cognate terms.[50] Yet this analogy must also factor in Donne's reluctance to see it as "collaboration," and his irritation at its tendency – as
in the theatres – to manifest as destruction and appropriation. "[T]hose
impertement Interjections," he continues, "swallow up one quarter of his
[the preacher's] houre, and many that were not within distance of hearing the Sermon, will give a censure upon it, according to the frequen-
cie, or paucitie of these acclamations."[51] The more an audience enjoys a
sermon, the less they will hear of it, because their enjoyment competes
with and "swallows" its remainder; the farther into the audience the performance travels, the more it becomes *their* performance alone, the actor's
agency "swallowed" again, registered only in the thing that obscures it.
Sermons were free, moreover, but plays were not; sermons were bound to
their allotted hour, but plays were not. If we believe Donne's claim that he
lost one quarter of his prepared material to audience response, we have at
least one cause (to which we will add more) of why play performances, as
Michael J. Hirrel argues, typically ran four or five hours: a substantial part

of those performances may have consisted quite literally not of the play at all, but of the dilatory performance of its own reception.[52]

Theatrical failure: or, audiences still behaving badly

None of the audiences we have observed thus far are hostile. Their excesses – uncontrollable sexual excitement, confession, tears, laughter, empathy, clamor, murmur, repetition, vocalic interlocution, continuous applause – may be cast as transgressive to greater or lesser degrees, but the affective involvement they symptomatize is absolutely normative. These are spectators engaging with dramatic spectacle exactly as they should, yet this engagement is always, almost programmatically, carried too far: even when theatre works, it teeters on the brink of practical failure – the audience's "swallowing" the stage with interference, and the players' inability to execute the play. When we turn to actual instances of theatrical failure, as a result, they strangely start to look like success – depending, crucially, on what definition of "theatre" we are pursuing, and whose.

If until now we have sampled how audiences reacted to what they *liked*, what they *dis*liked they greeted much the same way. John Lyly, ever steeled for disaster, provides a clutch of examples. Writing for the polite clientele of the Blackfriars in the 1580s, Lyly seemingly could not begin a play without reminding them what politeness meant: in a word, quiet, which under no circumstances he expected to get. *Campaspe* (1584) begs its audience that "although there bee in your precise judgementes an universall mislike, yet we maye enioy by your woonted curtesies a generall silence"; *Midas* (pr. 1592), "that presenting our studies before Gentlemen, thogh they receiue an inward mislike, wee shall not be hist with an open disgrace"; *Sapho and Phao* (1584), that the audience not "with open reproach blame our good meaninges" – and, even more hopelessly, should the play somehow manage to please, that it produce only "soft smiling, not loude laughing."[53] For Lyly, even at the hands of an upper-class audience, there was simply no way to win. And the archive is replete with accounts of what it was like to lose: the literary legitimations of dramatists are built on the carcasses of rejected plays, bitter recognitions of their own continuing theatrical irrelevance. Jonson's *Sejanus* (1605) can only look back in anger at the playhouse mob that chased it into print: one colleague scorns "the Peoples beastly rage, / Bent to confound thy graue, and learned toile," while another vilifies them as "the throate of the rude Sea ... the boggy and engulfed brests / Of Hyrelings, sworne to finde most Right, most rude."[54] The ascription of mindless confusion to the audience is, seemingly without contradiction, always coupled with the ascription of single-minded malice.[55] Of Jonson's "tedious" *Catiline* (1611) Leonard Digges recalls that "they would not brooke a line";[56] Fletcher, lauding the play's publication, imagines it still plagued by its original spectators more than plaguing them: "such men, / Deare friend, must see your Booke, and reade; and then, / Out of their learned ignorance, crie ill, / And lay you by, calling for mad *Pasquill*, / Or *Greene's* deare *Groatesworth*, or *Tom Coryate*."[57] His own *Faithfull Shepheardesse* had suffered the fate of being shouted down the year before, indeed, when "the people … hauing euer had a singuler guift in defining," mistook his pastoral tragicomedy for a country romp, "And missing whitsun ales, creame, wassel & morris-dances, began to be angry."[58]

Webster, meanwhile, dispenses with such contingent rationalizations. He blames the failure of *The White Divel* (1612) on its lacking "a full and understanding Auditory," but goes on to confess this phrase an oxymoron: "for should a man present to such an Auditory, the most sententious Tragedy that euer was written … the breath that comes frő the uncapable multitude, is able to poison it."[59] "Uncapable" of enjoying the play, perhaps, but all too capable of ruining it – activities that by now are coming to seem interchangeable. "This is the straine that chokes the theaters," notes Marston's Laverdure in *What You Will* (1601), "that makes them crack with full stufft audience … to crack the Authors neck, / This admiration and applause persues."[60] Both Marston and Webster still assume, of course, that "the Author" is the ultimate target of the audience's violence; they nevertheless imply, like the whole jeremiadic tradition they join, that the pleasure of the playgoer actually *consists* in destroying the play, one way or another. Nathan Field says as much, when in verses for *The Faithfull Shepheardesse* he prefers being heckled to the constant interruption of cheering – as if those really are the only two options: "Such art" as Fletcher's flop, he declares, "should me better satisfie, / Then if the monster clapt his thousand hands, / And drownd the sceane with his confused cry."[61] If the audience is not so "transported with" the play as to hijack it, it simply transports the play right out of the playhouse. For John Davies of Hereford, "It's easie to cry *Hisse*, but tis not so / To silence it," for those hisses will instantly transform into "Claps, that Clap vp all."[62]

There is little practical difference, then, between theatrical success and theatrical failure: the choice is either to be booed off stage, or to watch one's work be "drownd" with equally indiscriminate applause. When approbation and condemnation manifest in exactly the same way, and where the value of a good is invariably judged at the material expense of the good itself, the term "commodity" becomes no longer adequate to describe the baseline economic identity of early modern theatre. If anywhere, rather, we must locate it *in* this very act of judgment, in an audience's unilateral seizure of control over the stage, and in its exercise of sovereignty thereby. William Fennor's "Description of a Poet" (1616) conventionally grieves that "Sweet poesye" should be "condemn'd, and iudg'd to die / Without iust triall, by a multitude / Whose iudgements are illiterate, and rude," but it proceeds to analyze the group psychology of public theatre:

> Clapping, or hissing, is the onely meane
> That tries and searches out a well writ Sceane ...
> The stinckards oft will hisse without a cause,
> And for a baudy ieast will giue applause.
> Let one but aske the reason why they roare
> They'l answere, cause the rest did so before.[63]

The audience is engaged here in a "trial," a "searche," both of the authority of the stage and of its own as measured against it; "clapping" and "hissing" are equivalent probative methods, and their circular, collective answer to "why they roare," insufficient to a model of theatre as discrete production and consumption, is more consistent with viewing it as the interrogation of these relationships. The play Fennor eulogizes (*Sejanus*, again) may have been staged in 1603, but his recollection is firmly grounded in the public playhouse mentality of 1616 – a mentality on which the rising frequency of single-author plays, of bylines on playbook title pages, and of dedications and commendatory verses within those playbooks (not to mention the publication of Jonson's *Workes* that same year) have apparently made zero impact in the perception of drama as literary artifact.

To the "common" playgoer, if these examples can construct such a person, theatre remained not a body of texts but a ritualized (and disturbingly arbitrary) violence against textual bodies, a forum for constructing *themselves* as persons. For Anthony Munday, as for other antitheatricalists, the readiest danger of playhouses lay in "the disorder of their Auditorie," which they fully supply themselves: "[you] shall find there no want of yong ruffins, nor lacke of harlots, vtterlie past al shame: who presse to the fore-frunt of the scaffoldes, to the end to showe their impudencie, and to be as an obiect to al mens eies."[64] "Your Car-man and Tinker," Dekker explains in *The Guls Horne-booke* (1609), "claime as strong a voice in their suffrage, and sit to giue judgement on the plaies life and death, as well as the prowdest *Momus* among the tribe of *Critick*."[65] "To cry Playes downe," sighs Davenant, "Is halfe the businesse Termers have in towne."[66] To Henry Fitzgeffrey's *Notes from Blackfriars* (1617), an epigrammatic vanity fair of playhouse *ennui*, the play is an extension of the audience's pre-show posturing for each other, and he expects "to bee made *Adder-deafe* with *Pippin*-crye."[67] According to Shirley, "hee that can / Talke loud, and high, is held the witty man, / And censures finely, rules the Box, and strikes / With his court nod consent to what he likes."[68] At the premiere of Killigrew's *Pallantus and Eudora* (c. 1635), says its publisher, an auditor rose to denounce "the Indecorum that appear'd to Some, in the Part of *Cleander*, who being represented a Person of seventeen yeares of age, is made to speak words, that would better sute with the age of thirty," only to be rebutted by another auditor:

> But the Answer that was given … by the Lord Viscount *Faulkland*, may satisfie all others … This Noble Person, having for some time suffered the unquiet, and impertinent Dislikes of this Auditor, when he made his last Exception, forbore him no longer, but (though he were one he knew not) told him, *Sir 'tis not altogether so Monsterous and Impossible, for One of Seventeen yeares to speak at such a Rate, when He that made him speak in that manner, and writ the whole Play, was Himself no Older.*[69]

By 1635, at least one playgoer knows who "the author" is; the other clearly does not, and is surprised by the appeal to him. Yet what surprises us is that so lengthy and public an argument is being conducted at all, such that everyone must "for some time" "suffer" it. Seemingly in the midst of the play, the theatre has lapsed into open-floor critical debate. Neither does Falkland entirely end it: rather than shush him, he "answers" him, engaging in that debate. Indeed, on the pretext of defending the poet, Falkland merely uses him to do what his opponent is already doing – to grandstand, to perform his own wit, judgment, and nobility, to make himself known. If the play continues after this outburst, it does so on *his* authority, not the poet's; "He that … writ the whole Play" is not the one who makes it. (It worked: his name is in the playbook.) Theatrical self-fashioning was not a mental operation, a matter of internalizing the representations one saw projected onstage. It involved physically projecting oneself *onto* that stage, and claiming that stage for oneself.

This is not an exaggeration: it involved actual projectiles. A variety of food and drink was available for purchase at the playhouses, and in a letter to Spenser, Gabriel Harvey explicitly links the two forms of consumption: the theatre for him is "whereat thou and thy lively copesmates in London maye lawghe ther mouthes and bellyes full for pence or twoepence apeece."[70] Not only does each ware – admission to a play and of a snack – cost the same, but Harvey's Rabelaisian image renders them substitutable. Just as "lawghe ther mouthes … full" implies an activity equally ingressive and egressive, so matter intended for the belly could end up furnishing the means of that expression, taking the place of the mouth. The practice of hurling food at the stage certainly did not originate with the Elizabethans – it is as old as theatre itself – nor did it end with them. As late as 1849 William Macready could be assaulted with eggs, apples, potatoes, bottles, and sticks. The Astor Place riot, however, was an isolated flashpoint of international tensions, and the audience had come armed with its own ballistics; the house did not vend such items itself, and they were not an extension – nor, consequently, was their use a rejection – of its authority. Elizabethan playhouses, by contrast, made a business of equipping patrons with weapons to disrupt their business. "Unlesse … the popular humour [were] satisfied, as sometimes it so fortun'd, that the Players were refractory," recalled Edmund Gayton in 1654, "the Benches, the tiles, the laths, the stones, Oranges, Apples, Nuts, flew about most liberally, and as there were Mechanicks of all professions, who fell every one to his owne trade, and dissolved a house in an instant, and made a ruine of a stately Fabrick."[71] Gayton here recounts what audiences did merely when refused their *choice* of play, not their response to one: their barrage does not appraise a commodity, it *replaces* the commodity. Denied the particular play it wants to destroy, the crowd simply dismantles the playhouse. One is as good as the other, because each is the same as the other.

Spectatorial violence against the stage was never a purely anarchic gesture; it was part of a continuum of legibly theatrical behavior. Whether the bombardment in question were vocal or physical, both derived from the same structured, antagonistic impulse, and could just as often form a theatrically *productive* rather than destructive act. Tatham's "Prologue spoken upon removing of the late Fortune Players to the Bull" (1640) asks the audience to refrain from throwing fruit not because they are impatient for the play to end, but because they are impatient for it to begin:

> Onely we would request you to forebeare
> Your wonted custom, banding *Tyle*, or Peare,
> Against our *curtaines*, to allure *us* forth.
> O pray take notice *these* are of more Worth,
> Pure Naples silk, not *Worstead* …[72]

Pleading for respect of company property may have been poor tactics here, since the Red Bull audience the Prologue addresses appears every bit as conscious of it, and jealous of it, as the audiences the players had just left at the Fortune: "Those that now sojourne with *her* [the Fortune], bring a noyse / Of *Rables*, *Apple-wives* and Chimney-boyes, / Whose shrill confused Ecchoes loud doe cry, / Enlarge your *Commons*, wee hate *Privacie*."[73] The Red Bull crowd's barrage of the playhouse's own material excrescence, similarly, is not only "custom" – a prologue could hardly have been prepared for a freak incident – but forms an identical bid to "enlarge the Commons" of the stage, to strip the veil of propriety that segregates producers from consumers. From the audience's perspective, the play has already begun with the demand that it begin; "playing" is greater than "the play." Even at the upscale Whitefriars in the 1630s, a Prologue worries that they will "Damne unaraign'd" the play, "[j]udging it sin enough that it is *Ours*."[74]

This expectation of involvement, of generative dialogue with the stage, is best illustrated by a jest – to whose subject we will return – that exposes the circular economy of the theatrical event by reducing its entire content to a playgoer's missile:

> At the *Bull* in *Bishops-gate-street*, where the Queenes Players oftentimes played, *Tarlton* comming on the Stage, one from the Gallery threw a Pippin at him. *Tarlton* tooke up the pip, and looking on it, made this sudden iest.
>
> > *Pip in, or nose in, chuse you whether,*
> > *Put yours in, ere I put in the other.*
> > *Pippin you haue put in: then, for my grace,*
> > *Would I might put your nose in another place.*
>
> … *Tarlton* hauing flouted the fellow for his pippin which hee threw, hee thought to be meet with *Tarlton* at length. So in the Play *Tarltons* part was to trauell, who kneeling down to take his father blessing, the fellow threw an Apple at him, which hit him on the cheek.[75]

Predictably, another ribald rhyme ensued, this time about the play-goer's being escorted by a whore instead of his wife, at which "the people laughed heartily."[76] The jest prepares us for how stage clowns like Tarlton epitomized this sense of theatre as unstructured, bilateral game – in their focalization of its antagonistic impulses, and their proliferation into all areas of the theatrical program – which will be the subject of Chapter 2. But it will suffice here to note, amid its blow-by-blow account, the kinds of interchange the jest takes for granted. This altercation occurs not at the opening or close of a play, but in the middle; Tarlton is merely entering to take up his part, and does nothing to provoke the playgoer's attack. Rather, he is the object of provocation: the "fellow" throws his pippin to elicit retaliation – and does not hesitate to follow it up with another, knowing full well that the second rebuttal will be even more withering. He does so, however, "to be meet" with Tarlton, a battle for authority that he wins even as he loses it. Despite his public humiliation, he succeeds in temporarily wresting control of the player, "enlarging" the "Commons" of the stage, and forcing it to acknowledge him; the assault is never rebuked as a violation of decorum, only countered as personal challenge. The play we were not even told was in progress when the jest began presumably carries on once it is done, as if such "sudden" releases of bile and merriment were an obligatory part of theatrical experience, and not only exist independent of its aesthetic design, but take priority over it. The jest is interested not in the fictional conflicts theatre stages, but the real ones: once again, it remembers the interaction of player and auditor, not the title of the play.

At its ugliest, this contest could turn deadly, and (as Gayton's example shows) could erupt even more forcefully if denied its fulfillment. Davenant's epilogue to *News From Plymouth* (1635) toys with such danger when it returns an armed Sir Furious to the stage, threatening to cut to ribbons a Globe audience that might "cry down our Play," because it was "promise[d] shewes, / Dancing, and Buckler Fights":

> For if you dare but whisper one false Note
> Here in this House, or passing to take Boat,
> Good faith I'll mow you off with my short Sword ...
> for since my mettal lies
> To destroy yours, and our Enemies,
> Can I do less (be your own Judges) when
> You lay sad plots to begger the King's Men?"[77]

Still in character, the actor is obviously joking, but he flirts with a relationship between player and audience that often did revert to that of "Enemies." In April 1580, two Earl of Oxford's players, Robert Leveson and Lawrence Dutton, were arrested for "committing of disorders and frayes appon the gentlemen of the Inns of Court" – that is, for physically assaulting their own audience, which must have done something to invite it. A City order of 11 July 1581 accused "Parr Stafferton gentleman of Grayes Inne for that he that daye brought a dysordered companye of the Innes of Courte & others to assalte Arthur Kynge, Thomas Goodale, and others, servauntes to the Lord Barkley, & players of Enterludes within the Cytte" – a skirmish for which the players in question, clearly not blameless either, were detained as well.[78] Even (or especially) clowns were not immune to these outbursts of naked aggression, and in one case were its culprits. On 15 June 1583, at the Red Lion in Norwich, a disgruntled playgoer refused payment at the door, drawing the attention of Tarlton and his fellow comedians John Bentley and John Singer, who were already in the midst of performing. We do not know why the scuffle started, but it ended with the three charging off the stage in pursuit, rapiers drawn, and the playgoer dead in the street, with Bentley, Singer, and another bystander, Henry Browne, held on individual bonds of £80 until early July.[79]

Of tumults strictly between playgoers, we have relatively few cases. But that does not mean they did not happen; indeed, given the frequency with which playgoers attacked *players*, they must have happened often. "[C]onsidering the alarm so regularly voiced by the civil authorities," writes Gurr, "the number of affrays ... was almost nil."[80] But what counts as an "affray," to those authorities or to us, is precisely the question here. Those that merited documentation usually involve large numbers of people, or grievous injury, or noble personage – and that they still did so further attests to the incipient violence of the playhouse atmosphere. In 1584 William Fleetwood informed Lord Burghley of "one Browne, a serving man in a blew coat, a shifting fellowe having a perrelous witt of his owne, entending a spoile if he cold have browghte it to passe, [who] did at Theatre door qurell with certen poore boyes, handicraft prentises, and strook some of them, and lastlie he with his sword wonded and maimed one of the boyes upon the left hand."[81] Fleetwood notes that "there assembled nere a ml [thousand] people." In 1622, one Captain Essex tussled with a nobleman for refusing to clear his and his wife's sightline; "the lord then drew his sword and ran full butt at him, and might have slain the Countesse as well as him."[82] A similar fracas occurred in 1636 between the Duke of Lennox and the Lord Chamberlain, over a box seat at a new Blackfriars play.[83] From less official quarters, we know that playgoers like Fleetwood's Browne, armed with "a perrelous witt" and bound for the playhouse in search of a fight, were ubiquitous. Henry Chettle in 1592 bemoans the "barbarously rude ... disorders" caused by "lewd mates that long for innouation," who, "when they see aduantage ... will be of either side, though they be of no side"; "Ruffians," according to Richard Brathwaite in 1631, "to a play [will] hazard to go, though with never a rag of money," "make *forcible entrie*," and "Forthwith, by violent assault and assent, they aspire to the two-pennie room," to smoke discarded cigar butts, "applaud a prophane jeast immeasurably, and ... grow distastefully rude to all the Companie."[84] Seething with such fractious energies, the playhouse must have been in a constant state of "affray": if they rarely exploded, what looks to us like (in Paul Menzer's phrase) "theatrical strategies of crowd control" may merely be the fact that those energies were continuously vented at the stage.[85] Outside playhouses – from the Theatre to the Curtain to the Globe to the Fortune to the Red Bull to the Cock-pit – rioters periodically gathered to destroy them, in 1584, 1592, 1597, 1617, and 1626; inside them, that attitude was codified in the norms of playgoing itself. At the Red Bull in 1622, an errant sword grazed a feltmaker's apprentice standing too near the stage during a duel – whereupon, taking it as a personal affront, he stormed out in anger, vowing the collective revenge of all apprentices.[86]

Too near, too far, too much, too little, too intent, too detached: there seem to have been only wrong ways to experience early modern theatre, such that, cumulatively, they represent kaleidoscopic variations on the right one, and a single one. Playgoing unfolded along a boundary between fiction and reality that was routinely crossed – by the playgoer him or herself – and whose crossing was its basic function: the only norm of playhouse behavior was, ultimately, transgression, be it through deliberately disrupting the play or compulsively inserting oneself into it. Whether fueled by sublime, affective transport or merely by cruel, disaffected sport, each playgoer had a "perrelous witt of his owne," and for them the purpose of a play – whether it wanted it or not – was to actuate that sense of self-possession through their possession of the stage itself, as an extension of its dramatic representations or in despite of them. There is no difference between the "absurdity [of] a Country-Gentleman" who, according to a Caroline memoir, during a play at Blackfriars "was so caught with the naturall action of a Youth (that represented a ravish'd Lady) as he swore alowd, he would not sleep untill he had killed her ravisher,"[87] and the audience of a Gray's Inn Christmas revel of 1594 that precipitated the famous "Night of Errors":

> When the Ambassador was placed … there arose such a disordered Tumult and Crowd upon the Stage, that there was no Opportunity to effect that which was intended: There came so great a number of worshipful Personages upon the Stage, that might not be displaced; and Gentlewomen, whose Sex did privilege them from Violence, that … at length there was no hope of Redress for that present.[88]

Every conceivable disparity in circumstance is spanned in these two examples: historical, geographic, socioeconomic, institutional, occasional, numerical, sexual. In one case, the play's mimetic force moves a solitary, unsophisticated spectator to interrupt; in the other, there *is* no play, because the courtly audience has already overrun it. One is a result of extreme dramatic reception, the other of its extreme refusal. Yet both remain, from an early modern perspective, essentially "theatrical," insofar as they convert *reception* into *production* – the country gentleman because his swearing "alowd" projects him vocally onto the stage, the courtiers because they project themselves quite physically onto the stage, and will not give it up. Both plays succeed, ironically, because both plays finally *become* their audiences, and the audience the play; one just does it faster than the other.

Even the court masque, a genre constructed around this very principle, was not immune to the unpredictability of audience interaction. Where participation was the rule, the best way to perform oneself might be not to participate at all. At *Love Restored*, performed in 1612 before King James and Prince Henry, the masquers were ten lords, "the spirit of Court, and flower of men"; when, however, the lords offered to take ladies to dance the revels, reports John Chamberlain, "beginning with the ladies of Essex and Cranbourne, they were refused, which set an example to the rest, so that the lords were fain to dance alone and make court to one another."[89] At a lost masque known only through John Harington's letter about it as *Solomon and the Queen of Sheba*, performed in 1606 for James and the visiting Christian IV of Denmark, James likewise declined to play his part, much to the consternation of the actors:

> Victory, in bright armor ... presented a rich sword to the king, who did not accept it, but put it by with his hand ... [she] did endeavour to make suit to the king ... but after much lamentable utterance, she was led away ... I never did see such lack of good order, discretion and sobriety.[90]

Harington also reports that the Queen of Sheba spilled a dish of fruit in Christian's lap, that he was too drunk to dance with her or even to stand, and that he had to be carried to bed; perhaps the masque (if it is not altogether Harington's fiction) is lost for a reason.

The contrast between Jonson and Dekker's *King's Entertainment / Magnificent Entertainment* (1604), performed at James's royal entry to London, and Gilbert Dugdale's *The Time Triumphant* (1604), a journalistic narrative of the entry itself, illustrates how differently the same incident could be represented as text and as social event. Dugdale stresses not the collaboration of poets, or of poets and actors, but of various kinds of audience. His attention flits between the actions of the monarch and those of the commoners in attendance, giving us details of the pageant its texts never record: how "the women weeping ripe cryed all in one voice God blesse the Royall *Queene*"; how a tour of the Royal Exchange caused such a "hurly burly" that James was forced to view it from a window, where he "commended the rudeness of the Multitude, who regardless of time, place or person, will be so troublesome" – and whom Dugdale admonishes not to "prease your Soueraigne thereby to offend him."[91] On his progress home, there were impromptu street shows and "orations": "at the corner of the streete stood me one old man with a white beard" who proudly recites a verse of his own making, though "the noyse ... was not fauorable to him"; at "the great cundyt [conduit] on the top thereof, stood a prentise in a black coate," whose shop call – "What lack you gentlemen?" – turns into a welcome song.[92] Far from beholders of an event, they have come to be actors, and Dugdale makes them authors, transcribing their performances "so that all [their] fellow Subiectes may see."[93] The pomp of diplomats and aldermen, the fireworks, the waterworks, and Jonson and Dekker's central masque receive only passing mention, because they are not central. Given a chance to document the occasion, the audience documented itself.

Francis Beaumont's *The Knight of the Burning Pestle* (1607) is the great monument to this continuous back-channel of performance in the play-house, of course, and in its delightfully insane way an attempt to overload its circuits. The play is terrific fun, yet rather than view it as a proto-Brechtian experiment in audience estrangement, we should perhaps regard it as on some level the most *realistic* playbook in the early modern canon. If playbooks recorded a play's performance rather than its text, preserving what the audience did as well as the actors, every play would have its own George and Nell – probably many – either chattering onstage or calling out from the yard. One manuscript jestbook relates how, during a play at Woodstock, a line spoken onstage was bettered by one "Hoskins of Oxford," who "standinge by as a spectator rimes openly to it": the player's line was "As at a banquett some meates have sweet some saure tast," to which Hoskins retorted, "Even so your dublett is to short in the waste."[94] But this is a jestbook, not a playbook. Uniquely, then, *The Knight of the Burning Pestle* simulates what a play was *expected* to do for its audience: erase the distinction between the two domains.[95] The rest of Thomas Palmer's panegyric to Fletcher, indeed, enshrines him for that very virtue:

> How didst thou sway the Theatre! Make us feele
> The players wounds were true, and their swords, steele!
> Nay, stranger yet, how often did I know
> When the Spectators ran to save the blow?
> Frozen with griefe we could not stir away
> Vntill the Epilogue told us 'twas a Play.[96]

The singularity of Fletcher's authorship here comes to rest, ironically, on its multiplicity. So visceral is the spectators' sense of transport by the play that they helplessly transport themselves into it, running up onto the stage; desperate to alter its course, they must be told it is "a Play," which here means something quite different from what they took it to mean. For Palmer, "a Play" is a closed text, already written, performing only itself; for the audience, it is an occasion to perform themselves as well.

Once again, in another moment of "running to save the blow," we have Edmund Gayton to tell us which took precedence in the imagination of the playgoing public:

> A passionate Butcher of our Nation ... being at the Play, called *the Greeks and Trojans*, and seeing *Hector* over-powred by *Mirmydons*, got upon the Stage, and with his good Battoone tooke the true *Trojans* part so stoutly, that he routed the *Greeks*, and rayled upon them loudly for a company of cowardly slaves to assault one man with so much odds. He strooke more-over such an especiall acquaintance with *Hector*, that for a long time *Hector* could not obtaine leave of him to be kill'd, that the Play might go on; and the cudgelled *Mirmydons* durst not enter againe, till *Hector*, having pre-vailed upon his unexpected second, return'd him over the stage againe into the yard from whence he came.[97]

Perhaps no piece of evidence argues better for the purpose of early mod-ern playing, in both its form and its content, as the self-creation of its audience. Gayton's butcher here attempts to rewrite not just a play in pro-gress, but history itself: the Hector he defends is, after all, his ancestor, according to the myth of Brutus and of London as Troynovant; the "true *Trojans* part" he takes up is also his own, and that of every red-blooded Englishman in attendance. The play compels him to intervene: it would be a failure if he did not. And yet the consequence of his taking affect-ive "part" in it is his taking literal part in it, taking the play apart in the process. The damage he inflicts runs deeper than delay: though "the Play might go on," he has exposed the contingency of its dramatic order. The invincible Myrmidons are proven "a company of cowardly slaves," quak-ing backstage in terror; Hector must die only because someone somewhere *says* he must, and before this absent authority can be obeyed, it is forced to bow to that of the playgoer, from whom Hector must "obtaine leave." Here again, a playgoer needs the idea of "the script" *explained* to him. It seems a novel concept, and he does not like it.

For Gayton's butcher, not even history is scripted. How can theatre be? The final form of a play, as he understands it, is always determined by its audience, and as a result, form is never final. So inextricable was participation from performance, indeed, that we find it even figured *as* performance – as the reciprocal of what the onstage actors do, the com-plementary other half of a collaborative, organic social text. "*Player* is much out of countenance," writes Thomas Gainsford, "if fooles doe not laugh at them, boyes clappe their hands, pesants ope their throates, and the rude raskal rabble cry excellent, excellent: the knaues haue acted their parts in print."[98] In the remainder of this chapter, we will ask why, if those "parts" were so fundamental, they too were not put into print – and why, when they failed to "find themselves" there, playgoers did not seem to mind.

The improbability of playbooks

> Spectator, this Lifes Shaddow is; To see
> The truer image and a livelier he
> Turne reader.
> – Leonard Digges, "Upon the Effigies
> of my worthy Friend, the Author Master
> William Shakespeare, and his Workes,"
> *Comedies, Histories and Tragedies*
> (2nd Folio), 1632 (A5)

In the preceding pages I have tried to synthesize most of the available evidence for a claim we usually accept unreflectively – that early modern playgoing was governed by the democratic logic of social events rather than by that of textual, quasi-literary reception. It will seem, no doubt, that in pressuring this claim as far as possible, I have overstated its case: that all this evidence of audience participation remains exceptional to the rule (and does not, in sufficient quantity, at some point become the rule itself), and that I have neglected counterevidence of audiences behaving "well" – enjoying the play, appreciating the verisimilitude of the actors, and so forth. If this is not the same evidence we have already seen, of audiences marring the play as *coterminous* with their enjoyment of it, pro-pelling themselves into the dramatic illusion when they did not altogether reject it, then it is a class of evidence – of audiences being, essentially, no longer "audiences" at all – to which we have simply not yet come. Rather, by comprehensively surveying what audiences empirically *did*, across all circumstances – booing, hissing, clapping, laughing, roaring, hum-ming, whistling, stamping, crying, repeating, requesting, talking back to the actors, talking to each other, exiting early, entering late, "try[ing]," "search[ing]," judging, quarreling, food-throwing, "pressing" the stage, "drowning" the stage, physically *taking* the stage, one way or another – and seeing these forms of play-destroying as, ultimately, forms of play-making, we can follow that claim through to its somewhat less obvious conclusion: that the collaborative, dialogic nature of playgoing mandates a rethinking of the most basic discursive problems of early modern English theatre. We began with the question of how it became possible to speak of the "author" of a play, but perhaps the real question is how it became possible to speak of "plays" for there to be "authors" *of*.

Distinct from the classical, humanist, and morality drama of the pre-professional theatre, whose publications rhetoricize themselves as either anticipating performance (supplying cast lists, advice for the size and attire of troupes, duration, and even editing) or as altogether ignorant of it (as mere reading material, "treatises" in dramatic form), the commercial drama of the public playhouses *began* life in its performed state, swaddled in a living institution that rendered its *auctoritas* illegible and its formal identity plastic.[99] As we have seen, the play was not so much a commodity as a space for constructing one, and that commodity *was* the audience, the individual's self-fashioning in relation to others and the crowd's perception of itself as a whole. Richard Helgerson called this "the players' theater," but "players" – except as the term remained open to definition – clearly were not its key element.[100] To recognize this "audience's theatre," as we might instead name it, as "heteroglossic" does not mean we can quite call it "authorless," as Bakhtinian critics often claim.[101] Playgoers do not seem to have been partaking in a utopian carnival where speech lacked source, action lacked consequence, or individuality melted into anonymity – just ask the one who hit Tarlton with a pippin – but rather in an activity that tested the boundaries of these very categories, in dialectical opposition to the production onstage. Were the authority of early modern performance altogether dissolved, instead of merely dispersed, its concentration would pose no real challenge. The nature of playgoing, however, was not authorlessness, but a *superabundance* of authors: each one "covetous," seeking himself on stage and jockeying for possession of it, each one vying to impress herself upon the play, emphatically grounding performance in time and space.

If – as playgoers seem to have done – we take seriously such participation as acts of ownership, their vocalizations, disruptions, invasions, and destructions of the stage as imprinting upon performance an authorial stamp, then the publication of *every* playbook – *any* playbook – suddenly acquires a politics, regardless of whose name might appear on it. Whereas the New Textualist model materializes performance only up to the lip of the stage, distributing the authority of dramatic texts among all the agents of their production, to carry that project beyond the stage's edge – into the axis of reception – explodes the coherence of "production" itself, and so polarizes performance and print as to make them mutually unintelligible. If what the audience authorized was only a series of discrete performances, never realized identically twice, then how did they – not we, but *they* – homogenize the material in common to those performances as a single entity, as a "play"? How did an ownership that expressed itself by continuously warping its object tolerate the stabilization of that object in another medium, and here, moreover, under the aegis of the very agents against whom it competed? In order to ask how plays came to be thought of as originating from a writer, in other words, we must first explain how plays could be thought of as *terminating* in *writing itself.* How could an "audience's theatre," whose plural authorship intractably fragmented the identities of dramatic products and precluded their ability to be owned, yield to an "author's theatre," whose precondition – even more basic than its use of authors – was the reducibility of those products to *texts?*

Such a succession seems eventually to have occurred, and by this "eventually" there hangs a tale. The evidence for the ascendancy of the "author's theatre" is all around us: in the author-driven taxonomies and procedures we today use to regulate nearly all cultural production; in the "man and his works" ethos that structures our responses to and valuations of art, literature and theatre; most immediately for our purposes, in the early modern dramatic texts that survived to misrepresent the social practices which generated them. Histories of dramatic authorship – themselves products of their object of inquiry – have thus tended to cluster around its visible milestones, namely printed ones. Authorship registers on paper, so that is where we look for it. Accordingly, our histories have so far concerned purely bibliographic phenomena: the migration of authorial attribution, out of relative oblivion, first to title-page initials (e.g. R[obert]. W[ilson].'s *Three Ladies of London* (1584)), to end-text *explicit* (e.g. Peele's *Edward I* (1593)), to the sudden spike of full title-page ascriptions in 1594; the cosmetic emendations made by the printers of Marlowe's *Tamburlaine* (1590) and Kyd's *Spanish Tragedy* (1592) to conform them to a "readerly logic" instead of a theatrical one; the construction of Shakespeare as an author between 1598 and 1600; the title pages of Jonson's *Every Man Out* (1600) and *Sejanus* (1605), each announcing their divergence from what had been "Publickely Spoken or Acted"; the title page to *Volpone* (1607), visually subordinating the title of the play to the author; the increased frequency of class-marked paratexts, like aristocratic dedications and commendatory verses; the gradual typographic shift from blackletter to roman, as well as the uses of Latin epigraphy, commonplacing, and continuous printing, indicative of the rising literary status of printed drama; the crossover of playwrights into more esteemed poetic modes (sonneteering, epyllion, translation), exemplified in the lyric anthologies of the early seventeenth century and by Chapman's *Whole Works of Homer* (1616); the imitation of this classical, biographically driven format by publications including commercial plays (Jonson's *Workes* (1616)), and later consisting exclusively of them (Shakespeare's *Comedies, Histories and Tragedies* (1623)); the statistical drop-off to less than 10 percent of playbooks printed anonymously by the second decade of the seventeenth century; the steady, corresponding climb of playbooks acknowledging joint authorship and their acceptance of playwrights as historical subjects, culminating with Beaumont and Fletcher's *Works* in 1647.[102] These indices, of the emergence of an "author's theatre" where the play originates as writing, are as important as the sentence required to list them was long, and I am here dismissing neither their value nor that of the numerous studies that expound upon them. But to the core problem of the "author's theatre" we have been excavating – the textual representability of the play, which *enables* authorship of it – they are superficial. Whether our histories of dramatic authorship explain the appearance of authorial bylines as arbitrary demarcators of mercantile property zones, or as marketing strategies to give plays literary appeal (probably, both), does not finally matter. Insofar as they regard these bylines as marking the *inception* of a process rather than its terminus, they study merely the symptoms of that process, not the underlying pathology.

For evidence of this nascent "author's theatre," I would argue, we do not need to consult bylines, or title pages, or any of the changing topical features of playbooks. Every playbook was already latently "authorial" in its very form. In stark contrast to the textual conventions of genres like the masque or the civic pageant, whose past-tense inflections record (albeit selectively) historically specific events, the event-status of printed plays – uncomplicated by the repetitions of commercial performance – is utterly evacuated, along with the cumulative, constitutive contributions of their respective audiences. Hovering somewhere between imperative and indicative moods, the grammar of Elizabethan stage directions inhabits a kind of null present, indicating – with few exceptions – prescription, not action.[103] Only the thin membranes of prologues, epilogues, and title-page copy give the playbook access to the multifarious life in performance that lies behind it. It is equally indifferent to the lives that lie ahead of it: only two commercial plays printed after 1587 survive with cast lists suggesting the assignment of parts.[104] In 1571, the title page of *Damon and Pithias* still looks backward and forward to construct its sociology: its text is "*as the same* was played before the Queenes Maiestie" – a claim of historical exactitude reinforced by its proviso that "the prologue ... is somewhat altered for the proper vse of them that hereafter shall haue occasion to plaie it, either in priuate, or open audience."[105] Later playbooks similarly advertise "as it was played before the Queenes [or King's] Maiestie," but no strict identity between text and occasion is here implied. "[A]s it was played" does not mean "*as the same* was played" – much less the perfunctory boilerplate "as it hath been sundrie times played," which makes no effort to fix the text relative to any one of those occasions, nor to any prior variant edition with which it may materially conflict. (When such attempts are made, the result is usually something like Q2 *Hamlet's* muddled "newly imprinted and enlarged to almost as much againe as it was," which still references only the previous quarto.) Whatever gesture at theatrical provenance or textual integrity it might make, *every* early modern English printed playbook grammatically understands *its* verbal instantiation to be "the play," and "the play," in turn, an autotelic object comprised solely of such verbal instantiations.

A playbook does not even try, meanwhile, to preserve the random, heterogeneous, pluralistic totality of any single performance. It presents instead a temporally conflated and vocally streamlined version of what only the *players* said and did – or, rather, of what only *some* players *might* have said and done at some unknown juncture in the play's stage history. Quarto playbooks almost uniformly ignore, for instance, the act divisions that we know were a key structural feature of performance, let alone preserve the variegated material – inter-act music, sometimes dancing, and above all, as we will see in Chapter 2, stage clowning – that filled those interstices. Instead, with striking uniformity, they begin and end with markers of dramatic identity ("*Actus Primus, scæna prima*," and "*Finis*"), yet elide every break in between, suggesting an otherwise uninterrupted, unadulterated theatrical experience. Playbooks also ignore, at the same time as stealthily incorporating them, the often productive collaborations of their plays' audiences. It was apparently routine for poets to revise plays by redacting episodes playgoers found especially objectionable; performance sometimes solicited these improvements directly, indeed, as when the prologue to Marston's *Antonio and Mellida* (1602) asks its audience to "polish these rude Sceanes."[106] Yet playbooks in turn redacted the evidence of this co-authorship, and of the play's plasticity, publishing it as if it had originally existed and always been performed in exactly that state. Flattening the dialogue with the stage into a monologue of the page, removed from time, space, and contingency, printed playbooks are fossils of imaginary animals, the idealization into a perfect whole of that abstraction called "the play," merely what the players *intended* to perform on any given day – not how, or even whether, they actually did.[107] Playbooks do not just erase performance: they negate it, representing the play as if it happens only, or has already happened, on paper. Insofar as they transmitted verbal artifacts autonomous from their realization and from their audiences, *every* printed playbook differed, by definition, from what "hath been Publickely Spoken or Acted," and *every* playbook by definition already conforms to what Lukas Erne calls "readerly logic." That is to say, they make the reading of theatre possible.[108]

This logic dictates that a reader's experience, unlike a playgoer's, be dictated. Were the form of a playbook retentive of all the interference an audience could generate in a specific performance, it might look like *The Knight of the Burning Pestle*, only with more speaking parts; were each performance, furthermore, invested with equal authority as a representation of the play, no two printings of this *Pestle*-like playbook would look even remotely the same – unless it could be done as hypertext, with every word a palimpsestic link to its variants. And even could such a theoretically infinite number of books be made, there would be no reason to purchase any of them, since readers, unlike playgoers, tend to value the social currency of a text over its uniqueness. What here arbitrates between, cancels out, and supplants the competing authorities of performance is, by process of elimination, the authority of the playing company itself, which alone remains constant across performances. Regardless of the degree to which the title page specifies them or their playhouse, "the book of the play" is always implicitly *their* play, not even so much because it was legally theirs to print, as because only "their" play *can* be printed. Well before the advent of the authorial names attached to it, the playbook was already a template for literary property. Despite the complicating, formative agency of the several new collaborators (scribe, stationer, censor, printer) necessary to achieve it, the act of textualizing a play after its performance automatically foreclosed on 99 percent of the agents with an authorial claim to those performed states. The creation of one "reader" – a persona, notably, almost always addressed as singular – implicitly un-created one, or two, or ten, or twenty thousand spectators.[109]

The inevitability of playbooks

Now, that "eventually": these satisfied readers and disenfranchised spectators were largely the same people.[110] There are good reasons for not taking this commonsense assumption as absolute demographic identity, of course. At sixpence, a playbook would have cost six times the lowest admission fee to amphitheatres such as the Fortune or the Rose – a considerable sum for those furthest down the socioeconomic ladder, who have been traditionally supposed the least literate segment of the audience for the same reason that they have also been supposed the most stridently participatory. (As David Cressy has argued, and as this study will later show, neither compartmentalization is as easy as we might like.)[111] Given the relatively small press runs of playbook quartos, hardly every playgoer could or did purchase them. Neither were publication patterns uniform, with a disproportionate number of plays from the ostensibly more upscale (and later) indoor theatres finding their way into print. To embrace the opposite extreme, however, and posit a dramatic readership wholly divorced from spectatorship, is simply untenable. That playbook title pages structure their information no differently whether the play hails from the Blackfriars or the Red Bull, for instance, tells us not that readers disidentified with playhouses in general, but that they may have attended them all interchangeably.[112] An assumed commutativity between readers and playgoers, indeed, is the whole motive for playbook title pages to provide playhouse information. The disproportionate survival of playbooks in aristocratic libraries (despite Sir Thomas Bodley's dismissal of them as "riffe-raffes"), similarly, tells us nothing other than that the nobility saw no scandal in buying printed plays – nor in frequenting playhouses – and that libraries are good places for books to survive.[113] For the rest of the playgoing public, meanwhile, not every reader of a book was its first purchaser or its last owner. The used book trade, informal circulation, and amateur performance would have gradually filtered playbooks down to lower-income patrons.[114] Second-hand use vastly multiplied the number of spectators who could access plays in printed form; one of the factors in the high loss rate of playbooks, indeed, may well have been that they were successively read to death.

While early modern plays almost never internally reference their future as books, the rhetoric of their printed paratexts points to a general expectation that the community which had consumed it in one medium was now its target market in the other. Richard Jones' *Tamburlaine* (1590), for instance, at the same time as addressing "the Gentleman readers: and others that take pleasure in reading Histories," troubles the very distinction between a "theatrical" and a "readerly" logic it is often used to mark, when Jones hopes that – by excising "some fond and friuolous Iestures … vaine conceited fondlings greatly gaped at, what times they were shewed vpon the stage in their graced deformities" – the two plays "wil be now no lesse acceptable vnto you to read … then they haue bene (lately) delightfull for many of you to see."[115] These "you"s are the same. Precisely because so "many" of *Tamburlaine*'s potential readers were also its spectators, what has always been considered Jones' aesthetic scrupling between reading and seeing here masks a practical concern for the rift between them – namely, the untranslatability into print of "Iestures" and "fondlings", whose necessary omission he spins as editorial choice. Jones's optimism about the class of his reader, furthermore – the same readers who as spectators found "delightfull" the play's "deformities" – has its plebeian counterparts elsewhere. Valentine Simmes' quarto of Dekker's *The Shoemaker's Holiday* (1600) addresses the same base citizenry at whom its performance was aimed, "all good Fellowes, Professors of the Gentle Craft; of what degree so euer," while Heywood dedicates *The Four Prentices of London* (1615) "to the honest and hie-spirited Prentises The Readers."[116]

Whosesoever politics a play might flatter onstage, its potential readership was wide enough to allow it to extend the same appeal to the page. Richard Hawkins pitches his 1628 edition of *Philaster* right at the play's prior audiences, looping performance and print into an endless encore that treats the two media as mutually substitutable:

> This Play so affectionately taken, and approoued by the Seeing Auditors, or Hearing Spectators, (of which sort, I take, or conceiue you to bee the greatest part) hath receiued (as appeares by the copious vent of two Editions,) no less acceptance with improouement of you likewise the Readers ... the best Poems of this kind, in the first presentation, resemble that all-tempting Minerall newly digged up, the Actors being onely the labouring Miners, but you the skilfull Triers and Refiners: Now considering how currant this hath passed, under the infallible stamp of your iudicious censure and applause, and ... eagerly sought for, not onely by those that haue heard and seene it, but by others that haue meerely heard thereof ... (A2r–v)

Starting with playgoers, spreading outward to print and returning to a reinvigorated theatrical demand, Hawkins' market ranges from those who have "heard thereof" and wish to see, to those who have already "heard and seene" and wish to see again. That the object of their "Tr[ying]" and "Refin[ing]" now seems to have moved from the playhouse into the playbook, though, still begs the question of *why* playgoers would want the text of a play in the first place: what *uses* did it serve one who had already attended, or planned to attend, a performance? Nevertheless, by this time the fungibility of the two reception positions has become relatively unproblematic. In his epistle to *Catiline*, Jonson imagines his "Reader in Ordinarie" as recapitulating the judgment they brought to it as an ordinary playgoer: "you commend the two first Actes, with the people, because they are the worst; and dislike the oration of *Cicero*, in regard you read some pieces of it, at Schoole, and understand them not yet." Webster compares the fickle sensibility of Red Bull audiences to those of common readers, "resembl[ing] those ignorant asses (who visiting Stationers shoppes their use is not to inquire for good bookes, but new bookes.)"[117] For Beaumont, the quarto of Fletcher's *Faithfull Shepheardesse* is its "second publication," equivalent to re-performance; indeed, it is the *only* performance, since the first was mistrusted to actors "whose very reading makes verse senceless prose," meaning that "the people … saw it not." Those same people, he hopes, may now "see the thing they scornd."[118]

"Seeing" and "reading" are fast becoming indistinct terms: predicated on the demographic overlap of spectators and bookbuyers, playgoing can now be figured as mediated, textual practice and private study as immediate, visceral experience, each mode implicit in and supportive of the other.[119] By 1624, William Basse's puff for Massinger's *The Bond-Man* can go so far as to declare all performance merely mental rehearsal for the audience, to prepare them for the inward gratifications of the book:

> And (Reader) if you have disburs'd a shilling,
> To see this worthy STORY, and are willing
> To have a large encrease; (if rul'd by me)
> You may a MARCHANT, and a POET be.
> 'Tis granted for your twelue-pence you did sit,
> And *See*, and *Hear*, and *Understand* not yet.
> The AUTHOR (in a Christian pitty) takes
> Care of your good, and Prints it for your sakes.
> That such as will but venter Six-pence more,
> May *Know*, what they but *Saw*, and *Heard* before.[120]

In the same idealist vein, James Shirley would tell prospective purchasers of Beaumont and Fletcher's 1647 *Works* to "congratulate thy owne happinesse, that in this silence of the Stage, thou hast a liberty to read these inimitable Playes … which were only shewd our fathers in a conjuring glasse."[121] Whatever audiences were being "rul'd by" in order to "*Turne reader*," as Leonard Digges put it in 1640, it was probably not the condescensions of people like Basse, or the ministrations of prefatory matter buried too deep within a playbook to influence its sale. Yet playgoers increasingly bought playbooks anyway. Just *why* they did so, given the overwhelming and simultaneous evidence for playgoing as an irresolubly collaborative, improvisatory, interactive pastime, is perhaps the most crucial – and complex – question in early modern English theatre history.[122]

From 1576 to 1593, a total of just twenty professional plays were printed, barely one per year; eight of those years featured no commercial dramatic publications at all. In 1594 alone, however, fully eighteen new plays were published, seven of which went to second editions by 1600. For the next two decades the trade averaged roughly thirteen playbooks per year, and as Alan Farmer and Zachary Lesser have shown, despite periodic fluctuation they remained far more popular, and reliably profitable, than their raw market share once suggested.[123] Stressing that "the market for playbooks had to be created," Farmer and Lesser nevertheless locate this demand on the supply side of the equation – with the stationers' discovery after 1594 that "plays were suddenly selling very well," leading to second editions and the confidence to produce more firsts.[124] We thus have a demand-side theory without a theory: understandably, since the best evidence of demand is supply. Precisely *for* its "suddenness," indeed – *because* London bookbuyers in 1594 "might well have been surprised to find a play from the professional theaters among their choices" – the dormant appetite this glut awakened becomes all the more puzzling, and hard to originate within a bookbuying mindset not already structured by prior playgoing activity.[125]

Tiffany Stern moves us closer to an answer, by bringing early modern print and performance into more direct, physical contact. Given the evidence for the sale of books and pamphlets inside the walls of playhouses themselves, and "given that published plays anticipate being read by spectators, often the very spectators that watched the piece in the first place," she concludes that "playhouse sale of playbooks seems highly likely," and proceeds to consider its implications:

> the possibility is then raised that a theater audience might be partly shaped to and by printed playtexts that they bought in the theater … if playbooks *were* sold in playhouses then the paper potential of the performed text will always have been felt by the audience. The "book" will have seemed what the play was likely to become next – while the enacted play will never have become entirely separated in kind, at least in the mind of the watchers, from a written one.[126]

This is still a supply-side explanation, yet a richer one. No longer must the playgoer go to the bookshop in order to make the connection between the performed play and its printed version; on this theory, the printed version came to the playhouse, and made that connection for them. But still, how? Proximity is not superposition: unless the copies on sale were of the same play being enacted that day – and even then, since one would have to follow along to discover *that* it was the same play, or rather a completely different and denuded one under the same title – the playgoer must already grasp what a playbook is and means, and *want* to buy or read one. Stern's playgoers already understand this: if, in her words, they are merely "watchers" of the play, then it is for them already implicitly a written text.[127] I think we can go one step further, by going one step further back. Let us imagine a playhouse altogether without playbooks: how might it invent them? What if its interpenetration with textual practice had to occur not just near the stage, but on it? To have books inside the theatres, did theatre as a whole first have to be inside a book?

And thus, a paradox. If sheer supply could not create the legibility of playbooks, what could, but the very performance conditions that also militated against it? How did dramatic texts establish a conversibility with performance, except *through* performance? Where else could playgoers learn that a play could be a book, except at plays themselves – the very *last* place one might expect to learn this? A playbook can never make itself like the live experience of theatre: it is an inanimate object, incapable of interaction, and even its rhetoric is one of fixity, of morphological arrest. Performance, on the other hand, is mutable, its assumptions, procedures, and conventions subject to gradual change. This asks performance itself to become inanimate too, a proposition which its principal agents – its audiences – would intuitively, and (as we have seen) incessantly did, reject. So how could they be, and how were they, persuaded to accept it? Before any cachet attached to printed drama, and before local reading cultures assimilated it to new uses, why did playgoers purchase textual renditions of an experience that completely betrayed the fiber of that experience? How could they countenance the implication – being made explicitly by 1624 – that the organizing principles of their entertainment were illegitimate, that the sensorium of theatre was an illusion, and that its true substance was to be found on pieces of paper impervious to confrontation? If what audiences demanded was "suffrage," to "act their parts," why did they spend money on versions of plays that rendered those parts unacted, that edited them out – asserting, as blankly as the white space on its pages, that they did not count?

The only answer thus far advanced to these questions is as elegant as it is evasive of them: that no such relation obtained between performance and text – that we are being perversely literal about this, and that (to quote Stephen Orgel) "if the play is a book, it's not a play."[128] While a useful precaution for us as modern editors, it does not bear on the mentality of those early modern playgoers who were being invited to attend performances and then to buy texts of them as modules of a single cultural activity.

David Scott Kastan reminds us that the text of a play and its performance "are materially and theoretically distinct," with neither "more or less
authentic than the other," but this is true only in the present tense. In their
original sequence, where a play's performance always preceded its textualization, the fact that playbooks "deny performance altogether" becomes
more than just an academic crux. It meant the erasure of history.[129]

Against the hypothesis that playbooks merely advertised future productions or revivals, finally, stands the fact that no playbook ever actually
claims this much; if they did, we might reasonably expect at least one to
say so.[130] The closest we come to proof of the playbook's advertising function, indeed, returns us to *The Roaring Girl*: in their preface to the quarto,
Middleton and Dekker hope that it "may bee allowed both Gallery roome
at the Play-house, and chamber-roome at your lodging."[131] If the printed
version is meant to get playgoers into the playhouse, however, the performed version behaves as though that book does not exist. The same
spectators who bring a copy of the play in their hands – a text that should
delimit performance – will also, as we have seen, instantly find themselves
being accused of "bring[ing] a play in's head" as well. Why did Middleton
and Dekker think that audiences, who would know from the playbook
what to expect, would forget what was expected of them once they got
to the playhouse? Operative here seems to be a kind of mutual disregard:
if playgoers understood the articulation of performance and text enough
to buy books that ignored them, they also understood the disjunction
between performance and text enough to ignore those books in kind.

Theatre, then, comes to exist during the period in at least two related
but discrete states. The play *was* a book, since most of those who bought
playbooks were playgoers, either past or future. The play was also still *not*
a book, since its textuality appears not to have curtailed participation during performance. The former is what needs explaining, but it cannot be
explained without the latter. This, I think, is what has kept histories of
dramatic authorship thus far segregated from histories of performance:
their contradictory narratives are never forced to intersect. By reading
only the apparata of printed plays, one can tell the story of early modern drama as a rise of reading; by reading around them, conversely, one
can tell the same story as a static history of vibrant, defiant commoning.
Neither synthesizes the evidence to unravel how the two phenomena can
coexist, braided around each other yet separate. The reception evidence
we have surveyed in this chapter spans the entirety of the Elizabethan
and early Stuart period, continuing until the closure of the theatres and
beyond. Yet while audiences asserted their presence by destroying plays

and on occasion even playhouses, for their textual dispossession there is no record of anyone's ever burning, protesting, or even refusing to purchase a playbook. Indeed, in the one documented instance where an audience undertook to produce a playbook itself – transcribing Heywood's *If You Know Not Me*, where "some by Stenography ... put it in print" – Heywood tells us that they only "drew / The Plot."[132] Not the *performance*, in other words, which included them, but merely the *text*, which did not. Without needing to be told, they instinctively deleted themselves.

The ritual practices of the "audience's theatre" would endure for decades, "the play" conflating representational drama and improvised contest, soliloquy and heckle, player and auditor. And yet, *from within* it, grew an "author's theatre" that enforced these discriminations when "the play" reached the page. That paradox is the heart of this study. Before the figure of the playwright could emerge to consolidate and accelerate theatrical experience as a reading experience, "ownership" of theatrical production had to mean different things in different domains, and we need a more expansive, nuanced account of what – and how – "authorship" itself could mean in order to underwrite the bibliographic spaces in which it would eventually coalesce. Behind the history of dramatic authorship, that is, lies a more nebulous prehistory of theatrical individuation. Even as they went on disputing performance, by purchasing playbooks that turned those performances into paper, playgoers seem instinctively to have recognized that "theatre" possessed an innate authority *other* than theirs – an authority that predated and transcended performance, and that *originated* on paper as well. They first had to recognize, in other words, the existence of the one piece of paper they could never see: the script.

In this chapter I have tried to show that a history of how theatre became readable, and readable as already written, is larger than the paper on which its texts were printed. The authority inscribed in the playbook must trace to something outside and prior to the playbook itself, since playbooks needed playgoers to buy them. Rather, it must ultimately be grounded in the institution that spawned both, creating not only texts to be purchased, but the very people to purchase them. To print a playbook was not enough to make a play a book; that had to happen in and to the nature of performance itself, which is where the audience was. And where the audience was, so was the clown.

CHAPTER 2

Send in the clown

A master of fence is more honourable than a master of arte; for good
fightinge was before good wrightinge.
— Anon., *The Mountebank's Masque, c.* 1617

After the epilogue, before the prologue

For us, a prologue marks the start of a play, simply because it marks the
start of the text that contains it. Thus, a surpassingly small genre – typically twenty lines long – has been made to carry a disproportionate load in
our reconstruction of early modern performance dynamics. Then again,
insofar as we have confined issues like audience management to dramatic
evidence, the same might be said of "plays" themselves. Most recently,
Douglas Bruster and Robert Weimann have analyzed prologues as bridging the embodied world of the playhouse with the representational world
of the play:

> Prologues authorize the theatre to produce and perform plays as well as the
> right of the audience to evaluate these practices ... At the outset of dra-
> matic performances, the prologue ushered its early modern audience over
> an imaginary threshold – a threshold both of and for the imagination as
> well as one both of and for the specifically dramatic, theatrical uses of the
> "wooden O." This differentiating function of the prologue helped isolate
> dramatic from non-verbal types of performances.[1]

By "non-verbal types of performances," Bruster and Weimann mean
other entertainments – bearbaiting, for instance – with which playgoing
competed. Such "savage" sensibilities, latent in "the clamor and 'hurly-
burly' generated by many hundreds of fellow playgoers," are here purged
by the "rite of passage" of the "three soundings of a trumpet [that] would
usually announce the beginning of a play" – instantly transforming the
playhouse into a quiescent, introspective laboratory for the theorization
of culture.[2] Into the Elizabethan prologue, then, this account squeezes

60

the entire foundation of the New Historicism. Such analyses can be so efficient not only because they abstract prologues from the plays that follow, but because they proceed from a retrospectively distorted model of theatrical experience, discounting what the prologue *itself* would have followed.[3]

For Bruster and Weimann, that is, as for anyone basing their arguments solely on the evidence of playbooks, the prologue marks "the outset of dramatic performance," the absolute *incipit* of the theatrical event. Between the entry of the audience and the trumpet blasts, we must believe, no other practices consonant with a broader sense of "play" are already underway. What drops out of this model, as a result, is how prologues "authorize the theater to produce and perform plays," or why they would need to do so, when there has been no offer of competition. As we saw in Chapter 1, soliciting the audience's engagement with the play was not the problem; rather, it was constraining the audience to accept the *company's* play as the theatrical event. This chapter investigates those savage, "non-verbal types of performance" against which "theatre" is here defined: not only were they very much a part of theatre, I argue, but they were its fundamental prolegomena. By the time the Prologue arrived, he was already an Epilogue to something else.

Sometimes, for example, a play could begin the day before it began – in the tradition of nominating, at the *end* of a performance, what the *next* day's fare would be. Humphrey Moseley closes the preliminaries to Beaumont and Fletcher's *Works* (1647) by saying "As after th'Epilogue there comes some one / To tell Spectators what shall next be shown"; sometimes, indeed, the custom invoked the audience's sovereignty to choose it themselves.[4] In a letter *c.* 1611–15, the Venetian Antimo Galli describes an unfortunate episode that befell Ambassador Antonio Foscarini, who, indulging his predilection for (and ineptitude at) slumming *incognito* at the Curtain, waded in "among the rabble of porters and carters" in the pit:

> at the end, when one of the actors took leave of the audience and invited it to come back the next day and to pick a play, he actually named one. But the crowd wanted another and began to shout "Friars, Friars," because they wanted one that usually took its name from the friars, meaning *frati*. Whereupon our blockhead turned to his interpreter, [who] explained that this was the name of a comedy about friars. So loosening his cloak, he began to clap his hands just as the mob did and to shout "frati, frati." As he was shouting this, the people turned to him and, assuming he was a Spaniard, began to whistle in such a way that I cannot imagine that he would ever want to return to that place.[5]

We cannot be sure how tentative or matter-of-fact is the player's proposal, but the crowd feels no compunction about contravening him, and becomes so vehement in its insistence on *Friar Bacon and Friar Bungay* – clapping in unison – that the discovery of a foreigner in their midst ignites a torrent of xenophobia bordering on violence. While we may note the remarkably retrograde tendencies of canon formation here – instead of the proverbial thirst for novelty, the audience demands a comedy over thirty years old – the point is that their method of choosing is no less ritualistic than their choice. The crowd senses that the appearance of the *nuntius* is also its cue to overrule him, and does so instantly; its reaction to Foscarini is an extension of the solidarity the Epilogue's gesture is contrived to foster. One wonders, indeed, if the Curtain audience *ever* approved the company's first choice, even if it happened to be "Friars."

In his recollection of a more specialized variant of the practice, Edmund Gayton gives a sense of what "the play" might come to look like when its performance transpired under the formal mandate of the audience. In the same anecdote that concluded with the playhouse's demolition under a barrage of fruit and tile, which we saw in Chapter 1, Gayton suggests that democratic theatre may have been a license reserved for holidays – yet he goes on to note the danger of such a power transfer, where the choice of entertainment often became the entertainment itself:

> [T]o them [the average playgoers] bring *Jack Drums Entertainment*, *Greens tu quoque*, the *Devill of Edmunton*, and the like; or if it be on Holy dayes ... then it is good policy to amaze those violent spirits, with some tearing Tragædy full of fights and skirmishes: as the *Guelphs* and *Guiblins*, *Greeks* and *Trojans*, or the three *London Apprentises*, which commonly ends in six acts, the spectators frequently mounting the stage, and making a more bloody Catastrophe amongst themselves, then the Players did. I have known upon one of these *Festivals*, but especially at *Shrove-tide*, where the Players have been appointed, notwithstanding their bills to the contrary, to act what the major part of the company had a mind to; sometimes *Tamerlane*, sometimes *Jugurth*, sometimes the Jew of *Malta*, and sometimes parts of all these, and at last, none of the three taking, they were forc'd to undresse and put off their Tragick habits, and conclude the day with the merry milk-maides.[6]

Here is the reflexive taste for familiar fare again, but the selection of any specific play is in short order eclipsed by the freedom to select, which the audience pushes to the brink of brutality. The reason for "none of the three taking," one suspects, is that the crowd's real pleasure comes from the constant interchange of subject matter: if in the end they demand a comedy, after disintegrating three tragedies into "parts," they have of course been producing a farce of their own already. They turn the players into jukeboxes, and flex the same destructive power over the play – like overrunning the stage at the end of Heywood's *Four Prentices of London* (1615) – by shredding it into a manic medley. When the play transpires as an emanation of the audience's will from the start, in other words, they abuse that authority until no "play" can actually transpire from start to finish. Utterly undermined, meanwhile, is the authority of the players: the only "company" here, in Gayton's use of the term, is the crowd. And when the players bridle, he goes on, it vents its frustration (just as it turned on Foscarini) in a flash of collective anger – in this case, aimed at the play-house itself: "It was not then the most mimicall nor fighting man, *Fowler*, nor *Andrew Cane* could pacifie; Prologues nor Epilogues would prevaile; the Devill and the fool were quite out of favour."[7]

This passage is worth dwelling on. The players face an unruly mob so drunk with entitlement that it refuses to yield the stage, weaponizing that very stage against them; in such an emergency, their countermeasures reca-pitulate English theatre history in reverse. Gone is the possibility of any integral fiction, even to the level of the scene: what instead erupts is the histrionic tradition of medieval drama – a menagerie of stock types, devil and fool, figures who play to the audience, raw, "mimicall" performers (Fowler the swashbuckler, Cane the clown) known directly by name. They come too late here, but the expectation is that they can "pacifie" where both flat denial of and abject surrender to the playgoers cannot. What seems to us the basest, most desperate appeasement – a stage that panders to and incorporates the audience – here also serves, in theory, as an instru-ment of control. The closer we get to the embodied self, the performer presented as such rather than representing another in a symbolic field, the further we get from the idea of theatre as an aesthetically governed cul-tural production. And yet the closer we come to the seat of theatre's real power, the means by which it governed – and had to govern – itself first and foremost as a social production.[8]

Earlier in his work, Weimann sketched this relationship as the diffe-rence between *locus* and *platea*: the upstage site of referential mimesis, and the downstage area in more fluid, intimate dialogue with the performed event.[9] This *Figurenposition*, for Weimann, always requires a mimetic back-drop against which to function. When the authority of the stage is taken for granted, that is – as playbooks invite us to suppose – performance can be imagined as "playful," its valence always subversive, because there is always a textual regime for it to subvert: indeed, for Weimann, what defines Shakespearean dramaturgy is its anticipation and incorporation of such subversion. He may declare, then, that "once theatre history has become conceivable in the absence of an authority in dramatic writing … alternative locations of authority can be envisioned," but they are not really all that "alternative."[10] The "circulation of authority" in theatre that for him becomes "inclusive" includes only author and player, "pen" and "voice," and not the authority of the *audience* whose voices both had to negotiate.[11] Acknowledging this need, in fact, and broadening our focus to the vehicles available for doing so, might *connect* such activity to the "authority in dramatic writing" whose installation Weimann ultimately cannot explain. For if non-mimetic performance were purely differential, and limited to the drama proper – to self-conscious winks at the player's real identity from within it – it begs the question of how such "real" identity first revealed itself in order to register there.[12] How did the audience *know* a player was merely "being himself" at any moment in a play, unless that self had already been established elsewhere?

In an urban, professional environment, the audience could not know all players equally: this slippage between self and role was restricted only to certain performers, and presupposes a much wider, interpenetrative, presentational format. Inside the fragile membrane of the play, the *platea* may have been subservient to the *locus*; beyond those borders, however, *platea* was all there was – its function to *enable* dramatic production, this chapter will argue, by first claiming the stage as a site of production in itself. This liminal, ludic space permeated the play as much as it preconditioned it: it could be inserted anywhere – after a series of bids to settle the crowd, Gayton's players thrust out Cane in a last-ditch effort to re-initialize the system – because the clash it mediated was an elemental version of dramatic conflict as a whole, the contest of individuals to speak.

More than any part in which the play enlisted him, or to which it today reduces him, this generalized set of operations was the responsibility of one member of personnel, the stage clown. And it is why, from the inception of Elizabethan playing companies, the clown was always their nucleus. Of the twelve sharers drafted into the Queen's Men in 1583, six – Richard Tarlton, Robert Wilson, John Singer, John Adams, John Garland, and John Laneham – were comedians, a fact easier to reconcile with the troupe's mission to "give the impression of a watchful monarch" than it may at first seem. Clowns assumed leadership roles in company administration vastly disproportionate to their fictive roles in plays; whenever the stage was empty, clowns were sent on to fill it.[13] An enormous body of fanfare celebrates the clown as populist hero – again, on the basis of the dramatic record alone, one might ask why – yet for the playing company, in its regulatory structures if not its texts, he remained an intuitive figure of control. These facts are deeply related.

A king of shreds and patches

> Am I reuilde and bafled to my face
> And by a Dotard? one but for his tongue,
> In whom there is no difference twixt himselfe
> A meere Anothomie, a Iack of lent,
> And the pale Image of a bloudlesse ghoast?
> – Anon., *The Weakest Goeth to the Wall*
> (1600), F3r

The Elizabethan stage clown was primarily a solo performer. For most scholars, he descends from the Vice of Tudor morality, whose personification of unstable qualities – hypocrisy, mischief, temptation – lent him, together with his dynamic stage presence, a polymorphous psychology in excess of any single allegorical type. As his various names attest (Envy, Politic Persuasion, Ambidexter, Haphazard, Nicholas Newfangle, Sin), he stands for the evil inclination necessary to the *psychomachia*; self-referentially, he stands for the spectacular, fraudulent principles of playing itself.[14] For this reason, he has been seen as a progenitor of the Elizabethan anti-hero, voluble, enigmatic characters like Richard III, Iago, and Hamlet, who force us to abritrate competing value systems.[15] Yet for that exact reason, we cannot draw a straight line from the Vice to the clown. Though they share similar dramatic techniques, they express completely opposite ideas. We cannot explain how the Vice goes from the play's center to its margins; from plot mover to skeptical bystander or accidental victim; from crafty wit to witless innocent; from slick, sophistical urbanity to gullible rusticity.[16] From a hyper-performative persona – the player who presents himself *as* a player, as anything but himself – the last decades of the sixteenth century revert to a hypo-performative one: the player who presents *nothing* but himself, whose pretense consists in the disavowal of pretense. Far from shading linearly into one another, this incongruence argues for the clown a more complex extraction, and a different function.

To be sure, both ultimately trace their origin to the long line of comic types that the English folk-play inherited and adapted from classical and Christian tradition – the impertinent servant of Roman drama, the chorus and the *mimus*, the saucy apprentices of medieval St. George pageants and swordplays, mystery-play devils. And, on the surface at least, their performative idioms appear homologous. Like the clown's, the Vice's is a mangled patter of catchphrases and proverbs reminiscent of the *sermons joyeux* of the French *sottie* plays; like the clown, the Vice is the play's built-in audience manager, engaging the crowd and pacing its responses. His art thus accommodated improvisation, dictated by open-ended stage directions calling for flight ("*Infidelitie runneth away … Cry all thus without the doore and roare terribly*"), fighting ("[Courage] *fighteth to prolong the time while Wantonnesse maketh her ready*"), or song ("*Nichole Newfangle bringeth in with him a bagge … going about the place shewing it to the audience, and singing this* – Trim marchandise, trim, trim, trim marchandise, trim, trim … *He may sing this as oft as he thinketh good*").[17] "Vice" and "clown" both name a set of extradramatic procedures, and their mutual indispensability to the theatrical event is attested to by the infrequency with which they are doubled.[18] In contrast to more conventional dramatic roles – a contrast the clown's diminished stage-time heightens – each is a part for only one highly specialized, highly skilled performer, his costume changes minimized to facilitate instant recognition.

Even on the pragmatic level of crowd control, however, their difference lay in the sociology of their respective theatres. The Vice developed to meet the needs of itinerant troupes performing at shifting, provincial venues: in his hubris and showmanship, he was the exemplar of a theatre that to its audiences remained an exoticism. Different audiences demand different strategies, however, especially when they are the same audiences over and over. As David Wiles observes, the clown was fundamentally a response to London – yet not only to its demography, I would add, but to its performance conditions.[19] On the one hand, a growing segment of the populace composed of newly urbanized immigrants inspired a nostalgia for the country, and a new kind of stage figure able to tap its "coarse, anarchic, peasant" energies, to encourage its "active participation in the making of a culture."[20] But in the first years of daily playing in London, the "culture" being made was also that of the theatre itself, on which the phenomenon of repeat audiences bore far more pointedly than did an idea of the city at large. Sedentism entailed a new power dynamic between player and playgoer – increasingly familiar with one another, increasingly on equal footing – and a new vocabulary of engagement that adapted to its challenge.

That vocabulary, it turns out, would explicitly thematize challenge. If the Vice's flamboyance was too specific to itinerancy to serve as raw material, the development of his urban counterpart involved a different return to their common source in ritual festivity. Wiles argues that the clown recalled the figure of the Lord of Misrule, the ceremonial inversionary title granted, during Christmas revels or Whitsun mayings, to a townsman of low status. The Lord proved his worth by failing at his tasks, and thus the clown's trademark is always to "maneuver himself into a losing position." Whereas the Vice is destroyed by the countervailing forces of good, the clown is always the agent of his own untrussing, trapping himself in Bergsonian struggles with matter so that his opponent can emerge victorious – a joust with a dog being the paradigmatic example.[21] We must be cautious, however, of letting episodes from plays define his practice, which only partly represent its elements. Carnival needs an authority to antagonize, and insofar as the clown was the object of such antagonism from the audience, he was also an emissary of Lent.

The clown fused the Misrule tradition with another strand of popular culture, the Jack-a-Lent. Jack-a-Lents were originally effigies at which children threw stones during Lent, a pastime derived from a Shrovetide custom called throwing-at-cocks, in which a tethered rooster was pelted to death.[22] The effigy eventually became a pageant figure who appeared not at the start of Lent but at its end, an anthropomorphized scapegoat who transmuted bloodlust into play, and who negotiated the boundaries of chaos and order. Henry Machyn describes a Lord Mayor's procession in London on Palm Monday, 1553:

> and then cam the dullo and a sawden and then [a priest?] sheryffyng Jack-of-lent on horss-bake, and a do[ctor] ys fezyssyoun [i.e. his physician], and then Jake-of-lents wyff brow[ght him] ys fessysyons and bad save ys lyff, and he shuld [give him] a thowsand li for ys labur …[23]

The bargaining quackdoctor who will revive Jack is a detail borrowed from the St. George play; an 1855 account explains the Jack-a-Lent as an effigy "made up of straw and cast-off clothes … carried through the streets amid much noise and merriment" and subjected to ritual destructions such as being burned, drowned, shot, or thrown down a chimney.[24] What matters, however, is the liminality of his position, and the symbolic transition over which his humiliation presides. The moment it opens is carnivalesque, wherein the people take revenge on a weakened version of the Lenten austerity that has almost elapsed. Yet the season it heralds is not Carnival, but the rites of Easter and their purification. Thus Elderton's ballad "Lenton Stuffe" (1570) itself ends:

> Then Jake-a-lent comes justlynge in,
>   With the hedpeece of a herynge,
> And saythe, "repent yowe of yower syn,
>   For shame, syrs, leve yower swerynge."

And to Palme Sonday doethe he ryde.
With sprots and herryngs by hys syde,
And makes an end of Lenton tyde.[25]

That "comes justlynge in" conspicuously resembles the terms in which the
stage clown's entrance will be described. The Jack-a-Lent enacted the principle of Carnival under the auspices of its antithesis – a grotesquerie of
death, the mortification of the flesh for the welfare of the soul.[26] And so
he could never really be killed: he is always resurrected, always managing
to survive his comic torments because affliction is his very substance. His
degradation may be compulsory, but it was also only temporary.

Both the iconography and repertory of the stage clown descended
from the Jack-a-Lent through its apparent evolution, during the sixteenth century, into a freestanding idiom of performance and publication. In colloquial usage, the term denoted not only one prone to public
ridicule – "Make me a *Jack o' Lent*," says Rowland in *The Tamer Tamed*,
"and ... knock out my brains with apples" – but also, like the puppet,
one of diminutive stature: Falstaff's page Robin is called "you little Jack-a-
Lent" in *Merry Wives*, and Sir John later remarks that he has been "made
a Jack-a-Lent" by his gulling in the forest.[27] Hilt in Jonson's *Tale of a Tub*
tells Sir Metaphor "thou cam'st but halfe a thing into the world / And
wast made up of patches, parings, shreds ... thou didst stand six weeks
the *Iack* of *Lent*, / For boyes to hoorle, three throwes a penny, at thee."[28]
Visualized, he was festooned with the signs of dietary privation, the
Lenten fare of stockfish, herring, eel, and oysters. The woodcut for John
Taylor's *Jack-a-Lent His Beginning and Entertainment* (1620) sets his bony
frame astride a herring, chasing a bloated Shrove Tuesday, with Hunger at
his back; he is described as a footman who "hath the Art of Legerdemaine
beyond al the Jugglers ... yet for all this nimbleness and quicke agilitie,
hee was never seene to sweate ... because hee hath not any fat or pin-
guiditie in his incorporeall corps."[29] Because he was also associated with
the comic servant, meanwhile, the Jack-a-Lent coupled his leanness with a
proverbially insatiable gullet. "Though a man eat Fish til his guts cracke,"
Taylor adds, "yet if he eate no flesh, he Fasts, for he eates as faste as he
can."[30] Thus, perhaps, the frequent link between foodstuffs and the clown
parts of so much early modern drama; and thus the two most famous
clowns introduced by English comedians touring abroad, Pickelherring
and Stockfish, drew their profiles directly from the Jack-a-Lent canon. So
many English clowns passed to the Continent as conjugations of this root,
indeed – among them John Clam, John Conget, John Posset, John Panser,
John Grundo – that "English John" and "Jack Pudding" became generic

terms.[31] Playford's *English Dancing Master* (1651) includes a dance called "Jack a Lent," whose frenetic changes may simulate the jerky motion of the puppet as it was struck by stones – or, possibly, the rhythms of the stage clowns who patterned their routines, and jigs, after it.[32]

Along with the Jack-a-Lent's emaciated appearance came a reputation for candor and bluntness. The object of universal blame, he became a subterfuge for satire.[33] In 1547 Stephen Gardiner informed the Duke of Somerset of a recent ballad "sette fourth to deprave the Lent ... to rayle and to cause such as used to make provision for fish against lent, fearinge now lent to be so sick as the rime purporteth and like to die indeed." Not only did it literalize the Jack-a-Lent's visual conceit into a doctrinal argument, we learn, but it made him its speaker: Somerset chides Gardiner for "bee[ing] so ernest ... about jack of lents leude balade." Gardiner, meanwhile, worries that "Jack of lentes testament ... was openly solde in Winchester market, before I wrote unto your grace."[34] At home in the placeless world of print and a step ahead of its censorship, such pseudonymous "rimes," ballads, and "testaments" would continue to channel news and commentary for fully the next century. In 1548 appeared *Recantacion of Jacke Lent late vicare generall to the moost cruell Antichriste of Rome*; in 1562, "How the worlde ys well amended quod lettle Jack of Lente &c"; in 1578, "A shorte and sweete memorye of Jack a Lentes honestie."[35] "Honest Jack of Lent" narrates "Jack of Lent's Ballat," a 1625 diatribe on the marriage of Prince Charles: it claims to compile reactions to the match from every sector of English life – Catholics, Puritans, astrologers, lawyers, clerks, aldermen, sheriffs, sergeants, farmers – spread over ten pages of doggerel verse.[36] Branching out from religious polemic, the persona became a figure for cultural analysis, a faceless scourge of the body politic.[37] "Lenten stuffe" would serve throughout the period as a generic tag for social satire: Elderton's ballad calls on "Herrynge, herrynge, whyte and red," to "Seeke owt suche as be rotten."

The Jack-a-Lent author function was not confined to print. As these oral frames suggest, it grew alongside a performance tradition equally invested in dangerous speech. Roving minstrels developed the cognate figure of the "ragman," who dispensed, under the pretense of "news," topical satire – like Autolycus, he may have sold accompanying ballad sheets – in the form of rambling, incendiary railing, often directed at the audience. Nicholas Udall calls "ragmans rewe" "a longe ieste that railleth on any persone by name, or toucheth a bodyes honestee somewhat nere," and locates it in Tudor household feasts, where "some iestyng feloe ... maye scoffe and iest vpon the geastes, as they sitten at the table."[38] The term "ragman's roll," originally a medieval fortune-drawing game, came to encompass any catalogue of social types – *A Fooles Bolt is soone shot* (1636) being a late example, a mock-oral relic of the estates-satire genre related to the seventeenth century fad of "character" books; "My Bowe you see stands ready bent," says the speaker, "to giue each one their lot."[39] And it features a remarkable title page image: the fool's arrow aimed squarely at the viewer, his coxcomb a reminder that a pelted rooster can peck back.

Such performance carried risk for the performer, whose only warrant was his body. In 1555, a minstrel was tortured for "a song called Newes out of London, [tending] agaynst the Masse and the Queenes misproceadinges."[40] The 1549 Act of Uniformity appended to its ban on plays criticizing the Book of Common Prayer the phrase "Dialogues or other matter set forthe in form of Plaie."[41] The further forward the record goes, the clearer the link between this acerbic "news" format and a decidedly individual performer. Geffray Fenton's *Forme of Christian Pollicie* (1574) reproves magistrates for tolerating "these Players, *whether they be Minstrels, or Enterludours,* who, on a scaffold, Babbling vaine newes to the sclander of the world, put there in scoffing the vertues of honest men."[42] Five years later, with permanent playing companies in London by now established, Ulpian Fulwell's *Arte of Flatterie* (1579) still sees the solo stage comedian – quite differentiated from court jester – as the readiest approximation of the popular news broadcaster. To admonish folly, one should "resine the scaffold to the fool … / Lo now the foole is come in place, though *not with patcht pyde coate,* / To tell such news as earst hee saw."[43]

The rhetorical frame of this "news song" – its "honest," unpresupposing singer – gradually became part of it, allowing for parodies of the form. In one, the cry of "Newes! newes! ye never herd so many newes!" is followed by the breathless report of the milking of a cow and of a cat's licking a pot; another is a ballad "dialogue betwene a serving man and a Clowne of the state of Oxn.":

> SER: Howe, nowe, John a dogges what newes a broad?
> CLO: And thinke yo^w I haue nought abode
> because I seeme a carelesse clowne[?]
> I ride and heare the newes abroade
> I sit and see the trickes in towne.
> The devill is dead in devonshire late
> an happie tale if it be true:
> wch gives the checke and not the mate
> and are you dead S^r devill adewe …[44]

The association of country clown and devil was also traditional. An illiterate peasant, the clown was quintessential humanity, and a natural target for demonic misinformation; as a vestige of the Jack-a-Lent, however, he possessed a superhumanity, and enjoyed special, picaresque access to the occult.[45] Such is the very premise, indeed, of *Pierce Penniless*; *Telltrothes Newyeares Gift* (1593) has the bumpkin Tom mediate the satiric reflections of Robin Goodfellow, lately come from hell. The nexus of clown, magic, and immortality is radically foregrounded in both *Doctor Faustus* and *Friar Bacon*, and in the next chapter we will see it put to use in the literary afterlife of Richard Tarlton.[46]

As professional playing moved to the city, finally, the performance routine of versified abuse may have borrowed its formal features from the flytings of fishwives. The women of Billingsgate market were notorious for the scurrility and (as Lodge's remark about the ur-*Hamlet* reminds us) volume of their cries: aimed at rivals rather than at customers, such stylized verbal warfare seems to have doubled as community theatre. *London and the Country Carbonado'd* (1632) notes that "when they haue done their Faire, they meet in mirth" at taverns, "and vse scolding … to take and put vp words, and end not till either their money or wit, or credit be cleane spent out."[47] Davenant's *The Wits* (1636) compares the noise of "Mariners at Plays" to "Apple-wives / That wrangle for a Sive," suggesting competitions with a prize going to the victor, and a late reference in *The Transproser Rehears'd* (1673) describes a tilt between oyster-women and tankard-bearers wherein "the Rabble adjudg'd the Victory on their side, who manag'd the dispute with the greatest clamour."[48] Public theatre provided the only other setting for such trials of oral skill, and, as clowns did there, by the mid-seventeenth century fishwives apparently enjoyed cults of personality. Ballads advertised "scolding matches" and "scolding bouts" between "Doll and Kate," or "Margery Merry thought, and Nancy her Mistress," or "Alice and Betrice," whose altercations border on the titillation of female mudwrestling:

> BET. You smack, you smick, you wash, you lick,
>   you smirk, you swear, you grin,
> You nod, you wink, and in your Drink,
>   you strive for to draw him in.
> ALICE. You Lye you Punk, you're almost Drunck,
>   and now you Scold and make a Strife,
> With running in the Score, and playing the Wh[ore],
>   you lead him a weary Life.
> BET. Tell me so once again, you Dirty Quean,
>   and I'll pull you by the Coif.[49]

The lateness of its textual survivals (or inventions) makes their mutual influence difficult to determine, but scolding shared with clowning a reliance on the simple, heavy caesura of Skeltonic metrics, allowing internal rhyme and spontaneous, formulaic composition; quarrel over a man, or a ware, is as constant a theme in one as cuckoldry is in the other. Rather than devolving into mere railing or threats of physical harm, however, the stage clown's practice took the combative animus of the fishwife and applied to it the dramatic shape, and numerical odds, of the Jack-a-Lent. His opponent was the audience at large – the customer, tellingly, now become the rival – and he invited it to beat him.

Tarlton's trunk-hose

> 1 CHEATER. This is our Clown, Sir.
> SYMON.   Fye, fye, your Company
>   Must fall upon him and beat him, he's too fair y'faith
>   To make the people laugh.
> 1 CHEATER. Not as he may be drest, Sir.
>   – Thomas Middleton, *The Mayor*
>   *of Quinborough* (pr. 1661), 63

In August 1575 the Earl of Sussex's Men were at Bristol, where they performed *The Red Knight* at the guildhall. "The presse of people at the playe" was so great, we are told, that the doors broke their hinges.[50] The particular player they were in all likelihood clamoring to see, Richard Tarlton, was the first exemplar of the performance template we have been tracing, and – as much by his fans as by him – his persona was meticulously fashioned in its image. Tarlton was not a provincial, though a revisionist tradition says he was. According to Fuller's *Worthies* (1662), he hailed from Shropshire, where "he was in the field, keeping his Father's Swine, when a Servant of Robert Earl of Leicester ... was so highly pleased with his *happy unhappy* answers, that he brought him to Court."[51] Robert Wilson's *Three Lords and Three Ladies of London* (*c*. 1588), however, says that Tarlton was "a prentice in his youth of this honourable city," and a water-bearer: "I-wis, he hath toss'd a tankard in Cornhill ere now: if thou knew'st him not, I will not call thee ingram [ignorant]; but if thou knewest not him, thou knowest nobody."[52] Such declarations of Tarlton's self-identity went hand in hand with manifest contradictions about his life. If Fuller locates Tarlton in a medieval tradition of "natural" folly, other sources assure us he was variously a bachelor or married; married to a woman named either Thamsyn or Kate; both a happily married father and a henpecked cuckold;

a bankrupt who died in the arms of a prostitute, or – as historical records actually attest – a prosperous man who in 1587 was made a Master of Fence and a groom of the Queen's chamber, and who, at his death in 1588, left £700 to his son Philip, referring his care to Sir Francis Walsingham and to the boy's godfather, Sir Philip Sidney.[53] In *Tarltons Jests* (*c.* 1590), the same universality that divides the stories into "Court-wittie Iests," "Sound Cittie Iests," and "Country prettie Iests" also sees him dividing his time between managing the Saba tavern in Gracechurch Street, serving as scavenger for the ward, performing revels for the Queen, staggering drunk through the streets, playing pranks on citizens, being hoodwinked by beggars and children, and strolling aimlessly through the countryside. (See Figure 2.) His huge body of notices similarly registers a need to remember him as self-created, an absolute pleasure principle. *Ulysses upon Ajax* (1596) recites "Tarletons Testament" as "a little more drinke, then a little more bread, a little more bread, and a few more clothes, and God be at your sport Master Tarleton"; he is merry England, "May-game Lords and Sommer Queenes, / With Milke-maides, dancing o'er the Greenes," and "lou'd a May-pole with his heart."[54] For one character in *The Partiall Law* (*c.* 1615), his trousers contained the entire cosmos: "that's as old as the beginning of the world, or Tarltons Trunk-hose."[55]

Yet as much as Tarlton's persona was born to transcend the public stage, it was also a direct outgrowth of it, a tactical response to the new structural pressures of daily, commercial performance in London. Untold numbers of later comedians would inherit or adapt Tarlton's mold – John Singer, Will Kemp, Robert Armin, Thomas Pope, Thomas Greene, Will Robins, William Kendall, Thomas Sackville, John Shanke, John Green, Robert Reynolds, Robert Kingman, William Rowley, Thomas Pollard, Timothy Reed, Andrew Cane. By the same token, a single player could not have established the bumpkin as the dominant comic type of Elizabethan theatre, being recognized as early as Whetstone's remark in *Promos and Cassandra* (1578) that "Manye times ... they make a Clowne companion with a Kinge ... vs[ing] one order of speech for all persons," and in Sidney's dislike of plays that "thrust in Clownes by head & shoulders."[56] Tarlton's idiom must have had imitators among his contemporaries – the aforementioned Wilson, Laneham, Garland, Adams, and Bentley. Yet only in him did it galvanize into a cultural phenomenon, and thus it is through him and the documentation he precipitated (however much an active part of that phenomenon) that we can reconstruct early clowning practice.

Both the pleasure and the power of the clown lay in his being a player pretending not to be a player; his role remained constant, insofar as he was

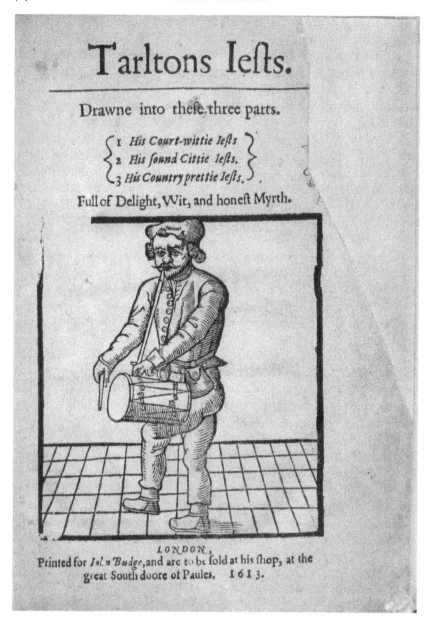

Tarltons Iefts.

Drawne into thefe three parts.

{ 1 *His Court-wittie Iefts*
2 *His found Cittie Iefts.*
3 *His Country prettie Iefts.* }

Full of Delight, Wit, and honeft Myrth.

LONDON.,
Printed for *Iohn Budge*, and are to be fold at his fhop, at the
great South doore of Paules. 1613.

Figure 2 Title page of the earliest extant edition of Anon., *Tarltons Jests* (1613), A1r.

always understood to be playing himself, no matter the fictional part he was assigned. The delight this duality generated in disrupting the play's order was hardly the extent or even the basis of his appeal, we will see, because the clown's appearance was not limited to the play. For the time being, however, two anecdotes will serve to illustrate, the first from *Tarltons Jests*:

> At the Bull at Bishops-gate was a play of *Henry* the fift, wherein the Iudge was to take a boxe on the eare, and because he was absent that should take the blow: *Tarlton* himself (euer forward to please) took vpon him to play the same Iudge, besides his owne part of the Clowne: and *Knell* then playing *Henry* … hit *Tarlton* a sound boxe indeed, which made the people laugh the more, because it was he …

The very next scene requires Tarlton to return "in his Clowne cloathes," and, "ask[ing] the Actors what newes," he is told of the incident in which he has just participated:

> no other like, said *Tarlton*, and it could not be but terrible to the Iudge, when the report so terrifies me, that me thinkes the blow remaines still on my cheeke, that it burnes againe. The people laught at this mightily, and to this day I haue heard it commended for rare: but no maruaile, for he had many of these. But I would see our Clownes in these dayes doe the like, no I warrant ye, and yet they think well of themselues too. (C2v–C3r)

Tarlton clearly contrives the exchange to collapse the distance between represented and representer, but there is really no such distance to collapse: the joke is impossible if the audience does not know he was the Justice, which it did, and which was inevitable given his distinctive appearance.[57] Nonetheless, the spontaneity of the jest prompts the narrator to affirm it the essence of clowning, and oddly, only a few years on, to lament clowning's already being in decline. One wonders why, and what he would make of a counterpart moment in Cookes's *Greenes Tu Quoque* (1614), in which the Red Bull clown Thomas Greene, as the character Bubble, is indirectly asked if he wants to go see himself perform:

RASH. But what shall's doe when wee haue dinde, shall's goe see a Play?
SCATTERGOOD. Yes fayth Brother: if it please you, let's goe see a Play at the Gloabe.
BUBBLE. I care not; any whither, so the Clowne haue a part: For Ifayth I am no body without a Foole.
GERALDINE. Why then wee'le goe to the Red Bull; they say *Green's* a good clowne.
BUBBLE. Greene? *Greene's* an Asse.
SCATTERGOOD. Wherefore doe you say so?
BUBBLE. Indeed I ha no reason: for they say, hee is as like mee as euer he can looke. (G2v)

Bubble is always Greene, and Greene always Greene; the very notion of "character" here, indeed, is just a bubble, existing only to be popped. Dromo in *Pilgrimage to Parnassus* (*c.* 1598) both anatomizes and parodies the formula as he leads onstage a character called "Clown," who protests he knows not what to do. Just be yourself, he tells him: "Why, if thou canst but drawe thy mouth awrye, laye thy legg over thy staffe, sawe a peece of cheese asunder with thy dagger, lape up drinke on the earth, I warrant thee theile laugh mightilie ... either saie somewhat for thy selfe, or hang and be *non plus*."[58]

Of course, he instantly figures out what to do. Feigning ignorance, he has already been doing it. Insofar as the clown pretended to be a confused bystander drawn into the fiction of the play, he surrogated the role of the spectator; insofar as the unitary self he projected was itself a fiction, however, it was a second-order container for something that resisted the play's containment – in a word, playgoing. Unlike the Vice, the clown's appeal lay in *repeat* performance, his bond with the audience a function of his integrity across events, an embodiment of collective memory. In him, the audience knew itself. On that integrity, accordingly, was placed a great deal of pressure. Tarlton's gift, as the form (and sheer fact) of *Tarltons Jests* attests, was to sustain the illusion that he was the same offstage as on: that he was always, in other words, "on."

Together with his homely features – squashed, misproportioned, squint-eyed and broken-nosed – Tarlton's crude, dissheveled attire intensified this paradox of stupidity and intelligence, of mimetic flatness and hidden depth. This ambiguity persists in John Scottowe's version of the *Jests* woodcut, which separates and narrows the eyes, resetting them into a vapid, glacial stare now cocked at the viewer; as before, the figure faces forward and back at once, left leg torqued, poised either to spin cavalierly away or to charge.[59] (See Figure 3.) To see him was to know him, yet the very anxiety this sentiment assuaged – that perhaps one did not know him, that his nature was artifice – underlies all of his encomia. "Who taught me pleasant follies, can you tell?" riddles one; "I was not taught and yet I did excell."[60] Another embraces Tarlton's dissimulation as simulacrum: "Earst he of Clownes to learne still sought, / But now they learne of him they taught / By Art far past the Principall; / The *Counterfet* is so worth all."[61] For a third, likewise, in him "Clownes knew the Clowne." Tarlton cannot be a copy, and so originality is reconfigured around him, positing him the fixed center of an increasingly illegible sociology. For just as the city imitates him – "present fashion sayes, / In euery streete where any *Gallant* goes, / The swagg'ring Sloppe, is *Tarltons* clownish hose" – so

Figure 3 Portrait of Richard Tarlton inside a majuscule "T," with accompanying verse.
John Scottowe, *Alphabet* (c. 1592).

the country now imitates the city in turn, making Tarlton's *successors*, conveniently, the true fakes: "Are Plowmen simple fellowes now a dayes? / Not so ... What meanes *Singer* then? / And *Pope* the Clowne, to speake so Boorish, when / They counterfaite the clownes vpon the Stage?"[62]

Tarlton's allure was thus on some level always a semiotic one: to behold him was to witness seemingly the failure and the apotheosis of representation at once, a performed self so hermetically sealed it both defied and demanded probing. In the broadest sense, he was an introduction to *mimesis* from its extreme – not from a body already constructed as duplicitous or diabolical, but from one that proclaimed its tranparency and guilelessness, that never had to *say* "I am myself," because it simply *was*. Scottowe's portrait appears in an alphabet book: Tarlton stands at the center of a majuscule "T," the letter as much a mnemonic for him as he for it. The book features no other historical personages: for it, Tarlton was not *of* history, but an archetype. Though he may be dead ("The partie now is gone, / and closlie clad in claye"), the verses imply that even his flesh was wardrobe, like his "cote of russet hew"; the true Tarlton is unrepresentable, such that they claim the image depicts not him but merely his "forme … vnto the Shap." When a 1651 farce called *The Prince of Priggs Revels* advertises on its title page "Tarltonian Mirth," it uses Tarlton not just as a synonym for "funny," but – because it was written during the closure of the playhouses, never to be performed – as a conjuration of "liveness" itself.

Tarlton's effect was surprise, his improbable yet inevitable turning of the tables on his aggressors, and surprise cannot be reproduced without becoming an effect; it lives in the moment, for its content *is* the moment, a participation in common experience. Yet playgoers craved just such replication – recall from Chapter 1 the cry "that again, that again" – and in Tarlton their desire to break their toys found a resilient object. He was routinely made to play against himself, a simultaneous celebration and disputation of his wit that, as we will see, was the basis of his routine. Gabriel Harvey mentions seeing the Queen's Men's *The Seuen Deadlie Sinnes* in London, and reports how he was

> verie gently inuited thereunto at Oxford, by *Tarleton* himself, of whome I merrily demaunding, which of the seauen, was his owne deadlie sinne, he bluntly aunswered after this manner: By God, the sinne of other Gentlemen, Lechery. Oh but that, M. Tarleton, is not your part vpon the stage: you are too-blame, that dissemble with the world, & haue one part for your frends pleasure, an other for your owne. I am somewhat of Doctor Pernes religion, quoth he: and abruptly took his leaue.[63]

The question is a trap, meant to tease out a disjunction between Tarlton's private and public self. Yet it also leaves space for him to reunify them, by inviting witty riposte; the charge of hypocrisy is really an excuse for Tarlton to produce more Tarlton, at tabletalk rather than the playhouse. Spurning the bait, he rebuffs the allegation without denying it (Andrew Perne, vice-chancellor of Cambridge, was a noted religious turncoat), seemingly irritated at the presumption that his theatrical persona is public property. Yet it was just that. In a fascinating episode from the *Jests*, his clothes are stolen from his chamber one morning, and worn by the thief "euery day" through the streets, "thinking that if he were espied to turn it to a iest." The confrontation never arrives, sadly, for "it past for currant," and the plot sputters into anticlimax.[64] Failing to materialize Tarlton, however, the thief does precisely that. In his expectation that he, not the clown, will be the one to "turn" their encounter "to a iest," he believes that Tarlton's wit magically resides in his clothing – potentially transferring his comic invention to anyone – and dares him forth without them. Even in its extratheatrical manifestations, the audience's relation to the clown was endlessly appropriative, adversarial, abusive.

The feeling was mutual. Tarlton always found a way to gain the upper hand: if he failed to meet the thief in the street, we later learn that he had words for him on the stage. However apocryphal, the *Jests* takes pains to depict a Tarlton whose humor channeled a deep antisocial hostility, con- sistently revealed at the moment his victimization turned to aggression. When a gallant at the Cross-Keys has his horse identify "the veriest fool" in the tavern and it sidles over to the clown, "*Tarlton* seeing the people laugh so was angry inwardly." He keeps his composure, and cleverly gets the horse to identify its owner as a whoremaster, but the ensuing cheers do little to dispel the impression of a psychology brimming with rage. A stew- ard at a country house surprises him with a cheeky answer, and brags to others "how he had driuen *Tarlton* to a *non plus*"; when Tarlton hears this, it "adde[d] fuell to the fire," and, "loath to rest thus put off," he devises a grossly excessive revenge that befouls the garden with feces. When he propositions a country wench "who gaue him quip for quip," indeed, with "I would my flesh were in thine," and she retorts "I would your nose were in my I know where," the punchline consists entirely of his muted fury – "*Tarlton* angered at this said no more, but goes forward."[65] Yet the episodic nature of the *Jests* always furnishes new outlets for his misanthropy, such as the gentleman diner whom, for no special reason, Tarlton sets out to prove has less wit than his mustard. "Some were pleased and some were not," says the narrator, "but all *Tarltons* care was taken (for his resolution was such euer) before he talkt any iest."[66]

The overall portrait is of an urban terrorist, a rogue insult comic whose medium was cruelty and incipient violence – structured by cycles of per- secution and retribution that encouraged his public toleration, sympathy, and repeated instigation.[67] On the one hand, there is the Tarlton who must pay his wife in order to learn that she cheats on him, or who, upon taking tobacco at an ordinary, is doused with wine when his companions see smoke at his nostrils – the lovable loser of his dramatic roles.[68] Yet on the other – and indicative of a different kind of role – there is the malevo- lent infant who never declined to escalate a slight, or who did not even need one: who, we are told, leads a country girl to church with promises of marriage only to ride off laughing; who decides to mock a quacksalver by filling a urinal with wine, and, after hearing the dire prognosis, drinks the sample down and hurls the bottle at the doctor's head; who, when a street raker blames his slackness on his sick horse, has the horse arrested – leaving the man not only to pull his cart himself, but to discover ("thinking *Tarltons* humor was to iest") that he now owes for the animal's bail as well.[69] There are no witnesses here; Tarlton is their only audience, and his mischief verges on criminality. In perhaps the most extreme example, he is at Salisbury with "his fellowes" "to play before the Maior and his brethren: but one of his company (a young man) was so drunk, that he could not: whereat *Tarlton*, as mad angry as he was mad drunk," sets bolts to his legs and has him borne off asleep to prison. It is not enough, however, for him merely to dry out there "while they were about their sport." When he awakens in confusion, Tarlton returns with the other players: "Oh Tom, sayes *Tarlton*, hard was thy hap in drunkennesse to murder this honest man, and our hard hap too, to haue it reported any of our company was hangd for it." Inconsolable, Tom weeps; they then pretend to spring him from jail and send him back to London alone – letting him believe that they have saved his life, rather than just summarily fired him.[70]

This dual personality – tormentor, bully, tyrant – comprised the other half of the role the clown performed onstage as in civic life (or vice versa). Both players and public alike indulged it because, as we will see, it satisfied the needs of both communities. In the above example, after all, Tarlton does more than just play a prank: he acts as a company executive, overseeing its personnel and policing its standards of professionalism. That the narrator not only deems such ruthless discipline good fun, but also calls their vocation "sport," prepares us to analyze the clown's stage practice, for what he did in the jestbook was not very different, in structure or purpose, from what he did at the playhouse.

First merriments

We return now to the twofold institutional problem with which this chapter began and the previous one ended: an early modern audience that privileged its own authority over that of the players, and consequently recognized no integrity to "the play" as an aesthetic or economic artifact. However counterintuitive, the initial solution was to exacerbate this very predicament, through a figure who solicited precisely the audience's incorporation, and who further decentralized and fragmented the theatrical program to do it. The clown was a tool of audience negotiation and control, meeting it head-on so its challenge could be codified and local-ized, opposed and neutralized. Such direct engagement was messy, and could not occur within the mimetic field of the play; the play, in turn, could not occur without it. They are nearly complementary territories, such that a reconstruction of one makes little reference to the other. We are thus departing from modern debates over the "ideology" of clowning – as either benignly "festive" or radically subversive – which base their evi-dence entirely on the drama, and thus misconstrue both the nature and the limits of the clown's action.[71] Insofar as they presuppose the play already a complete social text, such debates are anachronistic back-formations of the very texts from which they derive. The printed playbook is the edited transcript of a telephone conversation, and only one side of one *part* of that conversation. To recover the rest, we must listen elsewhere, and listen precisely for its static.

A final contrast between clown and Vice may prove instructive. In the Moralities, the Vice's operation is confined to the play, in that he tries to expand its domain as far as possible: acknowledging the environment, mingling self and role, descending among the spectators, his strategy is affective recruitment, dissolving the boundary between play and world so that, as Wiles puts it, "the audience is always on the move between … observer and participant."[72] All this antimimetic vagrancy, then, still serves the *mimesis*, rendering its didactic content palpable and immedi-ate. Investing represented events with personal stakes, he must above all keep the audience's attention – an imperative so overriding that it mer-ited a central role in the play. As such, it was largely scripted, and where it was not – as in Puttenham's account of how, when "the people waxed weary, then came in these manner of counterfeit vices … and all that had before been said, or great parts of it, they gave a cross construction to it very ridiculously" – it still referred (and deferred) to the dramatic action.[73] When he did not interpret for the crowd, he was its emcee, chatting them up, gathering details on which to riff, "like an Ape, a Parrot, or a Vice in a play, to prate what is prompted or suggested vnto him."[74] Though his pos-tures are threatening, their tone is inclusive and playful. He neither wishes nor needs to drive the audience off, but to involve them: he is a liaison, an interstitial figure of rapport.

All these statements (except for the size of the part) apply perfectly to the clown as well – considered *solely* as a character, framed by the pages of the dramatic text. But an urban audience did not need to be coddled, or to have their participation encouraged. Correspondingly, the textual space allotted to this task dwindled, and new tasks took its place, carving out new places for themselves in turn. When Dromo in *Parnassus* says "dost thou not knowe a playe cannot be without a clowne? Clownes haue bene thrust into playes by head and shoulders euer since Kempe could make a scuruey face," he implies (as does Sidney's formulation) that clowns were imports to the play – for to be "thrust in," after all, they must originate somewhere else.[75] Not only is the clown in the play no more than a trace of the Vice, he is but a trace of himself as well: when we read it, we do not see at all the mode of performance for which he was adapted.

Unlike the Vice's, the clown's audience needed to be *dis*couraged, to be resisted and combated. If he came to the Elizabethan playing company as a free agent, it was as a specialist who operated *outside* the play, in theatrical forms that were *wholly* unscripted. Here he was not a "hybrid" character, working within and against a mimetic frame, but shorn of *mimesis* altogether, a self unmediated by any fictional pretense to differentiate him from the spectators. Here a man stood before the multitude – the performer, offered as such – and it was against *them* that he played, their theme the meaning of performance itself. That the clown oversaw extracurricular entertainments is hardly a secret; in seeing them *as* extracurricular, however, we have had our priorities reversed, for they were not so much diversions from "the play" as its preconditions. Whereas the Vice embodied the authority of the play, the clown embodied – precisely by risking it – the authority of the players *to* play, a right that had to be forcibly asserted. Where the Vice translated the play's moral into the crowd's language, making it visceral and palpable, so the clown did with the order of playing itself. As the company's face to the audience, his taking the stage was a charge to defend it; as the audience's interface with the company, in turn, it was a challenge to make him lose it – the struggle between the two factions now given an object, a moving target. Distributed across a range of satellite vehicles that made up the daily theatrical program, such formal confrontation was a massive expansion of the cry for "Roome!" with which medieval drama opened – because the whiffler's traditional announcement neither called for, nor expected, an actual response.

Most scholars emphasize the jig as clowning's chief extradramatic contribution – again, a function of what plays tend internally to acknowledge or of what made it into print. A discrete dramatic afterpiece of song and dance, however, a jig, like a play, was not a forum for sustained audience dialogue. As we will see with its master craftsman, Will Kemp, while it retained elements of the clown's persona, it was a later development and, like his naturalization to the drama, actually the declining edge of the experiment he initially represented.[76] Rather, clowning splintered the theatrical program into an array of minor, evanescent forms that could not be reconciled to the play, because they were what the play passed itself through, pluralistic supplements to its vocalic unity. A case in point is the "merriment," evidently a species of farce interlude. In the sole surviving playbook claiming to contain one, *A Knacke to Knowe a Knave … With Kemps applauded merriments of the men of Goteham* (1594), the scene runs to a full page, introducing unique speakers and having nothing to do with the plot. Kemp's Cobbler and several other citizens debate who should present their petition to the King, which (since it asks only "to brew strong Ale thrise a week") is instantly granted, and the parties disperse.[77] Clearly more went on here than is recorded, and the device suffers from its half-hearted integration with the play – perhaps the reason it is also one of a kind. This was surely not Kemp's only "merriment," and when Nashe says of an imagined pillorying of Harvey "Will Kempe, I mistrust it will fall to thy lot for a *merriment* one of these dayes," we must imagine such *intermezzi* far more ubiquitous, caustic, and dramatically dissociated.[78] Indeed, they may actually have spurred the censorship of theatrical content more than anything in the plays ever did: its first decree was not Edmund Tilney's patent for the Revels Office in 1581, but a 1574 order by the Mayor and Common Council of London, forbidding innkeepers to "suffer to be *interlaced, added, mingled* or vttered in any such play, comedy, tragedy or show *any other matter* than such as shall be first perused and allowed."[79]

Clowning was more, then, than just a part of the play. This is a rhetoric inherited from plays themselves, which mention clowns most often to disclaim their freedom from them. *The Warres of Cyrus* (1594) boasts that "toies / Or needlesse antickes, imitations, / Or shewes, or new devices sprung a late, / We have exilde them from our Tragicke stage, / As trash of their tradition, that can bring / No instance or excuse for what they do."[80] *Cyrus* was a children's play, however, with no clowns in the company, so this "exile" is hardly a choice: it apologizes through reverse psychology.[81] A more famous declaration, meanwhile, from an adult company's play, implies nothing like the divorce that has been imputed to it – if anything, the reverse:

> From iygging vaines of riming mother wits,
> And such conceites as clownage keepes in pay,
> Weele lead you to the stately tent of War.[82]

Less the birth announcement of a "mature" drama than merely a way to start a martial play, what the prologue to *Tamburlaine* calls "clownage" is not the entire London theatre scene, but merely the action that immediately preceded the prologue. The prologue is a transition, a segue: when it says "lead you" and "from," it affirms, more than rejects, an organic continuity to the experience of the playhouse.[83] And the clown, already at its end and sprinkled throughout its middle, was also its beginning. Here is Nashe again:

> Amongst other cholericke wise Iustices ... was one, that hauing a play presented before him and his Towne-ship, by *Tarlton* and the rest of his fellowes her Maiesties seruants, and they were now entring into their first merriment (as they call it) the people began exceedingly to laugh, when *Tarlton* first peept out his head. Where at the Iustice not a little moued, and seeing with his beckes and nods hee could not make them cease, he went with his staffe, and beat them round about vnmercifully on the bare pates, in that they ... would presume to laugh at the Queenes men, and make no more account of her cloath in his presence.[84]

This is a provincial performance, but the format has by now become so standardized that Nashe can describe it as a formula. "*First* merriment" implies not only more to come, but order, a structure to the show in which the clown's presence was the founding principle. (Nashe's own household interlude *Summers Last Will and Testament* (*c.* 1592), perhaps in imitation of commercial plays, similarly does not begin with the Prologue, but with the ghost of the clown Will Sommers – who remains onstage throughout as chorus.) Even its opening movement has an overture, in fact, consisting of the introduction of that presence itself – Tarlton's signature stage entrance, *as* Tarlton, "peep[ing]" out his head.

The story's theme is control: interpreting the people's laughter as contempt for company and patron, the justice falls to beatings to compel their respect for authority. His motives are not what earn Nashe's derision, however, but his premises. Not only does he fail to grasp that Tarlton's appearance *means* to elicit laughter, and misread that laughter as directed at anyone other than Tarlton, but his outburst pre-empts the disciplinary function even that appearance performed, substituting its latent violence with his own. If the clown mediated a complex negotiation for possession of the stage, he had to be the first upon it – and he began by establishing his liminality to that contest, for which physical deformity seems to have been a prerequisite trait. In his unpretentious ugliness, the crowd saw a projection of themselves; in his naïve eagerness to please, they also sensed a weakness that incited their release. Tarlton could thrill an audience simply by coming into view – much as studio audiences (or laugh tracks) still whoop at the arrival of a favorite sitcom character: "such contentment to beholders as honest *Tarlton* did," recalls Sir Richard Baker, "though he never said a word."[85] Accordingly, he developed the art of drawing out that entrance into a full-length tease. Henry Peacham describes how "*Tarlton* when his head was onely seen, / The Tire-house door and Tapistrie betweene, / Set all the multitude in such a laughter, / They could not hold for scarse an houre after." An identical habit of "peeping" was employed by the Caroline comedian Timothy Reed, and one Middleton character, pontificating to a troupe of players like an anti-Hamlet, exults: "Oh the Clowns that I have seen in my time! / The very peeping out of one of them would have made / A young heir laugh, though his Father lay a dying."[86]

The clown heated this appetite by pantomiming and pulling faces on demand, a simian parody of human expression that further painted him as groveling idiot and retarded buffoon, a puppet endlessly malleable to collective whim.[87] *Parnassus*'s list of clown actions – "drawe thy mouth awrye," "lape up drinke on the earth," "hang and be *non plus*," along with Kemp's "scuruey face" – finds a zany parallel in a remembrance of Reed: "I'ave laugh'd / Untill I cryed again, to see what Faces / The Rogue will make ... To see him hold out's Chin, hang down his hands, / And twirle his Bawble ... I'd rather see him leap, laugh, or cry / Then hear the gravest Speech in all the *Play*."[88] Tarlton "in his Graue, still laughing, gapes," his death mask slack-jawed vacancy; Thomas Greene is mourned as having "new come from sea, made but one face and dide." The Continental transplant Pickelherring says of himself, "Last year I was a mighty good Pickelherring, / I could twist my face in a thousand ways. / Everything I did gave great amusement."[89]

Just as the clown's dumbshow ran the gamut of emotions, however, so it seems to have accelerated playgoers through a whirligig of affect, intoxicating them beyond reason. The very deformity that connoted his mindlessness could be turned upon them, suddenly, into a demonic specter of the grotesque. For William Prynne, the clown's deconstruction of bodily semiotics epitomized the barbarity of playing itself, his litany of "*ridiculous antique, mimicall, foolish gestures, complements, embracements, smiles, nods, motions of the eyes, head, feete, hands, & whole intire body which Players vse, of purpose to provok their Spectators to profuse inordinate laughter*" – performing a kind of progressive and mutual lobotomization, through the innate cruelty of watching "*inhumane gestures and actions, more fit for skittish goats then for men.*"[90] Another antitheatricalist, Anthony Munday, in 1580 relates how

The foole no sooner showeth himselfe in his colors to make men merrie, but straight-waie lightlie there foloweth some vanitie, not onlie superfluous, but beastlie and wicked. Yet are we so caried awaie with his vnseemelie gesture, and vnreuerend scorning, that we seeme onelie to be delighted in him.[91]

Joseph Hall is unequivocal about the clown's readiness to twist that twistedness into a weapon:

> mids the silent rout,
> Comes leaping in a selfe-misformed lout,
> And laughs, and grins, and frames his Mimik face,
> And justles straight into the princes place.
> Then doth the *Theatre Eccho* all a loud,
> With gladsome noyse of that applauding croud …
> When each base clown, his clumsie fist doth bruise,
> And show his teeth in double rotten-row,
> For laughter at his selfe-resembled show.[92]

Even through the funhouse distortions of Hall's description, it is hard to envision the audience's "gladsome noyse" at such ghoulish capering unmixed with disgust. In goading him on, they were entrusting themselves to someone with no shame, and as in a bearbait, there was always the danger that predator might become prey. Greene was likewise both revered and reviled for freakshow theatrics that, to one, crossed the line into blasphemy. "*Vos quoque*," inveighs I.H. in *This Worlds Folly* (1615), "and you also, who with *Scylla*-barking, *Stentor*-throated bellowings, flash choaking squibbes of absurd vanities into the nosthrils of your spectators, barbarously diuerting *Nature*, and defacing Gods owne image, by metamorphising humane shape into bestiall forme." The marginalia add "*Tu quoque*," which was Greene's catchphrase, and further down "*Greenes* Baboone" – referring either to his verisimilar imitation of an ape, or to his general playhouse persona[93]. Beneath even Tarlton's comic humanity, indeed, lurked the bare, forked animal who knew when to bite:

> Conspicienda amplo quoties daret ora Theatro
> *Tarltonus*, lepidum non sine dente caput,
> Spectantũ horrifico coelũ intonat omne cachinno,
> Audijt & plausus aula suprema Iovis.

[Whenever *Tarlton* appeared in a full theatre, and showed his witty head, which was not without teeth, the horrible laughter of the spectators shook the heavens; the high palace of Jove heard the applause.][94]

Like "double rotten-row," the clown's gruesome dentition again serves as the focal point of his power. If the audience becomes a mouth to terrify the gods, it is first terrorized by Tarlton's, its "horrible laughter" a visceral, shock response to the flash of his horrid grin.

Greene's catchphrase was no accident: the experiential structure of all clowning, at even the non-verbal level, was "*tu quoque*," "the same to you." Allowing himself to be debased into an inhuman plaything, the clown then violently confronted the crowd with the sublimity of his abjection – turning them into the instrument of their own overthrow, indulging their narcissism to the point of surfeit and reflux, suddenly transforming their authority into his own. Bruce Smith reminds us that the acoustics of the early modern amphitheatre were designed to amplify the sound of the audience no less than that of the players, and precisely by maximizing the disparity between it and him, the clown used that collectivity against itself.[95] (More than mere scurrility, perhaps, explains why as late as 1703 Tarlton's image adorned a jakes, "which by long standing there has contracted the Colour of the neighbouring Excrements.")[96] The clown's individuality was produced, onstage, directly by the audience, and once made, it refused to be dislodged. What began as an expression of the crowd's will – a staged body it could dominate – now became an autonomous incarnation of that drive, exerting control in its very resistance to control. When Tarlton enters as Derick in *The Famous Victories*, "rouing" wildly across the stage as if on horseback and hollering "whoa there, whoa there, whoa there!", only inexplicably to exit and then re-enter doing so again, he represents a new and different kind of pleasure – the charm of a spontaneous, complete person, entirely centered within himself and answerable to no one, as ungoverned by the constraints of the play as is the invisible horse he is riding.[97] Just as the horse figures Tarlton, so Tarlton figures, in a complex transference, audience desire. Fused in him at this moment are both the vicarious thrill of seeing the stage overtaken by one of its own – he does exactly what the crowd wants to do – and the impotence to predict when or how he would do it – he can never, by definition, do exactly what the crowd wants. The clown becomes a proxy for the audience, but a proxy that has broken its reins, acquired a life of its own – and thus whose every action, *especially* when irreverent or transgressive, also puts him further beyond the audience's reach, proclaiming his masterlessness. When a clown improvises, we assume he is flouting the author; but the author is not who created him.

This inspired what David Mann calls Tarlton's "jiz," the cocky set of mannerisms by which the clown exhibited his blithe self-possession, and in it is captured nothing less than the authority of the player, as an agency distinct from the audience, being flaunted in the moment just after its

conception, performed at a primal, animal level.[98] Tarlton in particular, as
the unbounded stage-time of entrances like Derick's enabled, was famed as
much for his stupefied gape as for the showboating to which it gave way,
flexing his body to fill even the mere act of crossing the stage with entertainment: "Tell Captaine Tospot with his Tarletons cut," says *Machiuells
Dogge* (1617), "his swaggering will not get him sixteene pence."[99] He filled
not just the act, indeed, but the stage itself with his presence – his stalking
of its planks resembling, evidently, the arrogant strut of a rooster claiming
its territory. In *The Commendation of Cockes, and Cock-fighting* (1607), as
his ultimate example of the noble bird's valor, George Wilson reports that

> no longer agoe, than the 4 day of May 1602, at a cocke-fighting in the
> Citie of *Norwich* aforesaid, a Cocke called *Tarleton* (who was so intituled,
> because he alwaies came to the fight like a Drummer, making a thunder-
> ing noyse with his winges) which Cocke hauing there fought many battels,
> with mighty and fierce Aduersaries ... at the length he had his eyes both
> of them beaten out of his head, his spurres broken off, and his bill brused,
> and rigorously rent from off his face, so that their remained no hope of
> him, but that he should bee instantly killed, and so of necessitie loose all
> the wagers that he fought for, yet behold a rare and miraculous wonder ...
> for all this he fought still most stoutly with his Aduersary, and would neuer
> shrinke from him, or giue him ouer, until he had (which to all men there
> present seemed an impossibilitie) most couragiously slaine him. (D4r)

"Tarleton" lived up to his namesake in technique as well as spirit. In its
arc from near-destruction to triumphant resurrection, the story not only
illustrates the adversarial nature of the clown's practice, but brilliantly follows its sacrificial structure. The clown too was an underdog who could
emerge all the more intact for his disfigurement, who held his ground the
more he seemed to give it up, who converted disadvantage to advantage.
Reed emulated Tarlton, we are told, when he would "cry, *Doodle, Doodle,
Dooe*" on the stage, "beyond compare."[100] This was the sum of the clown's
utterance – before he had spoken a word – and it said, in the theatre's first
language, "I am here; this is mine; come and get me."

The neverending sideshow

BUBBLE. How Apparell makes a man respected! the very children in the
        streete do adore mee: for if a Boy that is throwing at his Iacke-a-
        lent chaunce to hit mee on the shinnes: Why I say nothing but,
        Tu quoque, smile, and forgiue the Child with a becke of my hand
        ... so by that meanes, I do seldome goe without broken shinnes.
                        – Jo[hn] Cooke, *Greenes Tu Quoque* (1614), I3v

As we have seen, the clown provided more than just an initial release of energy, a pre-catharsis that facilitated submission to the formal structures of a *mimesis*. Audiences were not so easily placated – which is why clowning was not about placation. Their urge to self-project was pathological: at any juncture they threatened to overtake the stage, vocally or physically, such that performance could not continue. Were they given control of it as a *preliminary* exercise, the performance could not even start – the custom of play nomination, seemingly always terminating in riot, attesting to what could happen even at the *end* of the production. As those accounts suggested – the company's desperately trying to put Cane onstage to quell the mob – clowning was the *opposite* of capitulation. It was itself a formal structure, possessed of its own narrative shape; that structure appears elusive to us because it was dialogic, but in that dialogue lay dialectic. Setting himself up as a passive object for the audience's animus, the clown directed it back at them in a calculated burst of agency – suddenly becoming their doppelganger, a maddening image of their own insubordination, impervious to control.

When he resurfaced in the play, the antagonist of his improvisations remained the same: not "the poet," as yet a figure of no import, but still the crowd, his cheerful self-direction further agitating theirs, dangled before them as the displacement of their desire. Strumbo's greeting upon entering in *Locrine* – "How do you, maisters, how do you? how haue you scaped hanging this long time?" – is aimed at no one else, a plucky, audacious wave.[101] Robert Wilson's *The Three Ladies of London* (pr. 1584), with Tarlton himself in the role of Simplicity, embeds an identical moment of spectatorial defiance, even more explicitly capturing the institutional tensions it mediated. Simplicity is about to sing a song, yet pauses to address a nearby playgoer, and in what must surely have seemed (and may well have been) a comic ad-lib, pre-empts his intention to heckle him:

> But sir, marke my cauled countenance where I begin,
> But yonder is a fellow that gapes to bite me, or els to eate that which I sing.
> Why thou art a foole, canst thou not keepe thy mouth strait together?
> And when it comes snap at it as my fathers dogge wou[ld] do at a liver.
> But thou art so greedie,
> That thou thinkest to eate it before it come nie thee.
> *Simplicitie singe*
> … Now sirra, hast eaten vp my song? and ye haue ye shalle eate no more
>   to day,
> For euery body may see your belly is growne bigger with eating vp our play.
> He has fild his belly but I am neuer a whit the better,
> Therefore ile go seeke some vittels, and member for eating vp my song you
>   shall be my debter. (D3v)

With brilliant aplomb, Tarlton thwarts the playgoer's aim to interrupt him by interrupting himself; at once granting and frustrating audience desire, now he is the one doing what the other would like to do, and turns the tables on him. His battery of insults, moreover, deftly re-establishes their proper relationship: if the playgoer's open-mouthed "bit[ing]" signals the production of speech, it is instantly flipped into a gesture of consumption, applied not just to the song but to the performance – "eating vp our play" – as a whole, for which he has the nerve to suggest the audience owes double. As in every clash, he leaves the encounter stronger, and on his own terms. The clown began as an extension of the audience, but ended as something new. Feeding off their energy instead of depleting it, he produced not their docility but simply himself, a free subject to oppose them as trickster, as taunter, as nemesis. Through him, theatrical authority thus ritually drew itself from the authority of the audience, each defining and defined against its counterpart. As companies gradually built their format around him, in fact, they came not only to expect but actually to *need* the audience's belligerence. Their poetics were fundamentally defensive.

There was no permanent solution to the problem of audience entitlement, over the course of a single performance or across multiple ones. In this model of theatre as tactical warfare, rather, clowning offered only a stalemate, a series of blocks and checks. Forcing the audience to recognize the players' autonomy, it claimed the stage for them, drawing a temporary line between producer and consumer. The alternative – ignoring the audience – was not an option, for they would seek out engagement themselves, with potentially disastrous results. The clown was a lightning rod; yet a lightning rod needs lightning. If the structure of clowning made him an audience adversary, then the adversarial drive of the audience, only further stoked by his, guaranteed that the same structure would need to be repeated, in different ways, across the theatrical program. The perfect short-range weapon, he could crush any challenge – thus ensuring more challenges to come.

The genre of "themes" recapitulated the structure of clowning on a grander scale. It involved the clown's extemporal versification on a question or proposition, tending overwhelmingly toward the insult of specific spectators; the "theme" would be prompted by those spectators themselves. Proportionally, its textual corpus rivals that of the formal drama of the entire 1570s and 1580s, and by now we can start to guess why. If theatre was understood as a social event, "themes" satisfied a criterion of dramatic publication that playbooks could not: the textual representability of the playgoer. The genre took its very name, indeed, from what the audience rather than the player did.

> While the Queenes Players lay in Worcester City to get money, it was [Tarlton's] custome for to sing *ex tempore* of Theames giuen him … now one fellow of the City amongst the rest, that seemed quaint of conceit, to lead other youthes with his fine wit, gaue out, that the next day, hee would giue him a Theam, to put him to a *non plus*: divers of his friends acquainted with the same, expected some rare conceit. Well, the next day came, and my Gallant gaue him his inuention in two lines, which was this: / *Me thinkes it is a thing vnfit, / To see a Gridiron turne the Spit.* / The people laught at this, thinking his wit knew no answere thereunto, which angered *Tarlton* exceedingly, and presently with a smile looking about, when they expected wonders, he put it off thus. / *Me thinkes it is a thing vnfit: / To see an Asse haue any wit.* / The people hooted for ioy, to see the Theame-giuer dasht, who like a dog with his taile betweene his legs, left the place. (C4r–v)

This is to approach the genre from an extreme, but the deviations here speak loudly for the norm. Tarlton's default posture to the audience is one of challenge, so much so that the "gallant" begins preparing the day before, spreading word that he will best him, and rallying other upstarts to his cause; there is no mention whatever of the play, nor of where the clash falls in relation to it, because this is the main event. And it is downright nasty. If the advance hype was meant to intimidate Tarlton, the prompt itself shrewdly undercuts those expectations, stumping him with a nonsense abstraction. The genre was thus both a showcase for the clown's ingenuity and, as the bit of foul play here reveals, a genuine interrogation of it. The playgoers revel in Tarlton's resourcefulness but, in trying to "put him to a *non plus*," are also keen to destroy it, to expose its falsity. The object is to get the last word, for if the authority of the players rests in the clown, his defeat is also theirs; though here the playgoer ends up being forced to depart, he is *forced to depart*, implying the reverse should the outcome have been different. The fate of theatre again balances on a knife's edge, and before the spectators "hoot for ioy to see the Theame-giuer dasht," they "laugh" at the delicious prospect of Tarlton's having "no answere." That he finds one, of course, sidestepping the prompt with imperious dismissal – and a beatific smile that barely masks his rage – only redoubles their delight.

The crowd, indeed, is the real winner here. Regardless of the result, the sheer crossfire between playgoer and player realizes their presence; the clown may survive his overthrow, but the performance incorporates their attempt. Ultimately, the theme of every "theme" was the same – the audience. And in the hands of lesser talents, it could sometimes win outright. The commonplace book of Philip Powell in 1620 records how

> on[e] Kendal a foole in a stage play in Bristol being meerie accting the part of the vize, spake extempore as followeth, in dispriase [*sic*] of the noble Brittanes,

> > if thou art a Brittane borne,
> > it fitts thee to were ye horne

> John Brittan a prentiz of on[e] Thomas Dean of Bristoll his reply to Kendall: twise: as followeth:

> > A Brittans name I truly beare,
> > I leaue the horne for thee to were:
> > the horne becomes the saxons best
> > I kisd thy wife supose the rest ...

Powell's marginalium supplies the coda that Kendall evidently could not: "*Kendall the Saxon put to silence.*"[102] So total is the confounding, indeed, that Brittan repeats his zinger "twise" – perhaps in exultation, or perhaps because he really wants to hear the comeback, and refuses to let the overmatched clown off the hook.

"Themes" thus furnished yet another outlet for the fractious energies the clown excited, another extradramatic parenthesis wherein theatrical ownership could be reduced to single combat, here in a form akin to modern freestyle rap. If its couplets offered the rhetorical punch of finality, the satisfying smack with which a spontaneous rhyme closes around its target, they also implied circularity, the potentially endless repetition of the exercise itself. And Tarlton was only its most famous practitioner. A 1623 ballad relates how "Most of my money being spent, / To S. *Johns* street to the *Bull* I went, / Where I the roaring Rimer saw, / And to my face was made a daw."[103] In Munday's *Second and Third Blast of Retrait* (1580), "common plaies" consist equally of "vsual iesting, and riming extempore."[104] Nashe's allusion to "the queint Comædians of our time ... [who] when their Play is doone do fal to ryme" may indicate an effort to limit the audience's stage-time – and, increasingly, the clown's – by assigning it a terminal slot in the program.[105] In another of *Tarltons Jests*, this is where we see it occur:

> I remember I was once at a Play in the Country, where as *Tarltons* use was, the Play being done, euery one so pleased to throw vp his Theame: amongst all the rest, one was read to this same effect, word by word: / Tarlton, *I am one of thy friends, and none of thy foes, / Then I prethee tell how thou cam'st by*

thy flat nose: | Had I been present at that time on those bankes, | I would haue layd my short sword ouer his long shankes.| Tarlton mad at this question, as it was his property sooner to take such a matter ill then well, very suddenly returned him this answere: | *Friend or foe, if thou wilt needs know, marke me well, | With parting dogs & bears, then by the eares, this chance fel: | But what of that? Though my nose be flat, my credit to saue, | Yet very well, I can by the smell, scent an honest man from a knave.* (C4v)

Tarlton's spleen seems excessive: the question is couched in disclaimers of affection, and with such trepidation that the asker has actually taken care to recite it. But the subject is a sensitive one. The clown's deformity is part of his act, a mythology constructed onstage: to inquire about its origins is to dislocate him from the theatre by attempting to humanize him. Thus Tarlton, "mad at this question," perceives it as an assault on his authority, and his response grafts the demand itself into it. His flat nose, he says, is a wound sustained from "parting dogs and bears," figuring himself as the referee of a bearbait – which, in a sense, he is at this moment, trying to segregate player from audience; his face is a record of that absorbed violence, and he ends by lumping this among those attacks. Yet because the clown's defenses also invite them, the two arenas are gradually merging rather than being held apart. Interviewing Tarlton gives the playgoer a chance to bring his own text to the theatre, and for its delivery momentarily to occupy the stage; there are two acts of authorship going on here, and "themes" accords them equal space. Indeed, *Tarltons Jests* cannot really decide which to give preference to. Not coincidentally, it is the only anecdote in the volume framed by the narrator's own playgoing memory.

Moreover, the theatrical program we have been recovering is starting to look very distended – crowded out, as it were – by the clown's solo itinerary. (Hence, as noted in Chapter 1, four- to five-hour durations of standard performance.)[106] We have "peeping" and "faces" at the beginning, assorted "merriments" in the middle, and now "themes" at the end, somehow pinned up against the jig; this does not leave much room for "the play" as a coherent aesthetic experience, or even as a qualitatively different one. And thus the clown's slippery slope. Despite the effort to relegate "themes" to the end of the show, indeed, its anticipation invariably gave rise to premature commencement:

> It chanced that in the midst of a play, after long expectation for *Tarlton*: being much desired of the people, at length hee came forth: where (at his entrance) one in the Gallerie pointed his finger at him, saying to a friend that had neuer seene him, that is he. *Tarlton* to make sport at the least occasion giuen him … he in loue againe held vp two fingers: the captious fellow,

iealous of his wife, and because a Player did it, took the matter more hain-
ously, & asked him why he made hornes at him. No (quoth *Tarlton)* they
be fingers: *For there is no man, Which in loue to me, / Lends me one finger, but
he shall have three.* No, no, says the fellow, you gaue me the hornes. True
(sayes *Tarlton*) for my fingers are tipt with nailes, which are like hornes, and
I must make a shew of that which you are sure of. This matter grew so, that
the more he meddled, the more it was to his disgrace ... So the poore fellow, plucking his hat ouer his eyes, went his wayes. (B2v)

We are now in the midst of the play – why Tarlton has not yet appeared
is odd, unless the desire is to see him again – and, unlike when he was
pelted with pippins, the disruption is of the clown's making. Though
they express the same motive to open a communication between auditory
and stage, a pointed finger is less intrusive than airborne produce, and
Tarlton, "to make sport at the least occasion," is the one who interpolates
"themes" into the play. He cannot ignore the playgoer, however, because
of what the playgoer already ignores to make the remark: the play itself.
"That is he" implies total indifference to the representational project of
the drama – predicated on "that" *not* being "he" – and we are told this is
the majority sentiment, with everyone else merely enduring the tedious
fiction until Tarlton shows up. What looks like the clown's grandstanding,
then, and exploding the illusionistic framework, is here really an effort to
save it, by extinguishing a state of rupture that is already imminent. When
his rude gesture elicits an indignant response, he instinctively repairs to
the structure of a "theme" because it is a structure of repair, the closed
couplet slamming the door on audience interaction before it can further open. The playgoer eventually departs in shame, but it takes longer
than expected; he keeps adding puzzled protests to Tarlton's quips – as if
unaware that the game has any rules of closure. And ultimately he is correct: such containment is bound to fail, no matter the obtuseness of the
opponent. If Tarlton polices attention that looks through his fictional role
to "him," he can only do so by surrendering that role, from which there
is now no going back. He is made part of the play because his discipline
originates outside it, in the formative gulf of "play" itself; but that power
works through, and always imports, those margins. As long as he is present, the audience can always summon the clown it wants, because that is
his only weapon against them. In the very act of barring their access to the
stage, he becomes their portal to it: his confrontation is their reward, and
he knows only confrontation.

    The same futility underlies his actions at Gotham, where we now see
"themes" erupting before the play even begins – and ironically, so that

it *can* begin: "Tarleton, *who being vpon the* Stage *in a* Towne *where he expected for civill attention to his* Prologue, *and seeing no end of their hissing, hee brake forth at last into this Sarcasmicall taunt*: / I liu'd not in that Golden Age, / When *Iason* wonne the *Fleece*: / But now I am on *Gotams* Stage, / Wher *Fooles* doe hisse like *Geese*."[107] Two readings are possible. Seeing that the Prologue – and the play – is being rejected in favor of audience autonomy, Tarlton rushes onstage to oppose it and, invariably, validate it. Alternately, if he is already "*vpon the* Stage," Tarlton is *himself* the Prologue ("*his* Prologue"), and his appearance *ignites* the very unrest he must now defy – which he cannot do, of course, from within the person of the Prologue. Either way, he is both the necessary condition of the play's starting and the reason it cannot start, and in the latter instance, all he has managed to do is annex yet another dramatic position to the same extradramatic feedback loop.

In a very real sense, clowning must have been an addiction of the early playing companies, offering the only immediate fix to the problem it aggravated. Both the source of theatrical sovereignty and the site of its ongoing dispossession, the more you used the clown, the more you needed to use him. "Themes" at some point spawned a subspecies of rhyming tilt involving not one but multiple onstage contestants, with professionals pitted against amateur versifiers in gladiatorial, cage-match duels.[108] They thus had the virtue of sidelining the audience, but only by elevating one of its members to center stage – where, if he won, *he* might become its champion. The self-promoting William Fennor, failing to show up at the Hope for a bout with John Taylor, claims to have been stood up himself at the Fortune by the clown William Kendall (who, if the same "Kendal" from the debacle at Bristol, is not compiling a very distinguished record):

> And let me tell thee this, to calme thy rage,
> I chaleng'd *Kendall* on the Fortune Stage;
> And he did promise 'fore an Audience,
> For to oppose me, note the accidence:
> I set up bills, the people throng'd apace,
> With full intention to disgrace, or grace;
> The house was full, the trumpets twice had sounded:
> And though he came not, I was not confounded,
> But step't vpon the Stage, and told them this;
> My Aduerse would not come: not one did hisse;
> But flung me Theames: I then *extempore*
> Did blot his name from out their memorie,
> And pleased them all, in spight of one to braue me,
> Witnesse the ringing Plaudits that they gaue me.[109]

Fennor was a notorious liar, but his scenario may seem plausible by now –
at least it was written to be in 1615 – as is Taylor's account of how, left to
fend for himself at the Hope, "Some laught, some swore, some star'd &
stamp'd and curst / And in confused humors all out burst ... For now the
stinkards, in their irefull wraths / Bepelted me with Lome, with Stones,
and Laths ... I, like a *Beare* vnto the stake was tide, / And what they said,
or did, I must abide."[110] Such private "challenges" evidently did not alter
the basic pathways of theatrical reception. Not content to umpire third-
party contests, the audience seizes any opportunity to revert to "themes" –
and, if unmet by equal force, to revert to the impulse that "themes" tried
to sublimate, the destruction of performer and playhouse alike.

That distinction between public and private, indeed, was exactly what
"themes" worked to erode, even as the clown struggled to uphold it. If he
performed individuality onstage – and therein the individuation of that
stage – then the audience's mission, if he could not be destroyed, was to
subsume it, to nullify the distance between stage and pit. "Themes" thus
always topicalized Tarlton's own celebrity, his personal biography and
popular image, looking for the smallest scruple between the two. And
thus, as we have already seen, that inquisition spilled over into everyday
encounters, often taking the form of "themes" themselves. *Tarltons Jests*
abounds with people sallying up to Tarlton in the street and addressing
him in verse: a boy asks him in alternately rhymed trimeters about his
cuckolding; a gentlewoman offers him her opinion of the sexual prowess of horses in rhymed octameters; a beggar thanks him for twopence
in tetrameter couplets; even a goldsmith's apprentice named Robert
Armin, in a scene we will revisit, leaves rhymes for him in chalk con-
cerning the payment of a bill.[111] Not only is Tarlton endlessly available
for questioning in his daily affairs, but he is available in *the same way*
as at the playhouse: one sphere is an extension of the other, or must
become so. Likewise, his daily affairs are fodder for the playhouse, so
that often a jest will end in his facing a "theme" about it. When his
clothes are stolen

> the next day this was noised abroad, and one in mockage threw him in this
> theame, he playing then at the Curtaine:
>
> > *Tarlton*, I will tell thee a iest,
> > Which after turned to earnest:
> > One there was, as I heard say,
> > Who in his shirt heard Musicke play,
> > While all his clothes were stolne away.[112]

Everything is fair game for publication – "publication" being the point. If the clown's persona was self-identity, the audience must push that logic to its limit, if not to expose him as a fraud then to reveal him as genuine: for if he is the same offstage as on, then he is one of them again – and the emergent category of "player" for which he stands, a privileged class of labor entitled to define and restrict the uses of theatre, once again dissolves.

That, ultimately, was why the audience sought possession of the stage, and what their carnival expressed. To the Elizabethan playgoer, greeted with the contradiction of a playhouse that now exacted payment beforehand yet demarcated exclusive space, theatre came under instant expropriation; the capitalization of commercial playing had made it more than ever both a *res publica* and a *res privata*. (Remember from Chapter 1 the catcall of the Red Bull crowd, "Enlarge your *Commons*, wee hate *Privacie*.") The audience's demand for participation and control formed an entrenched statement of economic rights, and an effort to collapse this duality. If its fees seem so often to have been spent on the abortion of what it paid for, *that* was what it paid for: not a product but the rejection of "product," to perform its ownership by producing, or destroying, theatre itself – quite explicitly the motive of the Cock-pit riot of 1617, which not only attacked the playhouse and the players, but "broke open their trunckes, & whatt apparell, bookes, or other things they found, they burnt & cutt in peeces."[113] It brooked no difference between player and playgoer, performance and reception, "play" as text or play as sport, between art and life. Who owned theatre was a function of who got to make it, and a theatre of pure improvisation – consisting of only the contest for theatre, always the same and never the same – had no *techne*, no privileged source, its authorship perpetually open to claim. Stalemate favored the audience; they were playing for one all along.

No matter how many local contests clowning might win, then, globally it could only lose: its model of theatre was unsustainable. Participation could not be defeated with more participation, improvisation with improvisation, presence with more presence. By negotiating the right to play, clowning mortgaged itself to *having* to negotiate it, day in and day out, with the diminishing return of cannibalizing the theatrical program to that negotiation. Bypassed from top to bottom with connective tissue, all of it spontaneous audience interaction, that program now also guaranteed to differ radically from one day to the next, lacking more than ever the reproducibility of a legible market commodity. Concentrating theatrical

authority in a single performer not only further disintegrated the play, but
further blurred the line between producer and consumer he was meant to
draw. If his extemporality were not good enough, the audience simply arrogated performance to themselves, and the play did not go on; yet if it were
too good, the audience proved him not really a "performer" at all – and
the play still unfolded under their aegis, both the source and beneficiary
of their own entertainment. The crowd became the clown, or the clown
became it; either they took his clothes, or discovered him already in theirs.

The clown's authority was thus always double and permeable, open to
competing affiliations. To the company, he represented private interests, a
player pretending to be a playgoer, repelling the audience to erect a property wall; to the audience he represented public pleasure, a playgoer pretending to be a player, his bricks mortared with their lime, progressively
walling them in rather than out. Thus Tarlton could be celebrated both as
the first man of the theatre and as the last symbol of an enfranchised public. Simplicity in *Three Lords and Three Ladies* holds up "*Tarltons* picture"
for all to see, claiming his funeral rites on behalf of the playhouse; playgoers, meanwhile, devised more democratic memorials, a note in a copy of
Stowe's *Annales* calling him "so beloued that men use his picture for their
signes" – the same image relocated to inns and bowling alleys, brothels
and jakes.[114] These too were a semiotic repatriation, since in their multiplicity they could not signify distinct proprietorship, but like their original, merely the self-gratification promised therein, a kind of unified figure
of vendor and buyer. In both cases, Tarlton personifies theatre – just two
different versions of it: one coterminous with the physical space of the
playhouse, the other expanding that space to fit all of London inside it.

Protoauthorship and its discontents

> Please one and please all,
> Be they great, be they small,
> Be they little, be they lowe, –
> So pypeth the crowe,
> Sitting vpon a wall, –
> Please one and please all,
> Please one and please all.
> – R.T., "The Crowe sits
> vpon the wall" (n.d.)

Both the potency and the instability of clown authorship were best evidenced by its prolific extension into print. Just as onstage, he was theatre's

first author on the page – the name under which its agency could most easily be organized, and to which its textual output was reflexively assigned. Before the playwright, the clown *was* the playwright, not only discursively but often literally. Harvey ascribes to Tarlton *The Seuen Deadlie Sinnes* (*c.* 1585), possibly a two-part play, and Lodge's joke that he preferred Wilson's *Short and Sweete* to Gosson's *Catiline* registers, sarcasm aside, no basic incongruity in the idea that a clown might write a play. In addition to *Three Ladies of London* (1584) and *Three Lords and Three Ladies* (1590), to Wilson were also ascribed *The Cobblers Prophecie* (pr. 1594) and *The Pedlers Prophecie* (pr. 1595), and after the demise of the Queen's Men he seems to have joined Henslowe's writing stable.[115] As late as 1603 Henslowe was paying John Singer £5, the going rate, for "his playe called Syngers vallentary"; not only does Henslowe call it "*his* playe," but it is "Syngers" in its very title.[116] *Greenes Tu Quoque*, indeed, did not even have to be *by* Greene – whom as far as we know only starred in it – to carry that modifier. Whether or not he actually wrote, the clown was implicitly a writing subject, insofar as textuality gestures toward one. When theatre got written down, his was the only name capable of sustaining eponymous possession of it – the sole theatre professional, poet or player, for whom this distinction would ever be reserved.

The distinction is clearest in the jig, which underwent a burst of publication in the early 1590s – shortly before playbooks, perhaps not coincidentally, would experience the same thing. When Augustine Philips entered one in the Register in 1595, it was under the title "*Phillips* his gigge of the slyppers"; when another appeared soon after with the rather overlong title "A pretie newe J[i]gge betwene *ffrancis* the gentleman *Richard* the farmer and theire wyves," it was colloquially shortened to "Attowell's Jig"; when Henry Herbert licensed a jig in 1624, he indexed it "*Shankes Ordinary*, written by Shankes himself."[117] Will Kemp authored at least two of three jigs entered in 1591, the second of them entirely eponymous – "Kemps Iigge" – and he would be named in the titles of three more before 1595. When Everard Guilpin sneers that "Whores, Bedles, bawdes, and Sergeants filthily / Chaunt *Kemps* Iigge," we thus cannot know which jig it was they chanted – but despite such mass rebroadcast, it is "*Kemps*" jig.[118] Precisely because he broached the question of its possession, with the clown came a recognition that theatrical speech belonged *to someone*, and could remain so beyond the moment of its performance. He was, in sum, the dramatic protoauthor, demonstrating that theatre could be owned before such ownership even had a clear object to which to attach.

Yet the problem with such ownership, on the page as on stage, was its plurality. That the clown was an author did not mean that others could not also be at the same time. In performance he produced his individuality against a background of interference, and if playgoers were quick to embrace his name in print, it was because it always embedded theirs – becoming, like the Tarlton shopsign, a mark not of final propriety, but of ongoing collaboration. When theatre was written down, his may have been the default voice to which it was assigned, but we can never be sure what *counted*, for whom, as "theatre" – how much, if any, corresponded to what he had said or done, or if he served merely as a mouthpiece, a generative rhetorical position from which new theatre could be made. Tarlton's earliest notice was as an author rather than a player – a 1570 broadside dirge called "A very Lamentable and woful discours of the fierce fluds," with "*Quod*. Richard Tarlton" at bottom. Even before it was making mirth, the clown's name already lent itself to the anonymous news function of his minstrel roots, with 1579's "Tarltons Devise upon this vnlooked for great snowe" seemingly of the same type.[119] Similarly, if one had a new ballad or catch, "Tarlton's" became a convenient name under which to market it, theme it, or simply remember it. The subscript "R.T." appears at the end of the undated ballad "The Crowe sits vpon the wall"; Martin Parker composed two songs to the tune of "Tarletons Medley"; the ballad "Willie and Peggie" lists its accompaniment as "Tarltons Carroll"; music for a song called "Tarltons Willy" survives in manuscript.[120] No connection to his playhouse activities is ever stated, or necessary: they are the pretext for, not the text of, the discourse applied to him, a process whereby cultural production was arbitrarily labeled theatrical production – because he made the two equivalent.

Just as this process elided stage, street, and page, man and myth, neither was it bound by the term of his natural life: Tarlton's runaway authorship continued beyond the grave, protracting his death to the point of confessing its irrelevance. Three weeks after, on 23 September 1588, a pamphlet called "*Tarltons* Farewell" appeared, answered by "*Tarltons* repentance of his farewell" in 1589. In 1590 there followed "a pleasant Dyttye Dialogue wise betwene Tarltons ghost and Robyn Good Fellowe," beginning the period of explicitly posthumous appropriation that will occupy the next chapter. "Tarltons Recantacyon," entered 2 August 1589, seems the only one of these post-mortem tracts with any shred of theatrical provenance, purporting to be "vppon this theame gyven him by a gentleman at the Belsavage without Ludgate (nowe or ells never) being the last theame he songe."[121] Yet a printed "theme" does not really support a biographical motive either, since it records Tarlton's interlocutor along with him: even if Tarlton *had* sung "nowe or ells never," the "theme" as a whole is never quite his. The convoluted grammar of the title performs the structure of clown authorship itself, in which textuality does not render theatre unilateral, but merely captures a historically unique exchange.

More than any clown genre, "themes" let the audience "act their parts in print" – a concretion of the point where its desire to experience the clown intersected with its desire to experience itself – and represented, no less than playbooks, a perfectly plausible path for dramatic publication to take. Thus much was being argued, explicitly, by 1578:

> And at thy handes I challenge one requeste,
>   thy promise partlie yeelds it as my due,
> Which if performance answer all the rest,
>   then will I say thy wordes and deeds be true:
> It is thy Theames in order one by one,
> To keepe thy fame aliue when thou arte gone.
>
> Yet blame me not good *Dicke*, though I encroche
>   to take thy word, as if it were a band:
> It is because I faine would set abroche
>   the thing thou closely keepeste in thy hand,
> But in meane space thy trifles welcome bee,
> And thou farewell, for Theames remember mee.[122]

This is "Lewis Ph. Gentleman," in a commendatory poem to *Tarletons Tragical Treatises* (1578) – only a fragment of which remains, and perhaps the sole Tarltonian document with a claim to authorial authenticity. Nothing survives except a dedicatory epistle, three praises of the author, and a verse preface. The title disavows comedy, and the other two poems intimate a lofty subject: "braue discourse / of strange aduentures past"; a book not of "riddles" but of "grauer geere"; in a conceit that would later transfer to Shakespeare, Tarlton proves that "giftes of Arte so farre inferior be / To those which Nature planted hath in thee." Possibly it was a rendition of selections from Ovid's *Metamorphoses*, for the Preface extols the power of poetry to tell "how creatures first receiude their shapes," and "how crooked *Chaos* was disperste." Entitled "The Authors iudgement of such rashe verdicts as are gyuen in disprayse of Poets," it explains his turn to poetry almost as an extension of his theatrical duty, to defend against "the carping crue ... [with] *Argus* hundred eies" – where the performer must now turn writer because writing is unfit to withstand performance:

Thus are the Poets toste and turnde:
    their labours rent to ragges:
And all the sweetenesse of their time,
    truste vp in Tinkers bagges:
The silly labourer that toiles
    in shoures of haile and snow,
Doth make a pastime of his paine,
    a welfare of his woe

   .   .   .   .   .

Sith verse and I so different are,
    Ile presse in ragged rime,
To manifest the meere goodwill
    that I to learning owe,
No painted words, but perfect deeds,
    shall my inuention show. (*7r–*8v)

As onstage, Tarlton's "ragged rime" here offers to suffer exposure on behalf of poetic authority, absorbing the public denigration that will allow the literary to be heard. The passage reads like a manifesto of what Tarlton did at the playhouse, now transposed to a purely textual setting. We almost do not need the rest of the book: instead of a clown's history of the world, the Preface gives us something like a theory of himself, his theatrical identity likewise imagined – if only from his perspective – as an act of Ovidian *poesis*, an assimilation of wild elements, the ceaseless, foundational conversion of chaos into order.

And yet "Lewis Ph." clearly wants none of this. For him, those elements merely revolve within the clown instead of resolve, and his own poem is part of that circulation. Hijacking the very book he is supposed to plug, he calls for another – a collection of "thy Theames in order one by one," which he claims Tarlton has promised him to compile; the present volume merits but a single line, only to say its "trifles" are "welcome" until this successor arrives. Indifferent to Tarlton's literary endeavors, for Lewis Ph. the clown's authorship is conditioned by performance, and so must be shaped to it. He would see performance transmitted to print faithfully, "in order one by one," organizing theatre chronologically rather than objectively, as a string of discrete spatiotemporal events. The journalistic schema reduces Tarlton's byline merely to a selection principle, a common "theme"; the clown can no more own such a theatre than one can own the unfolding history in which one's words and actions are enmeshed. He cannot even own the byline, indeed, since the very improvisatory nature of his performance predicts that it would not really refer to "him" anyway. To read this "*Tarltons Themes*" would not be to recover "Tarlton," who becomes non-identical to the person who spoke those words, in those times, in those places, the instant he speaks them. Thus the romantic experiment of *Tarletons Tragical Treatises* strikes Lewis Ph. as utterly illegible; he never presumes to preserve "Tarlton," who for him exists from moment to moment, but merely his "fame."

Instead, the only theatrical entity that attains a permanence in his proposal is its most contingent one. In the playhouse, the audience changes from day to day; in a printed version of that playhouse that runs those days together, it becomes homogeneous. In both substance and form, *Tarltons Themes* is the playbook the audience would have written if the structure of performance did not already obviate doing so: organic, cyclical, infinite, not a book but a scroll, not of the play but of playing, not an artifact but the neverending chronicle of its arrested and contested manufacture – a monument against monuments, a leviathan constantly rending itself apart. The clown may author theatre, but the theatre he authors yields a *text* that can have no single author, and to which he is merely an author function, a heuristic. Though he designates a source for theatrical experience, the quality of that experience – spontaneous, interactive – ensures that he can never be the ultimate target of its textual representation. That remains the experience itself, always greater than the sum of the individuals who compose it, and Lewis Ph.'s poem already participates in that intractability. It requests a book of themes, yet does so *as* a theme – "challenging" Tarlton to deliver on his promise, compelling "performance" to "answer" it, testing if his "wordes and deeds be true." The book is to be Tarlton's reply, but since the prompt for the book lies outside it, it can never house *all* "thy theames." Such a book can never be written, because the dialogic structure of "themes" – of clowning as a whole – forms a totality that exceeds containment. And thus, perhaps, we find Tarlton withholding their publication ("the thing / thou closely keepeste in thy hand"), for as soon as they appeared they would cease to be "*thy* theames." If Lewis Ph.'s initial plea was "to keepe *thy* fame aliue when thou art gone," by the end it is "for Theames remember *mee*" – articulating, like a ghost, the essence of "themes" itself, the longing for materiality, each playgoer's need to register their existence. Fulfilling the same locution as performance, the Book of the Audience he imagines would extend it into eternity: "I was here."

For the clown, print does not stop the moment of performance, but perpetuates it indefinitely, becoming yet another way for the audience to possess the stage through him. Under his dispensation, there is no final text, because there is always another playgoer to remember, always a "theme" in answer to the last, always a tomorrow at the playhouse to link today's conversation to yesterday's. "O fustie worlde," exclaims Ingenioso in *The Returne from Parnassus* (*c.* 1600), speaking for an antiseptic author-ship that might escape such corporeal flux:

> were there anie comendable passage to Styx and Acharon, I would goe liue with Tarleton, and neuer more [b]less this dull age with a good line. Why, what an vnmanerlie microcosme was this swine faced clowne? But that the Vassall is not capable of anie infamie, I would bepainte him; but a verie goose quill scornes such a base subject, and there is noe ink fitt to write his seruill name but a scholeboyes, that hath bene made by the mixture of vrin and water. (269–77)

Here the conflation has become total: for the elitist Ingenioso – like so many frustrated playwrights from whom we hear – the clown is no longer recognizable as a professional, but now just a way of talking about the audience, "an unmanerlie microcosme." For him, "clown authorship" is a contradiction in terms – no less than "audience authorship," with which it is here paired. Not only is Tarlton beneath the writer, he is beneath writing itself, his infernal abode the antithesis of the study, alien to verbal composition. Shameless, puerile, accessible to all, he reduces what flows through theatre to what flows around it. His name is Audience, and to write it – like schoolboys practicing their signatures – is to write in bodily discharge, with no more visibility or permanence than in a sewage canal.

Scriptedness

> JOE GILLIS. Audiences don't know somebody sits down and writes a
> picture. They think the actors make it up as they go along.
>   – *Sunset Blvd.* (1950)

If theatre was to become economically and culturally legitimate, it needed not just authors – owning subjects – but *texts*, concrete, iterable, transfer-able, publicly recognized representations of its production to which own-ership could attach. Providing the former without the latter, the clown provided it at the expense of the latter. To the playwrights who wrote them, plays were certainly texts; but audiences never saw those playwrights, or those texts.[123] What they saw instead was a particulate, participatory per-formance – shot through with clowning – that authorized itself only by pluralizing its ownership, and that rendered "the play" even more difficult to discern as a discrete object. A first-generation authorial technology fit-ted to expediency, the clown opened a space for the discussion of theat-rical ownership, but could not close it; he personified the idea of theatre as property, but could not create any durable property himself. As long as his practice was dialogic and improvised, indeed, he actively discouraged any commensurability between performance and textuality – or at least, no textuality that did not affirm the audience as its ultimate content. His protoauthorship onstage worked, effectively, as anti-authorship on the page, barring the two media from intercourse with each other in all but a socially documentary sense. A theatre that did not unfold as a book could never become a book – or at least, not a book that belonged to the theatre.

Again, nowhere is this better illustrated than in the books theatre was already becoming – at the hands of its audience. The practice of amateur stenography is a good index of the disintegrationism that the nature of performance seems to have sponsored: for many playgoers, theatre consisted less of "plays" than of an assortment of phrases to be sampled, cribbed, and adapted for personal reperformance. And as often as not, what they copied was the clown, reducing the play to just the jokes. According to Q1 *Hamlet*, "Gentlemen quotes his ieasts downe / In their tables"; "There be them that will get iestes by heart," says Barnabe Rich, "that will not let a merriment slip, but they will trusse it vp for their owne prouision."[124] "I am one that hath seene this play often," brags the gallant in the Induction to *The Malcontent* – which for him means having "most of the jeastes heere in my table-booke."[125] If what makes a jest or a "theme" is the response of its audience, so what determines the content of "the play" is its audience – and the books of those plays are as variable as them. "Momus" visits the Globe, the Fortune, "and next to the *Curtaine*, where, as at the rest, / He notes that action downe that likes him best"; lawyers saffron their arguments with "a few shreds and scraps dropt from some Stage-Poet, at the Globe or Cock-pit, which they have carefully bookt up"; "from the poets labours in the pit," gentlemen "informe [themselves] for th'exercise of wit / At Tavernes, [and] gather notes."[126] Unlike their satirists, these playgoers do not seem at all cognizant of the "poet" whose "labours" they deconstitute, or of the play's preconceived, organic design; the albums they compile are snapshots of their own pleasure, collages of their personalities. No one is the author of a "scrap," or of a play viewed as a jumble of scraps. There is only their endless recirculation, barring any discrimination between producer and consumer. In this economy, indeed, authority belongs only to the audience selecting what to recirculate. Thus a poet-ape in Marston's *Scourge of Villanie* (1598) culls "a common-place booke out of plaies, / And speakes in print," yet "what ere he sayes / Is warranted by Curtaine *plaudeties*."[127] For him, the text of a play consists not in the words – even when those words are in print – but in those words as processed by performance, privileging the ones *audiences* approved. Both in performance and as text, the audience literally makes the play.

Like the putative *Tarltons Themes*, these are the decentered, idiosyncratic, do-it-yourself playbooks that a theatrical paradigm based on
clowning encouraged. Changing the episteme of performance, however,
was not just a matter of getting rid of the clown, because he had by now
become welded to performance. Institutional self-ownership thus neces-
sitated two incompatible locutions. In the long term, audiences had to
learn that theatre was an artifact of private labor above the need for their
participation. Yet in the short term, performance still negotiated itself as
social contract, the division of producer from consumer still a function of
the friction generated between them – thus requiring participation, and
thus daily renewing theatre's temporality. The players could not afford to
make their point by alienating audiences outright: they could not perform
with their backs turned, or refuse admission and play to an empty house.
Not only did you have to be there to *know* theatre was happening without
your needing to be there, but theatre was a business, and without patrons
it did not happen. The companies were slaves to demand, and as long as
that demand included a countenancing of the demanders, they needed
clowns.

The story of this chapter has been the emergence of that symbiosis –
that "a play cannot be without a clown" any more than it could do without playgoers. Even in 1620, when *Two Merry Milke-Maids* warns its
audience that it has "reform'd" the stage of "Guns, Trumpets, Drums" in
favor of "Sence and Words," in the hope that "you … will cease / your
dayly Tumults," it can still reassure them that "'Tis a fine play: / For we
haue in't a Coniuror, a Deuill, / And a Clowne, too."[128] And yet we read
these words, like so many commercial plays, in a printed playbook, an
objective, schematic representation of theatre that pretends its audiences
are not there, and that expects those same audiences to want to buy it.
How did theatre escape the corner it had backed into? How could the
"reform" of dramatic reception toward "Sence and Words" occur, while
performance still relied on someone who reduced it to "dayly Tumult"?

Dramatic reception could never be reformed: everything in the past two
chapters has attested to that fact, and, as we will see, standards of audience
conduct not only held constant across the period, but steadily worsened.
Changing the meaning of performance, however, did not require changing how people behaved toward it; in this case, indeed, it was constrained
to work within those conventions. Those conventions seem completely
intact in 1638, in the prologue to *The Obstinate Lady*, yet the relationship
between player and playgoer they subtend has utterly transformed:

'Troth Gentlemen, we know that now adayes
Some come to take up Wenches at our Playes;
It is not in our power to please their sence,
We wish they may go discontented hence.
And many Gallants do come hither, we think
To sleep and to digest there too much drink:
We may please them; for we will not molest
With Drums and Trumpets any of their rest.
If perfum'd Wantons do for eighteen pence,
Expect an Angel, and alone go hence;
We shall be glad with all our hearts: for we
Had rather have their Room then Companie. (A2r–v)

So much for "ushering" the audience "over an imaginary threshold": this prologue ushers them out. Encompassing all forms of disruptive attention and inattention – adding that the play "can be but Hiss'd at worst, and soon forgot" – it fully expects (and even invites) its audience to boo, snore, court sexual dalliances, say "This is the worst of all the Playes / You euer saw," or simply leave. It does not care. The performance will proceed anyway, with or without them – all the better, in fact, without them – because it is not *for* them; performance is not even for itself, a quickly forgotten shadow of something else. This is the ultimate insult to a theatre whose identity inhered in live events, and to an audience apparently still ready to insult it back – yet the Prologue anticipates no outcry against his statement. Somehow, without altering its modes of expression, the nature of theatrical patronage has been silently revised. Performance may be contestable, manipulable, violable, or ignorable, but theatre does not consist in performance; it is no longer of the audience, because no longer really of the players either, recused entirely from living matter. Such a shift involved the emptying out of performance as a whole. And thus, for *Milke-Maids*, the clown remains part of the solution rather than the problem, included rather than excluded from its "reform." Why would you banish the essence of what you wanted to deactivate – liveness – when he could be the instrument?

Since he could not be banished anyway, necessity became a virtue. The clown was a pawn – for a playhouse seeking to dissever its authority from that of the audience, for an audience seeking to reintegrate them – and that pawn had power. If the audience materialized itself through him, then they could also be *de*materialized through him – by dematerializing him as well, by evacuating performance of its status as unique event. That, in theory, is what a playbook does: in order to make that erasure comprehensible, and normative, the clown had to do it first, in practice, to his own practice. We are thus talking here not just about making texts of performance – the sheer act of printing a play some months or years after it premiered – which could not undo the ontological priority of performance. Rather, we are talking about making performance *itself* a text, by interpenetrating the two media from the start. In order for playbooks to be understood as a version of theatre, theatre itself had to be perceived as *already* a kind of playbook, merely the enactment of a pre-existent verbal ideal, whose particular realizations were equally secondary. It had to be perceived, in other words, as fundamentally *scripted*, written down beforehand – and thus capable of eliding performance when it was written down afterward. For Heywood's stenographer spectators in 1624, as we saw in Chapter 1, who transcribed solely "the Plot," the stage has become a site only of reproductions, not of production, and their text omits their own contingent vocalic production in turn.[129] The audience knows it can disrupt the script of the play, but not its scripted*ness*.

Such scriptedness, the rest of this study argues, had to take root outside the scripted drama – in the very performative interstices that most resisted scriptedness, and that frustrated the recognition of plays as scripted as well. The clown determined the quality of theatrical experience, and thus its redefinition had to work through him, not around him. As long as any part of theatre remained "live," it remained so in its entirety: those spaces of improvisation and participation could not be removed, so improvisation instead had to defuse itself from within, introducing a clinical distance between player and playgoer at the moment of their most intimate contact. *Because* the clown inhabited this intersection of performance and reality, he was the natural agent of its foreclosure; *because* he was the one thing theatre could not script, he was the one thing that could argue the prefabrication of all theatre – by scripting himself. What if he did what Tarlton had refused to do, and published his performance? What if he tried to simulate in print what he did onstage? What if what he did onstage became, in turn, a simulation of print? Who, and whose, was he then?

"But I would see our Clownes in these dayes doe the like," ran that afterthought to Tarlton's jest of a box on the ear. "No, I warrant ye, and yet they think well of themselues too." It is not that today's clowns copy Tarlton; somehow, they have become copies of themselves – and suddenly no longer worth bothering to document. The war against the audience had a second phase, one still marginal to our playbooks. Only now its goal was to forge the very equation between "play" and "book," by creating a margin both terms could exclude. That margin was performance, and it would contain both playgoer and clown alike. Fighting presence with absence, engagement with withdrawal, the clown's improvisation would point not to the audience but to its own script, to a stage that now exchanged only with itself. To be sure, this autotelic theatre emerged alongside the social one we have been mapping; it was itself an institutional improvisation – local, tentative, accidental – and since individual clowns had to be its engines, it was often reluctant and painful. For ultimately, the clown was choosing to surrender his stardom, to install a new hierarchy of theatrical production to which his own would be subordinate. Increasingly mediated through textual circuitry, he would become the ghost behind the playbook only by first becoming a ghost of himself – by disappearing, onstage, in plain sight.

If the clown could not make a book, he would become one. That metamorphosis was already underway in 1588, indeed, before his body was even cold. For when Robert Wilson's *Three Lords and Three Ladies of London* has Simplicity show "*Tarltons* picture" onstage, eulogizing the player who had earlier played him, it is as one of the ballads he is selling – which means it is not a portrait, but an illustration, a printed woodcut, possibly the first edition title page of *Tarltons Jests* itself.[130] In an instant, the audience's view of the clown – and of itself – began to change. Squinting to make out the image from so far away, they saw no longer a man, but a man made of paper.

CHAPTER 3

Wiring Richard Tarlton

In the preceding chapters, I have laid out the questions that inform the rest of this study. How did playbooks come to be seen as commensurate with theatrical performance sufficient to be purchased after it, read alongside it, and even constructed during it, when they in no way preserve the fundamentally dialogic, interactive nature of early modern performance? Did performance, on some level, first have to make itself like a playbook, foregrounding its own scriptedness? And how were clowns – precisely because they epitomized a theatre grounded in historically unique events, in the bodily presence of its performers and audience – not just necessary but indispensable to the process? That process, I have suggested, involved not banishing the clown (which no playing company could afford to do), but disembodying him, breaking apart his self-identity by passing and re-passing it through textuality. In this first of three case-study chapters, I examine how the foremost Elizabethan stage clown, Richard Tarlton, was strategically converted into an author-figure for a book trade in anonymous popular literature concerned to do just that: retroactively to render Tarlton anonymous as well, to alienate him from any agency in his past performances, and thereby to expose theatre, like print, as a domain of reproduction rather than production. Tarlton did not choose this fate, of course; it befell him after he was dead. But as we will see, the phenomenon of posthumous authorship gives us occasion – and gave its obscured practitioners occasion – to recognize its resemblance to the new theatrical category that the textualized clown opened up, and into which he would be pushed: the "actor."

Absolute interpreters

> The Puppets are seene now in despight of the Players.
> – Ben Jonson, *Discoveries*[1]

The year is 1592, and for Robert Greene, public theatre is already in decline. The threat he identifies in his *Greenes Groatsworth of Wit*, however, is neither cultural nor economic but institutional, internal to theatre itself. Rather than harassment from civic regulators or puritanical crusade, for him the ultimate danger lies in players themselves – in the very fact, as we will see, of players in general.

> Base minded men all three of you, if by my miserie you be not warnd: for unto none of you (like mee) sought those burres to cleaue: those Puppets (I meane) that spake from our mouths, those Anticks garnisht in our colours … Yes trust them not.[2]

Greene's critique quickly narrows into a personal attack, and a famous one: he singles out for rebuke one player in particular, an "upstart Crow" who has usurped the privilege of the educated by writing his own plays, "that with his *Tygers hart wrapt in a Players hyde*, supposes he is as well able to bombast out a blanke verse as the best of you." That the player appears to be William Shakespeare, and this passage his first, rather glamorous notice, has tended to occlude Greene's larger argument, which is a strange one. This new development is so unjust, he insists, because it adds professional obsolescence to what is already systemic exploitation. The latter is really the theme of *Greenes Groatsworth*, as Greene relates the descent of his alter ego "Roberto" into bankruptcy, both financial and spiritual, once he enters the world of playwriting. Having squandered his intellectual substance, his reward is now only to be replaced by those for whose living he provided, and Greene warns his colleagues – among them Nashe, Marlowe, and Peele – to "let those Apes imitate your past excellence, and neuer more acquaint them with your admired inuentions … seeke you better maisters."[3]

"Apes" should not be "maisters" to begin with, however, and Greene's other mixed metaphors likewise point to something less than contingent about the reversal of which he complains. "Puppets" do not "speak" from the mouths of others. Others speak from theirs – players' words, ostensibly, come from poets. To call them "garnisht in our colours," and "beautified with our feathers" posits the playwright as actually the *player's* outward form, not the other way round. What lies beneath the "Players hyde" may not be a player's heart, but it is not the poet's either: the figure of the player here possesses its own independent content. Greene's slander against player-*cum*-playwright, that is, carries special force only if it presupposes a clear, established hierarchy of theatrical production – a privileging of spirit over matter, of verbal origin over bodily enactment – that the rest of *Groatsworth* implies is never the case.

The failure of that hierarchy, in fact, underlies "Roberto's" downfall even before he meets the players. His fate throughout the book is to watch others take his place, his labor converted into their gain. He is repeatedly subjected to patterns of displacement and appropriation that are as much a result of his literary activity as of his moral weakness – which are not finally easy to distinguish. Left only one groat for an inheritance, Roberto brings his shy brother Lucanio to the whore Lamilia to cozen him of his fortune; Lucanio, instantly smitten but "wanting fit wordes," "stood like a trewant that lackt a prompter, or a plaier that being out of his part at his first entrance, is faine to haue the booke to speake what he should performe." Roberto plays that book, "repl[ying] thus in his behalfe," delivering a Petrarchan serenade to provide the necessary pretext for Lamilia's affection.[4] The immediate result of this performance, however, is the book's disposal, for Lamilia now realizes that she no longer needs Roberto, and cuts him from his share: "No poore pennilesse Poet," she says, "thou art beguilde in mee, and yet I wonder how thou couldst, thou hast beene so often beguilde … but a Brokers place, at best a lenders reward."[5] Such "brokerage" has also been occurring in the conventional, formulaic narratives that the episode gratuitously interpolates – an Aesopian fable, an "old wiues tale" with a bed-trick – and by the end of it, Roberto has been reduced to a personification of just that literary material, his value circulated and then consumed. "*Heu patior telis vulnera facta meis*," he cries, "I suffer wounds made by my own weapons."[6]

It is at this point that he meets a Player, sitting "on the other side of the hedge," who appears precisely as a recirculation of his anxiety about recirculation. Overhearing Roberto's eloquent sorrow, he offers him employment, "for men of my profession gette by scholars their whole liuing" – and he seems, we are told, "a substantiall man." He goes on to review his successes, not coincidentally, by reference to puppetry:

> Why, I am as famous as Delphrigus, & the King of Fairies, as euer was any of my time … The twelue labours of Hercules haue I terribly thundred on the Stage, and plaid three Scenes of the Deuill in the High way to heauen … I can serue to make a pretie speech, for I was a countrey Author, passing at a Morrall, for twas I that pende the Morrall of mans witte, the Dialogue of Diues, and for seuen yeers space was absolute Interpreter to the puppets. (E1r)

Performance here monopolizes the entire continuum of theatrical production. He is at once a player, an "Author," and an "Interpreter" who combines those two positions, seemingly a complete theatre unto himself. He even throws in a sample of his "plain rime extempore" – "*The people make no estimation / Of Morrals teaching education*" – adding that "if ye will ye shall have more." Clearly capable of generating his own text, why he needs Roberto's services at all is unclear; if anything, *he* offers the scholar "substance" rather than the reverse. The subsequent description of Roberto's actual playwriting for the company – such as it is, and inseparable from his moral degeneration – bears this out:

> His companie were lightly the lewdest persons in the land, apt for pilfere, periurie, forgery, or any villainy. Of these he knew the casts to cog at cards, coosen at Dice ... and pithily could he paint out their whole courses of craft: So cunning he was in all craftes, as nothing rested in him almost but craftines. How often the Gentle-woman his Wife labored vainely to recall him, is lamentable to note: but as one giuen ouer to all lewdnes, he communicated her sorrowful lines among his loose trulls, that iested at her bootlesse laments. (E2r)

Lodged by the players "in a house of retayle," Roberto becomes a retailer of the players themselves: his dramatic output consists merely in repackaging their deceptions for the stage – making the output of that stage itself a deception, a fraud recycled for profit. Frictionlessly "communicating" experience – even his own – into "lines" for them, he becomes purely a linguistic middleman, erased at the very instant of transmission, so that "nothing rested in him." The conceit is literalized, in fact, when a few pages later Greene suddenly "break[s] off" to announce that he is "the saide *Roberto*," his "life in most parts agreeing with mine."[7] Not only is Roberto's authorship merely a device for recirculating narrative material, but Roberto himself is now revealed to have been just such a device – for another author in turn. Like all playwrights, Roberto can only be realized by being deconstituted, as "the *saide* Roberto" – "saide," that is, always by someone else.

No wonder, then, that a player should eventually decide to arrogate to himself the poet's function: such an indignity, for Greene, fulfills the everyday appropriations of performance itself. The fundamental problem with theatre is one of bodies: the player has one, the writer does not, and this makes locating any textual origin beyond that body and its real-time productions impossible, dramatic authorship invisible and meaningless. Thus it is really the poets whom the players inhabit and temporarily vivify, the poets' "mouths" the ones "spoken from": instead of acting on the matter of the player's body, words are just matter to be enacted, and fit to be discarded once used up. The puppet epitomizes the abjection of being ventriloquized by "interpreters," of writing for a medium that makes one's production look like it emanates from someone else. Such performance anxiety – the anxiety of being performed – extends to publication as well, to the self-dislocation of having one's words printed. And here Greene knows whereof he speaks, since he is not even "Greene," but a mouthpiece for the pseudonymous ghost-writer "speaking from" him shortly after his death. The Greene of *Greenes Groatsworth* is thus already a puppet, analyzing dramatic authorship as the condition of being already a puppet.

Only two decades later, however, Jonson's *Bartholomew Fair* can apply this same figure to the exact opposite thesis. Here, the puppet represents every discursive position in theatre *except* the author's. Its actors conflated with their characters from the opening line, its characters continuously seized by irresistible "motions" (appetite, elimination, "vapors," humors, inspiration, monomania), its plot and induction alike turning on the prescriptive power of licenses, contracts, and texts, *Bartholomew Fair* uses puppetry to mediate a vision of total authorial control over the tools of dramatic mediation itself. This evacuated humanity is most concentrated in Bartholomew Cokes, the gleeful twit who drifts from one all-consuming distraction to the next, who compulsively recites every shopsign he sees, who "has learn'd nothing, but to sing *catches*, and repeat *rattle bladder rattle* … if hee meete but a Carman i'the streete … hee will whistle him, and all his tunes ouer, at night in his sleepe," and whose skull contains only "cockle-shels, pebbles, fine wheat-strawes, and here and there a chicken's feather, and a cob-web."[8] Cokes personifies a kind of performance so hollowed out that it is just involuntary, automatic repetition, and a performative presence so unconscious and amnesiac that it is tantamount to absence. "His soule," marvels Nightingale, "is halfe-way out on's body"; indeed, his soul *is* his body.[9] Merely a "bladder" to be filled and emptied, he is a living puppet – and thus he ends up among them in Leatherhead's booth at the puppet show, unable to distinguish their agency from the puppeteer's or their animacy from his own. "Doe you call these *Players*?" he asks. "They are *Actors*, Sir," Leatherhead clarifies – "and as good as any."[10]

Between 1592 and 1614, then, we find two theorizations of dramatic authorship whose key term is the same, but completely repolarized. For Greene, no generativity can belong to the writer, because the player is his "absolute interpreter," the point at which his labor articulates with the world and is appropriated. For Jonson, precisely *because* performance takes place in the world, the player's very bodiliness makes him negligible, reduced merely to a transparent conduit for texts. How, in just two decades, has the theatrical paradigm been inverted? How – it feels daunting even to write the question – did theatre decide that it no longer existed in "the world"?

The bridge is the word Leatherhead uses, "Actor," of which Greene as yet has no working theory. To be sure, theories of "acting" abounded in the early modern period, but they consisted of rhetorical techniques for manipulating physiological principles; they are theories as much *for* the orator as about him. When the word "actor" comes into use at this moment – Heywood's *Apologie for Actors* (1612) being its most salient codification – it denotes the performer's relation to the character he "personates," not to the text which scripts that character or to the person who scripted that text. Neither from this perspective did "personation" entail a corresponding disappearance of the performer: the purpose of "action," according to Thomas Wright, is "to discouer vnto the present beholders and auditors, how *the actor* is affected … by mouth he telleth *his* mind."[11] For Jonson, by contrast, the actor's mouth is for telling *another's* mind – the author's – and by itself is simply a speaking machine: "I know nothing," declares Wasp, "I do not know, and I will not know, and I scorne to know."[12]

Two familiar encomia of Richard Burbage, separated by half a century, may serve to mark the distance between these conceptions. In an unsigned elegy on his death in 1618, the agent of Burbage's performance appears to be utterly Burbage, to the point of his engrossing almost every pronoun to himself:

> How did his speech become him, and his pace,
> Suite with his speech, and every action grace
> Them both alike, whilst not a woord did fall,
> Without just weight, to ballast itt with all.[13]

Burbage is a unity: "his speech" is *his* speech, as are the "pace" and "action" that make it even more so; not only do his words "become" him, but he becomes himself, self-directed, self-possessed, obliterating any sense of mediation. Compare this with Richard Flecknoe's remembrance in 1664:

> It was the happiness of the Actors of those Times to have such Poets as these to instruct them, and write for them; and no less of those Poets to have such docile and excellent Actors to Act their Playes, as a *Field* and *Burbidge;* of whom we may say, that he was a delightful *Proteus,* so wholly transforming himself into his Part, and putting off himself with his Cloathes, as he never (not so much as in the Tyring-house) assum'd himself again until the Play was done: there being as much difference betwixt him and one of our common Actors, as between a Ballad-singer who onely mouths it, and an

excellent singer, who knows all his Graces, and can artfully vary and modu-
late his Voice, even to know how much breath he is to give to every syllable
… never falling in his Part when he had done speaking; but with his looks
and gesture, maintaining it still unto the heighth, he imagining *Age quod
agis*, onely spoke to him.[14]

The focus is still on actorly craft, yet the agency has subtly shifted. Though
there is more of Burbage's body here, there is somewhat less of Burbage;
indeed, "not-Burbage" has now become its paramount locution.[15] Flecknoe
is highly conscious of actors as media for texts, and his entire account
is framed by that relationship: by "writ[ing] for them," poets "instruct"
them, and an actor's "excellence" lies in a "docil[ity]" that resembles duc-
tility. No less than the "Ballad-singer who only mouths it," the text also
reduces the "excellent" actor to a kind of mouth, dictating his breathing
and vocals according to rules of art. The good actor knows these rules,
and obeys them; the bad do not. The knowledge may thus be Burbage's,
but the choices are not, any more than a pipe that "knows" its notes plays
itself. They are those of his "Part," into which *he* transforms, and which
continues to operate him, aloud or silent, alone or accompanied, "never
falling" or wavering, until it is done. This transformation starts and stops
where the text starts and stops, making no distinction between onstage or
off. In between there is but one thought, "*Age quod agis*," do what you are
doing, the very essence of non-thought. Burbage can "vary" his voice, but
not his performance: potentially it is the same every time, equally powerful, equally powerless, and the "self" that he "assumes" at its close merely
another "part." If for Jonson the actor is indistinct from his character, it
is because he too has no existence beyond performance, the character that
animates him neither originating nor terminating with him – a notion
that the list of "*The Actors Names*" prefixed to Webster's *Duchess of Malfi*
(pr. 1623), conflating not just the *dramatis personae* with their respective
actors but with the actors who succeeded them in those roles, likewise
underscores.[16] "Actors" do not create, they transmit; they do not possess,
but are possessed, like stage properties. Increasingly, the term names not
a mental or physical activity, but an economic position, a thing that does
things for another.

So where did this idea of "the actor" come from? How did it become
possible to conceive of players as less than alive, and of performance as
devoid of presence – when, as we have seen, theatre was far from coterminous with the play, and still featured genres based on precisely the player's autonomy, immediacy, and generativity? Even by 1614, this alternative
tradition was still synonymous with one player, Richard Tarlton – but for

Bartholomew Fair, it has become no longer so alternative. The Induction stages a dispute between the claims of improvisation and those of textuality, which ends with the Stagekeeper's ejection by the Bookholder in favor of the Scrivener's "Articles of Agreement." Yet even before he is unceremoniously dismissed, the Stagekeeper, who began by decrying "these Master-Poets" who "will ha' their owne absurd courses," is made to deconstruct his own argument:

> I am an Asse! I! and yet I kept the *Stage* in Master *Tarletons* time, I thanke my starres. Ho! And that man had liu'd to haue play'd in *Bartholmew Fayre*, you should ha' seene him ha' come in, and ha' beene coozened i'the Cloath-quarter, so finely! And *Adams*, the Rogue, ha' leap'd and caper'd vpon him, and ha' dealt his vermine about, as though they had cost him nothing. And then a substantiall watch to ha' stolne in vpon 'hem, and taken 'hem away, with mistaking words, as the fashion is, in the *Stage*-practice. (A4v)

It is unclear exactly what incident, intra- or extradramatic, the Stagekeeper recollects. Certainly, if this is his fantasy of Tarlton's having "play'd in *Bartholmew Fayre*," then his point is it would not be *Bartholomew Fair*, for Tarlton would always do his own thing – starting with his signature entrance of peeping and strutting ("you should ha' seene him ha' come in"). Yet very quickly, that "thing" Tarlton did starts to take on a routinized, predictable quality. Tarlton, being Tarlton, must be cheated and abused; "and" Adams must be his abuser; "and" he must do it in a certain way, riding piggyback on him, "and" beating even his fleas senseless. The cumulative weight of these concatenated "ands" is such that, in mid-stream, the mood switches from conditional past to present perfect infinitive – "and then a substantiall watch to ha' stolne in vpon 'hem" – almost, indeed, to imperative. Gradually, the Stagekeeper's free-associative reverie takes on a compulsory force: in the act of remembering Tarlton, he scripts him.

If at just this moment the Stagekeeper is intercepted by the Bookholder, he has in a sense already become a bookholder himself, and Tarlton a kind of book. Ironically, the anti-*Bartholomew Fair* he envisions actually comes to pass in *Bartholomew Fair*, almost to the letter. Only the person "coozened i'the Cloath-quarter" ends up being not Richard Tarlton but Bartholomew Cokes – and so not really a person at all, but something like a fabrication of cloth, a patchwork scarecrow of detachable body parts: "if a legge or an arme on him did not grow on," Wasp remarks, "hee would lose it i'the presse."[17] Together, induction and play recapitulate the process by which stage clown and "actor," theatrical subject and textual object, became commensurable identities – culminating here in their direct, one-to-one substitution – and by which a new category, the author, would move into the space the clown vacated. That process, I argue, worked much like the Stagekeeper's subtle conversion of Tarlton's memory into prescription, but with a twist. It involved passing Tarlton himself through the pseudonymous authorship from which Greene writes – before, indeed, even Greene got there – and making him the author, as it were, of his own de-authorization. The opportunity arose, in part, as a simple function of institutional age, and the inevitable passing of the public theatre's first generation. It is always easier to write for someone else when they are already dead; it is a trickier thing, we will see, in so doing to argue that they were never really as alive, or as "live," as they seemed. The remainder of this chapter considers how Tarlton lost his body "i'the presse" too, and at the same time retroactively gained one.

High fidelity

Here Simp[licity]. sings first, and Wit after,
dialoguewise, both to music if you will.

WIT. Now sirs, which singes best?
SIM. Tush, your copesmates shall not judge: (*to one of the auditory*) friend, what say you, which of us sings best?
WIL. To thy truth there's but bad choice. Now wil you sel the ballad you sang, for Ile not buy the voice.
SIM. Why wilt thou not buy my voice?
WIL. Because it will cost me more money to buy sallet oile to keep it frō rusting, than it is woorth. I pray ye honest man, what's this?
SIM. Read and thou shalt see.
WIL. I cannot read ...
SIM. If thou cannot read Ile tel thee, this is *Tarltons* picture: didst thou never know *Tarlton*?
WIL. No: what was that *Tarlton*? I neuer knew him.

– Robert Wilson, *Three Lords and Three Ladies of London*
(pr. 1590), CIr–v

On or about 3 September 1588, the institution of London theatre entered a crisis from which it would emerge irrevocably changed. On that day, according to the parish register, Richard Tarlton, freeman of the Vintners' guild, Master of Fence, member of the Queen's Men and the most celebrated stage player in England, was buried in St. Leonard Shoreditch.[18] For his devotees and colleagues alike, there was a sense of having moved into an era of "before" and "after": theatre was now old enough to have a memory, and playgoers young enough to warrant its conservation. Thus began the explosion of Tarltonian remembranciana we surveyed in the last chapter, overwhelmingly bent on eulogizing what had been lost with his death:

his pugnacious stage presence, his verbal facility, his quick wit. Stowe's *Annales* praises him for a "plentifull pleasant extemporall wit" that made him "the wonder of his time"; Meres says that "as Antipater Sidonius was famous for extemporal verse in Greeke, and Ouid for his *Quicquid cona-bar dicere versus erat* ["whatever I tried to say, turned into verse"]: so was our Tarleton."[19] Nashe and Harvey trade references to Tarlton no fewer than sixteen times during their feud, usually as a class-marked insult, but his "amplifications" and "piperly Extemporizing and Tarletonizing" also clearly serve as their rhetorical model.[20] "O brave Tarlton," Nashe mock-apostrophizes, "gramercy capricious, and transcendent witte, the onelie high Pole Artique, and deep Minerall of an incô[m]parable stile"; "good Dick Tarleton is dead," Harvey notes, "& nothing aliue but Cattes-meat, & Dogges-meat enough."[21] When Simplicity in *Three Lords and Three Ladies of London* (pr. 1590) brings "Tarltons picture" onstage to mark his passing by educating three youths on the legend they missed, it is precisely to deny the possibility of his representation, let alone of his replacement: "the fineness was within, for without he was plain; / But it was the merri-est fellow, and had such jests in store / That, if thou hadst seen him, thou would'st have laughed thy heart sore."[22] That the audience *can* see him, of course, in the picture, makes for a moment as semiotically complex as is the emotional response it tries to elicit. Tarlton originated the role of Simplicity in *Three Ladies of London*, but this Simplicity is not him; he tells them to "read" a text instead, but that text both is and is not Tarlton either. Where then should the audience look? Insofar as Tarlton personi-fied theatre, the play beckons toward a cloudy future; it implants a desire, but refuses to give it a medium.

Yet despite Simplicity's idealism, print had until now proven service-able enough in replicating the pleasure Tarlton provided. *Tarltons Jests* (c. 1590) may already have appeared by this time, its very title page quite pos-sibly the image he holds; innumerable pseudonymous ballads, songs, and dances besides, there had already been *Tarltons Toyes* (1576, lost), possibly a compendium of stage devices, and the commender of *Tarletons Tragical Treatises* (1578) imagines no difficulty in Tarlton's compiling "thy Theames in order one by one," which he stubbornly requests. Soon after his death, there followed at least three more lost items – "*Tarltons* Farewell" (1588), "*Tarltons* repentance" (1589), and "Tarltons Recantacyon" (1589) – seem-ingly purporting to be deathbed confessionals, leftovers, the last scrap-ings of the barrel. But the Tarltonian "store" would not run dry for long. Authentic or not, each of these publications still had a rhetoric of authen-ticity, with the living man as their alleged source. With the impish "A pleasant Dyttye Dialogue wise betwene Tarltons ghost and Robyn Good Fellowe" (1590), though, that rhetoric was apparently jettisoned. Suddenly, "Tarlton" was free to continue making merriment from beyond the grave. Print discovered something it could offer that theatre could not: not just preservation, but perpetuation.

If we wanted a point at which the momentum toward a market for playbooks begins to build, we could do worse than this ballad. There were playbooks before 1590, of course, albeit anomalous and few; neither was this the first time a historical personage had gone on accruing literary credits after their death. But it was the first time that person had been a player, and that is significant. As we saw in Chapter 2, until now the sole prerequisite for Tarlton's appearance in print had been performance – theatrical or otherwise, true or otherwise – somewhere, at some time, by Tarlton or not. His name signified only the claim of a shared event, which was now being shared again. Under his *imprimatur*, print had remained secondary to and documentary of performance: in its broadest sense, "theatre" was what happened, or could be said to have happened, and textuality merely its chronicle. The trauma of Tarlton's death, however, seems to have jarred this hierarchy. So personal was the public's attachment to him, and so keenly felt his loss, that the association of "theatre" with *him* began to take precedence over its dependence on actuality. For the first time, theatre – or at least one of its practitioners – now entered the realm of the explicitly imaginary. To "Tarltons ghoste and Robyn Good Fellowe," it does not matter that the speech it ascribes to Tarlton was never spoken, nor could ever have been spoken – an impossibility its title plainly announces. It is enough that this is what he *would have* spoken, had one access to his spirit. That spirit, the ballad argues, is now available in a new medium, which no longer requires – and even eschews – prior performance as its license. For popular print, the symbolic death of theatre was an opportunity to renegotiate their relationship.

By the time we reach *Tarltons Newes out of Purgatorie* (1590), the issue of the player's spiritual destination had apparently been settled so as to allow repeat visitation. Tarlton was absorbed into the literary genre of the dream vision, now relegated to ghost-authoring the stories of others. *Tarltons Newes* is a storybook, and not only are its tales no longer by Tarlton, they are not even about him, consisting of *fabliaux* recycled from previous collections or recently translated out of Continental ones. Tarlton here occupies what Alexandra Halasz calls "an attested storyteller position," framing the volume with a convenient and appealing meta-narrative of "how the stories came to be told."[23] Given its layers of appropriation – "Take Dick

Tarlton once for thine author," his ghost intones, in a pamphlet that says it is "Published by an old Companion of his, / Robin Goodfellow" (recalling the earlier ballad as well), and whose material derives from anonymous French and Italian adapters of Boccaccio – Halasz correctly sees in it a series of substitutions useful to the marketing of an English popular prose literature. On the one hand, "the pamphlet becomes a competitor with the theater … offering the spirit of Tarlton in a form that defies both the finality of death and the ephemerality of oral performance." At the same time, his "brand" fetishistically veils the book's provenance, "standing for the labor involved in the production of the commodity pamphlet."[24] In other words, *Tarltons Newes* seeks to reproduce exactly the author function that Tarlton enabled for the theatre. Serving to "naturalize … print culture as a phenomenon of the marketplace," Halasz writes, "the figure of Tarlton offers an image of free, that is endlessly circulating and uninhibited, speech … thematizing the circulation of printed material as if it were an unconstrained act."[25]

Yet the experience of a textual clown is not that of a live one: his speech may sound "free" and "unconstrained," but read it a second time, and it is not. And *Tarltons Newes* surely knows this. It cannot co-opt theatre without corrupting that template; to inflict such damage, I would argue, is its very aim. What happens to Tarlton's image of spontaneous "free speech" in a medium where such speech is categorically foreclosed? What impact does a version of his performance that "defied [its] ephemerality" have on the meaning of that performance, so intimately linked with ephemerality? The goal of his posthumous authorship was not just institutional citation – print piggybacking on theatre, as it were – but ultimately, institutional estrangement: Tarlton's theatrical pleasures may lead readers into a space of literary pleasure, but once there, it does not want to send them back to the stage again. The project of *Tarltons Newes* is thus more ambitious than simply using Tarlton to naturalize its recirculative economy. Precisely because it cannot fully do so, it uses him to leverage that same economy into its competitor as well. If *Tarltons Newes* fantasizes a print that feels just like theatre, it must simultaneously construct a theatre that works – and always worked – just like print.

The pamphlet opens, quite shrewdly, by recreating the scene of mourning so that its desires can be channeled in a different direction:

> Sorrowing as most men doe for the death of *Richard Tarlton*, in that his particular losse was a generall lament to all that coveted, either to satisfie their eies with his Clownish gesture, or their eares with his witty iests. The wonted desire to see plaies left me, in that although I sawe as rare showes,

and heard as lofty verse, yet I inioied not those wonted sports that flowed from him as from a fountain, of pleasing and merry conceits ... he was a mad merry companion, desired and loved of all: amongst the rest of whose welwishers my selfe being not the least, after his death I mourned in conceit, and absented my selfe from all plaies, as wanting that merry *Roscius* of Plaiers, that famozed all Comedies so with his pleasant and extemporall inuention ... (B1r)

On the title page, Tarlton solicits a specific community of consumers: "Onely such a iest as his Iigge, fit for Gentlemen to laugh at an houre, &c." Here, his absence immediately registers a crisis in consumer consciousness by which the pamphlet hopes to claim them. "Robin Goodfellow" introduces himself as a member of that community, one who shares our pastimes and now our loss. In so doing, he structures our grief into a re-evaluation of commercial behavior. He invites us to learn again how to go to the playhouse: how do we equate "as rare shows" and "as lofty verse" as we see today with their antecedents, without Tarlton's "wonted sports" and "merry conceits" to complement them? Does the content of performance reside in its words and sights, or in its individual performers? The reiterated emphasis on the clown's "pleasant and extemporal invention" – "hee had such a prompt witte, as he seemed to haue that *Salem ingenii* [pleasant eloquence]" – already telegraphs his answer, implying that if no two Tarlton performances were ever the same, no post-Tarlton performance can hope to reproduce him either. Neither are these purely theoretical speculations. Robin has attended plays, and knows: though the body of theatre remains, the spirit has gone out, just as "the wonted desire to see plaies left me." Querying the relation between theatrical products and their constitutive labor, he poses a dilemma between a theatre of unique personalities and a theatre of assembly-line manufacture – where Tarlton's absence either cannot be replaced, or is all too readily replaced. Both alternatives, predictably, seem hopeless. Having stoked a theatrical desire, *Tarltons Newes* swiftly moves to shut down its theatrical fulfillment.

Not surprisingly, Tarlton's singularity is invoked just long enough to displace his duplication to another medium, print. Such nice objections, *Tarltons Newes* senses, will not deter the hardened playgoer from reverting to habit. And so Robin performs that reversion for us, in order to set the terms of its failure:

yet at last, as the longest sommers day hath his night, so this dumpe had an ende: and forsooth upon whitson monday last I would needes to the Theatre to see a play; where when I came, I founde such concourse of unruely people, that I thought it better solitary to walke in the fieldes, then to intermeddle my selfe amongst such a great presse. (B1r)

Robin has come to test whether a theatre without Tarlton is still a possibility, only to find that it is already a mundane reality: the concourse of playgoers are "unruely people," both disorderly and remorseless, as oblivious of each other as they are careless of who brings them recreation. This is not an antitheatrical reaction, but a hypertheatrical one: through a metonymic devotion to Tarlton deliberately pushed to its extreme, devotion to the theatre is here constructed as antisocial pursuit, repudiating the very collective energy that was the fuel of Tarlton's performance. "Solitary," "walking in the fieldes," and "s[itting] me downe to take the aire," Robin is free to imagine a portable, meditative theatre of the mind, where the memory of Tarlton need not be desecrated by seeking him out, but where he instead comes unbidden to us.[26]

He dreams, that is, of an idealized, private theatre identical with the possibilities of print. His reluctance to "intermeddle my selfe amongst such a great press" recalls, and supplants, the trepidation his preface expressed about entering the marketplace of books: "for neuer before being in print," he writes, "I start at the sight of the Presse."[27] In one homophonic twist, the mechanical press is replaced by the "press" of humanity as the true obstacle to intersubjective experience. Tarlton's appropriation is thus carefully prepared for by a wholesale inversion of the usual relation between playhouse and page. If theatre is now a copy, then text must be original; if theatre is now alienation and distance, then text is nearness and exactitude. Before he even arrives, he has already been claimed by a print medium that, through its immateriality and replicative fidelity, offers an *ur*-theatre of absolute memorial purity.

More discursive legerdemain accompanies that arrival itself. No sooner has the narrator fallen asleep, in the shade of a tree, than the theatre of shadows for which he longs begins to unfold. *Tarltons Newes* takes extraordinary care to ensure that the Tarlton it conjures is the definitive one, his *blazon* diligently reconstructing a stage entrance:

As thus I lay in a slumber, mee thought I saw one attired in russet with a buttond cap on his head, a great bagge by his side, and a strong bat in his hand, so artificially attyred for a Clowne, as I began to call *Tarltons* wonted shape to remembrance, as hee drew more neere and hee came within the compasse of mine eie, to judge it was no other but the ghost of *Richard Tarlton*, which pale and wan sate him down by mee on the grasse. (B1v)

Except for the pallor by which we recognize him as a ghost, the magic of print has kept Tarlton true to form, suitably dressed and accessorized for the eternal "now" of showtime. But the performance it offers us is also a more intimate one – a Tarlton who descends from the stage, as it were, to "come within the compass" of our eye, who calls us "olde acquaintance" and takes a seat beside us "with his wonted countenance full of smiles."[28] It is a dream that would not just mimic but outstrip the reality, and if the syntax of the sentence runs memory and perception together – the vision coheres only "as I began to call *Tarltons* wonted shape to remembrance," making it difficult to tell where the narrator stops and the ghost begins – that is the point. The country wit and abusive banter are likewise in overdetermined evidence: "What … a man or a mouse?" he berates the narrator for his dumb shock. "Feare not me man, I am but *Dick Tarlton* that could quaint it in the Court, and clowne it on the stage: that had a quart of wine for my friend, and a sword for my foe: who hurt none being aliue, and will not preiudice any being dead."[29]

The narrator remains unconvinced, however, if not of the spirit's identity, then of its inclination. This prompts a bizarrely elliptical reassurance:

> Although thou see me here in the likenes of a spirit, yet thinke mee to bee one of those *Familares Lares* that were rather pleasantly disposed then indued with any hurtfull influence, as *Hob Thrust, Robin Goodfellowe* and such like spirites (as they terme them of the buttry) famozed in euerie olde wives Chronicle for their mad merry pranckes. Therefore sith my appearance to thee is in resemblance of a spirite, thinke that I am as pleasant a goblin as the rest, and will make thee as merry before I part, as ever *Robin Goodfellow* made the country wenches at their Creame boules. (B1v)

In case we missed it, it is said twice: the phantasmic Tarlton is no more to be feared than … Robin Goodfellow. Tarlton locates himself within a folk tradition of oral transmission, and specifically in relation to a persona that has already been used to identify with Tarlton – forming a circle of reference entirely bracketed by print, since "Robin Goodfellow" is the putative name of the author. First theatre was circumscribed, now popular culture as a whole. Not content merely to borrow him, *Tarltons Newes* instead fashions for itself a print medium in which Tarlton and all his associations are *already* contained, in which his performance finds its most ideal instantiation, and in which oral and textual identities are seamlessly interchangeable.

If we have already taken Robin Goodfellow for an author, that is, it is but a short step to "take Dick Tarlton once for thine author" as well, as he dismisses Robin's protests about election and damnation, and maintains the existence of a "*Quoddam tertium* a third place that all our great-grandmothers have talkt of, that Dant[e] hath so learnedly writ of ... Purgatorie."[30] This topic will eventually lead in to the stories themselves, and Tarlton's ensuing, tongue-in-cheek defense of Catholic dogma sounds the note of religious satire that will inflect them.[31] Coupling matronly fable and Italian *trecento* epic, furthermore, he also triangulates the book's market, which bridges the literary and the vulgar. But the polemical digression serves another purpose: to recreate Tarlton's stage practice further still, by getting him into an argument. Patiently tolerating the theological maxims that warn Robin he is a devil, Tarlton delivers his rebuttal:

> At this pitching his staffe downe on the end, & crossing one leg ouer an other, he answered thus: why you horeson dunce, think you to set *Dick Tarlton Non plus* with your Aphorismes? No, I haue yet left one chapter of choplodgicke to requite you withall, that were you as good as George a Greene I would not take the foile at your hands ... I see no sooner a rispe at the howse end or a Maipole before the doore, but I cry there is, a paltrie Alehowse: and as soone as I heare the principles of your religion, I can say, oh there is a Caluinist. (B2r)

This reads like an amalgam of performance citations: the crossed-leg Tarlton's signature drummer pose, the anticipation-heightening pause his customary style when responding to a "theme."[32] "Themes," indeed, the postludic genre wherein spectators would bombard the clown with prompts for *extempore* versification, is (minus the verse) expressly the context invoked here.[33] Tarlton will not be left "*Non plus*"; he treats verbal exchange as combat; he meets intellect with insult; his retort is pithy and crushing. Only here, an otherwise shapeless, ritualistic game is given a distinctly literary *auctoritas*. To be left "*Non plus*" by Tarlton is no longer merely to be shamed, but to be refuted in purposive debate, to have one's "choplodgicke" drawn into "chapters" and methodically broken down; "Maipoles" and "Alehowses" become terms for navigating arguments and arbitrating points of view. Tarlton's performance idiom can be better adapted for print if it is reconfigured as having already been textual, in a way the playhouse never grasped: what appeared to be sport is here revealed as its own, Socratic mode of knowing, a blunt, earthy *logos* fully integrable to the conventions of literary and cultural discourse.

Where the spiritual Tarlton began as a nostalgic substitute for a performing body, by the end of the Preface what he can claim to substitute for are simply other ghosts:

> Take *Dick Tarlton* once for thine author, who is now come from Purgatorie, and if any upstart Protestant denie, if thou hast no place of Scripture to confirme it, say as *Pithagoras* schollers did (*Ipse dixit*) ["thus he said himself"] and to all bon companions it shall stand for a principle. (B2v)

This is an erudite reference for someone the narrator told us was "only superficially seene in learning, hauing no more but a bare insight into the Latine tongue" – and just a part of the complex metempsychosis at work here.[34] The existence of Purgatory can only be predicated on the authority of the speaker asserting it, and on his continuity with the man we knew in life: Tarlton essentially asks us to take him at his word. Yet that word is here bypassed through a dizzying chain of textual surrogates. Tarlton's authority takes the place of Scriptural citation; Pythagorean citation serves as a precedent, in turn, for Tarlton's; Pythagoras – proponent, conveniently, of the doctrine of the transmigration of souls – survives only in the *amanuensis* of "schollers," much like the Robin Goodfellow who writes these lines. Whereas the book began by authorizing itself through Tarlton, ironically, within a few pages the Tarlton it revivifies passes his authority through that of the book, making them once again (as in the self-referential fairy catalogue) mutually dependent. And if the pamphlet has represented his speech as a kind of writing, now writing becomes a kind of speech. When he says – or rather, says for us to say, since the reader too is enlisted into his subsequent circulation – "*ipse dixit*," the direct appeal that "shall stand for a principle" is already built upon a pyramid of *scripsit*, prior acts of mediation that include the pamphlet's own. The passage is about testimony, yet makes it impossible to trace Tarlton's voice back to a body: for *Tarltons Newes*, this is precisely what it means to become an author – to be one in a succession of mouthpieces, extending indefinitely forward and back. Robin's dream occurs "vpon Whitson Monday last," the second day of Pentecost and the feast of the miracle of tongues – also about translating the flesh into spirit. Tarlton speaks as if already a text, aware of himself as both an agent and an object of transmission, and makes us reconcile this with how he spoke in life. To "take Dick Tarlton *once* for thine author" is not really possible; it requires taking him *always* for an author, which here is something much less than a player.

"Purgatory" turns out also to be the hybrid territory the pamphlet stakes between theatre and print, such that each ends up taking on qualities of the other. On the one hand, *Tarltons Newes* offers the bereaved playgoer both a Tarlton and a theatre boiled down to their essence: stripped of dramatic extraneity, freed from materiality and historicity – just Tarlton alone onstage forever, his superabundant wit capable of generating interminable pleasure because reducible to no one past instance of it. The first station he enters in his purgatorial progress, he tells us, is a "hall" with "an infinite number of seates, formed and seated like an Amphitheater": here sit all the Popes from antiquity to yesterday for him to mock, an audience seemingly gathered for no other purpose than his mockery.[35] Thence he passes into chambers designated for kings, monks, friars, tradesmen, rakes, cuckolds, scolds, artists, lovers – each of their residents waiting to be interviewed, an inexhaustible supply of comic material. When the dream ends, finally, its superposition with theatre is made explicit: "I waked," says Robin, "& saw such concourse of people through the fields, that I knew the play was done."[36] In the same two hours that the "concourse of people" with whom we began have spent at the playhouse betraying Tarlton's memory, *our* "play" – a book – preserves that memory as it never was and thus as it always was, endlessly and identically enacting itself, always unfolding afresh. Reading may transpire through time, but it is not a hostage to it. Tarlton concludes by saying "what punishment" was at last allotted him, and it is the very textuality that brings him to us: "they appointed that I should sit and play Jigs all day on my Taber to the ghosts without ceasing, which hath brought me into such use, that I now play far better then when I was aliue."[37] Quite literally, *Tarltons News* has been suggesting, the book is even better than the real thing.

On the other hand, it has also been suggesting that the book is the *same* as the real thing: it is, according to its subtitle, "onely such a iest as his Iigge." And while many of the tales he tells bear passing resemblance to the ribald stage jigs that were a source of his fame, their narrative deracination radically diminishes the very Tarltonian "storyteller position" so strenuously recruited to invigorate them. In a textual environment, that is, he cannot tell stories very well. As Tarlton descends from chamber to chamber recounting the follies that led to each figure's bizarre predicament, effects precede causes, and we must first encounter "a Cooke ... with a Cranes leg in his mouth" or "a Painter ... hauing the picture of a roode hung before him, and euery time he looked vpon it, he had three bastanados ouer the shoulders with a belroape" before the reason for their torments can be tediously reconstructed. Essentially, we get the punchlines before the jokes. Such a procedure owes more to the emblem book than to the temporality of the stage; when they take the stage, people's stories are not already over. And *Tarltons Newes* identifies itself as a miscellany by enshrining these human tableaux in its chapter divisions: "*the tale of the Vickar of Bergamo, and why hee sits with a coale in his mouth*," or "*the tale of two Louers of Pisa, and why they were whipt*

with nettles." Since the page numbers are keyed not to Tarlton's peregri-
nations between interlocutors but only to the formal *incipit* of the tales,
what the table of contents also announces is his structural irrelevance to
the volume. He does not interact with them in any significant way, nor
does he interject comment; the textual apparatus, indeed, is designed to
let us read around him. Once his presence has been established, he disappears almost totally behind the recirculated narratives that presence was
supposed to validate, his role confined to a *camera obscura*. The theatrical
Tarlton, after all, was never really a creature of narrative, much less a narrator; no sooner does the pamphlet make him one than even it proceeds
to lose interest in him.

This is pamphlet culture's use for authorship, however – ventriloquism –
and such authorship is corrosive when the person subjected to it was
renowned for his "pleasant and extemporal invention." Toward the end of
the *Newes*, Tarlton briefly departs from his reportage to note the fraternity
of poets condemned to Purgatory for having "written lascivious verse, or
other heroicall poems":

> But aboue them all I marked ould *Ronsard*, and he sat there with a scroule
> in his hand, wherin was written this description of *Cassandra*, his Mistresse,
> and because his stile is not common, nor have I heard our English Poets
> write in that vaine, marke it, and I will rehearse it, for I have learnd it by
> heart. (F2r)

What follows, remarkably, is a seven stanza, vaguely pastoral poem entitled "Ronsard's Description of his Mistresse," occupying nearly two complete pages and presented as a freestanding, inset literary work.[38] (See
Figure 4.) Most of the book's interpolated *fabliaux* are given separate
headings within its *mise-en-page* as well, which perhaps serve to demar-
cate them from Tarlton's first-person utterance. But Tarlton presumably
does not speak their titles, and these are moments when hearing Tarlton's
"voice" switches discretely to our reading a tale. This moment is different.
The table of contents contains no entry for the Ronsard poem; there is
nothing to prepare us for its eruption, and in fact Tarlton *says* he will now
recite it, stressing its continuity with his own voice. How does he recite
a section heading? How does speech convey the formal and spatial properties of verse – lineation, stanza breaks, roman type rather than gothic,
italic emphases? The poem ends with "A voice repl[ying] from the Aire,"
and that is precisely what we have been listening to, Tarlton's personality
and particularity finally dissolved, his own "voice" constituted only by the
texts in and out of which it moves.

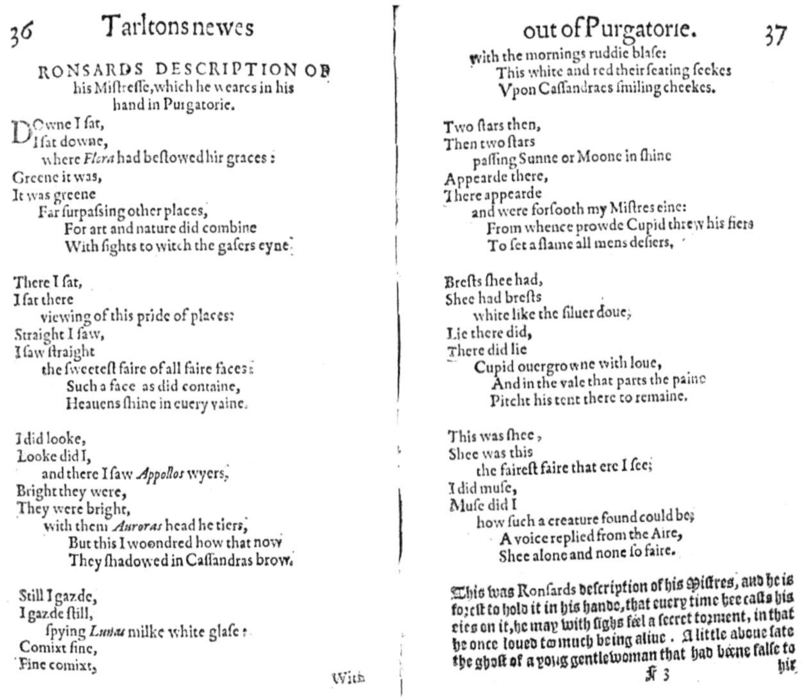

36   Tarltons newes

RONSARDS DESCRIPTION OF
his Miſtreſſe, which he weares in his
hand in Purgatorie.

Downe I ſat,
  I ſat downe,
    where *Flora* had beſtowed hir graces:
Greene it was,
It was greene
  Far ſurpaſsing other places,
    For art and nature did combine
    With ſights to witch the gaſers eyne.

There I ſat,
I ſat there
  viewing of this pride of places:
Straight I ſaw,
I ſaw ſtraight
  the ſweeteſt faire of all faire faces:
    Such a face as did containe,
    Heauens ſhine in euery vaine.

I did looke,
Looke did I,
  and there I ſaw *Appollos* wyers;
Bright they were,
They were bright,
  with them *Auroras* head he tiers,
    But this I woondred how that brow
    They ſhadowed in Caſſandras brow.

Still I gazde,
I gazde ſtill,
  ſpying *Lunaa* milke white glaſe:
Comixt fine,
Fine comixt,

(With

out of Purgatorie.   37

with the mornings ruddie blaſe:
  This white and red their ſeating ſeekes
  Vpon Caſſandraes ſmiling cheekes.

Two ſtars then,
Then two ſtars
  paſſing Sunne or Moone in ſhine
Appearde there,
There appearde
  and were forſooth my Miſtres eine:
    From whence prowde Cupid threw his fiers
    To ſet a flame all mens deſiers,

Breſts ſhee had,
Shee had breſts
  white like the ſiluer doue,
Lie there did,
There did lie
  Cupid ouergrowne with loue,
    And in the vale that parts the paine
    Pitcht his tent there to remaine.

This was ſhee,
Shee was this
  the faireſt faire that ere I ſee:
I did muſe,
Muſe did I
  how ſuch a creature found could be;
    A voice replied from the Aire,
    Shee alone and none ſo faire.

This was Ronſards deſcription of his Miſtres, and he is
forſt to hold it in his hande, that euery time bee caſts his
eies on it, hee may with ſighs feel a ſecret torment, in that
he once loued to much being aliue. A little aboue ſate
the ghoſt of a yong gentlewoman that had bene falſe to
hir
F 3

Figure 4 Anon., *Tarltons Newes out of Purgatorie* (1590), F2v–F3r.

The pamphlet's title is thus prepositionally inaccurate. There can be no news "out of" the purgatory it imagines, nor newness of any kind; its information, and its purveyors, remain part of its system. If nostalgia for Tarlton lets the book idealize theatre as a closed loop, its staging of him likewise refashions him in the book's image. The Tarlton that *Tarltons Newes* reproduces is not simply one who reproduces someone else's text, but a Tarlton who, as he says, "learn[s] it by heart," who absents himself entirely from the acts of transmission he performs, "rehearsing" them as representationally perfect, scripted routines. And who describes his performance in life, indeed, in these same terms: as perfectable, his "Jigs" requiring no real audience, so that even among the ghosts, mere repetition "hath brought me into such use, that I now play far better then when I was aliue." The very instant he offers to demonstrate his virtuosity, in fact, is the instant Robin's dream vision ends: "with that putting his pipe to his mouth, the first stroke he stracke I started, and with that I waked."[39]

A Tarlton who would sound a note of his own, in excess of the recirculative utility he serves the printed book, is simply not part of the book's
program. And so it constructs – as print must, and has all along been constructing – such improvisation as inaudible, and impossible. The Tarlton it
reanimates instead is one who can be disciplined into silence: who, when
no more "scroule" remains for him to recite, can be left "*Non plus.*"

Posthumous actorship

> A Poets worth takes birth, at first ti's weake
> Till by the life of Action it doth speake,
> In a square Theator; yet understand
> The Actor speakes but at the second hand.
> – William Fennor, "The Description of a
> Poet," *Fennors Descriptions* (1616), B2v–B3r

Seemingly in spite of itself, *Tarltons Newes* proved a relative hit, reprinted
three times over the next decade and reassigned among four publishers. At
least one reader was not fooled, however, by its romantic use of Tarlton's
stage practice. Later that year, *The Cobler of Caunterburie* (1590) subti-
tled itself "An Inuective against Tarltons Newes out of Purgatorie" – not
to decry the spurious premise of its predecessor, but to reject its tales as
"vnworthy Dicke Tarltons humour," advancing its own as superior representations of spontaneous popular entertainment.[40] Evoking Chaucer, the
narrative frame is a ferry ride to Canterbury, where the passengers debate
the merits of *Tarltons Newes* ("most of them are stolne out of *Boccace
Decameron*"), and then, instigated by the figure of the Cobbler, proceed
to spin their own yarns in a bid to outdo it.[41] But this rhetoric of one-
upmanship – fueled by the inclusion of an epistle supposedly from the
compiler of *Tarltons Newes* himself, Robin Goodfellow, promising to carry
word of the rebuke to Tarlton in Purgatory, where "*for anger he will almost
break his Taber, and will not rest till he haue reuenged*" – only exposes the
two books' affinities.[42] The tales in *Cobler of Caunterburie* are just as deriv-
ative as those in *Tarltons Newes*, likewise Continental imports given a fictional veneer of native authenticity and oral transmission. Only now it is
the Cobbler who enacts Tarlton's author function – even going so far as to
ape the idiom of a stage clown in his opening call for "Hall a hall gentlemen, roome for a Cobler, here comes the quaintest squire in all Kent," and
in extended riffs on his rusticity.[43] If the first pamphlet tried to abstract
from the theatre an *uber*-Tarlton, its successor now spins off from – and
against – that experiment a pseudo-Tarlton, and uses it further to point

up Tarlton's contingency. For where *Tarltons Newes* strove to conceal the heterogeneous agencies involved in the production of prose literature, *The Cobler of Caunterburie* cheerfully exposes those sutures. At the tales' end, the Cobbler vows to "remember them all, & very neere verbatim collect & gather them together," and then "to set them out in a pamphlet under mine owne name … and my selfe become an Author."[44]

Mimicking the appeal to oral presence only to reveal its expropriative agenda, *The Cobler of Caunterburie* shows Tarlton's posthumous author function already starting to buckle under the weight of its own artifice. The clock was seemingly running out on his ability to refresh recirculated literary material. With the appearance of Henry Chettle's *Kind-Harts Dreame* in late 1592, where he features as one of five apparitions delivering letters of complaint for publication, Tarlton's ghost-authorship ironically collapsed at the very instant it became literal: here he communicates directly, in his own words, yet this would be his last spectral visit to the pages of a book. What made this one so decisive?

The difference lay in the kind of Tarlton being channeled, and in the institution he is made to represent. *Tarltons Newes* had mounted a critique of disintegrated labor in the playhouse in order to prise Tarlton from the theatre, depositing him in a Purgatory that became, as we saw, a *topos* for print; critiquing *Tarltons Newes*, *Cobler of Caunterburie* parodies that posture as a mystification of print. A conversation had been initiated about the distribution and visibility of labor in the book trade, in other words, that was drifting away from Tarlton's original medium, leaving its own production model uninterrogated, and indeed retained as an ideal. *Kind-Harts Dreame* seizes on the analysis with which *Tarltons Newes* began: the conversation it wants is not just about how print gets made, but about how theatre gets made. If Tarlton was now implicated in a broader negotiation of early modern authorship, Chettle's goal is to bring him into maximal exchange with that negotiation, by imploding his authorial status at its source: by letting him speak as a player, for himself – as *Tarltons Newes* refused to do – and allowing that speech to fail. *Tarltons Newes* straddled a contradiction between presence and absence, between the autonomous performance that motivated the clown's authorship, and the anonymous performance such authorship dictated. *Kind-Harts Dreame* now feeds that contradiction back into itself, restoring a textual Tarlton to his natural setting in order to reveal it more textual than natural as well.

By a nice coincidence, *Kind-Harts Dreame* took its impetus from the previous pamphlet in which Chettle had been involved, *Greenes Groatsworth of Wit* – and by now we may discern a continuity of interest between them. The problem *Groatsworth* framed, we will recall, was the obverse of the labor structure advanced at the outset of *Tarltons Newes*: the superficial conflation of theatre with its performers, such that they dispossess and efface the work of writers. In the case of someone like Tarlton, the player embodies the life force of theatre, so much so that his aura persists beyond the grave; the poet, by contrast, given fleeting substance only through the player, is never really alive. Occurring four years to the day after Tarlton's, the death on 3 September 1592 of Robert Greene – libertine, scholar, pamphleteer, romance author, chronicler of the London underworld, and for Harvey (in a pregnant phrase) "king of the paper stage" – represented a chance to redress this inequity from the playwright's side, first and foremost through the fact of a literary after-life itself.[45] Appearing only three weeks later, *Groatsworth* adopts the same pose of deathbed textual recovery as Tarlton's remains had done, and uses it to pitch a battle line between poets and players, admonishing Greene's peers for their acquiescence in their own marginalization.

The backlash against *Groatsworth* sparked a challenge to its authenticity, with the scandal landing on its printer Chettle, on whose "peril" William Wright had published it according to its September 20th Register entry. "Because on the dead they cannot be auenged," Chettle insisted, "they wilfully forge in their conceites a liuing Author."[46] The present pamphlet, he says in the Preface to *Kind-Harts Dreame*, would have "come forth without a father" had it not served as occasion to disown *Groatsworth*; he maintains that Greene's manuscript was "il written," and that to make it legible, he merely "writ it ouer" in his own hand.[47] The guilty elaboration of Chettle's excuse has justified the suspicions of literary historians.[48] As the founding gesture of *Kind-Harts Dreame*, however, which is itself premised on editorial intervention – the dream relates only the delivery of the letters; Kind-Hart, a tooth-drawer, transcribes them, adding his own commentary; Chettle transcribes Kind-Hart's transcript – it establishes a link between the two texts that is not just genetic but thematic. Insofar as Kind-Hart's curatorial relation to his clients (he claims to "write the remembrance of sundry of my deceased friends" at the same time as to "deliuer euery Apparition simply as it was vttered") replicates Chettle's relationship to the pamphlet he says is Greene's, as well as to Kind-Hart himself, *Kind-Harts Dreame* not only amplifies the technique of *Groatsworth* but resumes its project, enacting a scribal version of the performative erasure of which *Groatsworth* complained.[49] Chettle was in a good position to grasp the structural analogy between print and theatre. By turns a frustrated stationer trying to break into poetry, and later a piecemeal playwright who would hardly be seen in print – of the approximately fifty plays he wrote for Henslowe, some three-quarters were collaborations, with as many as four other dramatists at a time – he is the poster-child for disintegrated literary production, his entire career a history of disavowal, resignation, and obscurity.[50] *Kind-Harts Dreame*, however, took a less direct approach to the issue than had *Groatsworth*: if playwrights could not be made to assert the priority of poetry to performance, perhaps the players themselves could. In Tarlton, Chettle set out to "write over" another original, once again to make it more legible.

Kind-Harts Dreame does this in the context of what Halasz calls an "investigation of the various … forms of agency involved in the production, distribution and consumption of printed texts," a panoramic survey of the burgeoning texual marketplace and of the entropic effect such expansion was having on traditional forms of authority.[51] Each ghost writes to express anxieties about the decay of his former vocation, contrasting it with a nostalgia for professional coherence that, usually, betrays their complicity in the very breakdowns they perceive. Anthony Now-Now, an old balladeer, lobbies for the tighter regulation of unlicensed ballads; Doctor Burcot, a physician, bemoans the profusion and misuse of medical textbooks, attacking the Stationers for putting their profits before his own; Robert Greene is brought back to lecture "Pierce Penniless" (a.k.a. Nashe) on precisely the tendency of textual personae to detach from their writers; William Cuckoe, a street hustler, rails against the spread of cony-catching pamphlets. Directly following Greene's, Tarlton's invective would seem to be a case in point of Greene's argument. Yet while he opens his epistle by invoking his textual identity, mentioning the interval since he last appeared in print – "Now Maisters, what say you to a merrie knaue, that for this two years day hath not been talkt of?" – Tarlton is here not to relay others' stories, but to speak on behalf of the players, to defend "honest Mirthe."[52]

Both the terms and the method of that defense, however, make it a case in point of Greene's *previous* argument – in *Groatsworth*. Tarlton begins by parroting the arguments of antitheatricalists, city fathers, and criminals, all united in their opposition to theatre, in order to expose their self-serving hypocrisy. Playgoing is "wondrous" expensive, he says; "players speeches" and "words" are "full of wyles"; they set out all manner of vice and "trecherie" for imitation; they impoverish brothels and other "houses of retaylers," which have just as much "infection" to recommend them; they

spoile our trade ... Beside, they open our crosse-biting, our conny-catch-
ing, our traines, our traps, our gins, our snares, our subtilties: for no sooner
haue we a tricke of deceipt, but they make it common, singing Jigs, and
making ieasts of us, that euerie boy can point out our houses as they passe
by. (E2v–E3v)

Among *Kind-Harts Dreame*'s other missives, Tarlton's at first appears
exceptional. Its institution is besieged by purely external enemies, neither side seemingly having anything to do with a runaway proliferation
of texts. The institution's defense, moreover, manages to satirize those
enemies while avoiding a satire of itself. Until, that is, one realizes that
theatre is here the very site of textual proliferation in question. Using
the same phrase as *Groatsworth*, Tarlton inadvertently analyzes theatre as
"a house of retayle" no different from the establishments with which it
competes – a parasitic entity that draws all its resources from elsewhere
and merely "make[s] it common," producing nothing but sterile recirculation. Not only does theatre materially depend on the vices it would
correct, but it is discursively equivalent to them as well. Tarlton's mock-
diatribe at one point digresses into a pandar's reasons for prostituting his
wife, which turn out to be quite compelling – landlords, who, making
nothing but capital, convert alms houses into tenements, charge their ten-
ants increasingly exorbitant rents, and live off their avails. The connection
is not lost on Kind-Hart: at the end of the letter, he notes the "one thing
I mislikte: that *Tarleton* stoode no longer on that point of Landlords,"
and spends his entire postscript expounding on their evil. When he raises
the topic again, though, it is to object that "how euer hee speakes well of
players, there is a graze widow in the world complains against one or two
of them, for denying a Legacie of fortie shillings summe" with which "she
intendes to set up an Apple shop"; if they withhold it, "she hath sworne
neuer to be good."[53] The players' profit from publishing social decay exac-
erbates that decay in return; here, potentially, they create one more petty
criminal for them someday to perform.

Tarlton's adversarial method thus gradually turns the stage into exactly
the organ of relentless textual reproduction on which Now-Now, Burcot,
Greene and Cuckoe opine, embodying the circularity of print. Even when
he drops his impostures to "speake in sobernes," his apology for theatre still reduces to this identity – "in plaies it fares as in bookes."[54] If by
this point it has become difficult to know whether his defense is genuine or parodic, of course, or to tell Tarlton's sarcasm from sincerity, it is
because he has until now been enacting a mimetic rebroadcast himself,
in the form of his would-be opponents. Not only does he speak from the

position of an antitheatrical agitator from the outset, but he spawns fictional characters who echo his sentiments – "I marry (says *Beaudeamus* my quondam Host) well saide olde Dicke, that worde was well plac'd"; "Quaintly concluded (*Peter Pandar*) somewhat yee must be, and a bawd ye will bee" – and whose surprisingly detailed biographies he relates in extended sequences of impersonation.[55] The cumulative effect of these embedded acts of "mak[ing] common" is more than just to undercut any argument for the economic legitimacy of theatre, but also to degenerate Tarlton's theatrical persona along with it. We expect Tarlton the clown, the player, yet the one who shows up is the posthumous author function – the human jukebox of the printed pamphlet.

Kind-Harts Dreame wants to suggest that those two subject positions – "player" and pseudonym, performer and mouthpiece – are one and the same. Until this moment in the history of English theatre, the stage clown had sustained a fundamental inconsistency in the logic of playing. There were as yet two categories of player: those who represent others, and those who present only themselves. The book trade began by borrowing this latter authenticity merely in order to naturalize literary borrowing; *Kind-Harts Dreame* puts the appropriated Tarlton *back* into the theatre to collapse that double standard, to homogenize the latter category of player with the former, and to depict the theatrical model of production as no less a kind of borrowing. Sensing that his histrionics have gone too far, Tarlton tries to right himself, precipitating a moment of loss from which he never fully emerges:

> Whither now *Tarlton*? this is *extempore* out of time tune, and temper. It may well be said to me: / *Stulte, quid haec faris, &c.* / *Rusticus ipse, tuis malus es, tibi pessimus ipsi.* / [You speak foolishly. / The very clown, you are bad, the very worst.] Thy selfe once a Player, and against Players: nay, turne out the right side of thy russet coate, and lette the world know thy meaning. Why thus I meane, for now I speake in sobernes. (E3v–E4r)

This is Tarlton attempting to speak as himself, and it takes a great deal of coaching. For now that he has defined – and exemplified – players as vehicles of pure imitation, what does it mean for him to speak as himself? Even here, his self-recriminations must be passed through an absent interlocutor ("it may well be said to be"), with whom he goes on conversing, taking instruction and redundantly responding in kind; it is hallucinatory speech, not "sobernes." Tarlton is a "bad clown" here not just for seeming to speak against theatre, but for *seeming* to be other than he is at all, for speaking out of different sides of his mouth, which he also cannot seem to stop doing. By the time he regains his own voice, it has ventriloquized

so many other subjectivities, and become so "common," that there is no
authentic Tarlton to return to – and perhaps there never was. The moment
parallels, indeed, the point in *Groatsworth* where pseudo-Greene "break[s]
off" from "the saide *Roberto*" to do the same thing, only to enfold one
persona within another. If Tarlton has all along been wearing his "russet coate" – the emblem of his simplicity – inside out, and that inside
is where his vocal multiplicity emanates from, then reversing it changes
nothing. *Both* his insides, according to the topology of this remarkable figure, are merely kinds of outside, such that he has no inside at all.

If Tarlton was a player, and the player can have no intrinsic content,
then even Tarlton – *especially* Tarlton – must be shown to be an empty ves-
sel as well. Tarlton the *author*, paradoxically, allows Chettle to do just that.
By cultivating the impression that the textual clown reproduces theatrical performance, as *Tarltons Newes* did, *Kind-Harts Dreame* uses print
to undermine that performance, retroactively ascribing to him *in vivo* the
same derivativeness as his simulation. Tarlton calls his extravagance into
mimesis "*extempore* out of time tune, and temper," as if he were not com-
posing a revisable text – he is writing a letter, after all, so if he doesn't like
it, why not erase it? – but engaged in organic, improvised speech, as at the
playhouse. By saying so, he suggests he has here done only what comes
naturally to him: speaking as another. And thus, what really did come
naturally to him in life – his self-possession, his "prompt wit," his improvisation – can also be circumscribed by whatever his text now lets him
do. Just as the Tarlton who performed no one but himself here performs
everyone but himself, the growing pressure to generate his own entertainment reveals that entertainment to have been never his own:

> Now to you that maligne our moderate merriments, and thinke there is no
> felicite but in excessiue possession of wealth: with you I would ende in a
> song, yea an Extempore song on this Theame, *Nequid nimis necessarium* [no
> more than necessary]: but I am now hoarse, and troubled with my Taber
> and Pipe: beside, what pleasure brings musicke to the miserable. Therefore
> letting songes passe … (E4v)

The detour is completely gratuitous, which makes its inexplicable abortion all the more amazing. In the temporality of reading, anything can
seem "Extempore" – just as Tarlton earlier used the term to equate his
epistolary activity with impromptu performance – and technically, he
has as long as he needs to compose a "song" on any "Theame," especially
since this one comes from him rather than a live playhouse audience. Yet
Chettle *wants* the fiction of a Tarlton who authored himself onstage to
fail, deliberately invoking his extemporal skill in a setting where it can be

short-circuited and extinguished. Instead of displaying mastery of his text, he suddenly reveals his text to control him, limiting what he can say only to what it prescribes: he cannot sing "no more than necessary," ironically, because the text has deemed it more than is necessary. Figuring his failure to perform as mechanical rather than volitional, moreover – blaming it on both his "hoarse" throat and "trouble with my Taber and Pipe," as if they were collectively one instrument – reduces his performance to a kind of instrumentation. Tarlton cannot really have laryngitis, since he has been writing, not speaking. Describing his writing as present speech, rather, which is what carried his speech into writing in the first place, lumps both together as modes of expression that originate beyond him and merely pass through him – for when one stops, so does the other. The clown does not produce, he transmits: and transmits, specifically, a liveliness that effaces its textual source. Chettle gives us a Tarlton who confesses that charisma to have been merely an onstage effect, by dispelling it once he is off: a Tarlton who simply *reads*, rather than speaks or writes, who can only take dictation. He makes him a puppet, that is, precisely by showing him with his strings cut. The sound of this moment – a rasp, a rattle, a cough, a silence – is the sound of a pipe trying to play itself.

What we are witnessing here, only three months after *Groatsworth* registers the need for one, is the first theorization of the actor. More than a theorization, it is an enactment – as it must be, since new discursive formations come into being only through the breakdown and recombination of existing ones, from the uses the living make of the dead. The capital *Kind-Harts Dreame* liquidates to do so is the clown, whose institutional utility would be fulfilled not when he was made an author – which playgoers had been doing for him all along – but when he had been *un*made as one. Because he stood for an extreme counterformulation, in which authority inhered in the performing body, Tarlton's distillation into textual ghost enabled the evacuation of that authority. Subjecting him to a mediated production of himself, whereby the simulation collides with, "writes over," and annihilates the original, Chettle reverts the historical Tarlton into what print had already made him: a shell, a husk, a signifier of everybody who was himself a nobody. When *Kind-Harts Dreame* pictures him, indeed, it is distinctly *not* as a ghost, but as a corpse, or a zombie. Kind-Hart calls the figure before him "either the *body* or resemblaunce of Tarlton," and as this cadaverous thing departs, he "with his Taber fetch[ed] two or three leaden friskes."[56] In *this* afterlife, Tarlton is heavier, closer to dull matter; and if he here plays *worse* than when he was alive, it is because his animacy has moved from him into the letter he reads. The birth of the actor thus heralded the death, so to speak, of the posthumous author. His extemporality not so much exhausted as dismantled, now that Tarlton had become a creature of texts, he could no longer create them, and his brief literary career suddenly reached its end.

At the same time, the death of this particular posthumous author gave birth to the actor: seeing that they were already mirror images across different domains – each the breathing of spirit into lifeless matter – Chettle simply used the one to theorize the other. *Kind-Harts Dreame* turns Tarlton's print incarnation from a competitor with theatre into a frame for the competition within the theatre itself, an opening salvo in the contest over whose agency would, and could best, possess the stage. For Chettle – perhaps feeling, like his pseudo-Greene of *Groatsworth*, the encroachment of Shakespeare from the other direction – there could be no middle terms in that contest: there were only writers and players. If Tarlton was more a player than a writer, he had to be made an actor; and if he could be made an actor, so could any player. And an actor, like a posthumous author, is a fantasy of control, a superconductor through which intention can be both realized and delimited, always implying an ulterior origin. The conflation of Tarlton's author function with his clowning effectively re-materialized him, after the fact, as a species of performer who made writing visible rather than eclipsed or transcended it: to reveal not that behind every book there are many producers, but that behind every theatrical production there is a book – in other words, a script.

For his service to playwrights (if not as one), Henry Chettle was given a fleeting afterlife of his own. Thomas Dekker ends *A Knights Conjuring* (1607) with a description of a writers' Elysium, whose members – from Chaucer and Spenser to Marlowe, Greene, and Peele – are greeting new arrivals. Thomas Nashe, "newly come to their Colledge," is asked "what newes in the world," and specifically "how Poets and Players agreed now." They do not, he reports, and the struggle continues to the poets' disadvantage. As "the patient loues his Doctor no longer then till he get his health," so the players love the poet only when "the sicknesse lyes in the two-penie gallery," and they need new plays – and audiences destroy those plays just as quickly, so that "hee workes like *Ocnus*, that makes ropes in hell; for as hee twists, an Asse stands by and bites them in sunder."[57] "He had no sooner spoken this," however,

> but in comes *Chettle* sweating and blowing, by reason of his fatnes, to welcome whom, because hee was of olde acquaintance, all rose vp, and fell presentlie on their knees, to drinck a health to all the *Louers* of *Hellicon*: in doing which, they made such a mad noyse, that all this *Coniuring*

which is past, (beeing but a dreame,) I suddenlie started vp, and am now awake. (L1r)

These are the book's last lines. It may come as a shock to imagine a literary pantheon in 1607 that includes dramatists, let alone one that waits for Henry Chettle – even more so a Chettle who cuts such a ridiculous figure as here. Yet in its very corpulence, Dekker's valediction grants Chettle in death what his literary endeavors had lacked in life: a body. And thereby, seemingly, it returns a favor. For despite the continuing devaluation and denial of their labor, Nashe's analogy can now affirm playwrights the soul of theatre, on whom its body, cognizant or not, is dependent for sustenance and care. It is just a matter of time, one senses, until soul overtakes body – and the conclusion opens toward this dream, precisely as the dream ends. In their cacophonous "mad noyse," the ghost writers suddenly unite to form a theatre unto themselves, surging upward and outward to touch the plane of the real; they *act*, waking the speaker up. And in so doing, they propel the voice of the speaker – which here becomes that of the author – into total textual presence, and indeed the present tense itself: "I … am now awake."

Tarlton, meanwhile, was headed in the opposite direction. His ghost's final bow in prose fiction registers the extinction of his self-authorizing personality – as well as the dead writer to whom its torch had now been passed.[58] At the close of *Greenes Newes both from Heauen and Hell* (1593), Greene and his traveling companion Velvet-Breeches are watching an infernal synod of devils and Catholic bishops plot the doom of England, when for no discernible reason

> in comes *Dick Tarlton*, apparelled like a Clowne, and singing this peece of an olde song.
>
> > *If this be trewe as true it is,*
> > *Ladie, Ladie:*
> > *God send her life may mend the misse,*
> > *Ladie Ladie.*
>
> This suddaine iest brought the whole company into such a vehement laughter, that not able agayne to make them keepe silence, for that present tyme they were faine to breake uppe. (H1v)

Why Tarlton briefly resurfaces here to do the state some service is a mystery, but it is a telling glimpse. Once *"rusticus ipse,"* this Tarlton is merely "apparelled *like a* Clowne"; he still cracks jokes, but they are not his anymore, and it is a laughter from which we are unequivocally excluded.

Fragmentary and opaque, his performance now disperses community instead of creating it. This is the faded afterimage not of Tarlton so much as of his author function itself: they have, indeed, become indistinguishable. A literary recycler who has lost the ability to recycle himself, like a stranger in the night he drifts listlessly past his successor, a figure still generative enough to accrue new material. Having used him up, this is where literary history too leaves him behind – not in Helicon, but marooned in Hell, singing other people's songs to the damned, confined to a walk-on part in someone else's story.[59]

CHAPTER 4

Nobody's business

One man lead in two W[omen] forwards and back twice: Honnor
to one, honnor to the other, then turn the third. Lead your owne
with your left hand, and the woman you turnd, and as much. Then
as much with the other two W[omen] turning your owne. The next
man as much. Then the third man as much.
  – "Kemps Jegg," in John Playford, *The English Dancing Master*
                                               (1651), E1r

The epigraph above does not quote all of "Kemps Jegg" in Playford's book
of dance instructions, but however sanitized a version Playford's may be
of what Kemp did onstage, it nevertheless captures something representative about the jig – or, at least, about the grammar of dance instructions. There is a tendency for pronouns to drop off, and for antecedents
to become hazy; for individuals to become indistinct within a group, and
to lose sight of what is their "owne"; most basically, for texts to be only
a shorthand of live events, in no way trying to contain them. There is
also, at the same time, order – but an order that works through concatenation, in the sequential doubling of the moves of "one man" by "the next
man" so that, whether first or last, they all end up equivalent. For us, it
prefigures the problems that Will Kemp, the clown in Shakespeare's early
plays but to the playgoing public much more than that, would encounter when he tried to disentangle himself from that public – ironically
and perhaps unwittingly, by thrusting himself into it. Thus far we have
seen how clowning, because it played to the audience and interacted directly with it, became a focal point for labor relations in the early modern theatre, and for their resolution. Who were theatre's producers, and
how could they be distinguished from its consumers? Where was theatre
made – onstage, or in books? In Chapter 3, the posthumous textualization
of Tarlton's stage persona, and its canned reproduction of his extemporal
quality, encouraged audiences to imagine performance as separable from
its particular performers, who merely channel someone else's words. In

this chapter, we move from ambient cultural interventions that sought to deconstitute live performance, to living performers actually doing it to themselves. Kemp, unlike Tarlton, still had a body to defend, and his own words. What *he* wants to imagine, for that very reason, is a mode of performance separable from its audience. He may not have realized it, I speculate, but in abandoning his playing company, its stage, and the clowning genre he dominated – the jig – in order to do so, he abandoned what had already protected him from that audience. In the nine-day morris dance from London to Norwich on which he embarked, he was now confronted with them, unable to escape their relentless, invasive participation, or the breakdown of his economic coherence as an entertainer. The only way out was to write *Kemps Nine Daies Wonder* (1600), a textual sanctuary in which he could preserve his words as his, but only by surrendering his body – and from which he never truly returned. If Tarlton's pseudo-authorship set his afterlife in Purgatory, Kemp's genuine authorship would cast him into limbo.

"What I haue to say is of my owne making"

In 1599 William Kemp left the Chamberlain's Men, the company to which he had belonged, in its various configurations, for over ten years. In the preceding decade he had become England's preeminent stage clown: already by 1590 Thomas Nashe could call him "jest-monger and vicegerent general to the ghost of Dick Tarlton."[1] His prodigious athleticism made him the undisputed heir of the stage jig and other popular dance forms, as well as to Tarlton's penchant for improvisation and buffoonery.[2] His fame packed playhouses, and was even deemed sufficient to carry playbooks. *A Knacke to Knowe a Knave* (1594) prominently advertises "*With KEMPS applauded Merrimentes*" beneath an ascription of the play to "ED. ALLEN and his Companie." The work of authorship – both a stabilizer of theatrical property and an index of celebrity – is here divided between two players, each representative of the play's producers at the time of its publication.[3] Which of the two, were one forced to choose, would count as its author? Kemp comes second visually, and as we saw when we considered this text in Chapter 2, the actual "merriment" preserved in it – if it is preserved at all – is slight. But then again, "Ed. Allen" is merely the leading edge of a much larger entity, "his Companie," with which Kemp's name is affiliated, but from which it also remains separate. What Kemp owns here (the "Merrimentes") may be less, but he does not share their ownership with anyone. We might say, indeed, that the "Companie" owns the play, but Kemp its performance – or at least, *his* performance in it. This chapter investigates whether that was enough for him, or if such a claim is even true. For as the title page implies, his ownership was far less exclusive: the "Merrimentes," after all, are "applauded."

Kemp's roots lay in a playing culture that identified more with patronage relations than with the autonomous cooperative of the professional theatrical company. We first find him in Holland with Leicester in the mid-1580s, accompanying the Earl's liveried players but remaining distinct from them, his non-verbal comic talents apparently employed for diplomatic purposes that merited individual payment and the freedom to come and go at his discretion.[4] Primarily a solo comedian, his decision upon Leicester's death in 1588 to attach himself to a commercial troupe – first Lord Strange's Men, later the Lord Chamberlain's – was thus an expediency to which he evidently never quite adapted. Though he attained a high standing within the company (not atypical for the clown), often serving with Burbage and Shakespeare as payees on court rolls and acquiring shares in the Globe when its lease was signed in early 1599, he remained an unresolved element in the dramaturgy that ultimately precipitated this change in venue.

That dramaturgy constituted a temporary settlement between the interest of the company, and the stage clown who served both that interest and his own. As we saw in our reconstruction of clowning in Chapter 2, no matter the part the drama required of him on any given day, the clown's overriding role lay in pretending not to have one, or in spurning it. Instead, he posed as an avatar of the audience, so as to grant them access to the stage and to deny it at once; less a vehicle of dramatic representation than its social precondition, the clown was primarily a showman, a free agent with his own repertory of extemporaneous, interactive, often confrontational, non-mimetic or paramimetic genres. The problem with recognizing the audience this way, however, as seems to have plagued Tarlton, was its tendency to defer rather than suppress – indeed, sometimes to escalate – their demand for further engagement, which they were liable even to initiate themselves. As a result, the play had to make room for constant interstitial disruption, both by the audience and (pre-emptively) by the clown, continually frustrating its coherence as an integrated artifact, and as the core of the theatrical program.

The Chamberlain's Men's solution, like other companies' in the 1590s and after, was to compartmentalize the clown's parts into marginal scenes where his improvisations (and any corresponding audience participation) would minimally derail the plot, and to install the increasingly regular postlude of the stage jig in order to displace them from the play altogether. Kemp's special province – as audiences quickly recognized, and came to anticipate – was the end. Though he apparently still provided crosstalk during the play and mobile, set-piece interludes during it (what both Nashe and the title page of *Knacke* call "merriments," which could be more or less part of the play's fiction), we never hear of his practicing standard clown modes like peeping or "themes." Unlike Tarlton, or Kemp's own later successor Thomas Greene, he was not particularly ugly, but something of a robust physical specimen, and he naturally gravitated toward the jig – brief courtship farces rife with song, noise, trials of physical prowess, misbehaving props, opportunities for improvisation between performers, exchange with the audience, smutty innuendo, and the climactic release of dance. A basic plot, variously elaborated, supplied the frame for repeated themes of seduction, deceit, and cuckoldry, with the clown – barely distinct in persona from the performer – as the protagonist. And yet, his persona primarily grounded within them, such vehicles attest to Kemp's weaknesses as well as his strengths. Unlike clowns before or after, he tellingly seems to have avoided interactions with the crowd that called for extreme isolation and humiliation. Buttressed by supporting comedians, and ensconced in a genre that put no direct pressure on his relation to the audience, he would have experienced only its adoration, without the aggression that (as with Tarlton) always underlay it. It was a formula for potentially confused allegiances: believing that the crowd really loved you, rather than merely itself.

Nevertheless, as this transition from rule to misrule became a codified feature of theatrical events, its sophistication rendered it vulnerable to the same creative frictions it sought to mediate. As David Wiles has shown, poets increasingly moved to colonize the jig by anticipating and prescribing its nature from within the play, attempting unilaterally to homogenize the theatrical program. By the mid-1590s, Shakespeare's denouements begin to carve out conspicuous spaces for Kemp's return after the action: Costard has yet to vie with Armado for Jaquenetta at the close of *Love's Labour's Lost*; *The Merchant of Venice*'s Gobbo must wed his pregnant Moorish mistress; the text of *A Midsummer Night's Dream* never supplies the "Bergomask dance" of Bottom's dream that he promises; *Much Ado About Nothing* ends merely looking forward to punishments for Don John, which Dogberry might be expected to conduct.[5] All these are almost certainly Kemp's parts. The Epilogue to *2 Henry IV*, meanwhile, may form Shakespeare's most ambitious integration of the jig: the clown's fictive identity is left wholly unspecified (devoid even of a speech prefix), yet he delivers an apologetic preamble to his dance that suspends it between the present play and its sequel, his agency thoroughly subordinate to that of the playing company. We cannot be certain it is the clown who is to speak these lines, and whether the "daunce" he proposes as compensation for a "displeasing play" is meant as a prelude to his postlude or actually to elide it; in the former case, equally interestingly, he can begin his jig only after having spent himself on this one.[6] Nevertheless, if Kemp is the one here offering to "daunce out of your debt," to "commit my body to your mercies," and inviting the audience to "commaund me to vse my legges," it is not just their authority to whom he submits. Wiles contends that he might have just finished *playing* Falstaff when he concludes with a preview of how "our humble Author will continue the storie, with Sir John in it," foreshadowing his *own* death "of a sweat" just before actually commencing a sweat – all this framed by the admission that "what I haue to say is of my owne making," in a scripted speech that either forfeits his improvisatory freedom or, even more deviously, co-opts it.[7] By allocating time for Kemp's preparations – or, as in *2 Henry IV*, compressing it – and entwining with his performance the resolution of the play's social inferiors, such seemingly deferential gestures subtly project the play's representational regime onto the jig, encroaching on Kemp's shift from quasi-mimetic role to self-identical jig-maker. Kemp, in other words, cannot become simply "Kemp": he is forced to stay in character.

This, at any rate, is the one-sided narrative of annexation the texts record; Kemp may have ignored or circumvented such coercive prompts. The extant jigs that can be associated with him, surviving either in later English variations or in German *singspiele*, reveal a sensibility more indifferent to any framing dramatic context than complementary of it. In contrast to other period jigs, which enhance the clown's socially oppositional function in the play with a symmetrical narrative that sees common values triumph over aristocratic incursion, Kemp's avoid any thematization of class conflict. Instead of making the clown a poor husband who must fend off a wealthy, amorous gentleman, as in *Attowell's Jig*, or a prosperous miller whose wife is wooed by a charming apprentice, as in the German *Pickelherring*, Kemp's Rowland and Simpkin, for example, contend only with suitors of equal social station. This was hardly a concession to the gentrified wing of the playhouse audience, however, or to the Chamberlain's Men's desire to placate them. Kemp's jigs were of and for the groundlings alone, celebrating a proletarian world from which gentility was summarily excluded. Whereas Shakespeare stretched the script to accommodate him (to put it charitably), Kemp denied him consideration. After mucking his way through the play, his jig could now subvert its predecessor's vision not with critical inversion but with outright dismissal, introducing a dramatic solipsism in which divergent values obtained – and in which the clown emerged not as the butt of the action but as its controller, the hero of a story all his own. Kemp first disrupted the poet's designs, and then got the last word to replace them. By the late 1590s, the appetite of playhouse audiences for such populist anthems had become proverbial, warily depicted as both riot and cult, both rapturously utopian and fanatically slavish in its focus, drowning out everything before it. "A hall, a hall, / Roome for the Spheres, the Orbes celestiall / Will daunce *Kempes Iigge*," sneers Marston, and Everard Guilpin nauseously listens to "rotten-throated slaues / Engarlanded with coney-catching knaues, / Whores, bedles, bawdes and Sergeants filthily / Chaunt *Kempes* Iigge."[8]

Given that he went on to publish several of these jigs, so sweeping a coup of the theatrical event seems less a case of resistance to authorship than of rival authorship. As we saw in earlier chapters, stage clown and author were hardly incompatible subject positions during the first decades of professional theatre; indeed, given the printing of numerous quasi-literary materials under Tarlton's name in his own lifetime (at least one of which, *Tarltons Toyes* (1576), seems to have contained jigs), the first was a template for the second. Among the eleven jigs entered in the Stationers' Register between 1591 and 1595, five bear the name of an individual comedian, four of them Kemp's:

- – 5 Jan. 1591. a newe Northerne Jigge
- – 16 Dec. 1591. the seconde parte of the gigge betweene Rowland and the Sexton
- – 28 Dec. 1591. the Thirde and last parte of *Kempes* Jigge
- – 14 Jan. 1592. a merrie new Jigge betwene Jenkin the Collier and Nansie
- – 16 Jan. 1595. *Kempes* A plesant newe Jigge of the Broome-man
- – 4 Feb. 1595. a pleasant Jigge betwene a tincker and a Clowne
- – 17 Feb. 1595. a ballad of Cutting George, and his hostis being a Jigge
- – 2 May 1595. *master Kempes* Newe Jigge of the kitchen stuffe woman
- – 26 May 1595. *Phillips* his gigge of the slyppers
- – 14 Oct. 1595. A pretie newe J[i]gge betwene *ffrancis* the gentleman *Richard* the farmer and theire wyves [a.k.a. "Attowell's Jig"]
- – 21 Oct. 1595. *Kemps* newe Jygge betwixt, a souldiour and a Miser and *Sym* the clown [a.k.a. "Singing Simpkin"][9]

Not only does Kemp dominate the genre, but by 1595 (even discounting *Knacke*) he had more dramatic bylines than any member of his company – Shakespeare as yet had zero – if not any living member of the profession.[10] As the posthumous credits Tarlton was also given suggest, however, the instability of the clown's protoauthorship lay in the plastic, participatory conventions of the performance his texts claimed to capture, and in the generative persona of the perfomer who subtended them. Where the audience is ceded a role in the theatre's creative matrix, the clown, as its bridge, becomes collective property, a resource of public speech instead of an absolute source. Embodying a rhetorical power on the stage designed to work only onstage, and implicitly containing the collaborative energies of which its singularity is constituted, he licenses his own dispersal in print, such that his authority there comes to serve as a principle of profusion rather than of thrift.

Even if copies of Kemp's jigs survived, that is, we could not be certain how many were Kemp's compositions, or written by others in his vein and merely marketed as "his." What relation, if any, they bore to their performed states – and consequently to a playgoer's expectation of what he or she would see on any given day – is likewise radically contingent. If we can take the version of "Singing Simpkin" that resurfaces sixty years later as any guide, the sheer frequency of lines ending with "&c.," in the context of song, dance, and other potential stage-business, suggests (like the "mad men of Gotham" episode of *Knacke*, where the "funny" is decidedly not on the page) that the text of a jig existed in – and perhaps to confirm – a secondary, hollow relation to live performance.[11] The printed "jigbook," we might infer – neither jig nor book – made no attempt to delimit performance, but merely provided a framework for performance to exceed; its utility lay in the pleasure of anticipating what was *not yet* in it, the material to be contributed either by the clown or by the spectator in response to him. Infixed with no intentionality, it was an anti-playbook, a series of prompts to *disregard* the script it superficially represented.[12]

And yet the exact same evidence intimates (whether he knew it or not) Kemp's increasing resistance to these collaborative poetics, however much they complemented the jig's politics, and however content he was to continue embracing both to further his renown. Jigs still did not especially *need* to be published, except for other reasons that potentially reverse the meaning of doing so. The clustering of so many entries in 1595 is too conspicuous to ignore: this was the same period in which, after the reorganization of the London companies, a disproportionate number of *plays* were being printed in order (in part via authorial attribution) to disentangle their shared features and clarify their lines of descent. Since the clown's febrile postlude was no less mandatory a component of the theatrical experience than the play – part of the problem with it – it stands to reason that this pattern of publication followed the same logic. Coupled with these entries' tendency to collapse their titles into *dramatis personae* or simply the name of the chief performer, the printing spurt suddenly becomes legible instead as an effort by the Chamberlain's Men to protect their investment in a different, equally vital area of their repertory (at the same time that other areas worked to erode its vitality). Whatever use the printed text might open up to its purchaser, informing its very printing was also a foreclosure on the jig as private property, in which Kemp was complicit – all the more so because the attachment of *his* name to it, in the name of company property, specified its ownership even more narrowly than that category.

That jigs might be treated as company assets, indeed, no different from plays, only alerts us to what seems already, unmistakably play-like about them. Based on the samples of "Attowell's," "Simpkin," and "Rowlands Godson," Frances K. Barasch has shown that English jigs likewise borrowed extensively from Italian drama, adapting the plot devices and character types of *commedia dell'arte* troupes who probably made their first appearance in England in 1573, a date roughly coincident with its generic emergence.[13] While Kemp's variations adapted such urbanity into rural crudeness, their capacity for serial elaboration ("the seconde parte of the gigge betweene Rowland and the Sexton," "the Thirde and last parte of *Kempes* jigge") – not unlike the Shakespearean history plays they might have concluded – evidences his deepening investment in them as integrated, self-propagating, operatic fictions.[14] As William N. West observes of the Epilogue to *2 Henry IV*, "it demonstrated, or seemed to demonstrate, a kind of real *labour* on the part of the actors, who were regularly mocked because their only work was play." Both the increasing complexity of Kemp's jigs and their rising frequency of publication signify the same way, I would argue, as the Epilogue's obsessive reference to his tongue, legs, breath, and sweat: they offer themselves, as West puts it, "for consumption" – not as finished products, but as products that think they are their own to finish.[15]

Since the jig brought up the rear of the theatrical program, however, and thereby avoided any direct monetary measure of its value – playgoers paid only at or near the start of the day's entertainment, in a lump sum not divisible by any particular part of it – all Kemp needed to test the ambiguities of its ownership, seemingly, was the conversion of his artistic investment into a material one. Subject in performance to the collaborative claims of his audience, and subject in print to the claims of shared company profit, he was beset on all sides by modes of publicity that inherently dispossessed him. At some point, caught between these competing theatre economics, it may have occurred to him to wonder exactly *who* made a jig happen, *whose* agency was most responsible for its mirth, and whether his personal labor was being adequately recognized. What was a jig worth? No one had ever been asked to pay for an afterpiece. What if they were? What if, instead of remaining a spinoff of the play, the jig became its own freestanding entertainment?

The distracted globe

> A clown with his pants falling down,
> Or the dance that's a dream of romance,
> Or the scene where the villain is mean.
> That's entertainment!
> – Howard Dietz and Arthur Schwartz,
> "That's Entertainment" (1952)

Kemp's departure from the Chamberlain's Men, and beyond, tells the story of his grappling with this fundamental problem – how to determine the economic identity of his practice. And yet the very conditions that framed his understanding of it would also mask its insolubility. As long as he remained in an institutional setting, the two fronts of appropriation presented an illusory choice. Whereas the company's efforts to capitalize on his play as work both effaced its individuality and sought to curb its license, the love of the crowd seemed to reinforce his individuality, and made his work feel like play. Free to choose between the audience and his fellow sharers, he chose the former – without realizing that they were one and the same act of "sharing," or how the former might look in the absence of the latter.

Such a slippage, indeed, informs the subtle critique he is made to give himself in *The Second Part of the Returne From Parnassus* (*c.* 1602, pr. 1606), a Cambridge play that depicts him not as the rebel against professionalism he may have thought he was, but as all too representative of it. In London and needing employment, Philomusus and Studioso are interviewed by Kemp and Richard Burbage for positions as hired men. Kemp is his usual self, mocking the declamatory stiltedness of university actors (who "neuer speake in their walke, but at the end of the stage") and disdaining the pedantry of their poets, who "smell too much of that writer *Ouid*, and that writer *Metamorphosis*."[16] That self, however – seemingly so artless and ignorant that he calls Studioso "*Otioso*" – is soon revealed to be equally an affectation, the product of someone for whom the stage is more *negotium* than *otium*.[17] Kemp extols the virtues of his craft in mercenary terms:

> But be merry my lads, you haue happened vpon the most excellent vocation in the world for money: they come North and South to bring it to our playhouse, and for honours, who of more report, then *Dick Burbage* & *Will:Kempe*, he is not coū[n]ted a Gentleman, that knowes not *Dick Burbage* & *Wil Kemp*, there's not a country wench that can dance Sellengers Round but can talke of *Dick Burbage* and *Will Kempe*.[18]

"Indeed M. *Kempe* you are very famous," Philomusus smartly replies, "but that is as well for workes in print as your part[s] in kue" – a conflation that foreshadows what ensues. When it comes time to test the apprentices' aptitude, Burbage and Kemp do so precisely through their ability to cite – and recite – "Dick Burbage and Will Kemp." Burbage gives Studioso a copy of *The Spanish Tragedy*, reads a soliloquy, and has him imitate; Kemp's measure of a clown, however, maintains the same relation of text to performance. "Now for you," he tells Philomusus, "me thinkes you should belong to my tuition, and your face me thinkes would be good for a foolish Mayre or a foolish justice of peace: mark me. ——" A strike runs to the margin, as though Kemp's transition were an effect of typography. There follows an eighteen-line, Dogberry-like mock oration to the town council, with a lecture on government whose malapropisms and cuckold jokes sound, as they are here meant to do, polished into cliché. "Come let me see how you can doe," he concludes, "sit downe in the chaire."[19] Philomusus' next line – taking up Kemp's first one – reads only "Forasmuch as there be, *&c.*," which could not form a starker contrast to the other "&c."s of the "workes in print" for which Kemp was "famous." Philomusus' qualifications as a clown end up having little to do with his face: even without Hamlet around, they *already* consist in speaking "no more than is set down."

Kemp never asks him to extemporize, not only because he himself (or rather, conveniently, the actor playing him) seems incapable of it, but because he does not *want* him to. Instead of proffering a book to (mis) read, as a counterpoint to Burbage's exercise, he applies the same textual rigor to his own patter, making his free-associative outpouring a "worke in print" that he here expects his pupil instantly to memorize and repeat *verbatim*. The scene of instruction is completed by the "chair" in which Philomusus is made to sit, at which point it becomes no longer the seat of the mayor Kemp was playing, or whom Philomusus now impersonates, but the seat of a *spectator* who has been watching *Kemp* – the same spectator, indeed, whose reception he has already belittled as just such vapid, reverential repetition, reducible to the chanting of his name. Deeply skeptical of Kemp's populism, his *Parnassus* parody analyzes its underlying drives in a way the real Kemp would not grasp until too late, and in ironic relation to his professed politics. The only collectivity in which he wants immersion amounts to an echo of himself: he wants back from his audience an impossibly perfect mirror, without distortion or contamination, of what he gives them. He wants them, in other words, to behave as precisely the kind of actor he refuses to be. He can deviate from the script, yet he expects those very deviations from his "part[s] in kue" to be tantamount to a script, to and from which no one else is free to add or subtract. Every jig contains an authoritarian impulse, saying "watch what I can do"; inside every clown, more than most professional performers, beats the heart of a tyrant.[20] "Thou wilt do well in time," he assures Philomusus, "if thou wilt be ruled by thy betters: that is by my selfe, and such graue Aldermen of the playhouse as I am."

The Chamberlain's Men's move to the Globe in 1599 disposed of this incipient rivalry, and its discursive complications.[21] The Burbages had been planning a market upgrade ever since their purchase of the Blackfriars in 1596, and the abandonment of the northern Curtain for the Bankside came with a refinement of repertory. There were surely as many lower-class spectators in the south, but playhouses built their reputations on a prevailing style, and the key novelty of the Globe's – perhaps the most significant turning point in Shakespearean dramaturgy – was to phase out the jig. Evidence for this shift in policy is, of course, even more inferential than that of the jig's ubiquity during Kemp's tenure, and as later chapters will demonstrate, it was more short-lived a policy than is usually recognized. Nevertheless, the first Globe plays seem to trace a precipitous decline from the jig's sanitization to outright elimination. The Swiss tourist Thomas Platter saw *Julius Caesar* on 21 September 1599, and noted how "after the play, according to their custom they did a most elegant and curious dance, two dressed in men's clothes and two in women's."[22] Though homologous to a jig in cast and context, "elegant and curious" are scarcely the adjectives Kemp's obscene skits should inspire, whose vulgar motifs would have been obvious to – and had indeed been practiced on – non-anglophone spectators. This was also the first English play Platter had ever seen, so a decorous coda might have appeared to others less "according to custom" than an attempt to change custom.[23] The Chamberlain's Men had acquired a new comedian, Robert Armin, less adept a dancer but a better

singer, enabling not just the development of more literate comic characters but, as we shall see, a different kind of postlude. Touchstone, his first
Globe role, is made an integral and musical part of *As You Like It*, and
is pointedly included in the nuptials at the play's end; no jig is prepared
for as in previous plays, and Rosalind's epilogue may have served partly
to quash such expectations – reminding the audience that "a good Play
needes no epilogue," yet still titillating them with the language of sexual
gratification.[24]

Swallowing the jig could not have been easy, and turns out to be something that another early Globe play, *Hamlet*, thematizes even as it institutes. It is a play, perhaps *the* play, about the surreptitious power of scripts.
Here clowns are explicitly told to "speak no more than is set down,"
and where they do not (Hamlet himself being the chief example), those
deviations from prescribed codes produce not so much improvisation as
adherence to new codes – most obviously, as Hamlet's misguided efforts
to ascertain the truth of the Ghost dictate a regressive chain of empirical
trials. In one of the many violations of his own advice to the Players – a
runaway postscript to that speech, in fact – the 1603 Quarto expressly
performs Kemp, when Hamlet inventories the idiot gestures that delight
those capable only of "inexplicable dumbshows and noise":

> And then you haue some agen, that keepes one sute
> Of ieasts, as a man is knowne by one sute of
> Apparell, and Gentlemen quotes his ieasts downe
> In their tables, before they come to the play, as thus:
> Cannot you stay till I eate my porrige? and, you owe me
> A quarters wages: and, my coate wants a cullison:
> And, your beere is sowre: and, blabbering with his lips,
> And thus keeping in his cinkapase of ieasts,
> When, God knows, the warme Clowne cannot make a iest
> Vnlesse by chance, as the blinde man catcheth a hare:
> Maisters tell him of it. (F2r–v)

The fusion of dance and clowning in "cinkapase" marks Kemp as a target clearly enough; it is also the only version of Hamlet's advice in which
"Clowne" is singular.[25] The clown Hamlet apes may deviate from his part,
but he is not really *improvising*: his words turn out to be "set down" somewhere after all, just somewhere else. In a reversal of playhouse stenographic
practice, here the clown's catchphrases and mannerisms prove so familiar and predictable that "Gentlemen quotes his ieasts downe / In their
tables" *before* they go to the play, not during it.[26] The pleasure, presumably, consists in the uncanny feeling of remote control as one by one each

item on their checklist transpires, and words on a page become action onstage, magically impelled into the player and out of him again. "Quote" seems inadequate to this transaction, since the phrases originate with the playgoers, and return to them once they have passed through him. The clown does not so much act a script, indeed, as he *is* a script incarnate, no more extricable from it than from his "one sute"; when he is out – even "warme," in a rhythm – his wit deserts him, because not really his. Here, under our noses, is the first reference to a playbook's interchangeability with performance, and that performance is a clown's. Only the playbook is not yet a playbook: it is the performer himself, whom the audience can already read as one.

Both the form and theme of Q1's "cinkapase" speech permeate the play. Hamlet habitually rehearses lists like this, catalogues of human behavior as "cinkapases": actions that a man might play, gestures that impart secrecy, the affectations of women – "jig"s being among them. Corambis, like the clown, spews language in predigested, automated particles – proverbs, rhetorical copia, obsessive pleasantries, aphasic sputterings – and is also, coincidentally, "for a Iigge, or a tale of bawdry."[27] This is what, for *Hamlet*, a "jig" really is: not an impromptu performance, but the *most* scripted kind, a script that lives in the body, such that one can be inside it and not know it. Hamlet calls himself "your only jig-maker" after the play-within-the-play, and after his running commentary has spoiled its diagnostic utility – himself becoming one of those players who "cannot keep counsel, thei'le tell all."[28] And then he dances a jig. No sooner does he "wipe away all Sawes of Bookes" from "the tables / Of my memorie" than a new "sawe," "that one may smile, and smile, and be a vilayne," replaces them; even his insanity, according to Corambis, must follow a formula, a grammatical declension, "a melancholy, / From that vnto a fast, then vnto distraction, / Then into a sadnesse, from that vnto a madnesse."[29] In Q1 *Hamlet*, not only is a "cinkapase" a script, but scripts unfold as cinkapases – as algorithms, manic, circular, amnesiac computations, experiences of simultaneous self-absorption and self-loss. To be an actor, after all, is to remember and forget at once, to exist in the oblivion of the present, in the lines one is speaking. Precisely by its excess, the "cinkapase" speech anatomizes the self-dislocation not just of the clown but of the very actor mimicking him: the ragdoll clown is here not the actor's opposite, but his epitome.

The condition of Q1 *Hamlet*, that is – even more than its sister texts – is a theatre where *no one* can speak "more than is set downe," clowns least of all. Hamlet heralds the arriving players with another fivefold inventory, this time of stock character types:

> He that playes the King shall haue tribute of me,
> The ventrous Knight shall vse his foyle and target,
> The lover shall sigh gratis,
> The clowne shall make them laugh
> That are tickled in the lungs, or the blanke verse shall halt for't,
> And the Lady shall haue leaue to speak her mind freely.[30] (E3r)

A version of the clown line also appears in F, but only in Q1 does it subtend "or the blank verse shall halt," implying that clowns speak in verse. Only in Q1, as a result, does "the Lady" "speak her mind freely" in a medium whose freedom has already been foreclosed. Characters have no minds to speak, of course, and in a theatre that analyzes the clown as a kind of character – whose "ieasts" come pre-"quoted," laughed at only by those already predisposed to laugh – improvisation is impossible. "Come on maisters," exhorts Hamlet, "Weele euen too't, like French Falconers, / Flie at any thing we see": in other words, let's be spontaneous.[31] Yet his demand for "a passionate speech" instantly stalls. The player needs a prompt, prompting Hamlet to recall the player's own past performance: "if it liue in thy memory beginne at this line."[32] By the end of these dissociative transfers, it is only the speech that "lives," a free-floating text distributively stored between them; actors are mere playback devices, of each other and of themselves. "Pronounce me this speech trippingly a the tongue as I taught thee," he instructs; in Q2 he "pronounced" it for them to "speak," but in Q1, performance means rote delivery.[33] Its agency always lies without: as with the clown, the audience must supply the impetus, already "tickled," priming the performer to prime them; the player is "quoted" before he opens his mouth, his words fed back to him so he can regurgitate them. Somehow closer to Kemp's defection, Q1 *Hamlet* uses him as its own prompt to explode the fiction of performative autonomy. Its players are introduced as "the law hath writ those are the only men": here there is no "liberty," no making things up for oneself.[34] And its clown, uniquely, tells his joke wrong. "Who builds strongest, / Of a Mason, a Shipwright, or a Carpenter?" he asks.[35] His punchline – "a Graue-maker" – falls flat, because he had framed the question, falsely, as a choice.

To be sure, there are glances at Kemp in Q2 *Hamlet* as well, but of a more local flavor. Capering to his nonsense lyrics at the close of "The Murder of Gonzago," Hamlet asks Horatio: "Would not this sir & a forrest of feathers, if the rest of my fortunes turne Turk with me, with prouinciall Roses on my raz'd shooes, get me a fellowship in a cry of players?" Horatio's acerbic reply, "Half a share," implies that some fellowships are more discriminating than others.[36] Hamlet may be good enough for the

Fortune or the Rose, that is – by mid-1602 Kemp had joined Worcester's Men, financed by Philip Henslowe, the owner of the Fortune, and they occupied the Rose, the Southwark playhouse next to *Hamlet*'s – but not for the Globe. Undeterred, Hamlet continues:

> HAMLET.   A whole one, I.
>   For thou doost know oh *Damon* deere
>   This Realme dismantled was
>   Of *Iove* himself, and now raignes heere
>   A very very paiock.
> HORATIO.   You might haue rym'd. (H3r)

Horatio seems a good deal more aware than Hamlet that his interference has obscured "some necessary question of the play."[37] By Q2, insofar as any sequence underlies them, *Hamlet*'s critique of clowning has hardened into policy, based on the pragmatics of performance rather than its theory. Lacking the "cinkapase" passage that connects them, the clown is no longer the same species as the actor, his improvisation not so much self-deluded as merely inimical to the integrity of the play. Here, Horatio tells Hamlet, in the "realm dismantled" and reassembled from the timbers of the original Theatre, the clown ("pajock") controls nothing, and is just an "ass" – the rhyme he asks him to complete.[38]

As we will see, the Chamberlain's Men's real policy was hardly so absolute. The traditional repertory of the stage clown, as they intuited by hiring Robert Armin – and as Q1 *Hamlet* analyzes Kemp's – was anything but antithetical to a textually governed model of theatre. Q2 *Hamlet*'s insults, rather, appear a reconsidered response to Kemp's departure, and to his having concluded otherwise. Whether his removal preceded or was provoked by The Chamberlain's Men's move to the Globe, the fact remains that the company only wished (or at least welcomed the chance) to decomission the jig, not the entire spectrum of clowning. The more minor, and ostensibly *more* participatory, forms of interactive improvisation – like "themes" – would ironically end up being retained. Rather, it was precisely the extravagance of the jig – Kemp's expansion of it into a separate dramatic species, a postlude to which the play was but a prelude – that selected it for termination. It is not that jigs did not contain a scripted quality: it is that they denied it in performance instead of foregrounding it, and did so, indeed, at the direct expense of the play's sense of scriptedness as well. To the astute observer, like the *Parnassus* author, the jig was not even clowning anymore, but something more insidious: it was playwrighting masquerading as clowning, restoring the audience as king in order to carve out a petty fiefdom for itself.

Kemp seems to have confused an attack on improvisation in general with an attack on the particular genre in which he claimed to offer it; whether he realized he was not really offering it either, of course, remains to be seen. It is a forgivable error, and one we make too, because the canonical *Hamlet* serves as an aggressive public relations statement to that effect. But even there, clowning becomes the blunt object of its scorn only because its more specific loss cannot quite be named. Indeed, the overriding strategy of the first Globe plays was to *disavow* the jig, to excise it as silently as possible from the expectation horizon of public theatre – or, where mentioned, categorically to repudiate it.[39] To be "for a Iigge, or a tale of bawdry," after all, is to be classed uneasily not only with Hamlet's verbal indiscipline but with Polonius's, and to be unceremoniously killed off with him midway through the play – the only other corpse besides Yorick's to get an unmarked grave, and a counterpart father figure who is denied a ghost. The play ends seemingly closed to the possibility of anything to follow it but itself, Horatio's "let this same be presently perform'd" yawning onto an abyss of perpetual repetition.[40] Yet *Hamlet* is everywhere haunted by the jig's epiphenomenal shadow: in its fixations on afterness, on irreconcilable chronologies, on the externality of the performing body, on objects and people both past recovery and incapable of burial, beyond either memory or forgetting. *Hamlet*'s metaphysics register the amputated conditions of its own production, a phantom limb that still tingles and even sings its own loss: "But age with his stealing steppes / hath clawed me in his clutch," hums the Gravedigger, "And hath shipped me into the land, / as if I had never been such."[41] Similarly, all Hamlet's fulminations against the players' clown serve to do is underscore the fact that he never appears in "The Murder of Gonzago" – and, in Q1, to supplement that absence. "[T]hough I am native here / And to the manner born," says Hamlet, "it is a custom / More honored in the breach than the observance"; *Hamlet* compusively enacts both. In a play whose action is the continuous frustration and deferral of its action, and where the skull of a clown is unearthed only to be cast aside, Hamlet embodies that clown in order to purge his institutional memory, inaugurating through his failure – and Fortinbras's succession of him – the transition to a more centralized theatrical format, wherein time can feel no longer "out of joint."

Will in the world

HORATIO. What if it tempt you toward the flood my lord,
            Or to the dreadfull summit of the cliff

> That beetles o'er his base into the sea,
> And there assume some other horrible form,
> Which might deprive your sovereignty of reason
> And draw you into madness? Think of it.
> The very place puts toys of desperation,
> Without more motive, into every brain,
> That looks so many fathoms to the sea
> And hears it roar beneath.
>
> HAMLET.   It waves me still.
>   – *Hamlet*, 1.4.54–64

Kemp had acquired a fifth actor's share when he co-signed the Globe lease in February 1599, but by the fall of that year he was gone. He may initially have returned to the Curtain with an unspecified troupe, where familiar and loyal audiences would have welcomed him back: Jonson's *Every Man Out of His Humour* (1599) has Macilente wish he "had one of Kemp's shoes to throw," perhaps alluding to the other play Platter noted seeing that fall at the Curtain, in which a drunken servant hurled a shoe at his master, followed by dances "both in English and in Irish fashion."[42] Kemp would later return to the Continent, sojourning from Calais to Rome – "welcome M. Kempe from dancing the morrice over the Alpes," says Studioso in *3 Parnassus* – and would see England again in late 1601 just long enough to gather ten younger players for a five-week tour of Germany and the Low Countries, serving in the capacity of actor-manager.[43] The foreign setting heightened the reliance on non-verbal media: music, dance, and farce. Not surprisingly, one observer at Münster reports, the clown appeared during every costume change.[44]

Back in London by 1602, he would join Worcester's Men at the Rose – possibly in time for *Hamlet*'s jabs next door – finding in them a professional outfit whose nativist idiom complemented his style of showmanship. Since they leased their playhouse from Henslowe, later moving to the Boar's Head, Worcester's Men were technically a rogue troupe, one of several such companies strafing the city in search of jig-hungry audiences either disaffected with the Globe's rarefied tastes or priced out of the boys' private halls. But the lack of a fixed venue would have been no deterrent to an inveterate wanderer. Their repertory consisted of domestic tragedies of marital infidelity rather than romantic love, and political histories that, even after the Essex uprising, still valorized the defiant subject at the expense of the aristocratic order. Intermingled were trusty comedies like *Cutting Dick*, *The Blind Eats Many a Fly*, and *No-body and Some-body* – for which last Henslowe gave Kemp five shillings "to bye

buckram to macke a payer of gyente hosse," a purchase whose significance
we will revisit.[45] Worcester's Men's surviving plays do not always specify an
obvious clown part, but the essence of the difference between them and
the Chamberlain's was that they did not need to do so: such populist fare
suited the tone and politics of his routines, and as the fledgling troupe's
marquee member, Kemp's grandstanding after the show would have been
the main attraction.

   Before finding this conservative haven in the playhouses, however,
Kemp embarked on a more radical justification of his retrograde career
move, and of the purist theatrical vision that informed it. The morris
across Europe was merely a grandiose sequel to its domestic counterpart:
on 11 February 1600, just a few short weeks after his severance from the
Chamberlain's Men, Kemp set out on a morris from London to Norwich.
The publicity stunt was, primarily, an entrepreneurial venture. Suddenly
bereft of steady employment, Kemp must have needed money, so he
advertised that the journey (some 115 miles in length, in winter, and on
dilapidated roads) would take only nine days of actual dancing – a figure
that was, given the enormous vigor the morris required even when station-
ary, sure to arouse interest. Kemp took bets against him at odds of three to
one, distributing pledges for preset sums (in the feudal counters of points,
gloves, and garters) on his way through the countryside, which he could
then, if successful, redeem for treble on the trip homeward. Rhetorically,
however, the expedition was calculated as a merry rebuke to the forces of
class mobility and aesthetic pretension that sought to repress the popular
tradition. Kemp wanted to display the value and vitality of the capital
he was withdrawing from the commercial theatres. His path took him
northeast from the city center, past the Curtain, past the razed site of the
old Theatre, to the traditionally democratic gathering place of Finsbury
Fields, through familiar precincts that would have been lined with ador-
ing fans. Symbolically and geographically, he was reversing English social
history, returning a beloved and endangered pastime to its provincial roots
and renewing the bond between the people and their ritual festivity. It was
a triumphant piece of capitalism in defense of pre-capitalist ideals.

   Accordingly, this affirmation of common culture had to be kept distinct from the commercial culture it was rejecting – a contamination
Kemp was ultimately and tellingly unable to prevent.[46] He delivered
on his promise (so he claimed) to reach Norwich within nine days of
dancing – non-consecutively spread across a full month of travel – but
the fusion of public entertainment and private enterprise implicit in his
project was, to say the least, dubiously received. Allegations of fraud and

political insurgency – ironically not unlike those often leveled at the play-houses, only now emanating from them – seem to have surrounded him from the outset. Balladeers, jig-makers, and stage satirists charged that he had variously cheated, drunk excessively, caused mischief, evaded highway tolls, lost money, made too much money, couriered gifts to the Queen to court her favor, and was fomenting a threat to the Queen's peace.[47] He was given the mock title "Knight of the Red Cross," and his folk-heroic presumptions were ridiculed in *Tom-a-Lincoln, the Red-Rose Knight* (1600), a burlesque prose romance about a delusional Summer Lord of Misrule.[48] "One hath written *Kemps farewell* to the tune of Kery, mery, Buffe," Kemp complains, "another his desperate daungers in his late travaile, the third his entertainment to New-Market, which towne I came never neere by the length of half the heath … many say thinges that were neuer thought."[49] In a pun meant to underscore his modest aims as well as (perhaps) his renunciation of the Globe, Kemp rebutted claims that "I have trode a good way to winne the world" with the reminder that "without good help I have daunst my selfe out of the world."[50] Nevertheless, the world he tried to leave behind continued to dog him. As a result of these controversies, most importantly, many of his debtors were now refusing to pay up. "Some that loue me, regard my paines, & respect their promise, haue sent home the treble worth," he admits, "some other at the first sight haue paid me, if I came to seek thē[m]; others I cannot see, nor wil they willingly be found, and these are the greater number."[51]

Kemp thus had practical reasons to redress these accusations, hinted at in his concern that "else euery Ballad-singer will proclaime me bankrupt of honesty."[52] But it was the form in which he chose to do so – from which most of our knowledge of them derives – that betrays how little he had "daunst [him] selfe out of the world," or perhaps how much of that world he had still carried with him. "A sort of mad fellows seeing me merrily dispos'd in a Morrice," he says, "haue so bepainted me in print since my gambols began from London to Norwich that (hauing but an ill face before) I shall appear to the world without a face."[53] Kemp's only recourse, ironically, was to plunge himself into that arena of facelessness. Soon after returning in March, he composed an account of his journey and had it published as *Kemps Nine Daies Wonder* (1600). The pamphlet gives every sign of merely supplementing his project's rhetoric of authenticity. For the same reason that his disclaiming it the "first Pamphlet that euer Will Kemp offred to the Presse" is not quite true, it wants to model its secondary, you-had-to-be-there relation to performance after the printed jig, advising its readers to look for nothing but "blunt mirth in a Morrice dauncer, especially such a one as *Will Kemp*, that hath spent his life in mad Iigges and merry iestes."[54] With a misdirected aristocratic dedication consistent with Kemp's plain-man persona, followed by a lively itinerary of his activities (divided into ordinal chapter headings) as endured by his taborer Tom Slye, his page William Bee, and a notary, George Sprat, its basic plan is both to certify his achievement and to recreate an experience – so as, in the words of its subtitle, to "reproue the slaunders spred of him ... written by himselfe to satisfie his friends."[55]

This quasi-legal locution, however, fundamentally alters the pamphlet's status as the record of a past event – since, with an official witness on hand (why else hire Sprat?) there should have been no need for Kemp himself to write it. *Kemp's* authorship rather than Sprat's, that is, yields not a testimonial to the dance but a textual repetition of it. That his first-person narration of the event is not felt to diminish its evidentiary validity is less important, for us, than how it retroactively alters the status of the event, synchronizing it with the act of writing. Though the subtitle of *Nine Daies Wonder*, "Performed in a daunce from London to Norwich," asserts the chronological priority of performance over text, Kemp is surprisingly attuned to the pressure of offering an entertainment whose consumption occurs at a remove, and the close of his dedication invites us to participate in the remembered performance as if it is only just now taking place:

> In which light conceite I lowly begge pardon and leaue, for my Taberer strikes his huntsup, I must to Norwich: Imagine, Noble Mistris, I am now setting from my Lord Mayors, the houre about seauen, the morning gloomy, the company many, my hart merry. (A2v)

This is more than just fancy: to the skeptics in Kemp's readership, the real performance *is* only now taking place – an underwriting of the event that inevitably ends up overwriting it, and rewriting the very role of participation in it that it seems to solicit. A funny thing happens on the way to Norwich, that is, this second time around. Kemp's morris may not have been initially contrived to exist in two different states, but the superimposition of textual absence onto real-time experience produces a curious effect, triggering an anxiety for control either latent in the original or, more interestingly, retroprojected into that memory, inflecting and warping it. The performative dislocation of vindicating the dance in writing, in other words, irrevocably imbues the account of the dance, which stands in for the dance itself; experienced through this text, as Kemp intends it to be, the dance becomes a second-order performance trying to *reinforce* the boundary between performer and audience rather than erase it, revealing the incompatibility of universal pleasure and private profit. Whether he realized it or not, Kemp's agenda when he sat down to write *Nine Daies Wonder* conflicts with that of the dance it purports to document: instead of merely describing what happened, he must here describe what *had* to have happened in order for him to recoup his investment. In the very act of defying an institution that was destroying the intimacy of spontaneous play, he unwittingly endowed his resistance with something that did just that – a script.

If it befits this irony that Kemp's text will terminate in a playhouse, it is because on some level the dance never really left it, replicating elements of the economic paradigm of commercial theatre. The morris was associated with the pagan courtship rituals of spring, and was never performed during Lent.⁵⁶ Kemp timed his to coincide with the first day of Lent, to capitalize on the closure of the theatres. Insofar as the crowds he drew on his way out of London may largely have been idle playgoers, then, the event remained, like the jig, as much a circumscribed extension of the playhouse as an exodus from it. His morris, moreover, privileged individual over group choreography. In contrast to cognate forms like the ring morisk, wherein dancers took turns leaping and preening for a Maid Marian, Kemp's version dispensed with such internal structure to facilitate both indefinite duration and the visual centrality of its star. Even before he starts narrating it, it already reduced a complex and interactive form into a closed circuit of technical virtuosity that neither required other participants nor, indeed, necessarily wanted them.

Something of this ambivalence to audience lingers in the title-page woodcut – an image ripe for dialogue with the one of Tarlton that had been circulating for a decade, and that had in fact adorned a new edition of *Tarltons Jests* that same year. (See Figure 5.) *Nine Daies Wonder* splits that Tarlton in two. On the left is the taborer Tom Slye, a simplified figure who retains the Tarltonian signifiers of pipe, drum, baton, and *contrapposto*. Instead of being trained on us, however, his gaze directs our attention to Kemp, whose feathered hat, billowing sash, and *jongleur* costume – replete with belled buskins – dominate the frame. The homage thus pays homage to Kemp in turn, lending a cultural authority to his progress, situating it in a nostalgic tradition of jovial wanderlust reminiscent of Tarlton's provincial tours with the Queen's Men. Yet insofar as the image now gifts him with a following – even one here composed, iconographically, of the very clown he had succeeded – it also opens that lineage to question. Kemp is not a one-man show. His dance needs an audience, yet it is an accompaniment he disdains: rather than meeting Slye's glance or miming Tarlton's

Kemps nine daies vvonder.

Performed in a daunce from
London to Norwich.

Containing the pleaſure, paines and kinde entertainment
of *William Kemp* betweene *London* and that Citty
in his late Morrice.

Wherein is ſomewhat ſet downe worth note; to reprooue
the ſlaunders ſpred of him: many things merry,
nothing hurtfull.

Written by himſelfe to ſatisfie his friends.

LONDON
Printed by *E. A.* for *Nicholas Ling*, and are to be
ſolde at his ſhop at the weſt doore of Saint
Paules Church. 1600.

Figure 5 Title page of William Kemp, *Kemps Nine Daies Wonder* (1600), A1r.

steely glare, he stares out not at us but into empty space. The image furthermore depicts no other spectators of any sort; Kemp twirls on a barren ground, contoured seemingly only the better to convey its featurelessness. The abject figure of the taborer embodies the problematic status of the observer that will continue to ramify throughout this text. If Tom Slye – to say nothing of William Bee, George Sprat, or the multitudes that trailed him out of London – matched Kemp step for step, providing the music, authentication, and for some periods even the complementary measures of the dance itself, how much of the *Wonder* is really *Kemps*, such that he was exclusively entitled to its profits, or to profit at all?

If the audience is the repressed presence of the woodcut, it surfaces with gathering force in the text, whose goal gradually becomes not the validation of Kemp's feat for its remote critics, but the reclamation of his labor from its most proximal contributors. Since (from what he tells us) all the disputations of his achievement were coupled with charges of personal incontinence, the defenses of both are handled together: anything unrelated to his execution of the wager is blamed on outside instigation – including, conveniently, impromptu outgrowths of the dance itself. While necessary to maintain the impression of his popularity, the very community intrinsic to Kemp's project thus also begins to register as a swelling tide of interference.

As he departs London, this friction is still dormant. Kemp already notes that his pace is only "as fast as kinde peoples thronging together would giue mee leaue," but the collective energy – dispersed for the time being among other celebrations – remains a help rather than a hindrance to a performance that, nonetheless, assumes a defensive posture:

> Being past White-chappell … multitudes of Londoners left not me: but eyther to keepe a custome that many holde, that Mile-End is no walke without a recreatiõ[n] at Stratford Bow with Creame and Cakes, or else for love they beare toward me, or perhappes to make themselues merry, if I should chance (as many thought) to giue over my Morrice within a mile of Mile-End. How euer, many a thousand brought me to Bow, where I rested a while from dancing, but had small rest with those that would have urg'd me to drinking. (A3v)

Kemp claims he rebuffed these temptations for the "congruity" of his health, occasioning brief pause on the strangeness of that term in the mouth of a simple man: "yet it may be a goode worde for ought I knowe, though I never made it, nor doe verye well understand it; yet I am sure I bought it at the word-mongers …" The tangent is a stab at extemporaneity meant to impart to the text the whimsy of the dance, but under the conceit of folly it hints at the commodification of the immaterial – a hint that then extends itself to the dance, by alerting him to his having strayed from its material facts: "Farwell Congruitie for I meane now to be more concise, and stand upon eeuener bases: but I must neither stand nor sit, the Taberer strikes alarum."[57] A further anecdote of Bow Bridge is aborted as "no matter belonging to our Morrice."[58] Though not yet serious business, Kemp reminds us – via himself – that it is a form of business none-theless, and one that cannot tolerate disruption.

Neither can it do so as a form of entertainment, apparently, as the next incident obliquely illustrates:

> Many good fellows being there [at Stratford Langthorne] met, and know-ing how well I loved the sport, had prepared a Beare-bayting: but so unrea-sonable were the multitudes of people, that I could only heare the Beare roare, and the dogges howle: therefore forward I went with my hey de gaies to Ilford ... (7)

Kemp says he "loved the sport," but it sounds as if he has never been to a real bearbait. It was a violent spectacle over which people continuously jockeyed for vantage, and were made all the more frenzied, not coinciden-tally, by the fact of wagering. With presumably no scaffolding to provide tiered seating for the event, however, Kemp expects his fellow onlookers to keep a distance conducive to his personal enjoyment; after all, he says, the affair was arranged for his benefit. To whatever extent the bearbait's agitations are continuous with his own performance, furthermore, his instinctive retreat from it also serves to connect them: Kemp is prevented from watching a gang attack because he is attacked by a gang. A witness to a bearbait in 1575 intriguingly describes the animal's struggle like a kind of dance, who "if he were ta'en once, then by what shift with biting, with clawing, with roaring, with tossing, and tumbling, he would work and wind himself loose from them."[59] Likewise, as Kemp flees the hordes at Stratford Langthorne – followed by drunken invitations at Ilford to which "I soberly gave my boone Companyons the slip" and a reception at Romford from "Londoners that came hourely ... in great numbers to visit me, offring much more kindnes then I was willing to accept" – this same pattern of evasion begins to grip, and indeed constitute, the narra-tive rhythm of the dance itself.[60]

Its underlying regard for the commercial integrity of that dance, more-over, begins to mark Kemp's language as well, increasingly assertive of his antisocial exertions as socially recognizable work. Dancing "by Moone-shine" to deter the crowd, he encounters two clashing jades, and compares the distinctly morris-like kicks of their "fore feete ouer my head" to "two Smiths ouer an Anuyle." He spends two days in Romford "to giue rest to my well labour'd limbes"; straining his hip the morning of his second day of dancing, he perseveres, "finding remedy by labour that had hurte me."[61] In Brentwood on a market day – where "the multitudes were so great at my coming ... that I had much ado (though I made many intreaties and staies) to get passage to my Inne" – this tacit vein of economic legitimation finds its opposite in the form of two arrested thieves:

> In this towne two Cut-purses were taken, that ... followed me from London (as many better disposed persons did:) but these two dy-doppers gaue out when they were apprehended, that they had laid wagers and betted about my iourney ... I iustly denyed their acquaintance, sauing that I remembred one of them to be a noted Cut-purse, such a one as we tye to a poast on our stage, for all people to wonder at, when at a play they are taken pilfring ... after a dance of Trenchmore at the whipping crosse, they were sent backe to London: where I am afraide there are too many of their occupation. (B1r)

Kemp skillfully contrasts the pickpockets' corrupt practice with his proper one: while they have attended every leg of his journey, since they cannot prove their moneys are a surety of "laid wagers" upon it, he "iustly denye[s]" that their perversion of public entertainment into a means of private livelihood is in any way connected with his own. Perhaps sensing he is on thin ice here, Kemp sutures the moment with a tactical reference to commercial theatre, "where I am afraide there are too many of their occupation": this is the deplorable interpretation of pastime that has "followed" him out of London rather than one brought with him, a point reinforced by another Globe pun in his "wish ... that the whole world were cleer of such companions."[62] The remarkable insinuation is that Kemp produces not only *something* in exchange for his deferred price of admission, but something actually *more* substantial than that offered by the playhouse; whereas his gives pleasure, its is a "dance" that ends – and perhaps begins – at the tail of a whip.

Yet he happily enlists the Globe's notion of commodity in order to attract the "better disposed persons," with whom he too cultivates association. He relates a meeting with Sir Thomas Mildmay, who "receuied gently a pair of garters of me: gloues, points, and garters, being my ordinary marchandize, that I put out to venter for performance of my merry voyage."[63] Kemp's disingenuity here masks a truth: since "performance" is expected from the recipients of these tokens, they are precisely the "marchandize" into which Kemp's own performance – both physical and literary – is trying to inject real monetary value. In a logic far more reifying than the Globe's, indeed, the "marchandize" Kemp "venters" is merely the currency in which to pay him. It is an absurd proposition, of course, and nowhere acknowledged so flatly, but Kemp backs himself into it from a professional's assumption that *some* commodity, however circular, is better than none. The compulsion to frame performance as an economic relationship again locates him within a larger institutional discourse, and the very fatuousness of his metaphor only confirms his inability to frame it any other way. He simply *has* no other language, nor a sense of the need for it, to describe what he is doing.

In order to justify (and individuate) his commercialization of festival, then, Kemp must maintain a fiction of transaction, with a clear line between producer and consumer – whose incessant transgression by those consumers only further fuels his aversion to them. There would be something amusing in the Beatles-esque image of Kemp pursued through the fields by swarms of ardent fans were his evasiveness born of modesty rather than of naked antipathy. He departs Brentwood by night, "stealing away from those numbers of people that followed mee: yet doe what I could, I had aboue fiftie in the company ... that would needs when they heard my Taber, trudge after me though thicke and thin." By the dawn of day three those numbers have swelled "past two hundred, being the least company that I had" – an entourage that is now openly impeding his progress, for "it was more than an houre ere I could recouer my Inne gate". Later, at Bury, "poor Will kemp was seauen times stayed ere he could recouer his Inne" by "the wondring and regardless multitude."[64] On the decrepit road to Braintree "two pretty plaine youths ... with their kindness somewhat hindred me" by joining too closely in the dance, "one a fine light fellow [being] still before me, the other euer at my heeles." When they fall into a mudpit only Kemp can traverse, he exults less in their misfortune than in its affirmation of the singularity of his performance: "My youth that follow'd mee, tooke his jump, and stuck fast in the midst, crying out to his companion, come George, call yee this dauncing, Ile goe no further: for indeede hee could goe no further, till his fellow was fain to wade and help him out. I could not chuse but lough to see howe like two frogges they laboured." Kemp is quite happy to leave them behind, "and they faintly bad God speed me, saying if I daunst that durtie way this seauen yeares againe, they would neuer daunce after me."[65]

Where Kemp does willingly engage his devotees, indeed, it is only in managed environments that fortify the distinction between performer and audience, environments seemingly always mediated by theatrical devices of enclosure and privilege. While a guest at Chelmsford in the gentry household of "one Sudley" and his wife, he accepts a request to dance with their maid; the hour-long morris takes place in the privacy of "a great large roome" – a morris within the morris, as it were, temporally and architecturally – with all the airless deliberation of a command performance.[66] While he has no trouble outlasting the girl, by contrast, the effort of eluding the mob on his way into town makes him "so weary, that I could dance no more": needing ever smaller rooms, he repairs to his inn and "was faine to lock myself in my Chamber, and pacifie them with wordes out of a window instead of deeds."[67] Having forfeited the insulation of the Globe's platform stage for physical immersion in the streets, Kemp is now driven to seek refuge in the purely verbal remove of the balcony.

Where such constructs prove unavailable, in fact, he repairs to the furthest verbal remove of all to distance himself from collaboration. The habit begins inconspicuously enough, during the incident with the puddle in Braintree: Kemp is about to introduce his two acolytes to the story, but seems to anticipate their challenge by first doing something else they cannot – namely, introducing things to the story. Narrating the start of the day's sloppy events, Kemp breaks off mid-sentence to interpolate a catch lamenting the foulness of the road: "*With hey and ho, throughe thicke and thin, / the hobby horse quite forgotten, / I follow'd as I did begin, / although the way were rotten.*"[68] The verse is set off both spatially and typographically, its formal lineation and roman face suspended in a sea of block gothic – rather like a man trapped in mud. We can only wonder whether the verse is a cultural citation or a poetic invention, but that proprietary blurring seems part of its point.[69] Kemp never says he sang these rhymes during the dance, and certainly they have nothing to do with a textual record of it. They contribute only to the value of the text itself, a space Kemp here gradually (and literally) starts expanding, I would suggest, for purposes unrelated to the quality of our reading experience. In a narrative increasingly about the interruption of his progress, such moments of self-interruption may look like the random emanations of a generous, carefree persona, but they potentially acquire the opposite valence.

The pattern quickly becomes pathological, rearing itself with every frustrating act of participation Kemp must endure. From Sudbury to Bury a hardy butcher endeavors to dance alongside him, and after a half mile relents, "protesting, that if he might get a 100. pound, he would not hold out with me." But at his departure "a lusty Country lasse" takes up the challenge to last the whole mile "though it had cost [her] life":

Nay saith she, if the Dauncer will lend me a leash of his belles, Ile venter to treade one mile with him my selfe ... The Drum strucke, forward marcht I with my merry Maydemarian: who shook her fat sides: and footed it merrily to Melfoord, being a long myle. There parting with her, I gaue her (besides her skinfull of drinke) an English crowne to buy more drinke ... my kindness she requited with dropping some dozen of short courtsies, and bidding God blesse the Dauncer, I bad her adieu: and to give her her due, she had a good eare, daunst truly, and wee parted friendly. (B3v)

The woman's zeal comes close to effecting an extraordinary inversion. Bizarrely, Kemp ends up paying *her* – perhaps because, unlike the butcher (or for that matter himself) she performs not for money but for sheer joy, the embodiment of an uncompromised version of his own nostalgic project; donning his regalia, her "venter" is freely given, and looks for no reward. She dances so "truly," indeed – with no clear sign of whose decision it is for her to stop – that the identity of the deferential epithet "the Dauncer" is, by its second occurrence, syntactically ambiguous. Kemp is pressed to counter this momentary contest of his authority, and has nothing with which to do so but textuality: "But ere I part with her, a good fellow my friend, havin writ an odd Rime of her, I will make bold to set it downe." Just who this conveniently produced "friend" is Kemp never explains, of course; he pretends merely to transcribe. But the ensuing lines nevertheless textually reinstate a performative sovereignty his dance cannot, its patronizing blazon of "Her stump legs ... / browne brows ... / browne hips ..." executing a lyric containment that accessorizes her as "Marrian in *his* Morrice daunce."[70]

Yet in the process, the friction between documentary and simulation again erupts to the surface. Assailed by spectators whose relentless participation both adulterates and critiques the differentiation of labor he is trying to validate, Kemp's narrative quietly begins to uncouple from the historical event with which it is supposed to be coterminous. Like the hobby-horse verse before it, the Marrian doggerel is of no relevance to the evidentiary argument of the text. But for Kemp that argument has exposed discursive faultlines he can no longer outrun – Who owns mass entertainment? when does it cease being a diversion for its audience, and its audience become the diversion? – questions that force him to take refuge in a performative domain he can still control. A third poem appears the next day (likewise attributed to the mysterious "my friend late mentioned before"), a tribute to his host at Rockland and a sentimental ode on innkeepers that runs the length of a page.[71] A fourth, supposedly recited by "one Thomas Gilbert in name of all the rest of the Cittizens" when

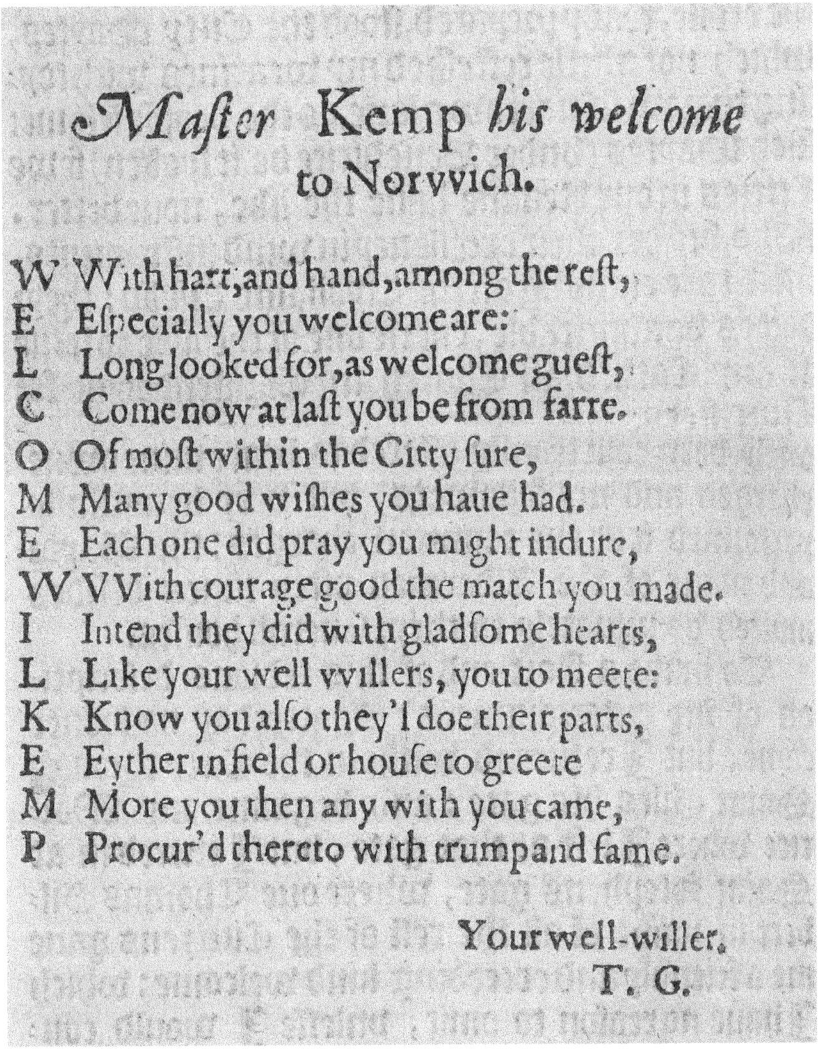

Master Kemp *his welcome*
to Norvvich.

W With hart,and hand,among the reſt,
E Eſpecially you welcome are:
L Long looked for,as welcome gueſt,
C Come now at laſt you be from farre.
O Of moſt within the Citty ſure,
M Many good wiſhes you haue had.
E Each one did pray you might indure,
W VVith courage good the match you made.
I Intend they did with gladſome hearts,
L Like your well vvillers, you to meete:
K Know you alſo they'l doe their parts,
E Eyther in field or houſe to greete
M More you then any with you came,
P Procur'd thereto with trump and fame.

Your well-willer,
T. G.

Figure 6 Composite image of acrostic poem in *Kemps Nine Daies Wonder* (1600), C4r–v.

"I entred in at Saint Stephens Gate" to celebrate his arrival at Norwich, is an acrostic spelling out "WELCOMEWILKEMP" – a greeting legible only in a textual medium.[72] (See Figure 6.) Unless one had an extraordinarily trained ear, such a conceit could not have been part of an oral ceremony; it is designed to work only on paper. And even then, it does not work

well enough: an extra column down the lefthand margin redundantly fil-
ters the word-initial letters, so that "WELCOMEWILKEMP" appears twice,
setting Kemp quite literally beside himself. The space of the *Nine Daies
Wonder* has now ceased to be the dance, or a written account of the dance,
and become, simply, writing; the commodity it offers is now a literary
enactment of the disintegration of its commodity. When none of its other
actors will follow it – precisely because they insist on following it too
closely – the plot of the clown's script devolves into his own desperate
attempts to escape from it.

As Kemp cuts through ever-denser thickets of adulation, his crisis of
professional identity peaks in the panicked responses that end up achiev-
ing its breakdown. On the "foule way" to Hingham he is so "much hindred by the desire people had to see me" that he himself loses the ability to
distinguish producer from consumer – in fact pointedly reversing them –
and the performance itself momentarily slips beyond all coherence:

> For euen as our Shop-keepers will hayle, and pull a man with Lack ye?
> What do ye lack Gentlemen? My ware is best cryes one: mine best in
> England sayes an other: here you shall haue choyse saith the third: so was
> the dyuers voices of the young men and Maydens, which I shoulde meete
> at euerie myles end, thronging by twentie, and sometime fortie, yea, hun-
> dreths in a companie: One crying the fayrest way was thorow their Village:
> another, this is the nearest and fairest way ... an other sort crie, turne on
> the left hand, some on the right hand: that I was so amazed, I knewe not
> sometime which way I might best take. (C3r)

If West argues that stage jigs represented "the triumph of sound," this is
their revenge on their master.[73] Consistent with the degeneration of the
prose into heteroglossic mess, the bystanders are now the ones directing
traffic, and doing the trafficking themselves: the analogy with London
shopkeeper cant makes nearly explicit Kemp's demotion in such a fray
from the sole seller of a ware to its purchaser, if not to the ware itself.
Struggling to make his own voice heard above theirs, when given the
choice the "way" Kemp takes is increasingly whichever one leads him *away*
from the mob, even if it means choosing his autonomy at the expense of
dancing at all. Finally drawing within sight of Norwich, the persistence of
"so great a multitude and throng of people still crowding more and more
about me" forces Kemp to delay its completion because there are simply
too many spectators to enjoy it for it to be enjoyed:

> mistrusting it would be a let to my determined expedition, and pleasurable
> humour: which I long before conceiued to delight this City with (so far,
> as my best skill, and industry with my long trauelled sinews could affoord

them) I was aduised, and so tooke ease by that aduise, to stay my Morrice a
little aboue Saint Giles his gate, where I tooke my gelding, and so rid into
the Citty, procrastinating my merry Morrice daunce through the Citty till
better opportunitie. (C3v)

In their ecstasy, the audience swarms so closely around him that they form
"a let" to his "determined expedition," which is itself supposed to "delight"
the audience. Once again, there is something oddly dissociative about the
passive construction into which Kemp displaces the counsel to "procras-
tinate" his dance, as if the voice inside his own head were becoming a
wholly separate person. If "better opportunitie" entails fewer people, and
if the commercial integrity of public entertainment varies inversely with
the size of its audience, we are approaching the point where for Kemp the
ideal performance has an audience of none – including, conceivably, even
himself.

The crushing obstructions of his final progress, sure enough, push this
exponential logic to its limit. On the open road he might have been able to
outpace his interlopers, but the constricted Norwich streets subject him to
a public torture from whose interminability there is no reprieve – curiously
recalling the bearbait, or perhaps those cutpurses strapped to the London
stage. "My wearines with toyling thorow so narrow a lane" requires the
aid of "Wifflers (such Officers as were appointed by the Mayor) to make
me way through the throng of people, which prest so mightily vpon me";
his body both guarded from and confined by the body politic, the passage
conflates carnival with a scene of execution.[74] One unlucky reveler, a girl
with a "long wasted peticote," gets too close to the action and, when she
collides with Kemp, is instantly engulfed in the mindless vortex: "it fell
out that I set my foote on her skirtes: the point eyther breaking or stretch-
ing, off fell her peticoate from her waste … and she could hardly recouer
her coate againe from vnruly boies." He is moved, yet being moved too
forcibly to dwell on it: "I was sorry for her, but on I went."[75]

It is not the last article of clothing that will be lost in Norwich, or
that mediates a moment of rupture. "With great labour," Kemp relates,
"I got thorow that narrow preaze into the open market place," which he
has only to traverse in order to reach the Mayor's house and complete
his venture. Fittingly, however, the traditional venue of itinerant theatre,
the marketplace, permits his venture no closure without forfeiting the
larger marketplace to which it simultaneously seeks access. "The presse
still increasing by the number of boys, girles, men and women, thronging more and more before me to see the end," Kemp – in an agoraphobic
fit – suddenly

deceiued the people, by leaping over the Church-yard wall at St. Iohns, getting so into M. Mayors gate a nearer way: but at last I found it the further way about: being forced on the Tewsday following to renew my former daunce, because George Sprat my ouer-seer hauing lost me in the throng, would not be deposed that I had daunst it, since he saw me not. (D1r)

Kemp at last breaks free of his audience, and pays a price. Just as he privatized the morris in order to publicize it, he now violates the terms of that privatization in order to rescue it from its public. So total is the crowd's participation, and so total is Kemp's equation of such participation with interference, that he here forfeits even the minimal spectatorship required – in the case of Sprat, dedicated – to witnessing his achievement. And though he goes on to boast of his prodigious jump, "the measure of which is to be seene in the Guild-hall at Norwich, where my buskins, that I then wore, and daunst in from London thither, stand equally deuided, nailed on the wall," it presents a crucial problem. Sprat's unwillingness to corroborate Kemp's having danced the remaining distance means that, unseen, he technically *has not danced it* – thus demanding a *tenth* day of dancing ("the Tewsday following") on which to repeat it. This may be why the voucher for which Sprat was originally retained is withheld from Kemp's pamphlet, and why Kemp must write it himself: the title of his pamphlet is a lie, traduced by its own narrative. Insofar as this climactic act of self-sabotage also circularly creates the *need* for a written defense – one that, for that very reason, should have omitted it – its almost fatalistic repetition dooms Kemp's enterprise both as populist preservation and as financial investment. Yet it also crystallizes what he has been most anxious to preserve all along. The leap over the wall – a graveyard wall – marks the point where, his autonomy crumbling around him, Kemp's embattled self-possession as performer recedes into terminal textuality, from "the press" of flesh into the printing press, from the world of the living to the land of the dead – leaving behind only an empty pair of leggings – and where the Nine (or possibly Ten) Days' Wonder is finally eclipsed by *Kemps Nine Daies Wonder*, a performance now as protected from the agency of its consumers as it is powerless to compel performance from them in return. Kemp has spent his journey fantasizing about a dance with no one there to see it, and the instant of its realization coincides with the genesis of the book we read. Fetching one last caper, the clown – with his pants falling down – disappears into the antithesis of what he thought he had embodied: authorship.

Disappearing acts

> POL. ... will you walke out of the ayre my Lord?
> HAM. Into my graue.
>
> – *Hamlet* (1604), F1v

In which transfigured form, naturally, he now reverts to the practice that already approximated authorship: jig-making. He appends an epilogue to his own drama, "Kemps humble request to the impudent generation of Ballad-makers," in which he conducts an imaginary manhunt for his libelers that eventually, inexorably, leads him back to the playhouse – where misanthropy, not community, is the basis of professional performance. If he has just exposed the latent authorial desire of his stage practice, the object of his rage now becomes those *other* authors who tricked him into it. Collectively calling them "My notable Shakerags," he claims to make "a priuie search" of "what private Jigmonger of your iolly number, hath been the Author of these abhominable ballets written of me" – a search that, taking swipes at Shakespeare and Armin along the way, ultimately re-maps Kemp's own flight into privacy. After running down various leads, he questions a would-be suspect "about the Bankside, sitting at a play." This proves a dead end, however, "till by chaunce a friend of mine" – no doubt the same "friend" who materializes whenever texts do – "puld out of his pocket a book in Latine called *Mundus Furiosus*," whose pseudonymous writer is the culprit.[76] Recapitulating the poetics of his travelogue as a whole, Kemp's "privie search" for the public sphere takes him from street to theatre into text, from a dispersed, multiple agency to a single, faceless figure; the author of his flight into authorship is, fittingly, nothing more or less than "the madness of the world" itself.

And authorship is already the dislocated space in which Kemp's coda unfolds. He haunts London here not as an embodied person but as an explicitly departed spirit: the Epilogue opens by declaring that "I William Kemp, whom you had neer rent in sunder with your unreasonable rimes, am shortly God willing to set forward as merily as I may, whither I myself know not ... imploy not your little wits in certifying the world that I am gone to Rome, Jerusalem, Venice, or any other place."[77] Before he even starts looking for him, Kemp is just as withdrawn and unreachable as the slanderer he seeks, a word on a page signifying absence; he ends his pamphlet even more "without a face" than he began. The Epilogue's subtitle offers it "to the tune of Thomas Deloney's *epitaph*," but it is entirely in prose; the tabor that carries him out of England is a funereal and broken music.

Kemp would return from his reprised morris on the Continent, as mentioned, but to his audiences he never really did. (Katherine Duncan-Jones believes he survived until 1612, performing "in private households rather than on public stages"; professionally, then, he may as well have died of plague in 1603, as most scholars continue to suspect from the Southwark burial record on 2 November of one "Kemp, a man."[78]) For when Queen Anne's Men – formerly his adopted company, Worcester's Men – resurrected him for a posthumous cameo in 1607, it was in a play called *The Trauails of the Three English Brothers*, where the diplomat Anthony Shirley meets the expatriate clown in Venice. The terms of Kemp's ongoing exile are never explained, and seemingly need not be: as in the Cambridge play of 1602 that anachronistically imagined him as both arrived from "over the Alpes" and still with the Chamberlain's Men, he now persists only as a fractured amalgam of popular memory, lingering in a limbo of placelessness. Shirley asks him to stage a scene with an Italian Harlequin and his wife; Kemp protests he is "somewhat hard of study," preferring "some extemporal meriment"; as they arrange a cuckolding plot in which he will be the peasant, he surreptitiously fondles Harlequin's wife; he blasts Italian culture as lewd and Italian women as whores.[79] They never get around to the actual play, of course, because Kemp's "meriment" is already happening: his idiom was that of the "live," the spontaneous, the performer just being "himself." But his old, familiar persona, with its nativist politics and shared immediacy, is here revived only by someone playing him, reading from a script that reads *him* as a script, being enjoyed by people watching a play about the foreign. In order to be retailed now, Kemp must be multiply packaged as other, remembered and represented as an alien, alienated commodity.

And it was thus that Kemp, upon joining Worcester's Men in 1602, had likewise apparently retailed himself in the last years of his life. After the possessive meltdown and resultant disappearing act of the *Nine Daies Wonder*, the only play in which we know for certain that he partook was the anonymous *No-body and Some-body* (pr. 1606) – and in which, thanks to Henslowe's note about the "gyente hosse," we can suppose he took the part of Nobody, the embodiment of anonymity, the folk-figure whose hyperextensive legs leave him, like Kemp's empty buskins, with "no body." (See Figures 7 and 8.) Somebody, his unseen nemesis, commits all the misdeeds in the play, while Nobody takes all the blame – a literalization of the old refrain "who did it? Nobody." Insofar as the joke attains its physical dimension from an Englishing of the German *niemand* (no one),

Figure 7 Title page of Anon., *No-body and Some-body* (1606), A1r (detail).

though, *No-body and Some-body* must also have poignantly allegorized for Kemp the paradox of clowning in a world that was increasingly polarizing the economic and performative identities of bodies – a *mundus furiosus* that let him own himself onstage at the cost of disowning the pleasure he produced, or that let him claim it on the page at the cost of not producing it at all.[80] In his own double translations from Continental itinerant to professional player and back, he himself had gone from a nobody trying to become a somebody to a somebody trying to become a nobody again.

Figure 8 Last leaf verso of Anon., *No-body and Some-body* (1606), I3v.

And like the premise of the play, the iconography of its bookended wood-
cuts renders undecidable the discursive valence of each position, which
is an author and which a clown, implying only their complementarity.
Atop a dancer's exaggerated legs, Nobody holds a scroll, a text, a script;
Somebody's meaty trunk grips at once the club of authority and the slapstick of the clown. Arrested in these two images is nothing less than early
modern theatre as a whole in mid-transformation. Kemp here straddles the
spreading center that has "rent" him "sunder," the new order from whose
emergent dichotomy he will be excluded. As Nobody, he personifies both

the textual condition to which he self-contradictorily aspired, and the self-negation it entailed. Yet this is a figure not just for authorship, but also for its corresponding type of clown, who had already begun to replace him – Armin's fool, the epitome of the actor, the persona that personates not a self-identical somebody, but everybody and nobody at once.

CHAPTER 5

Private practice

At the close of "A Jest of Tarltons Box on the Ear," we noted in Chapter 2, the narrator of *Tarltons Jests* glances disparagingly at Tarlton's successors: "But I would see our Clownes in these dayes doe the like," he says, "No, I warrant ye, and yet they think well of themselues too." Like the audience that cried "that again, that again, that again" in Chapter 1, he demands an impossible thing. On the one hand, he wants the pleasure of the spontaneous, the serendipitous, the "live," which Tarlton unfailingly provided. On the other hand, he wants an exact reproduction of that pleasure, "the like," which can no longer be "live" – a project in which his own book already participates. In the preceding two chapters, we saw both Tarlton and Kemp subjected to the pressures of reproducing their own performance textually. For Tarlton, who does not do it himself, the failure to improvise implies that he never did it himself, that all his theatrical production was reproduction; for Kemp, who does it himself, the participation texts disable makes reproduction the ideal mode of theatrical production. In both cases, they make these discoveries alone, in the pages of books: the devaluation and deconstitution of "live" performance is a conclusion the reader draws only after the fact. In this final case study, I turn to Robert Armin, the clown who replaced Kemp in the Lord Chamberlain's Men, and whom *Tarltons Jests* views as Tarlton's heir as well. He picks up their reluctant embrace of textuality, I argue, where they left off, and carries it much further – into the playhouse, making its experience a thoroughly mediated one. Armin was an author at the same time as a clown, identities he considered it necessary to intersplice. After tracing the development of his strategy in *Foole Upon Foole* (1600), in which he constructs his authorship out of multiplicity, I examine *Quips Upon Questions* (1600), which reduces multiplicity into performative singularity. *Quips* pretends to be a theatrical document, purporting to record the dialogic postlude of "themes," but as a reading experience, it collapses into schizophrenic monologue when its constituent voices are represented unintelligibly. It *became* a theatrical document only afterward, I contend, when Armin performed those "themes" exactly that way, as a solo, polyphonic medley, simulating both himself and the audience, and interacting with it as simulation. For Armin, all performance became a reproduction, or the reproduction of a reproduction, an endlessly looped script; for his audiences, theatre too became reading.

But before we come to that material, we must finally redress the critical tradition that categorically rejects clowning as compatible with fixed, iterable texts – as we have seen, clowning is precisely where the desire for them had been accumulating – and which insists that clowning's outright removal was a precondition of such texts. As a result, the relation of Armin's "fool" characters to his extradramatic persona has been obscured, as well as the fact that he performed postludes at all. As we will see, if what made clowning transgressive was improvisation, improvisation was considered destructive not because it destabilized the text of the play, but because it keyed audience participation, which destabilized the terms of the theatrical event itself. Armin's improvisation – if it can still be called that, or something much more complex – made the audience participate in its own erasure from that event.

The rise of the uncommon player

SIR HUMPHREY. How now, why stays that Fool?
FOOL. Because that Fool has more wit than to go away.
SIR HUMPHREY. I'll keep no Fool, 'tis out of fashion ... 'tis exploded ev'n upon the Stage.
FOOL. But for all that *Shakspear*'s Fools had more Wit than any of the Wits and Criticks now adays ... a vast number of Fools have been in Print, and written their own Histories.
           – Thomas Shadwell, *The Woman Captain* (1680), B2v

According to most narratives of early English theatre history, this book should now be at an end. So that narrative is worth reviewing. In "Staging Exclusion," an oft-cited chapter of *Forms of Nationhood* (1992), Richard Helgerson posited the year 1600 as the climax of an institutional "crisis" that replaced a "players' theater" with an "authors' theater," and that had thus pitted authors against players – in particular, against clowns. Central to that crisis was the "sociopolitical identity " of theatre, its ability to represent class distinction and thus to enjoy such distinction itself.[1] In 1590, the start of "the decade of maximum tension," the theatre is still "common": uniform in repertory, dependent on popular audiences, and produced by men of low origins whose newfound wealth afforded them rapid, controversial social mobility. Accordingly, its dramaturgy was "inclusive," showcasing the same "mixing [of] high and low" that the playhouse embodied.[2] At the same time, Marlowe's clarion call for "high astounding terms" announced a "shift in the weight of production and recognition toward the new non-player writers," a generation of university poets for whom "the gentility of poetry was endangered by their subjection to the begging rabble of players," and who therefore sought to ennoble their "base trade" by affirming elitist boundaries.[3] The opening of the Globe and the Fortune, the revival of the indoor halls, the rise of city satire, the bifurcation into "rival traditions" of citizen and coterie, the nationalization of patronage under James – for Helgerson, synthesizing work by Alfred Harbage, Annabel Patterson, Michael Bristol, Robert Weimann, and Walter Cohen, all these milestones in professional prestige were anticipated by a dramaturgy of divisiveness over the preceding decade.[4] The cultural legitimation of theatre was thus a function of the plays it staged, plays that "encode[d] a significant symbolic action." That action was exclusion.[5]

If playwrights wanted to stress class difference over and against the class fluidity that theatre represented, then the fluidity it actually *pre*sented, in its "mingling of kings and clowns," became a natural target of reform. Rather than sequester the two, dramatists devised a way of engaging popular culture that simultaneously renounced it. This vehicle was the chronicle history play. From *Jack Straw* to the May Day riot in *Sir Thomas More* to Falconbridge in *Edward IV*, popular revolt is carnivalized as self-defeating, its leaders caricatured as *Grand Guignol* villains and its utopian aims discredited.[6] Such parodies of populism not only barred commoners from a national vision, but obliquely pejoratized the clown, whose free speech disrupted the political hierarchy that the theatre sought to internalize. Once linked to rebellion, his festive inversion could be condemned, his improvisation censured, and the *platea* of the platform stage rendered an illicit space that violated the sovereign *locus* of a playwright allied with censor and crown.

This strategy played out acutely in the case of Shakespeare, Helgerson argues, who profited from it most, and whose own transition from lowly player to landed gentry personified the anxiety it assuaged. Having made sedition comically licentious in the figures of Jack Cade from *The First Part of the Contention* and Richard Crookback from *Richard III*, he proceeded to make comic license seditious, and to punish it accordingly – most memorably with Falstaff, whose banishment at the end of *2 Henry*

IV (upheld by *Henry V*) inaugurates Hal's Lenten civil policy.[7] These rites of exclusion culminated, finally, with the actual defection of Will Kemp from the Chamberlain's Men. Helgerson is understandably cautious about this coincidence, yet also unequivocal:

> There is no reason to think that the banishment of Falstaff caused this sep-
> aration. But the fictional event does have a proleptic relation to the factual
> one. The banishment of carnival from the proximity of politic rule fore-
> shadows the departure of Will Kemp from the Shakespearean theater. And
> when neither returns, the likeness is confirmed. (223)

Helgerson thus offers a bootstrap model of how a centralized "authors' theatre" unfolded through a kind of self-fulfilling determinism, in which the reiterated symbolic eventually becomes reality. Shakespeare's writing unilaterally
shaped the conditions necessary for that writing – plays – to be perceived as
products of a single creative agency, setting in motion his own "posthumous
elevation to the rank of major canonical poet."[8] And while Falstaff reappears
every time either of the *Henry IV* plays is staged, "he is there to be banished."[9]
Aligning the order of performance with the order of the state, the poet made
the clown the scapegoat for a popular tradition whose disgorgement became
the signature – and ultimately efficacious – digestive ritual of a theatre intent
on describing its activity as labor rather than holiday, as work rather than
play. The history of clowning ends with Kemp, and dramatic authorship
emerges in exact, satisfying conjunction with that end.

Previous chapters in this book should by now allow us to critique
the circularity of this account. Helgerson concedes the clown a role in
the development of an "authors' theatre," but that role remains entirely
penal: he is inscribed into it only as he is written out of it. We thus have
a narrative in which playwrights beget themselves, when the engine of
that parthenogenesis – the authority of the dramatic script to define the
nature of performance – was precisely at issue. The clown stops improvising because the poet says so; audiences stop expecting him to improvise because the poet says so; the effect of this process – that "a sharply
increasing share of public attention … was being paid to the texts as texts
and the authors as authors" – is also its cause.[10] This also presupposes the
dramatic fiction coterminous with the theatrical event, which was simply
not true. The problem is not that the repertory might call for Falstaff to be
reprised the *next* day, but that the *same* day's program required a clown –
for Helgerson, the same clown who had *just* played Falstaff – to dance a
jig that afternoon. That too seems a "significant symbolic action," of the

opposite kind. Insofar as the clown's theatrical role always exceeded his dramatic role, he was a survivor, and the theme of his performance was survival.

Helgerson adduces two factors to argue Kemp's exit more than coincidental, and part of a coordinated campaign of reform. The first was the subsequent abolition of jigs from the Globe. "The jig was anathema to the new authors' theater," Helgerson claims, because it was improvised, and improvisation constituted an intolerable challenge to an authorship that sought to emulate royal absolutism:

> On the *platea* ultimate authority belongs to the actor. In the *locus* it belongs to the author … the *platea* is an illicit space, a space given over to unauthorized speech and action. Without a fixed text, official censorship could have no effect. The unitary voice of the author and the unitary voice of the state would gladly combine to exclude the clown's disruptive and discordant improvisation. (224–25)

Thus the Chamberlain's Men eliminated the jig, wherein "the clown competes with the author for attention and control, producing a dialogic text in place of the monological scripted play."[11] As we saw in Chapter 4, this challenge was actually quite authorial in itself – producing not so much "dialogue" as two clashing monologues – and explains the vexation with which Kemp pursued it into print. Nevertheless, and still deferring the question of how plays came to be perceived as "monological" and "scripted" in the first place, Helgerson's model of internally driven reform requires a highly punctuated evolution. When the jig is gone, so is clowning as a whole, and the "players' theatre" it represents. After 1600, the Globe stage seemingly no longer has a *platea*.

Robert Armin was the comedian who replaced Kemp in 1599, and his chief value for theatre historians has been as the second factor to buttress the first. Thanks to the cathartic stress laid on Kemp's flight, Armin's career has been made to conform exactly to this narrative of rupture – a total submission to the rule of the playwright, preserved in the new line of comic character he supplied, "the Fool." For Helgerson, as for Leslie Hotson and others, the distinguishing trait of Armin's parts is their lack of distinction. In contrast to the clown, the fool is "socially unmarked," his motley signifying liminality rather than the class-specificity of the russet jerkin.[12] To the extent that he is courtly, he is also a feudal dependent, an idiot *savant*. Witty and wise, unlike the vulgar and witless clown, the fool speaks truth confusingly where the other spoke confusion truthfully; his ridicule is directed not at superiors but at the universality of folly, a mockery steeped in stoic tradition rather than in peasant protest. The Fool is thus a mimic, performing not himself but others. Whether dressed as a prince like Cloten, stripped to a beggar again like Autolycus, or whipped like Thersites and Caliban, whether aping the courtier like Touchstone, the lecher like Lavatch, or the drunkard like Carlo Buffone, he grotesques humanity itself, deforming all values but introducing none of his own. All these generalizations of "fool" characters seem true enough.

But above all, we are told, the Fool is just that – a character, confined to the plot of the play. Tarlton and Kemp *were* clowns, one might summarize the received binary, but Armin merely *played* the fool, a character who ended when the play did. Tarlton's and Kemp's roles always carry English names (Derrick, Peter, Launce, Dogberry) that pose little barrier to their reverting, in the postlude, to Tarlton and Kemp; Armin's roles are assimilated to the cultures of their fictive milieux, and their plot resolutions do not anticipate his solo return at the end. The fool never interacts with the audience, because he does not speak like it. The clown speaks in prose; the fool alternates between prose and verse. The clown answers obtusely and directly, the fool riddlingly and evasively. The clown thinks with his gut; the fool's language is both syntagmatic and paratactic, prone to figurative leaps and convolutions. Foremost among those he imitates, then, is the poet, who dictates his outpourings. Armin's speech patterns, for David Wiles, do not "suggest in any pointed way that the actor is extemporizing"; after 1600, "there no longer seems to be a dichotomy of poetic and extemporal styles."[13] Colin McCabe extends this principle from the play-texts to the daily structure of performance. With Armin, "the function of the clown must now be integrated into action and character, and there is no integral place for a concluding jig." He may take on the clown's duty of constituting an alterity from which to comment on the play, but it is "an alternative world located in his own misshapen body rather than in his relation to the audience."[14] The "fool's privilege" that, as Charles Felver put it, is both "his passport and his license" thus also bears the stamp of subjection: he appears "free" to say anything only because it has been allowed by the playwright.[15] In place of the clown – a stand-up comic only moonlighting as an actor – Shakespeare supposedly substituted an actor who merely played a comic, an extension of the author's words and will.

This is a remarkable about-face, meant to supply the strong authorial agency an "expulsion" narrative demands. That narrative can work, indeed, only with a selective and retrospectively linear approach to the evidence. "The Fool" no more became the King's Men's dominant comic type under Armin than did "the clown" vanish with Kemp's exit. If anything, their fates are intertwined. Though Armin is a court fool in *As You Like It* and *Twelfth Night*, he remains "Clown" in speech prefixes and stage directions; though he has no name but "Clowne" in George Wilkins' *Miseries of Enforced Marriage* (c. 1606) and plays a servingman, he is described as "a philosophicall foole" for his cryptic wit.[16] On the one hand, in his frequent juxtaposition with genuinely rustic scene partners – the *parvenu* Sogliardo in *Every Man Out*, or Corin and William in *As You Like It*, all the way to "Shepherd" and "Clown" in *The Winter's Tale* – there seems an effort to dislodge Armin's comic function from its former social signifiers. Yet on the other hand, those significations were actively perpetuated in the other, more traditional clown parts still being written for him: plebs and bumpkins like *Hamlet's* Gravedigger, *Macbeth's* Porter, *Measure for Measure's* Pompey Bum, *The Fair Maid of Bristow's* Frog, *Henry V's* Nym, as well as the nameless walk-ons in *Othello* and *Antony and Cleopatra*.[17] Since the repertory entailed Armin's inheritance of most of Kemp's roles, indeed, the ongoing provision of these class-marked comic parts indicates a corporate investment in sustaining convention too.[18] By the same token, Shakespeare was not alone in writing these parts, and so not alone in originating Armin's "fool" characters either – it seems a compositional parameter available to anyone writing for him. As reductive taxonomies for the dramatic roles a leading comedian might take on a given day, "clown" and "fool" had little bearing on his overarching theatrical persona, which transcended individual plays. Insofar as that persona might take dramatic reinforcement, however, the disparate associations of "clown" and "fool" mattered, and their constant alternation for Armin suggests an attempt to suspend two performance codes under one performer – keeping his Kemp profile intact, while incrementally modulating it toward the mimetic possibilities his talents began to present.

Those possibilities came, this chapter argues, out of precisely that mode of clown performance the expulsion narrative says he was not supposed to be still indulging: the postlude. After 1600, no less than before, the clown's fictional roles still derived from his solo practice – and the clown, even the Chamberlain's/King's Men's clown, retained such a practice. If Armin's dramatic characters are more chameleonic, it is because his extradramatic one was as well. That very inscrutability, as we will see, was simultaneously the basis of his routines and the reason they left so little cultural trace compared to those of his predecessors. Unlike Tarlton's or Kemp's, much of the evidence for Armin's extracurricular activities is preserved in the plays themselves, because their effect was to elide the boundary between the two. To be sure, Armin probably never danced jigs at the Globe. From the musicality of his parts we can infer that he was hired for his singing, and from what we can surmise of his puny physique, it seems equally likely that he was *not* much of a dancer. But as we have seen, the jig was not the limit of the clown's repertoire, nor even his most complete occupation of the *platea*. The Chamberlain's Men's commitment to phase out one genre of clown postlude was not, nor could it have been, a wholesale rejection of clowning in general; indeed, weaning audiences off one genre might well have intensified the appetite for another. And in that refocused demand – depending on the clown – lay opportunity.

Interlocutions

> *WITHIN.* Mr. *Pollard*, wher's Mr. *Pollard* for the Epilogue?
> (*He is thrust upon the Stage, and falls.*)
> EPILOGUE. I am coming to you Gentlemen, the Poet
> Has help'd me thus far on my way, but I'll
> Be even with him.
> – James Shirley, *The Cardinal* (*c.* 1641), F3v

That inescapable inertial force, the audience, brings us to the final inadequacy of any account of institutional reform driven by a tension between playwright and player. The expulsion narrative unfolds in a vacuum, already cut off from the very entity whose cutting off it is about. Neither the turning of the year 1600, nor the turnover of particular players, nor the social ambitions of playwrights, nor a succession of anti-populist plays could do anything to alter the fundamental dynamic of playgoing; the "alienation of ... the people from the nation," in Helgerson's phrase, did not mean their alienation from the *theatre*, for the form of early modern theatre is not reducible to its dramatic content.[19] That form, as we have seen, constituted a drama of its own, to which the clown and his entertainments remained indispensable. Otherwise, the Chamberlain's Men might have gotten rid of Kemp any time they chose; that they did not implies a need for him in the first place, and enough urgency to that need for a new clown to be ready to replace him.

The expulsion myth, after all, neglects a major complication: persistence. Clowns came and went, but clown*ing* did what it did best: it survived. And it did so across theatrical stratifications. For the Admiral's Men, royal promotion in 1603 portended no significant realignment of personnel. Upon the death of their clown John Singer in the same year that they became the Prince's Men, they promptly replaced him with John Shanke, even fifty years later remembered as "*John Shank* for a Jig."[20] Worcester's Men, upon becoming Queen Anne's Men, replaced Kemp with the even more outrageous Thomas Greene; when Greene died, in turn, he was replaced by Will Robins.[21] And while both companies, at the Fortune and the Red Bull respectively, were identified with the stalwart citizens' theatre whose jigs the Middlesex Sessions banned in 1612, that stigma did not prevent the King's Men from acquiring Shanke for themselves in 1613 upon Armin's retirement.[22] Whatever Armin was, he was the aberration, not the new norm; and whatever he did, it was actually followed by the *return* of jigs to the Globe. If the clown was "anathema" to Shakespeare's political agenda, his company apparently disagreed: we must ascribe to him a subtler agenda, then, and probably a shared one.

To the audience, indeed, there was no "players' theatre" or (much less) "authors' theatre"; there was only the audience's theatre, for which the term "player" here comes misleadingly to stand. To the audience, player and author were already on the same side – the side with the stage, the side that claimed theatrical production for itself. As we saw in Chapters 1 and 2, the audience wanted to make the same claim, or at least constitutionally to resist the first. For Helgerson, the clown's improvisations are always "disruptive and discordant," because they are not "the monological scripted play." Yet this imagines his performance as just another monologue: something not in the play, perhaps, but still originating from the stage. Were this all improvisation meant, it would pose no problem to a model of theatre desirous of "fixed texts," because the theatre still produces that text. Its production is merely distributed across multiple creative agencies – no differently from a play with multiple authors – and the theatre can decide for itself what that final text is. A particulate series of monological texts is no better or worse than a single one. Yet to say that "on the *platea* ultimate authority belongs to the actor" is to misconstrue – simply by using the word "actor" – the *platea* as another *locus*. When the clown spoke, he produced a "dialogic" text not because he improvised, but because he did not speak alone. The trouble with improvisation was *participation* – the audience it invariably licensed to speak in turn.

When dramatists openly censure improvisation, this is the consequence they have in mind: not the sheer fact of deviation from the script, but the surrender of institutional autonomy thereby. The gentleman playwright LeToy in Brome's *The Antipodes* (1638) is happy to let his clown Byplay improvise, so long as he affirms rather than undermines the basic integrity of his own performance:

> LET.   Well Sir my Actors
> Are all in readinesse; and I think all perfect,
> But one, that never will be perfect in a thing

> He studies; yet he makes such shifts extempore,
> (Knowing the purpose what he is to speak to)
> That he moves mirth in me 'bove all the rest.
> For I am none of those Poeticke furies,
> That threats the Actors life, in a whole play,
> That adds a sillable, or takes away.
> If he can frible through, and move delight
> In others, I am pleas'd. (D2v)

"Fribbling" could be the mark of a poor actor as well, of course, like the country players in *The Mayor of Quinborough* (*c.* 1606) who purchase printed plays, read them once, and merely "fribble out the rest."[23] Nonetheless, it is still the mark of an *actor*, whose aim is to reproduce a *script* – even when that script, as in the *commedia* tradition, prescribes only a scenario and a character on which to build.[24] Throughout the 1590s and 1600s – the period of clown "censorship" Helgerson considers, in some of the very same plays – we find playbooks whose stage directions explicitly task clowns to "speak more than is set down": "*He playes and sings any odde toy*"; "*Jackie is led to whipping over the stage, speaking some word, but of no importance*"; "*Exit clown, speaking anything*"; "*speake any thing, and Exit*"; "*Here they two talk and rail what they list.*"[25] In a repertory system with perhaps no more than one rehearsal, it was natural for dramatists to leave expansion brackets for error, logistics, and whimsy, and even for such ad-libs to accrete to the book itself.[26] Clowns were extemporizers, and could be trusted to find the comic potential of a scene. Within the framework of the play, as without, they kept the performance intact as a performance, and augmented it where necessary.

What LeToy will not tolerate from Byplay, however – and where he now becomes jealous of the labor he was otherwise content to distribute – is precisely when Byplay cedes possession of the performance as a whole:

> LET. But you Sir are incorrigible, and
>   Take licence to your selfe, to adde unto
>   Your parts, your owne free fancy; and sometimes
>   To alter, or diminish what the writer
>   With care and skill compos'd: and when you are
>   To speake to your coactors in the Scene,
>   You hold interloquutions with the Audients.
> BIP. That is a way my Lord has bin allow'd
>   On elder stages to move mirth and laughter.
> LET. Yes in the dayes of *Tarlton* and *Kempe*,
>   Before the stage was purg'd from barbarisme,
>   And brought to the perfection it now shines with. (D3v)

Like Sidney, LeToy is attuned to the difference between moving "delight" and moving "laughter": one invites an aesthetic response, the other a physical one. Improvising *before* the crowd is mastery; improvising *for* them, on the other hand, is the opposite, confessing the material dependence of performance on them, and thus reducing it to a collaborative, unpredictable social event. The need for a "fixed text" was not to censor the clown, but to censor the audience. For as we have seen, the true obstacle to the cultural legitimation of theatre was never its politics, but its economic coherence – the ability to claim ownership of its production by demarcating it from consumption. Or, we might say that its politics always remain captive to its economics. A theatre cannot withdraw from popular culture when that withdrawal is staged *for* the populace, its suffrage still enshrined both in entry fees and in the conventions of reception. For John Stephens in 1615, "a common player" is one who, "when he doth hold conference vpon the stage, and should looke directly in his fellows face, hee turnes about his voice into the assembly for applause-sake … so howsoeuer hee pretends to haue a royall Master or Mistresse, his wages and dependance proue him to be the seruant of the people."[27] Even soliciting applause is "interloquution": by recognizing the presence of the audience, the performer realizes it, opening the play to their validation and the stage to their vocalizations. This is Hamlet's "pittifull ambition," the clowns who "will themselues laugh, to set on some quantitie of barraine spectators to laugh too"; insofar as it extends production into the audience, improvisation did not just introduce another script on top of the original, it subverted the idea of "script" itself, and of theatre as an art form privately or even finally produced.[28] Thus the obsequious Post-Haste in Marston's *Histriomastix* (1599), aware that his company's performance of "The Prodigal Child" is flopping, does not hesitate to move straight into the postlude: "My Lords … if you a theame affords," he intercedes, "I … extempore can sing."[29] For Stephens, players can amass all the wealth and prestige they want: no matter how their plays dramatize high subjects or thematize "distinction," in their formal porousness they remain "common." As long as they cannot distinguish their own production from that of their audiences, players produce nothing but a means for those audiences to produce themselves.

The more egregious "interloquutions" of clowning thus merely exposed what was base about all commercial playing: the fact that, since the public provided the financial substance of theatre, it was entitled to be its material substance as well. As late as 1634, the legal foundation of this relationship is still expressed by the Prologue to Shirley's *The Example*, who meekly asks the Cock-pit audience not to "entaile like land / Upon heires male all action, and command / Of voice and gesture."[30] If the stage is here literally real estate, only temporarily and uneasily leased from its rightful owners for the duration of the play, then the disagreeable compromise of the clown's entertainment was to restore it. Dekker gives us the best textual representation of that restoration, and for him the point is precisely its resistance to textual representation:

> And as I haue often seene, after the finishing of some worthy Tragedy, or Catastrophe in the open Theaters, that the Sceane after the Epilogue hath beene more blacke (about a nasty bawdy Jigge) then the most horrid Sceane in the Play was: The Stinkards speaking all things, yet no man understanding any thing; a mutiny being amongst them, yet none in danger: no tumult, and yet no quietnesse: no mischife begotten, and yet mischiefe borne: the swiftnesse of such a torrent, the more it ouerwhelmes, breeding the more pleasure.[31]

The description "ouerwhelmes" even the very "nasty bawdy Jigge" at its center: whatever performance occurs onstage is completely subsumed into the audience's own, because the difference between them has been erased. The 1612 Middlesex ban on jigs at the Fortune specifically targets "divers cutt-purses and other lewde and ill disposed persons in great multitudes [who] doe resorte thither *at th'end of euerye playe*" – telling us that at this point, entry was no longer policed, and the playhouse was seemingly opened to all.[32] If participation acknowledged theatre's embeddedness in the market, a marketplace is also what it reverted theatrical space into: a commons, its inside indistinct from its outside, all trace of proprietary production now abandoned. Both fiscally and discursively, the clown coda was where theatre forfeited itself, where it simply ceased being theatre.

And yet despite LeToy's remonstrations, it is precisely Byplay's *failure* to engage the audience that almost results in his play's premature collapse. *The Antipodes* is meant as aversion therapy for its humorous spectators, but the one thing their humors refuse to let them be is spectators. The neglected young wife Martha registers aloud every personal reflection the play prompts; the flirtatious Diana chats with the players; Joyless deflates the whole enterprise with constant, caustic commentary. In the course of warning them to desist, even LeToy becomes guilty of "interrupt[ing] your Actors, and ty[ing] them / To lengthen time in silence, while you hold / Discourse by th'by."[33] Worst of all, Peregrine, who suffers from Mandeville syndrome and believes he has journeyed to the opposite end of the world, so accepts the play's reality that he wishes to join it. Instructed not to break character, Byplay has no choice but to admit him backstage, whereupon disaster ensues:

BIP. He has got into our Tyring-house amongst us,
  And ta'en a strict survey of all our properties …
  When on the suddaine, with thrice knightly force,
  And thrice, thrice, puissant arme he snatcheth downe
  The sword and shield that *I* playd *Bevis* with,
  Rusheth amongst the foresaid properties,
  Kills Monster, after Monster; takes the Puppets
  Prisoners, knocks downe the Cyclops, tumbles all
  Our jigambobs and trinckets to the wall …
  He takes the imperiall diadem and crownes
  Himselfe King of the *Antipodes*. (G1v)

The burghers at LeToy's rural estate are not a paying audience, but Peregrine's delusion follows the tyrannical pathology of one, relentlessly seeking out their own avenues of involvement in the performance when such outlets are neither accommodated nor forcibly opposed. The play thus paints a no-win scenario: because it refuses interlocutory improvisation, it eventually comes to consist of nothing *but* such improvisation when it is altogether overrun by its impetuous auditors, hastily reorganizing its plot around Peregrine in order to salvage its design. The script can recover itself, of course, because the intrusions are a part of it. Yet it is worth noting that the entire corpus of early modern drama features not one play-within-a-play wherein the onstage audience does *not* talk to the actors, or to itself, or otherwise disrupt and invade the proceedings.[34] To the extent that these devices represent contemporaneous theatrical reception, they are more realistic than corrective; indeed, their only disciplinary function – aside from parody – seems merely to pre-empt such interference from the real audience, by doing it for them.

While the reduplicative elegance of this solution is worth bearing in mind, it only further illustrates the problem. You could not just *stop* addressing the audience, for the audience never stopped demanding inclusion – and, as we have seen (and will continue to see), was always ready to satisfy itself on its own terms. Improvisation was compulsory, because participation was inevitable, and the desire for it constitutional. Manifesting their presence was simply what early modern audiences did, and the idea of a theatre capable of transpiring in their absence utterly alien to their understanding. Unless every play could unfold as a play-within-a-play – and several, *The Taming of the Shrew* and *The Knight of the Burning Pestle* among them, try it – clowning remained necessary to absorb such self-projecting energies. The clown may have triggered the release of those energies, but he was not their cause; he was their symptom. The *platea* could not be closed simply by vacating it – it was always there, and had to be filled by someone, or else it could be filled by anyone. Keeping it open to include the audience, the clown impeded theatre's articulation with textuality, denying the dramatic script identity with the theatrical event. Yet he did so only to keep the *platea* from opening completely: impeding the audience as well, he was the guarantor of performance in the first place.

We might conclude our discussion of the expulsion narrative, then, which has recapitulated much of my first two chapters, like this: if the London theatre before 1600 was at all a "players' theatre," it was characterized by precisely this ambiguity of what a "player" was, and by sucessive efforts – invariably focused on its most liminal figure – to resolve it. Who does the clown work for? Was he a factor of the audience, mediating their access to the stage? Or was he akin to the playwright, facilitating dramatic representation from outside it? Could his own work be made visible *as* "work," so that the integrity of theatrical labor might pass through his performance instead of passing out with it? Until now, as we saw in Chapters 3 and 4, there had been only retroactive attempts to revise the meaning of his practice, and to push the term "player" into the column of "author" rather than "audience." The clown must become either an actor, or an author himself – or both, but thus far never both at once. Tarlton is made a posthumous author to be made an actor, his speech running out with his text; Kemp, fearing he may be just an actor, runs away into authorship, into a text from which he never emerges. One loses his soul but gains a body; the other retains his soul but loses his body. Each becomes a kind of ghost, the origin of their performance removed to words on a page – someone else's or their own. Either way, who they were onstage is changed. The performing body is dislocated, never centered in itself, always looking before or after; performance is evacuated of presence.

That, at least, is the goal of these interventions. Their impact is purely imaginary, because they cannot or will not put that dissociated body onstage again; their retreats into the space of the book are self-terminating, creating irreconcilable disjunctions only with *previous* theatrical experience. To be meaningful, they had to become the basis of *new* theatrical experience. What was missing, in other words, was a mode of clowning that *internalized* textuality, and imported it back into performance – that performed, from within its traditionally "live" genres, the performer himself as missing, and performance as not really live. The survival of clowning after Tarlton and Kemp is not a blemish to be ignored or explained away, but an explanatory asset: if it persisted alongside the rise of dramatic textuality, then we must think of it as related. A playbook is a theatre without bodies or audience: for theatre to become commensurable with playbooks, someone had to simulate – with his body, for those very audiences – the feeling of already being inside a playbook, in the midst of the playhouse itself. And they had to do it to the one area of performance where "liveness" was maximal, that was supposed to resist textual finality or propriety, that could never be a book: the postlude. What was needed was not less clown authorship, but more – a clown who textualized his practice not after the fact but in real time, who scripted both himself and the audience together.

If the Chamberlain's Men became invested in an "authors' theatre" around 1600, indeed, it was only as the term "player" fully merged with "author" rather than diverged from it. Because the underlying concern of such a theatre was ownership of performance, it had to be effected through performance, so that "clown" and "author" actually became, if only for a moment, phenomenologically equivalent positions. William Shakespeare's was not the only print authorship that the company was promoting in 1600, nor was the replacement of Will Kemp purely a subtractive calculation. Launching their bid for distinction from a theatre that had yet to be paid for, they had to give audiences what they wanted – "interlocution" – while simultaneously withholding it, somehow reclaiming the *platea* from *within* the *platea*. Their ironic solution was to pick up exactly where Kemp had left off – to make the *platea* its own *locus*, by converting its dialogue to monologue. Robert Armin would prove that you could have improvisation without participation; you could even have improvisation, indeed, without improvisation. Not every play could be a play-within-a-play, but perhaps what came after it could.

Dark enigma

Armin's stage career is graced with a foundation myth that, at the same time as establishing his comic pedigree, also foreshadows its trajectory. In 1600, his first full year with the Chamberlain's Men, the latest edition of *Tarltons Jests* added a story about him. Armin is here a boy, a goldsmith's apprentice sent to collect a bill from the manager of Tarlton's tavern, who refuses to pay. In revenge, "with Chalke on a Wain-scote," Armin scrawls a verse graffito deriding the debtor's poverty. Tarlton, "partly acquainted with the boyes humour," reads it, and so admires its wit that he writes a reply: "A wagge thou art, none can preuent thee; / And thy desert shall content thee … As I am, so in time thou'lt be the same, / My adopted sonne therefore be, / To enioy my Clownes sute after me."[35] Armin "so loued *Tarlton* after" that he "used to his Playes, and fell in league with his humour," becoming his protégé; "priuate practice brought him to present playing, and at this houre performes the same, where, at the Globe on the Banks side men may see him."

It is a strange anecdote to find in a volume premised on Tarlton's uniqueness, subjecting him to a replication that potentially renders the book itself obsolete. Tarlton declares his own living successor, an "adopted sonne" to whom he passes both his comic style and its material substance, and to whose well-honed enactment of "the same," "at this houre," the archival project of *Tarltons Jests* must defer. We do not have to settle for textual recovery: if we want to see the closest thing to Tarlton, we are told where to go. And yet the story also posits a hereditary structure to clowning that embeds Armin in the wrong medium. The transfer of vatic authority occurs entirely through writing, the once and future clowns appraising each other across dueling epigrams; it is left unclear when, or even if, the two ever meet. The intimacy of mentorship, likewise, devolves into the solitude of that curious phrase "private practice." Is this "private practice," rather than "Tarlton," the antecedent of "the same" that Armin now performs? If not "Tarlton," then is the product of Armin's "private practice" even "Armin"? And how does one "practice" clowning privately, when its fundamental prerequisite is an audience? Can one rehearse spontaneous wit? By the time the jest directs us beyond the book, we are not so sure the Globe stage is a qualitatively different space. It wants to naturalize and validate Armin's theatrical lineage, yet it does the opposite: even in his myth of origin, it is precisely his origin that is questioned. Already, for Armin, an attenuation seems at work, whereby a textual distance intercedes between performance and the agency of the performer.

That may be because Armin's "practice," in fact rather than myth, was initially not as a player but as a writer. Prior to surfacing on the theatrical scene in the late 1590s with the Lord Chandos' Men, and even before becoming free of the goldsmiths in 1592, Armin had evidently achieved a modest literary reputation for himself. Nashe in *Strange Newes* (1592) mentions him alongside the balladeers William Elderton, Thomas Deloney, and Philip Stubbes, whom he calls upon to scandalize Harvey; in *Pierces Supererogation* (1593), Harvey likewise lists him among "the common Pamfletters of London."[36] None of these early publications survives, but the commendatory epistle prefixed to *A Briefe Resolution of a Right Religion* (1590) and signed "R. Armin" implies considerable weight to his

name – the tract's author, by contrast, remains anonymous. The earnest-
ness of the epistle's tone, as well as its context, furthermore imply no particular theatrical profile to the writer: sober praise for the "learning" and
"plainness" of an otherwise unremarkable anti-Catholic *sic credo* hardly
seems consistent with the heir of Tarlton's "clownes sute." One is tempted
to speculate that this "R. Armin" of piety and judgment was an altogether
different Armin – which, in a manner of speaking, is almost true.

The year 1590 was not one for casual sallies into religious debate. Sure
enough, the epistle goes out of its way to rebuke a constituency the tract
itself never addresses:

> The other vitious and detestable sect, are Martinestes, who see so farre into
> matters, that they ouersee themselues, wresting thinges from the right sence
> to the wrong, making shew of zeale when it is meere follie ... (A2v)

The possibility raised by such a partisan statement – that Armin cut his
teeth as a satirist during the Marprelate controversy, hence his authority to
endorse *A Briefe Resolution* – has important implications for the sensibility
he brought to the theatre. Had he taken part in this seminal collision of
print and public sphere, he would have engaged in rapid-fire skirmishes
where today's attacker was tomorrow's victim, where the power of textual utterance to outpace its speaker also made it vulnerable to returning
carved into ridicule or perverted into character assassination. Before he
was ever Armin the clown, Armin the pamphleteer would have been alert
to the anxiety of controlling a rhetorical persona that instantly became
public domain. And for that reason, he would have grasped the value of a
rhetorical mode whose every locution anticipated, contained, and thereby
disarmed counterfactual rebuttals. Under such paranoid conditions, that
is, the best defense was a constant offense, a calculated schizophrenia. The
Marprelate episode taught English polemic to talk to itself – or, rather, to
talk *as* both itself and its adversary at once: as the glossolalic, motormouth
prose styles of Nashe and Greene illustrate, maintaining one's authority
came to rest partly in dissolving its integrity, in assuming and assimilat-
ing the subjectivities of imaginary opponents. If an analogous mode of
mimetic pre-emption would inform Armin's stage practice, it was because
print already simulated the same siege mentality as clowning. Indeed, insofar as these textual strategies had themselves emulated the combative animus of the clown – a great deal of the anti-Martinist backlash was carried
out from the playhouses – Armin represented merely the repatriation of
theatrical techniques that had been processed through another medium.[37]
Coming to the theatre from the world of print, however, gave Armin the

perspective to see the two as equivalent forms of self-publication, and to use them in tandem. Even as he became a performer, he never stopped being a writer: shuttling ceaselessly between page and stage, for Armin the way to negotiate each was to interpenetrate it with the other.

We can see half of this formula at work in one of the two books Armin published in 1600 – his most active year in print, and also his first at the Globe.[38] *Foole Upon Foole* is an album of long-form jests, compiled from the "lives, humours and behauiours" of "six sortes of sottes," from village idiots like Jack Oates, Jack Miller, Lean Leonard of Sherwood and Blue John of Christ's Hospital, to court fools like Will Sommers and Jemy Camber. Modern readers are often seduced by the collection's documentary flavor into the belief that Armin here founds his theatrical credentials upon these historical originals: as an actor, he is obviously an "artificial" fool, but he wants to show himself a student of "natural" ones. On the one hand, this is to take the book a bit too seriously as personal performance: foolbooks were a fad at the turn of the century – two others appeared the same year and five more over the next decade – and no discrete "Armin" ever emerges in contradistinction to these portraits to state a motive of professional research.[39] Yet for that very reason, on the other hand, *Foole Upon Foole* has also not been taken seriously enough as personal performance. Its figures are not character studies for Armin, for he is already in character even before introducing them: the imitative poetics of his craft are sketched not in the pamphlet's text, but in its paratexts, where "fool" becomes merely the name for an operation of self-dispersal.

That process begins on the rather busy title page. (See Figure 9.) Beneath the main title and subtitle, the six fools are paired into assonant epithets – "A flat foole / A fatt foole," "A leane foole / A cleane foole," "A merry foole / A verry foole" – to be read from left to right. The separation of left and right pairs by a set of triple braces, however, also divides them into two groups of three, so that we may just as easily read from top to bottom. To read the phrases correctly, we discover – that is, in the order corresponding to their actual sequence in the volume – thus requires treating the braces as multiplication brackets, and performing that multiplication on the "and" suspended between them: though there is one "and" on the page, the braces force our eye through it thrice. Then, after a boilerplate analytic of the volume's contents ("Not so strange as true"), a Latin motto: *omnia sunt sex* [all are six] – not a motto at all, but merely a Latin reiteration of the number of fools once again, which we already know. Next, in place of a byline, we get an evasion that seemingly distributes the author through multiple prior constructions. He is the offspring of two parents

FOOLE

VPON FOOLE,

OR

Six sortes of Sottes.

A flat foole				A fatt foole.
A leane foole	and		A cleane foole.
A merry foole			A verry foole.

Shewing their liues, humours and behauiours, with their
want of wit in their shew of wisdome. Not so strange as true

Omnia sunt sex.

Written by one, seeming to haue his mothers witte,
when some say he is fild with his fathers fopperie, and hopes
he liues not without companie.

Clonnico de Curtanio Snuffe.

*Not amisse to be read, no matter to regard it :
Yet stands in some stead, though he that made it mar'd it.*

LONDON

Printed for William Ferbrand , dwelling neere
Guild-hall gate ouer againft the Maiden-head.

1600.

Figure 9   Title page of Robert Armin, *Foole Upon Foole* (1600), A1r.

("seeming to have his mothers witte" and "fild with his fathers fopperie"), and also a product of public discourse, since "some say" he possesses these qualities; if a byline is a space of distinction, this one expresses a wish for even less distinction, hoping that "he liues not without companie." And yet such radical vagueness is followed by the very specificity it resisted: "*Clonnico del Curtanio Snuffe*," Snuff, clown of the Curtain – just like the gap between the previous blurbs, whose "*omnia sunt sex*" flowed directly into "Written by one."

The title page (perhaps even the title itself) of *Foole Upon Foole* thus becomes an exercise in visual poetics, and a kind of essay on authorship therein. Awash in numerical relationships whose configurations keep shifting, it repeatedly expands singularity into multiplicity only to collapse them again, alternating between scenarios where many make one and one makes many. The final verse performs another series of self-cancellations: "*Not amisse to be read, no matter to regard it: / Yet it stands in some stead, though he that made it mar'd it.*" Even in the third person, Armin refuses to be fixed as a speaking subject with a stable viewpoint; where we expect to hear him, we hear many. Yet at the same time, where we think we see others, we see one: like the white space of a title page, or the "and" inside two dilemmas, Armin materializes in the space behind and between other agencies. Even the curious snail ornament above the colophon participates in this effect. In hindsight, we know it belongs to the printer Edward Allde – he would use it on another book in 1602. In 1600, though, it was new, and Allde's name is otherwise absent; we are consequently unsure whether to read it bibliographically or thematically. Is it a printer's device, or an emblem? Are the snail's horns a fool's coxcomb? Does its shell symbolize a cryptic nature? Where the title page should locate the author, *Foole Upon Foole*'s fails; and yet at the bottom, precisely where the book turns itself over to the signs of collaborative production, the author pops up to usurp them.

The subsequent paratexts pick up on this idea, and develop it vocally rather than visually. Armin now addresses those collaborative agents, writing a letter to the printer and to the binder of the book he is writing, and appealing for diligence in its assembly. Or, more precisely, the book itself conveys the request: "*He that made me doth persuade thee, to print pure, / With increase of care to worke fayre, and to sow sure.*"[40] Making a book is a conversation, the epistle seems to acknowledge, and Armin stages the economic basis of that partnership literally *as* conversation:

> Take heede then and let vs lay our heades together: not to be faulty in our labour: I in writing, you in working, least our tytle be layd to our charge …

euery man shall carry his owne burthen, let vs be wise if we can, and ioyne
to defend this hard world: You'll say if my writing had been better, your
printing had had more profit: true so I: And againe, I say that if your printing be perfect, my vnperfect writing will the better passe: is not this good
than, when one can help another? (A2r)

Sealing their solidarity with the pledge that "so we two liue t'is no matter if all the world dye," the intersubjective performance yields for Nora
Johnson a "frank cynicism" pushed to "Swiftian levels of irony": "Yet,"
he continues, "if … all els dye, what shall the seller doe that bestowes
the impression? nay what shall people doe when none liues to buy his
bookes[?]"[41] Johnson, focused on the fool tradition as the content of
Armin's authorship rather than as its method of inscription, reads in this
moment of callousness a remorse for his exploitation of figures associated
with a charity economy. Making "the death of the entire reading public
… a tragedy of unprofitable investment in the printing of a book" thus
regretfully registers the human costs of "the privatization of … shared
property."[42]

But Armin is beyond the morally conflicted stance Johnson assigns him,
I think, for such theft extends to the shared property of the book itself. At
the same time as he acknowledges publication collaborative, mingling his
labor and his voice with those of his workmen, Armin also speaks from
the voice of the very book supposedly dependent on them for embodiment. The same epistle that incorporates their perspective and values their
contribution also nullifies it, by suggesting from the outset that the book
is already fully formed without them. With each block of type they set,
they reveal a book that claims to exist before they ever set those blocks of
type; they are made to participate in exposing their participation as a fiction.[43] "Commaund me," reads Armin's valediction to the printer – a submission that is itself a command.[44] The closing sentiment that "so we two
liue t'is no matter if all the world dye," then, does not even leave room for
two, and it reinforces the conceit of the epistle: a book that transcends its
materiality, here preceding its own producers just as it disdains the need
for consumers.

This entity – the book not as object, but as *text* – becomes coterminous with the author precisely to the extent that it systematically admits
other, non-authorial agencies it then surrounds and swallows. If the book's
material life involves sources, mediations, and receptions that compromise its exclusive ownership, Armin's technique is to dramatize that life, and
in so doing circumscribe it. Thus with the book's readers as with its printers, whom he next addresses, wishing "as much health as to my selfe." We

are of course free to say about the book whatever we want, he tells us, even if those opinions are harsh; he even anticipates what we will say, in fact, so that suddenly the book is speaking for us:

> yet I wonder not that thou thinkest ill: for the common course is such, the more is the pitty. What ist a new booke sayes one? I sayes another, tis call'd foole vpon foole: nay like enough sayes the first, fooles write as their wit workes. (A2v)

Where earlier the book performed its own manufacture, now it performs its own critique. The same feigned gesture of opening toward an imaginary readership is reiterated in the volume's coda, only this time with an even sharper, more ironic foreclosure:

> Thus Gentlemen as the kinde Hoastes salutes her guestes, saying you see your cheere, and you are welcome: euen so say I, desiring that you wil pardon my folly, in writing of folly: which folly can no way be excused but by your fauour: so as *Cæsar* said *Veni vidi vici*. I am bolde to busie your braine with any darke *Enigma*. Wherefore if my pardon may be purchased then so, if not, the worst is you will say the Author may keep his six fooles company. (F4r)

Armin here assumes the fool's posture, not only begging our forgiveness but following it with the bizarre *non sequitur* of "*Veni vidi vici*." Yet the seemingly random phrase proves apt here, for by delimiting our choice of response, he also determines it: either we pardon his folly, or we naturalize it to that of the other fools in the volume, which is the volume's mission. Success and failure are conditioned as the same, and once again the book invites participation only to render it superfluous. Indeed, the passage performs that surreptitious consolidation of property in its very terminology. As the book ends, it reveals itself never to have been ours at all, but merely a rented space that "Hoast[ed]"ed us. Here, at the moment Armin submits to a public judgment he himself frames and conducts, he can also for the first time call himself "the Author."

If *Foole Upon Foole* culminates with the equation of "fool" and "author," indeed, it has been developing it all along, transacting it across Armin's subjects themselves. The fool is a solipsism, an absence, his "dark enigma" consisting in the illusion of interactive discourse. Jack Oates plays cards "all alone," talks to the deck, and a passing servingman thinks he calls him a knave; Leonard "lock[s] himselfe into a Parler," plays shuffleboard with no coins, "out-sweares" phantom playmates "with a thousand oathes," and destroys the room in fits of rage; asked the cost of anything – be it his coat, his cap, or his beard – Blue John always replies "a groat."[45] Armin's authorial strategy is no different: the more a text seems to talk to others, the larger the universe in which it talks only to itself, and he peppers his narration with dialogic devices – editorial asides, rhetorical questions, verse prologues introducing each figure – that simulate oral performance.[46] At one point, in the middle of a jest, the narrator even merges with those figures. Upon a visit by "the Lord Shandoyes Players" to his town, Jack Miller becomes enamored of their clown, whom he names "Grumball" – Jack's name for himself, we learn, when "he would imitate playes dooing all himselfe, King, Clowne, Gentleman and all."[47] To prevent him from running off with the players at their departure, the townspeople lock Jack in a garret, yet from the window he sees them crossing the thinly frozen river Haven:

> But he I say seeing them goe by, creepes through the window, and sayde I come to thee Grumball ... he got downe very daungerously, and makes no more adoe but boldly ventures over the Hauen ... my heart aked to see it, and my eares heard the Ize crackt all the way: when he was come unto them, I was amazed, and tooke up a brickbat (which there lay by) and threwe it, which no sooner fell upon the Ize but it burst. (D4v)

Armin may have toured with Lord Chandos' Men before joining the Chamberlain's – "this is true," he reiterates, "my eyes were witnesses being then by" – but the moment's significance is more than biographical.[48] If Armin is an artificial fool, it records nothing less than the instant of his making, here figured as the conversion of folly into a purely textual effect. The marvel of Jack's passage is its bodilessness, that he is "borne of that Ize which would not endure the fall of a brickbat." Yet as it unfolds, that quality transfers to the narrator, the person Jack longs to reach – whose presence is felt only as a pair of disembodied "eares" and "eyes," and whose name is someone else's. Jack is painfully restored to his body: to punish his trespass, "the Players in iest breecht him till the bloud came." By contrast, Armin here physically surfaces only to re-submerge, fragmenting into a disintegrated consciousness. His only material contact with the narrative coincides with the shattering of the ice beneath it.

Foole Upon Foole does not lead us to Armin's clowning by way of any particular dramatic character he played; his goal is not to channel these historical fool figures, but to amalgamate them, to refine their collective personae into a textual mode of being. To be a clown, as with an author, for Armin required learning to become a narrator – inhabiting a null subjectivity that performs through the performance of others, that is everyone and everywhere because no one and nowhere, that can "imitate" not just people but whole "playes dooing all himselfe." *Foole Upon Foole* dramatizes the creation of this textual space, indeed, at the expense of the individuals it chronicles. If the volume begins with Jack Oates savagely beating a rival "artificiall foole," it ends with the natural fool's interment by that very rival, as the narrator decides to write Blue John's epitaph himself, on a printed page rather than stone.[49] While each fool is gathered and concentrated, given historical definition and fixity, what gradually emerges behind and above them is Armin, their voices now overwritten by his own – a new kind of fool, compound and incorporeal, greater than the sum of its parts because simultaneously less. Fulfilling the poetics of its title page, the book produces its author not initially, but cumulatively; thus the "upon" in the title itself, both concatenation and superposition at once. If not quite a stage practice, this was practice for the stage. Dilating a purely interior world of heterogeneous agencies, Armin would let each man "carry his owne burthen" only so long as each of those men was him.

"We conclude togeather"

On the page, one can invent the challengers one impersonates in order to perform a monopoly on public speech. On the stage, one's sources, collaborators, and critics were all identical, and all present in the playhouse audience: there was no mechanism by which to mediate and dispossess their contribution. The authorial subterfuge of "the fool" thus had to adapt to the theatrical realities of the clown, whose demands were the opposite. Clowning was nothing if not the performance of self-identity: the clown could not stand alone onstage and pretend to be someone else, much less not to be there at all.

Armin's career strategy – to be in print but also in the theatre, to be in the theatre but also in print – attacked this problem on two fronts. If he encircled his textual identity with performance, replicating on paper the dialectical structure of clowning that produced individual agency out of plural, he was also, simultaneously, encasing his performances in textuality. We have so far been calling him "Robert Armin," but that is more than he says: the byline of *Foole Upon Foole* is his stage name, "Clonnico de Curtanio Snuff" – which the second edition of 1605 would retain, altered to "Clonnico del Mondo Snuff" to reflect his new venue. Though the book has little to do with theatre, it is framed as an extension of Armin's playhouse persona. Yet that persona is itself a fictional construct: Armin is the only professional player who performed under a pseudonym – and certainly the only clown ever to do so. Or did he? Clearly the theatre public knew him by name, for several plays pun either on "Armin" or on his being a goldsmith; none of the notices he generated, not even Davies of Hereford's lengthy epigram about him, ever calls him by any other.[50] Not only is the sole source for Armin's sobriquet Armin's own writings, in fact, but apparently "Snuff" was not even his only sobriquet: in addition to "Grumball," while with Chandos' Men he may also have gone by the moniker "Pinck."[51] Were all these merely pseudo-pseudonyms, aliases only in Armin's own mind? Then again, if his stage name were merely a pen name, why coin it in reference to that stage? Then again, how exactly could he have self-applied a stage name? How *does* a clown introduce himself, we are forced to ask, or perform for the first time? Is there ever a first time?

If the attribution of *Foole Upon Foole* makes the relative priority of performance and print tricky to decipher, then the other book Armin published in 1600 – *Quips Upon Questions*, likewise ascribed to "Clunnyco de Curtanio Snuffe" – makes ambiguating that relationship its entire project. Here a material connection between the volume's contents and Armin's actual clowning seems unequivocal, because *Quips Upon Questions* appears to be a book of actual clowning – specifically, a compendium of "themes," evidently the one genre of clown postlude Armin sustained. The survival of such a book ought to make it a treasure: here at last, we expect to find an unalloyed record of audience participation. That, at least, had been the promise of "themes" since the inception of public theatre, when in 1578 Tarlton was already being beseeched to compile "thy Theames in order one by one."[52] Far more improvised, interactive, and open-ended than the jig, "themes" reduced the cultural transaction of playgoing to pure dialogue, pitting spectator against player on equal terms; more than in any other clowning genre, here theatrical authorship was intractably multiple – not just in the bilateral structure of individual contests, but in the numerical superiority their textualization would aggregate. A book of "themes" has more amateur authors than professional ones, and theoretically no limit to them; it is the "anti-playbook" theatre could never produce – and, despite the obvious demand for it, had so far resisted – because a book that incorporated the audience called into question all those that did not. The danger of such an enterprise thus cannot be overstated: *Quips Upon Questions* was the book the playgoing public had been awaiting for at least twenty-two years – a playbook of their own. As such, it flirts with calamity.

For Armin to publish it may seem discordant with what we have already seen of his interests as an author; for him even to have practiced this genre, indeed, ran counter to his assets as a performer. Unlike his predecessors, Armin was not physically imposing: he was not an athlete, but a singer. Though he had the clown's requisite ugliness, it was accompanied by a diminutiveness – his characters are compared to dogs, frogs, pigs, sparrows, lice, vermin – that made his command of the stage, his ability to maintain a presence, a genuine concern; Wiles notes the tendency of playwrights to embed him in comic trios rather than let him carry a scene *solus*.[53] That he should have been entrusted with the entire postlude, then, becomes all the more remarkable: here not even a shred of dramatic apparatus intervened between clown and audience to keep him the center of attention. Yet his very inadequacy – and how he compensated for it – made him an ideal candidate for the task. For Armin, the exposures of page and stage were versions of each other, and could be handled in the same way: not by defying vocalic interchange, but by retreating into it, and therein controlling it. Rather than stop the audience from talking, he had to interpose a textual buffer through which its speech could be anticipated, mediated, and co-opted. But how? He could hardly compel the audience to conform its utterance to a playbook; neither could such a playbook be codified after the fact as merely a raw transcription of past utterances. It is not clear, in fact, whether *Quips Upon Questions* aims to be a script or a transcript – which is perhaps what made it both.

Where the ambiguity in *Foole Upon Foole* was authorship, in *Quips* it is the text's identity itself. Its prefatory materials refuse to plot it anywhere on the continuum between theatrical and literary experience. (See Figure 10.) The first subtitle calls it "A Clownes conceite on occasion offered" – leaving uncertain whether that "occasion" is the present printing or prior performance. "[B]ewraying moralised metamorphoses of changes vpon interrogatories," similarly, forms a palimpsest of nearly impenetrable opacity. "Clapt vp by a Clowne of the towne in this last restraint, having litle else to doe, to make a litle vse of his fickle Muse" suggests private composition while the Curtain lay shut in June 1600; just as easily, though, "Clapt vp" suggests performance already approved and applauded while the theatre was open. If anything, the temporality *Quips* strives for is neither before nor after, but now. The twinned quips concluding the title page cannot decide if they address a reader or a spectator – or they address each separately, and yoke them together to form interchangeable modes of engagement: "Like as you list, read on and spare not, / Clownes iudge like Clownes, therefore I care not: / *Or thus,* / Floute me, Ile floute thee; it is my profession, / to iest at a Iester, in his transgression." The first invites readers to do critical violence to the book; the second constructs the book

QVIPS

VPON QVESTIONS,
OR,
A Clownes conceite on occasion offered.

bewraying a morrallised metamorphoses of changes
vpon interrogatories: shewing a litle wit, with
a great deale of will: or in deed, more
desirous to please in it, then to
profite by it.

Clapt vp by a Clowne of the towne in this last restraint,
hauing litle else to doe, to make a litle vse of his
fickle Muse, and carelesse of carping.

By Clunnyco de Curtanio Snuffe.

Like as you list, read on and spare not,
Clownes iudge like Clownes, therefore I care not:
Or thus,
Floute me, Ile floute thee; it is my profession,
To iest at a Iester, in his transgression.

Imprinted at London for *W. Ferbrand*, and are to
be sold at the signe of the Crowne ouer againft
the Mayden head neare Yelhhall.
1 6 0 0.

Figure 10 Title page of Robert Armin, *Quips Upon Questions* (1600), A1r.

as a product of such violence – in the "flouting" of Armin's stage authority – and therefore as a textual perpetuation of theatrical contest. Armin
encourages us, either way, to talk back to the book, as if it is not just a
static record of discourse but an ongoing one, requiring our active, agonistic participation. Playgoing and reading are thus calibrated as reciprocal
forms of experience: what goes for one, goes for the other.

Three prefatory epistles further superimpose the clown's theatrical situation onto his textual situation; as if taking up the fugitive impulse of
Kemps Nine Daies Wonder in mid-stride, Armin begins the book already
under fire from his audience, and on the run from it. He dedicates the
first to his slapstick, "Sir Timothie Truncheon: *Alias* Bastinado, euer my
part-taking friende," asking him "to protect me from insicion, or in deede
from dirrision, in which I am now to wade deeply."[54] Yet so wary is Armin,
seemingly, that he delegates the encounter to Sir Timothie, and the invo-
cation becomes a valediction. In this hybrid scenario of print anxiety
and stage fright, it is the slapstick that must now perform on his behalf,
anthropomorphically "like a Burgomaster walke[ing] from Stationers shop
to Stationers shop, to see what entertainment my Booke hath; and who so
disgrases it enuiously, and not iesting at it gently, at the least bastinado
them, that bobbadillo like as they censure," fending off enemies "whose
teeth are all blacke with rancor of their spight; and whose tongues are
milke white with hart burning heate: God keepe me from their bytings."[55]
As for Armin, meanwhile, "say I am out of towne, and heare not their
ribald mockes, and by that means excuse me from them." Fantasies of per-
secution, however, pursue him even there: proposing a flight to Hackney,
he still fears that along the way "some one in ambush [will] endanger my
braynes with a Brickbat unsight or unseene."

Further fusing the imageries of literary and theatrical reception, his next
epistle – to his "Readers, Reuilers, or in deede what not?" – conflates his
impotence over the book with his impotence in the book. Now book and
body seem bound together again, but only because they prepare for a mutual
evisceration, like a defenseless player about to take the stage: "my blood be
layd to your charge," he rails; "Glut with gazing, surfet with seeing, and rell-
ish with reading ... Well, go on, vse me at your pleasure."[56] Publication is
figured as performance, and performance as physical assault – so brutal that
it proleptically becomes victimization. "Themes" was about fighting back,
but Armin already surrenders. "A man may liue after to requite his aduer-
sarie," he vows, yet defers such requital; "A man shal not be slaine hugger
mugger pissing against a wall," he protests, "but shall rather be warnd to
defend" – yet instead of offering such a defense, he grovels for mercy:

> He that must of force endure, is willing of force to be patient: but if your
> patience willingly endure vnforst, I shal be the more beholding to you:
> otherwise, let Sir *Timothie* reuenge it, (and so a thousand times making
> legges, I goe still backward, till I am out of sight, hoping then to be out of
> minde) … (A3r)

If the book is a battlefield, it is starting to look pretty one-sided. As onstage,
so dwarfed and overwhelmed by the crowd does Armin already appear that
instead of summoning himself to the contest, he resigns it. He takes leave of
the text before it commences, abjectly dwindling into a forgotten thought;
even the earlier threat of future "reuenge" is withdrawn, forfeited again to
his slapstick. A final epistle, bestowing "Incouragement to the Booke," com-
pletes the excision: now book and body are wholly divorced. In contrast to
the vivid, oncoming tongues and eyes and teeth of his oppressors, what little
body Armin here projects – a trickle of urine, a pair of legs that run themselves away – "goes backward," receding behind other "part-taking" entities
that likewise "take" his "part" from him, and take him apart in the process.
If *Quips Upon Questions* at all approximates Armin's clowning practice, he
sets it up as failure, his agency already obliterated. Instead of question-and-
answer exchange, we now expect from the rest of the book a total victory of
the audience – and the victory it always sought: a representation of its cacophony, of its "speaking all things," purged of any voice but its own.

   And that is just what we get – just not as we expected it. Armin imple-
ments this hermeneutic so thoroughly as to turn it inside out. The volume contains forty-five themes, ranging from one to ten stanzas in length;
individual stanza length, verse form, and meter vary, but each theme is
headed by an originating prompt and concluded by a single couplet or
quatrain. Their formal irregularity, however, is not the problem. Rhyming
dialogues, trialogues, tetralogues, pentalogues, they interpolate multiple
perspectives that object, correct, deflect, cancel, and reverse the argument
flow at random intervals, each interrupting, questioning, answering, sec-
onding, qualifying, and replacing the last. None of these alternations from
speaker to speaker, furthermore – sometimes sustained across several stanzas, sometimes flitting back and forth within a particular line – is ever
aurally prefixed or visually tagged, so that we quickly lose track of not
only who is speaking, but how many. For example:

> *Who dyed first?*
> Not he that first was borne, I am sure of that.
> Who then I pre-thee? Faith I do not know.
> Harken to me, and I will tell thee what.
> What is it thou wilt tell me? pre-thee show. (E1v)

Who is happy?
… Then who is happy, let me heare of you.
The strong man, meane you him? No, he is weake.
Strength is a blessing I can well alow.
But not a happy blessing? Good sir speake. (C3v–C4r)

   He eates much.
True, he eates much, but drinketh ten times more.
How know you that? I know it by his skore.
What, doth he pay his skore? yes, euer he doth.
Then tis no matter, let him feed his tooth.
But you say that he drinkes more than he eates.
I, so they say: the Brewer the more gets.
      Tush, let vs peace, in vaine we spende our winde,
      Gluttons will feed, & drunkards drinke them blinde. (E3r)

   Wh[a]t's neare her?
Her Smocke is neare her. I that's true indeed,
Of outward thinges, it is her nearest weed.
Nothing is nearer (I thinke) then her smocke.
Yes, her skin's nearer, that it is by cocke.
      That is a weede to, to keepe out the weather.
      Then nothing's nearer, we conclude togeather. (C2r)

The last two of these are almost complete themes (most are far longer), but even they do not include the closing quips, which – set off by italics, a brace, and the inscrutable rubric "*Quip*" – often add yet another, wholly distinct voice to the chorus: "*True hast thou sayd, the first was nothing wise, / No more the second was, let it suffise: / One that giues golde, the next that giues the bird, / Three fooles well met, for thou shalt be the third.*"[57] Yet just as often, that final voice is not acerbic, but morally aloof – "*This be their quip, that none can dispence, / Lightly liue, but dye with heauie conscience*" – or authoritatively equal to the preceding ones – "*Yes, one thing's nearer then her smocke or skinne, / Of which I speake not, but will keepe it in*" – and thus not really final at all; it too occupies no stable rhetorical register from theme to theme.[58] Sometimes there are two quips. Sometimes a theme will continue the previous one; sometimes they abruptly switch topic. Sometimes the first speaker answers the prompt as if he proposed it; sometimes he altogether rejects it. Is the quipper always the same as the prompter, or someone else? Is the quipper always one of the speakers, or someone new? There are no set rules to help us reconstruct these conversations. Their internal voices have been individuated and sequenced, as they must, but punctuation, lineation, and typography provide only an illusion of hierarchy, and the text otherwise spools out free of editorial intervention. Where the Tarltonian theme was uniformly bilateral, always a duet between the player and a particular playgoer, those of *Quips Upon Questions* pass through no fixed point, radiating in all directions. Instead of talking to the clown, the audience seems to be talking to itself.

Where is Armin in all of this? What is his role, if any? True to his word, he has disappeared from the book – or rather disappeared into it. No voice is unmistakeably his; potentially none of them is. "Out of sight," however, does not mean "out of minde." On the contrary: conditioned to the format of "themes," wherein the audience generates the prompt and the clown generates the verse – an expectation courted by the book's very title – we are driven to search him out, in the hope of some cognitive anchor. Since every theme in *Quips Upon Questions* consists of more than just question and quip, there is always at least one more speaker than there should be; the more the text deviates from convention, ironically, the more hiding places for Armin it makes available. In "*Why barkes that Dogge?*" for instance – only the second in the book – Armin may be either the prompter, or the first respondent ("Aske him, and he will tell thee why he barkes"); he may be a second respondent, who may be the same as the prompter, and who turns the subject to man's own cynical nature ("Thou that wilt make comparisons so odious, / As twixt a Christian and a barking Curre, / I hold thy wit to be no whit commodious, / But to be scrapt out like a parchment blurre"); he may finally be the quipper, who now conflates the first two ("*One to offend in asking such a question, / Th'other defend and choke in his disgestion: / Well reasond both too fooles, and if you marke, / Both wanting wit, better be Dogges, and barke*"), but in the process disavows all of the above.[59] Predictably, the vocalic development of each theme is different, and equally unpredictable; trying to identify Armin, indeed, has the curious effect of scattering him further. Is he the quipper, refereeing with a final trump? Or does he frame the debate, posing the initial question? Which sometimes also makes him one of the internal interlocutors, and sometimes not? Are there as many interlocutors as there seem to be, or fewer?

A slippery slope is emerging: as in *Foole Upon Foole*, "or" so proliferates that it gradually becomes "and." By radically multiplying our interpretive choices, *Quips Upon Questions* radically condenses them. The same thing happens with the book's relationship to performance, an identity it likewise cultivated but about which we grow increasingly uncertain. Some themes appear completely documentary, not only implying an immediate performance situation – "*Who sleepes there?*", "*Whats aclocke?*", "*Can that Boy read?*" – but incorporating concrete details from the audience. The

diptych "*What haue I lost?*" and "*How shall I finde it?*" requires knowing that the asker is a one-eared felon, and in "*What ayles that Damsell?*"
the theme acts on the lady in real time, making her laugh in embarrass-
ment.[60] In others, however, such deixis proves a deceptive effect: the subjects of "*Who comes yonder?*" and "*He washes cleane*" cannot realistically be
members of the audience.[61] Some themes are parabolic and epigrammatic,
exfoliating characters who also become internal speakers; some, like the
story of the drunk who gets his pocket picked at the Curtain, overlay the
physical space of the theatre with a fictional one.[62] Some, finally, are so
referentially abstract – "*A Poet Pawnde*", "*He builds a great house*", "*Do it
and dallie not*" – that they cannot be improvised at all: at one point, the
speaker even admits "Writing these Emble[m]s on an idle time, / Within
my windowe where my house doth stand: / Looking about, and studying
for a Rime."[63] If we are looking for Armin, along the way we lose sight of
ourselves. How much of *Quips* derives from actual playhouse production,
and how much from private composition? Is its polyphonic chaos real,
or just an artful simulation? Is it live, or scripted? Performance, or text?
Many, or one?

Such zero-sum hypotheses do not so much alleviate the book's unread-
ability as illustrate it at work. Irresolubly mixed, the distinction between
these categories becomes impossible to draw, and the categories themselves
break down. If *Quips Upon Questions* is an "anti-playbook," giving totalized textual representation to perfomance rather than hierarchizing it, that
is precisely what makes it also the *ur*-playbook: where the playbook simply
expurgates all past audiences after the fact, *Quips* feeds the audience back
to itself so completely and indigestibly as to make them perform their
own excision. Promising to translate the experience of theatre into that of
reading, the book delivers, creating a sonic environment *exactly* like the
theatrical one. Only now, the orgy of indiscriminate speech that thrilled
the crowd in the playhouse confounds us on paper. Removed from the
aural scene of its production, forced to parse that bewildering racket of
speech, the audience must separate and organize itself – for reading needs
a grammar, just as a playbook needs speech prefixes. And because attribution is frustrated, it follows an insidious principle of thrift: the heuristic
of ascribing to Armin either the quips, or the questions, or both, or everything in between, until no one else is left. If at first none of the voices is
Armin's, they gradually coalesce and "conclude togeather" until they are
all potentially his, and become no longer voices at all: to be nowhere is
to be anywhere, and everywhere. Under the pretense of unifying them,
Quips exploits the gap between performance and textuality in order to

let playgoers watch their own labor alienated – and to be the very agents of that alienation, precisely as they desire to experience it again in print. Initially abdicating authorship, Armin makes us reinstate it, as a cognitive necessity of the medium we are in. The book even recognizes this design, and laughs at our expense. The penultimate poem, "*He begins well, but endes ill*," features no vocal alternations, and merely apologizes for our disappointment: "*All is as much to say, the Author feares, | The Reader vowes to haue him by the eares.*" The final poem, "The Conclusion," is just that – a poem, featuring neither question nor quip, but flattened into pure monody; the third-person narration has become a lyric "I."[64] The embodied, multivalent space of theatre has dissolved into the space of reading: we are no longer the content of the book, but on the outside looking in.

The fidelity of *Quips* to historical performance cannot be recovered, but then again could not have been assessed by its early modern readers either. All that matters to its project is the expectation of fidelity it solicits. Publishing clowning, Armin grasped, was not the institutional surrender to the audience it might have seemed, affirming their integrity to performance. Executed with rigorous verisimilitude, it was a way to dissever the audience from performance. Giving us exactly what we want, the book invites us to consume only ourselves – "glut with gazing, surfet with seeing" – only to make us hate it; it is a Trojan horse, spilling out so many versions of us that we must disown them and it together. If "themes" satisfied the audience's need for authorship of the theatrical event, then printing those "themes" pushed that fantasy even further, to expose its futility. The audience may dominate performance, but it can never become a book: *here* is that book, and it is illegible. The act of textual reproduction thus works to reveal a deeper order of theatrical production. Theatre consists not in performance, but in reperformance, the ability to be experienced twice; an audience exists only once, all at once. Here the audience is put to that test, so it can fail – and made to experience its own textual evaporation. In *Quips Upon Questions*, the reader participates in negating his participation as a playgoer. In a sense, it lets the audience collaborate in making a playbook, and – just as Heywood's spectators would do twenty-four years later – erase themselves.[65]

Going backward

CLO[WN]. I am gone sir, and anon sir,
Ile be with you againe.
                    – *Twelfth Night* (1623), Z4r

Throughout the history of early modern clowning – early modern English theatre as a whole, in fact – events precede their textualization: the discursive implications of this arrangement have been the basic concern of this study. *Quips Upon Questions*, appearing at the outset of Armin's tenure with the Chamberlain's Men rather than in the middle or toward the end, is potentially the first book to reverse this relationship. Unlike *Kemps Nine Daies Wonder* or any collection associated with Tarlton, it is not (throughout, at least) the record of performed events, but merely masquerades as one, hyperbolically fulfilling that function in order to implode it. If the book acts like an epistemological virus, however, it extends beyond the printed page. It announced as much on its very title page, indeed, in the commutativity it proposed between playhouse and bookstall: what goes for one goes for the other. Whether "flouting" or "reading," exactly as we would expect to be agents in theatrical performance, so we should expect in the book. If upon reading, then, we discover ourselves not really involved, we can expect the same degree of involvement in performance. Precisely because *Quips* is not the record of any event, it paradoxically becomes one – as a blueprint for *future* events. There are no subsequent calls to put Armin's postludes into print. That is where they had already begun, and we are in all probability looking right at them.

On paper, Armin's "themes" are so public that they do not work as a text; put into practice onstage, they would have become so private as to cease being "themes" at all – a perpetuation of the process the book begins. I believe (and there can be no proof here but the sheer audacity of the claim) that he performed *Quips Upon Questions* just this way, *verbatim* and *solus*. Doing so would have extended its expropriative reading experience into the real world: just as Armin engrossed all its parts to himself, so he now physically acts out all of those parts himself. The effect is the same whether the audience has read the book or not, but it is all the more powerful if they have. As in print, Armin's stage authority is founded not on its autonomy but on his renouncing it; inverting the clown's practice of opposing individuality to the crowd's polyvocality, he performed himself by performing everyone else. The smallness that made him a target became an advantage: he kept shrinking that target, as it were, until it vanished. Yet at the same time, miniaturizing within himself the entire playhouse and speaking on its behalf, he silenced it. Here was Armin's solution to the problem of "distinction": *in*distinction, a "going backward" so deep into the plurality of theatre that it emerged as a singularity.

Elevated to manic, mimetic spectacle, improvising for the crowd thus became an improvisation *of* them – and yet not an improvisation, but something different. All those instances of seemingly concrete detail in *Quips* acquire new life during rote performance. When Armin sings "*What haue I lost?*", he does not need an actual clipped convict in the assembly – he may simply point in a general direction, or to someone in a hat. "*Can that Boy read?*", likewise, or "*He eates much,*" or "*Why weares he bootes?*", or "*Why sweates he so?*", or "*What is shee?*", require no more than locating someone young, or fat, or in boots, or sweaty, or female. When Armin sings "*What ayles that Damsell?*" and makes a woman blush, he makes an *actual* woman blush – no matter which one he has singled out – merely by singling her out; when he says "she laughes and smiles," she *will* laugh and smile.[66] This is not an "improvisation effect," but the opposite.[67] Rather than molding a textual prescription to fit the moment of performance, the moment of performance is revealed to be textually determined. Armin projects artificial identities onto the audience, and they inevitably accept and adopt those characters, spontaneously doing whatever he describes them as doing at any given juncture.

Quips Upon Questions includes passages that not only arrest the illusion of "live" performance, but straightaway resume it again, as if to show just how easily an audience can be simulated, predicted, mystified, and mystified again by the prediction of its own mystification. From "*Who is happy?*":

> He that liues well and dies well, I say still.
> But who is that? Nay when I know Ile tell thee:
> Then I am not the neare, I want my will.
> True, and thou must but harken what I will thee.
> No man shall answere one an others part,
> But each man for himselfe shall: O my hart!
>
> Quip. { *What, startst thou backe for feare? And dost thou quake?*
>   *I see thou knowst no answere what to make.* (C4r)

Like "euery man shall carry his owne burthen," this is a shocking provocation, yet here sheltered from reprisal by the shock it provokes. Armin concludes the catechism with an ironic appeal to the very democracy his soliloquistic method forecloses – and when his dumbfounded listeners fail to respond because they have never been allowed to, he then incorporates their silence. It may *seem* as if Armin performs in real time, his virtuosic fits freely integrating the reactions of the audience, but the text conditions those reactions in advance – and breaks its spell just often enough to remind them of that fact, that they too are merely performing a text, reading it no less than it reads them. The more about them it contains, in

a sense, the more it contains them, materializing them only to dematerialize them, circumscribing their participation and thereby neutralizing
it. Onstage as on the page, *Quips* grants the audience its desire – to be
a player, here the only player. The price of admission, though, is to be
scripted, rendered incapable of resisting the text they enact; inclusion in an
automated performance is also exclusion. Watching Armin ventriloquize,
animate, and operate them, they watch themselves reduced to puppets.[68]

Yet in order to do this, he must be scripted too, becoming in essence
a puppet of himself. Technically it is not Armin who ventriloquizes the
audience, but the text – which Armin merely recites, ventriloquized and
animated by it as well. Performing *Quips Upon Questions* onstage repli-
cated its reading experience not just in its erasure of the playgoer, but in
its corresponding erasure of the player – turning the act of performance
itself, quite literally, into a reading experience. Because performance follows the book – materially as well as historically – every performance is
already a reperformance, a repetition, an echo, creating a metaphysical
disjunction in the performer; there is no "first time" anything happens,
because it never really happens. The body that perfoms the action "writing
these Emble[m]s on an idle time, / Within my windowe where my house
doth stand" is not the same body that delivers these lines in the playhouse.
To speak words that say one has composed them – and, here, to speak
them exactly *as* composed, without deviation – is not to speak them in the
present tense. Just as *Quips'* polyphonic dimension requires Armin to play
many people at once, its poly*chronic* dimension puts him in two places
at once, divided from himself. In "*Are you there with your Beares?*", the
first retort is "One takes my penn and writes this question" – making the
problem not just where the bears are, but where everything else is: there
is also no "penn" onstage, nor presumably "one" to "take" it.[69] A monological writing posing as dialogic speech now figures that speech as a kind
of writing; if the text circumscribes performance, making the audience
arbitrary and imaginary, now performance folds back onto the scene of
composition, rendering the player himself a hallucination. There may be
someone onstage, but he is no more real than the pen he does not hold:
that pen is more real, indeed, because it holds him, his presence merely
its hologram. Actors often played themselves in plays; authors, though,
never did.[70] Armin here does both – and in the process does something
more, something unprecedented and unique in early modern theatre.
Performing himself writing the very words he speaks, he doubles and cancels himself. Actor and author simultaneously, two absences at once, he
performs author*ship*. Here was something no one had ever seen, because

until now it could not be seen: not a man onstage, but a text in the shape of one.

Clowning, we are told – especially the kind outside the play, where literary object decays into unreproducible event – is the antithesis of authorship. Yet even more than authorship, clowning was an emphatically individual practice, and always carried the germ of authorship within it. When the clown scripted himself, he suddenly transformed into its supreme incarnation, a play-within-a-play *without* the play, policing rather than relaxing the porous borders of the theatrical program and removing it from instantaneous, "live" performance. The "audience's theatre" rested on the intrinsic authority of bodies; the nature of theatre could not change unless the nature of its bodies did. It did not hinge, in other words, on the mere replacement of one body (e.g. Kemp's) by another, but on the disappearing of *all* of them, making visible and universal a textual condition beneath them. Because the clown's was connected to the audience's, his was the most intransigent, and therefore the most crucial to bypass. By textualizing both, Armin dissolved both. The authority he now embodied had no body – a theatre immune to participation, interference, and contest, because it has already happened on paper.

In the process, he was also committing a kind of suicide – yet no different from the assisted and belated attempts we have already seen. Climaxing the encroachment of writing upon clowning that began at Tarlton's death and continued with Kemp, Armin made writing not just retroactive to his practice, but anterior and inextricable. No entity that lives on the stage can survive onto the page; neither poet, nor actor, nor character, nor spectator can fully inhabit both domains at once. To live in the book, one must be of the book: in *Quips Upon Questions* Armin makes that choice inescapable for us, and makes it for himself. Clowning is now a commodity, capable of textual reproduction, but only because for Armin it is already a textual reproduction; dedicated to inculcating that one idea, it is condemned to repeat it, incapable of producing anything new. Authorship homogenizes the stage clown into just another actor – even if his own – and forfeits his other claim to immortality, a place in cultural memory.[71]

And *Quips Upon Questions* knows it. In "*Wher's Tarleton?*", Armin negotiates his own authority against that of his predecessor, through a debate between an "Asse" and a "Foole." "Foole," fittingly, leads a stoic meditation on the distinction between the clown's body and his name: "What, is his name Letters, and no more? / Can Letters liue, that breathe not, nor haue life? No no, his Fame liues, who hath layde in store / His actes and deedes ... You say not, Whers his Body that did die? / But, Where is

Tarleton? Whers his name alone? / His Name is *here.*"[72] Yet where, again, is "here"? Is it the playhouse, or a book? When the clown merely performs that book, his body inspired by "Letters" that "breathe not," is there a difference? The best transmission of others' "actes and deedes" he can offer, accordingly, is like his own – in letter rather than spirit, hollow and forced. As if to illustrate, "*Whats vnfit*" ends in a rote reprise of Tarleton's most famous "theme," devoid of context and meaning: "*me thinkes it is vnfit, / To see an Iron Gridiron turne a Spit. / No, no, mee thinkes that it is more vnfit, / To see a blockhead asse haue any wit.*"[73] A human phonograph, Armin cannot generate theatrical experience, only replay it – in stereo. In both form and content, he is a living citation, a severed head.

His career forms a citation of that citation, a series of further withdrawals into the fragmented identity *Quips Upon Questions* established. The evidence comes not from his postludes, however – which left no trace other than the one he deposited in advance – but from the King's Men's plays themselves. Now that their interests were harmonized, the relation between company and clown reverted to its former balance: the clown's dramatic parts returned to streamlining the transition to his solo routine, instead of impinging on it – because we can now see how they merely elaborated on that routine. The Armin whose Carlo Buffone stages a heated altercation between two cups of wine and "talk[s] nothing but Crackers and Fire-worke," or whose Touchstone "quarrel[s] in print, by the book" with himself, or whose Caliban writhes and flails under the barrage of invisible spirits, are no less continuous with the essential "Armin" of his postlude than Tarleton's Derick or Kemp's Launce were with the "Tarleton" and "Kemp" of theirs.[74] The difference is that there is no essential "Armin" to be found there either. That "Armin" is also a role – only one written by Robert Armin, rather than Ben Jonson or William Shakespeare – and just as much a character as those before it. The bleeding of immediate theatrical reality into the dramatic fiction now unsettles rather than reassures, because there is no longer any such reality, and we cannot be certain which Armin is an extension of which.

Indeed, where earlier we saw Shakespearean dramaturgy forced to work around the clown, now it worked through him. Preposterously, the postlude came to drive the play instead of being driven out by it. Or, more accurately, they merged. In *Twelfth Night*, for instance, the dissociative nature of Armin's "themes" is elevated and diffused into a global theme. More than any Shakespeare comedy, its procreative *telos* is passed through repetition and recirculation, closed economies that breed: a melancholic duke, "in voyces well divulg'd," who is "best / When least in companie"; a countess whose face is but a portrait of itself; a woman who to "publish" herself becomes a sexless actor, "a blanke," a message shuttled between households; twins who are at once more than one person and less, "an apple cleft in two."[75] Texts become people, and people texts: Maria "personates" both Olivia and Malvolio, and Malvolio performs her letter, to the letter; Sir Toby drafts a challenge from Sir Andrew to Cesario, then conveys it orally. Sebastian does not need a pseudonym, but gets one; Viola goes five acts without a real name, and Orsino ultimately prefers the false. A play whose climax asks "how haue you made diuision of yourself?", how "one face, one voice, one habit" can be "two persons" – and that ends with a song Armin would repeat nearly *verbatim* elsewhere – is more than just a play: it is play and postlude combined, the reduplicative poetics of Armin's "themes" blown up to a cosmic scale.[76] When Feste torments the captive Malvolio, most pointedly – making Malvolio's off-stage confines as real to us as Sir Topas is to Malvolio, discoursing on madness both with a phantom and as one, alternating personae so rapidly they greet each other as they pass – we seem to be inside "themes" itself, an intra-dramatic assimilation of Armin's extradramatic solipsism. And yet there is no "inside" to such multiplicity, for when Feste becomes Sir Topas, he becomes "Armin" only by adding *more* disguises, not removing them – and gratuitously so: "thou mightst have done this without thy beard and gowne," Maria observes; "he sees thee not."[77] For Shakespeare, Armin is always in disguise – he *is* disguise.

In *Troilus and Cressida*, similarly, the influence of Armin's "themes" extends far beyond the character of Thersites, who apostrophizes absent interlocutors and catechizes present ones, and who performs Ajax's prosopagnosia – "that takes mee for the Generall" – as a talking to no one.[78] It imbues Shakespeare's very construction of "character" itself, which here (as in many of his later plays) has become radically extrinsic. Besieged on all sides by invasions of their privacy, their affections merely conditioned responses to each passing stimulus, knowing themselves only through their reflection in others, everyone in this play is on some level "the general," a public person in the most material sense. From Armin's performance practice, Shakespeare seems to have adapted not just a comic type, but an entire model of consciousness as composite and relational, that can preserve its integrity by communicating only with itself.[79] In *Timon of Athens*, something even closer to "themes" occurs in the play, and this time it is not even Armin who performs it. When in 2.2 Timon bids that the servants be "entertained" in his absence, a nameless "Fool" is brought in to field idle questions about mistresses, usury, and whoremongering, while

Apemantus looks on. Armin here stands literally beside himself, watching someone else play Armin: "that answer," he at one point notes, "might have become Apemantus."[80]

We have seen this tableau before. It is the same pattern of self-estrangement that attended the textualizations of Tarlton and Kemp, the retroactive desconstitution of their performing bodies into a set of iterable, and dislocatable, signs. Unlike his predecessors, though, Armin embraced that fate, and made it the goal of his career. Its fulfillment came in 1609, with the printing of *The History of the Two Maids of More-clacke*, a full-length comedy of his own devising. (See Figure 11.) If his postludes had hitherto subordinated performance to textuality, *Two Maids* completed that process by removing performance altogether – and Armin with it. According to its epistle, the play's printing complements Armin's intention to reprise his stage roles in it,

> wherein I whilome pleased: and being requested both at Court and Citty, to shew him in priuate, I haue therefore printed him in publicke, wishing thus much to euery one, so delighting, I might put life into this picture, and naturally act him to your better contents. (¶2r)

He never delivers on that promise, however. He goes on to say that the revival was staged without him, by the Children of the King's Revels, for "*Tempora mutantur in illis*, & I cannot do as I would." The playbook ends up substituting for what it supplements, placing his original performance beyond recovery – its reperformance, fittingly, now deteriorated into an ever smaller chain of bodies. Instead, we are told, we must "accept this dumbe show" – when a dumbshow is not the words on the page, but everything *except* the words on the page.

If this leaves us to imagine Armin's theatrical performance for ourselves, in turn, words on a page are all we discover it to be. For *Two Maids* is nothing but a quilt of citations. It is strewn with random phrases from the Shakespeare canon, and a whole plot is devoted to parodying *Hamlet* – a youth named "Humil" bewails his widowed mother's adultery, not for his dead father (who turns out to be not really dead, and her lover), but out of naïve loyalty to his stepfather, who wants Humil dead anyway. Armin plays Blue John of the Hospital, who recycles his jokes *verbatim* from *Foole Upon Foole*. He also plays the jester Tutch, whose name recalls Touchstone, and who later plays John. Where we might expect room for a postlude, finally, we find none: the play is Armin's postlude, its own hall of mirrors. Every time it parts its dramatic illusion, it reveals not a live event, but other books – and a player who has disappeared into

THE
History of the two Maids of More-clacke,

VVith the life and simple maner of IOHN
in the Hospitall.

Played by the Children of the Kings
Maiesties Reuels.

VVritten by ROBERT ARMIN, seruant to the Kings
most excellent Maiestie.

LONDON,
Printed by N.O. for *Thomas Archer*, and is to be sold at his
shop in Popes-head Pallace, 1 6 0 9.

Figure 11 Title page of Robert Armin, *The History of the Two
Maids of More-clacke* (1609), A1r.

them, for whom authorship and performance, "shew[ing] in private" and "print[ing] in publicke," have become mutually reinforcing activities. The image of this new, self-contained theatrical economy occurs not on its title page – either John, or Armin as John, or John as Armin as John – but in its action, where Armin's first stage direction is *"Enter Tutch the Clowne, writing."* It is just a shopping list: "Capons, Turkeis, Smallebirds, Beefes, Muttons, Partridge, Plouer, Wood cocks."[81] But it also dictates his first lines: whether he actually writes it or it is written down beforehand – in Armin's case, both – clown and script emerge simultaneously. And if an actor who enters reading is already inside the thing he enters, a clown who enters writing enters oblivious to us, talking only to himself.

Epilogue
The principal verb

Going forward

So it is, *boni viri*, that one foole presents another; and I a foole by
nature, and by arte, do speake to you in the person of the Idiot our
Play-maker. He like a Foppe & an Asse, must be making himselfe a
publike laughing stock, and haue no thanke for his labor.
  – Thomas Nashe, *Summers Last Will and Testament* (pr. 1600), B1r

Clowning, as we have reconstructed its modes and motives, typified
an embodied paradigm of theatre whose internal relationships increasingly needed resolution: relations between production and reception,
poet and player, player and audience, performance and text. If the terminus of this process was a new sense of theatre as purveying essentially
immaterial, ahistorical, autotelic literary objects – a culture of playgoing
compatible with a culture of reading, evidenced by both the form and
consumption of playbooks – then such an evacuation of performance,
I have suggested, had to occur *in* performance itself, and clowning was
its crucible. Gradually, the clown's liminal, multivalent identity broke
apart against, and into, the fundamental categories of modern theatre.
Tarlton's print afterlife thus enables a theoretical delineation of author
from actor, ultimately privileging spirit over matter as the site of theatrical agency. For Kemp, meanwhile, performance is devalued from
the other side by the expropriative participation of its audience, forcing his flight into authorial absence and an equally nobodied presence.
In Armin's stage practice, finally, that flight into textuality became real-
time: once the seat of the "liveness" of theatre, clowning now thematized
its circumscription by print, embodying performance as disembodied,
atemporal, and iterative. From the extradramatic peripheries that defined
it, then, the playhouse made itself a book – one that transcended player
and audience alike, and that therefore could exclude them from its textual self-representation.

As with any developmental narrative, however, there are limitations to this story as I have presented it. To suggest that over this period "theatre" came to exist primarily as a literary entity rather than as a social one – that theatrical performance on some level ceased to "happen" as a scene of unique cultural production – is scarcely to imply that theatrical *performances* ceased happening. They had to keep happening, of course, not just because they remained the companies' main source of revenue, but because on the very terms of this argument, performance could only be dislocated *in* performance – though we should pause to note the irony of an institution invested at this moment in depreciating its own capital. Nevertheless, to call this an "institutional" project when it has thus far involved just three figures – two of them from the same company – may seem unwarranted. Armin was one clown among many, in a single playhouse. While his postludes seem to fulfill a much longer and larger process, we can hardly conclude that clowning alone – much less a lone clown – rendered dramatic authorship the default creative agency by which performance would henceforth be organized and apprehended, across the entire theatrical landscape. Even if my reading of early modern clowning is sound, it is also selective, and evidence for its impact on playgoing sensibilities is necessarily thin: playgoers who felt marginalized are unlikely to generate documentation. Evidence to the contrary, on the other hand, as we saw in Chapters 1 and 2, is plentiful. Certainly, for audiences at the lower end of the playhouse spectrum – those of the jig-filled, clown-centric Curtain, Fortune, and Red Bull – the meaning of performance was in no way diminished, the authorship of theatre no more settled or closed to ritual dispute.

Not only did performance keep happening, indeed, but even across corporate and class boundaries, it kept happening in the same *way* it had always happened – especially where it did not. The anonymous, early seventeenth-century chronicle history play *Thorny Abbey* neatly encapsulates this *plus ça change*. It begins with a figure its audience might have expected at the end, the clown. He enters "*with a Paper in his hand for a Prologue,*" yet he proceeds instead to denounce the play for otherwise omitting him:

> D'ye call it a *Tragedy*? So they tell me it is, and that no *fools* must be in *Tragedies*: for they are *serious* matters, forsooth. But I say there may, and there must be *fools* in *Tragedies* ... they are all *fools* in the *Tragedy*; and you are *fools*, that come to see the *Tragedy*; and the Poet's a *fool*, who made the *Tragedy* ... when in *Pacy's*, and *Sommers's*, and *Patche's* and *Archer's* times, my venerable Predecessours, a *fool* was alwayes the *Principal Verb*. (B1v)

The transgressiveness of improvisation is in rather heavy-handed evidence here. The play wants very badly for us to believe this is an unscripted moment, to the point of overscripting it. Concluding his disquisition, the clown announces, "I have a *part* to say to you, if the *Prompter* would come to tell me, when I am out"; with the Prompter standing behind him, he insists on corrupting "*We're to present you*" to "*I am to present you*," and "a play" to "a Pick-pocket"; "*The* Prompter *offers to strike him, and he runs in*"; "what more he had to tell you in his mind," the Prompter makes sure to add, "I find not in the notes h'has left behind."[1] We now have, clearly, an audience that knows plays are scripted, and a clown constructed as their opposite. Yet we also have a play that still feels compelled to produce that clown, if only as a production. *Thorny Abbey* is not an amphitheatre play – its stage directions call for house lighting – but its epilogue, like its prologue, seems calibrated to the culture of one: the expectation of a closing jig. This it cannot provide. "After so grave a scene," it apologizes, "t'were not fit / To unhinge your thoughts with flashy wit."[2] And thus, perhaps, its prologue mitigates that disappointment, fleetingly enacting the clown's "principal verb" at the same time as foreclosing it.

That it should need to do so is strange, because along with the orthodoxy that jigs were never offered at the "private," indoor halls – an orthodoxy *Thorny Abbey* supports – comes the critical conviction that their audiences were demographically and aesthetically distinct from those of the houses that did. But "polite" audiences seem to have remained quite cheerfully unreconstructed, and impolite, longer than we are accustomed to think.[3] The border between what Alfred Harbage called "popular" and "coterie" cultures was porous enough for the Globe, from which Hamlet had supposedly banished clowns in the same year that the Chamberlain's Men had supposedly banished Will Kemp, to reinstate jigs as early as 1613; as late as 1640, Shirley's *The Doubtful Heir* predicts the Globe playgoers' dismay at the fact that it has "*No bawdery, nor no ballets … no clown, no squibs, no devill in't*" because it was originally written for the Blackfriars.[4] Not only were the standards of the Globe in evident decline, but they seem to have declined in sympathy with those of the Blackfriars, as a spillway for the increasingly atavistic demands of upscale audiences. Just as Shirley belittles the Globe audience as "*Squirrels that want nuts*," fearing they will "*crack the benches … deaf us with lewd noise, or tongues*" for lack of traditional fare, Richard Lovelace sees that same sensibility in the Whitefriars, its audiences craving bombast and spectacle, for whom "the Throne / To their amazement should descend alone, / The rosin-lightning flash, and Monster spire / Squibs."[5] When Christopher Beeston moved Queen Anne's Men to the

Cock-pit in 1617, similarly, he must have calculated that some of their Red Bull audience would travel with them.[6] If the apprentices who ravaged the Cock-pit were irate Red Bull patrons, they were clearly not its only, or even largest, constituency.

The segregated formats of the public and private houses maintained the fiction of segregated patronage, but in reality patronage overlapped a great deal, aggravating appeals to community at the elite venues. Massinger's *The Bond-Man* (1624) is sure its Cock-pit audience wants "*no* Gipsie Jigges, *no drumming stuffe,* / Dances, *or other* Trumpery *to delight,* / *Or take, by common way, the common sight*" – yet it must still remind them.[7] Massinger and Fletcher's *Fair Maid of the Inn* (1626) laments that nowadays "*for approbation* / *A jigg shall be clapt at,*" and exhorts its Blackfriars audience to "*H[i]ther* / *Come nobler judgements.*"[8] By 1629, Massinger is through importuning: the epistle to *The Roman Actor* now fully expects that "*the grauity and height of the subject* [will] *distaste such as are onely affected with Jigges, and ribaldrie … their condemnation of me, and my Poem, can no way offend me.*"[9] Thomas Goffe's *Careles Shepherdess*, revived at Salisbury Court in 1638, mounts an elaborate, metatheatrical Prelude that forces its audience to choose between superego and id. If, like the obtuse Thrift and Landlord, we agree that "I would have the Fool in every Act," we must seek such pleasure elsewhere. At the end, Thrift elects to "hasten to the money Box, / And take my shilling out again … I'le go to th'Bull, or Fortune, and there see / A play for two pense, with a Jig to boot."[10]

Of course, *The Careles Shepherdess* neither wishes nor expects its own audience to follow suit. And by virtue of watching the Prelude, they need not do so. Before it can exorcise such playgoers as "ghosts," relics of a former age that "nothing understand but fools and fighting," it first gives voice to their desires;[11] before it can abjure the pleasures of the clown, it first vicariously supplies them, in its loving pastiche of his antics:

> LANDL. I'ave laugh'd
> Until I cry'd again, to see what Faces
> The Rogue would make: O it does me good
> To see him hold out's Chin, hang down his hands,
> And twirle his Bawble. There is nere a part
> About him but breaks jests. I heard a fellow
> Once on this Stage cry, *Doodle, Doodle, Doe*,
> Beyond compare; I'd give the other shilling
> To see him act the Changling once again.
> THRI. And so would I, his part has all the wit,
> For none speaks C[ar]ps and Quibbles besides him:
> I'd rather see him leap, laugh, or cry,

Then hear the gravest Speech in all the *Play*.
I never saw *Rheade* peeping through the Curtain,
But ravishing joy enter'd into my heart. (B2v–B3r)

Timothy Reed, the clown around whom these memories gradually cluster, was hardly dead, or even an amphitheatre player: he performed *at*
Salisbury Court, in fact, just for a different company.[12] So worried is *The
Careles Shepherdess* that his absence from this *single* performance would
send spectators to the exit, that it simulates him by recollecting his past
performances. And the Prelude goes even further: as in *Thorny Abbey*, its
transition to the prologue features an "improvisation effect" – a series of
Prologues, in fact, who, forgetting their lines, are left (like the clown of
Pilgrimage to Parnassus) to hang and be *non plus*. The first gets no further
than a single line, "Must alwayes I a Hearer only be?", before "being out,
[he] is laught at" by the onstage audience; he curses the prompter, and
exits. "Another" enters to speak it, and gets to the second line, "Mayn't
a Spectator write a Comedy?"; he too, "*being out, looks in his hat.*" He
is in turn laughed at by "*an Actor plac'd in the Pit,*" who takes the stage
himself, offering to "something vent, though't be *ex tempore.*"[13] The forty-
eight-line rhymed verse prologue he proceeds to speak of course cannot be
improvised, and is a snooty defense of the play's pastoral verisimilitude,
which its previous audiences had savagely mocked. But at first, we do not
know he is an actor. It genuinely appears that a spectator is now "writing
a Comedy" – and he again disavows his own scriptedness, assuring us: "If
I too should be out, this answer take, / I do not now so much repeat, as
make."[14]

    If this seems an odd way to reproach audiences for presumption, it has
to be: for Goffe, part of the Stuart phenomenon of amateur, gentlemen
playwrights, was himself a spectator writing a comedy – and, in a gam-
bit we should keep in mind, he is identified as such, as one of the crowd.
But it also reveals something about the pathology of the hyper-critical
hall audiences, and their simultaneous appetite for clowning. Although
these two sensibilities are here made to seem opposed, each is corrected
by means of the other, and both, surreptitiously, are gratified together.
Despite the Prelude's claim that "The Motley Coat was banish'd with
Trunk Hose," and that poets have "Purg'd their inventions of those grosser
follies … and rather move us to admire, then laugh," if the audience now
"laughs" at the actors' failure or are "ravished" to see someone "making"
theatre for themselves, they have a great deal more in common with the
tastes of Thrift and Landlord than they realize. The Prologue to Shirley's
Changes (1632) flatters its Salisbury Court audience as "able to distinguish

straines that are / Cleare, and Phebean, from the popular, / And sinful dregs of the adulterate braine." But in the play itself, Caperwit, a poetaster writing a play for just such an august gathering, knows better, outfitting it with all manner of songs, dances and "pretty devices" instead of "dull and flegmatick Poetry." "Many Gentlemen," he explains, "are not ... Now satisfied without a Jigge, which since / They cannot, with their honour, call for, after / The play, they look to be serv'd up in the middle."[15]

Apparently, clowning had not become so indistinguishable from scripted performance as to vanish. If in Caroline hall drama it was becoming an increasingly mediated effect, it still thrived in the jigs of the suburbs, with which poets anxiously and cleverly attempted to compete. As *Thorny Abbey* and *The Careles Shepherdess* illustrate, when the clown was unavailable or undesirable, he was simply supplemented – "serving up" the audience, as it were, not at the end but the beginning.[16] And as *The Careles Shepherdess*'s stage insurrections suggests, this was less a matter of reforming the audience than of checking it. In this last section, then, I want to return to the foundations of my argument. The textual assimilation of the clown forms only part of the story of how an epistemic framework for dramatic authorship took root, and ironically, it actually *predicts* a steady deterioration of audience manners in its wake. The evacuation of the authority of the performer did not vacate performance as a whole of authority. All it did, indeed, was leave such authority suddenly up for grabs. The dynamics of playgoing remained the same: Armin had merely used them to his advantage, not altered them. It was still a contest between audience and stage, for that stage. Here, as throughout this study, theatrical authority never stops being a function of *bodies*, or being mediated by them. The clown's disembodiment had had to be embodied; the authority that came to replace his would have to be embodied in turn.

We need not look far for the proving ground of this hypothesis. We need only revisit the junction of 1600 – when the textual disappearance of the clown, first Kemp's and then Armin's, seems to have climaxed in his *physical* disappearance from the stage altogether. In the Caroline plays treated above, the clown's absence was merely contingent, a factor of the genre and personnel of those particular plays. Implicit in their preliminary *occupatio*s, moreover, is a recognition that the disorder and delight the clown triggered was ultimately a force for order, so concentrating the demand for audience participation that even his surrogation might fulfill it, or at least defer it until tomorrow. Yet what if that absence were permanent, a condition of the venue itself, and there were no tomorrow to await? In the Caroline halls, the only kind of clowning unavailable was the jig; in the early Jacobean halls, by contrast, it was clowning as a whole. The revival of the boys' companies at Paul's and the Blackfriars represented a new bid for socially superior clientele, and an opportunity to revise the role of the audience along neoclassical lines. Since boys could not improvise, it also represented a theatre without clowning – the first time drama tried to sever itself from the satellite forms with which it had grown up, its built-in tools of audience management. The proponents of this experiment believed that the finer sort, beyond the need for such discipline, could elevate themselves above the common rabble. Their hopes would prove uncannily, disastrously correct.

The city staged, the stage repossessed

> AUT. Whether it like me, or no, I am a Courtier.
> – *The Winter's Tale*, 4.4.732

It is no accident – though to my knowledge the conjunction has gone unnoticed – that the genre of city comedy arose with, and largely for, the sudden spike in the number of playhouses that no longer offered a dedicated clowning component: it was a genre suited to its place as well as to its time. By portraying London and its fashions, city comedy did more than tap into the increasingly theatrical nature of urban life. It was also the first dramatic genre to attempt, in its own poetics, an end-run around the defining condition of performance – the audience's impulse to claim the stage – precisely by yielding to it, by pre-emptively constituting the entertainment around them: they were *already* its content.[17] City comedy did not literally depict the audience onstage, of course, but "neere, and familiarly allied to the time," afforded instead an "*imitatio vitae, speculum consuetudinis, imago veritatis.*"[18] By subdividing the metropolis into types and "humours," it subdivided its own audience in turn, converting theatre into a different kind of space for the performance of identity – private and reflective, passive instead of active. The spectator must look for themselves onstage by proxy, in the character who most closely corresponds to their social status and who calibrates their affective position in the play. Faced only with a mirror, denied any uncritical relationship to the players in their roles, the playgoer's animus is now directed inward, encouraged to cultivate an impersonal detachment from his caricature and, by extension, from himself. "If there be any that will sit so nigh / Vnto the streame, to looke what it doth run," says the Prologue to *The Alchemist*, they will find "naturall follies, but so shown / As even the Doers may see, and yet not owne."[19] Dramatized in its concentric entrapment plots and sardonic dialogue, in its self-reflexive inductions and intermeans, the overarching theme of city comedy is surveillance: its audience watched itself performed in order to perform itself by how it watched, broken down into monads of interpretation.

If Jonson's "contract" in *Bartholomew Fair* (1614) articulates this vision of theatre as differential social space in parodically rigid terms – "It shall be lawfull for any man to iudge his six pen'orth, his twelue pen'orth, so to his eighteene pence ... and not censure by *Contagion*" – perhaps this is because it was his first play for an outdoor theatre in nearly a decade.[20] At the indoor halls, such a sociology of reception was already established; the idea that an audience could effect its *own* purgation, indeed, was the central idea of the Jonsonian masque.[21] Jonsonian dramaturgy reinforced that self-sufficiency, furthermore, by barring the clown as an object of cathexis. Servants like Face and Mosca are agents of mischief because they are masters of pretense, never themselves; "essential" clowns like Sogliardo, Would-be, Mammon, Cokes, and Fitzdotterel, meanwhile, now become fops and gulls – no longer immigrants who want out but *arrivistes* who want in, punished not for their simplicity but for their excessive self-complication. Self-identity, indeed, is the antithesis of humor comedy. Based on psychic imbalance rather than unity, it is a genre engineered to preclude clowning, to disrupt a rapport between player and audience. Thus its inaugural specimen, *Every Man Out of His Humour* (1599), begins by having Carlo Buffone deliver the prologue already *as* "Carlo Buffone," and ends with his lips sealed in candle-wax – the clown here is merely a character, confined to the play.[22] His ability to critique events instead belongs to Jonson's onstage spectators, Cordatus and Mitis – who model, for the actual ones, how to keep a critical distance from the fiction. In theory, city comedy had evolved beyond clowning: prevailing upon its elite audience's vanity, it now *required* them, as a test of their quality, to reject the play.

This assumed, however, that such disengagement would remain purely mental. In practice, Jonson's audience responded all too eagerly to the invitation to "dis-play" itself. Coinciding exactly with the advent of city comedy at the clowning-free, coterie London theatres at the turn of the century, the phenomenon of gallants sitting on the stage – quite literally "nigh unto the stream" – has never adequately been situated within this historical constellation.[23] Most of our knowledge of it comes from the inductions of the period, which react with growing alarm, indignance, and parody to the gallants gathered around them.[24] Yet those inductions could hardly have been effective deterrents, meant (on Nova Myhill's view) to make the habit "ridiculous" by opening it to "self-consciousness," for their very frequency implies the continuity of the practice.[25] As we will see, the gallants were perfectly aware of what they were doing, and attracting scorn was their entire motivation. Such public mockery merely entrenched the behavior by acknowledging its desire for distinction. The new dramaturgy of reflexivity proved an instant success by instantly backfiring, engendering the very pompous self-regard that its poetics of self-regard were intended to harness. Satire had bred a playgoer immune to – indeed, emboldened by – satire itself.[26]

The incentive for their toleration was money. Primped in their finery (Buffone tells Sogliardo to "sit o'the stage, and flout" only "prouided, you haue a good suit"), playgoers paid handsomely to lounge on a stool, take tobacco, play cards, chat, yawn, sleep, and vent their boredom or contempt for the play as obtrusively as possible.[27] The fee was twelvepence, twice the cost of the gallery. This is the sum quoted by Jonson's Prologues in *Cynthia's Revels* (1601) as they ape the transaction, and Will Sly's petulant gallant in *The Malcontent* (1602) evidently considers it the minimum, threatening to withhold a tip because his conduct has been obstructed. Insisting that "we may sit upon the stage at the private house" and assuming he can do so at the Globe, he is the centerpiece of the fun it pokes at the Blackfriars milieu of the boy companies, where "any man that hath wit may censure if he sit in the twelvepenny roome."[28] The revenue seems to have gone directly to the actors' take: in 1639, Richard Heton, manager of the Revels Children, decided that the boys should get "one dayes p'ffitt wholly to themselves every yeare in consideration of their want of stooles on the stage, wch were taken away by his M^ts command."[29] The royal ban gives us a *terminus ad quem* implying stage-sitting throughout the entire Stuart period, as well as a sense of how impotent were the forces of rebuke to curb it.[30] For the innovation – which the adults would adopt upon moving indoors – represented far more than a profitable sideline, like selling cushions, apples, and nuts. Rather than enhancing one's experience of the play, stage-sitting was a self-aggrandizement deleterious to the play itself, and a prostitution of the players' only real estate. Like the dramaturgy that precipitated it, it incorporated the playgoer as a theatrical producer in his own right.[31]

The more dramatists tried to incorporate their reprimand, accordingly, the worse the problem seems to have become. Chapman's *All Fools* (1604) chides them for their conspicuous habit of early exits: "For if our other audience see / You on the stage depart before we end," begs the Prologue, "Our wits go with you all."[32] Day's *The Isle of Gulls* (1606) asks "either see it all, or none": for "if any one rise (especially of any fashionable sort) about what serious busines soeuer, the rest ... cry mew, by Iesus vilde; and leave the poore hartlesse children to speake their Epilogue to the emptie seates."³³ Marston's *What You Will* (1601) takes a more sophisticated approach, planting three ersatz gallants who *"sit a good while on the Stage before the Candles are lighted, talking together"* before they ambush their neighbors, whom they nickname *"Sineor Snuffe, Monsieur Mew, and Cavaliero Blurt."* They ridicule their feathers and tobacco-snorting, and inveigh against *"Skoffes* Artillery" of *"drunken Censure"* with "sower breath" and "rancorous breasts," who say nothing but *"that's not so good, / Mew, blirt, ha, ha, light Chaffy stuff."* Aware that they "straine the spectators patience," finally, they elect to "place ourselves within the Curtaines, for good faith the Stage is so very little we shall wrong the generall eye els very much."³⁴ Yet as *The Malcontent* recognized, the stage gallant was above courtesy, personifying a state of manners that had overripened into boorish rot: "Dost think I fear hissing? ... Hiss at me!"³⁵ *The Knight of the Burning Pestle*, the most extreme parody of the practice, immolates itself to make that point: its stool-sitters are gauche, middle-class louts who hijack not just the stage but the play, flogging it into an inverterbrate, cartoon medley of amphitheatre citations. If, according to its publisher, the play was *"utterly rejected ... for want of judgement,"* we should perhaps take him at his word – as intimating not a fifth column of commoners at the private houses offended by their portrayal, but the spite of the gentlemen whose audacity George and Nell burlesque, and whose vulgarity they socioeconomically locate.³⁶

Not every play could fail deliberately in order to wage war on the gallants, but more than anyone, Ben Jonson tried it.³⁷ Already in *Every Man Out*, they were becoming his new nemesis: Asper warns Cordatus and Mitis to watch for "a gallant of this marke, / Who (to be thought one of the iudicious) / Sits with his armes thus wreath'd, his hat pull'd here, / Cryes meaw, and nods, and shakes his empty head."³⁸ A year later, *Cynthia's Revels* impersonates the "gentle auditor" who, between exaggerated puffs, heaps abuse on the boy actors: "these rascally *Tits* ... so many *wrens*, or *pismires* – not the fift part of a good face amongst them all ... their *musicke* is abominable ..."³⁹ *Poetaster* (1601) personifies him in Envy, who will "blast your pleasures and destroy your sports, / With wrestings, comments, applications."⁴⁰ Long past the point when other poets had made their peace with it, indeed, and long after earning his laureate credentials, Jonson remained obsessed with the onstage audience. *Bartholomew Fair* was played at the Hope, but Bartholomew Cokes is a demented product of the Blackfriars – flirting with the puppet actors, missing his hat, feather, and "boys now to bring stools, fill tobacco, fetch ale … as they have at the other houses," and blathering through the show.[41] *The Devil Is An Ass* (1616) rails against its "grandees" who "force us act / In compass of a cheese trencher" and who treat the actors as transparent "*Muscouy* glasse"; its protagonist aspires to join them, off to "the *Black-fryers*" to "Sit i'the view" of the very play he is in.[42] In *The Staple of News* (1625), four onstage gossips spew idle commentary on the actors' clothes and physiques – paying no more mind to the play than the real audience, who "marke it not, and sit not still; / But haue a longing to salute, or talke … what is done, and where, / How, and by whom, in all the towne; but here."[43] Jonson blames the failure of *The New Inn* (1629) on "a hundred fastidious impertinents, who were there … to make a generall muster of them-selues … and possesse the Stage, against the Play."[44] In *The Magnetic Lady* (1634), Damplay openly equates the theatrical transaction with his right to condemn: "Can any thing be out of purpose at a *Play*? I see no reason, if I come here, and give my eighteene pence, or two shillings for my Seat, but I should take it out in censure, on the *Stage*."[45] Utterly one-dimensional, he is – like his name – exactly himself, unrepentant and unredeemable: "I care not for marking the *Play*: Ile damne it, talke, and doe what I come for."[46]

If the attributes of Jonson's stage-sitters are starting to sound familiar, Thomas Dekker explains why. In *The Guls Horne-booke* (1609), a mock courtesy manual for gallants, Dekker realizes that the performative sensibility in question represents not hypertheatricality, but merely a reversion to hypo-theatricality – an old stage figure in a new suit. Ceremonially clothing him in "motley," and depicting his face "ill-fauoredly made … as if a tooth-drawer were fumbling about his gommes," Dekker analyzes his performance by situating it within its proper theatrical lineage:

> But when at a new play you take up the twelue-penny roome next the stage … there draw forth this booke, reade alowd, laugh alowd, and play the *Antickes*, that all the garlike mouthd stinkards may cry out, *Away with the fool* … *Tarleton, Kemp*, nor *Singer*, nor all the litter of Fooles that now come drawling behinde them, neuer played the clownes more naturally then the arrantest Sot of you all shall. (B1v–B2r)

Writing from the perspective of the public rather than private playhouses, Dekker has no trouble discerning the structural homology between clowns in one domain and gallants in the other. In a theatre without clowning, the audience will simply fashion a creature of its own who arrogated the clown's function – in a performance of spectatorial individuality so hyperbolic, ironically, that it devolved back into the individual stage performer.

Present not your selfe on the Stage (especially at a new play) until the quaking Prologue … for then it is time, as though you were one of the *properties*, or that you dropt out of y^e *Hangings*, to creepe from behinde the Arras, with your *Tripos*, or three-footed stoole in one hand, and a teston mounted betweene a forefinger and a thumbe in the other … for if you should bestowe your person vpon the vulgar, when the belly of the house is but halfe full, your apparell is quite eaten vp, the fashion lost, and the proportion of your body in more danger to be deuoured then if it were serued up in the Counter amongst the Powltry. (E3v)

Tabor and pipe have been traded for sixpence and a stool; these might be instructions for a clown entrance. "Creeping" rather than peeping from behind the curtain, his movements stylized into an inflammatory routine of provocation, the gallant courts consumption, his "body" the substance of his presentation – just as Timothy Reed inspired "ravishment." Publishing himself, for all his "apparell" the gallant aspires to a naked relation with the audience: "the Stage … will bring you to most perfect light and lay you open," Dekker says, so that "the simplest dolt in the house snatches up your name."[47]

All his gestures, in turn, likewise "lay open" an incipient dimension of violence entirely separate from the play because the play affords no figure in dialogue with it. For Dekker, the stage-sitter surrogates the clown as both terrorist and scapegoat, measuring himself by how much contempt he can inspire and how much abuse he can withstand as a result. "Spreading your body on the stage," he must invite others to "pul you in peeces to enioy your custome"; playing at cards, he must make a spectacle of cheating and an even greater spectacle of pretending, nevertheless, to lose; he must generate his own comedy of dissonance, "to laugh alowd in the middest of the most serious and saddest scene of the terriblest Tragedy" – or else "turne plain Ape, take vp a rush, and tickle the earnest eares of your fellow gallants, to make other fooles fall a laughing: mewe at passionate speeches, blare at merie, finde fault with the musicke, whew at the childrens Action."[48] Above all, he requires the assaults of the audience. "Like a piece of Ordnance," he is to be "planted valiantly (because impudently)" on the stage, "beating down the mewes and hisses of the opposed rascality."[49] One picking a fight with many, he flaunts his isolation, claiming an indefensible piece of ground to defend it for as long as possible: "neither are you to be hunted from thence, though the Scarecrows in the yard hoot at you, hisse at you, spit at you, yea, throw durt euen in your teeth."[50]

The Guls Horne-booke describes a playgoing dynamic that, in 1609, has not appreciably changed since 1589.[51] But the playgoing program had, at least at the indoor halls. With no clown to oppose them, not only does the audience literally "possess the Stage," but the ritual contest for such possession he had mediated must now be supplied *by* that audience. In the absence of any other countervailing noun, they simply became the "principal verb" – "serving themselves up" to themselves. What they pay for is still patronage itself, and patronage thus becomes the event's over-whelming content:

> Sithence then the place is so free in entertainment, allowing a stoole as well to the Farmers sonne as to your Templer: that your Stinkard has the self-same libertie to be there in his Tobacco-Fumes, which your sweet Courtier hath: and that your Car-man and Tinker claime as strong a voice in their suffrage, and sit to giue judgment on the plaies life and death ... It is fit y^t hee, whom the most tailors bils do make roome for, when he comes, should not be basely (like a vyoll) casd up in a corner. (E2v)

This is an economic leveling precipitated not just by commerce, but by an institution that matches no "voice" to the audience, that cannot counter their "suffrage"; Dekker's gallant can "aduance himselfe up to the Throne of the Stage" not just because he has paid, but because there is no one there to stop him, no delegate of the players to challenge.[52] Henry Fitzgeffrey celebrates this gallant – himself – as the new clown, who, with his "3. story Plume," and his satiric authority his capacity to sustain satire, alone

> dares grapple with
> A muster of *Opinions*, in the teeth:
> Who though a *Theater* should striue bring out
> His closest grosest *Faults*, and all about
> Set on to barke: dost boldly stand it out ...
> Who thinks to trauerse so vpright the Stage
> (Free from *Controle*) of this *Censorious Age*.[53]

In both these portraits, it is as if there are no other players, and we are in an inversion of de Witt's Swan drawing, a packed house teeming around a vacant stage. City comedy had wished to make the crowd the play, and that is precisely what it got.

Our bending author

> If you know not ye author, you may raile against him: and peraduenture so behaue your selfe, that you may enforce the Author to know you.
>   – Thomas Dekker, *The Guls Horne-Booke*, E3r

For Jonson, according to most critics, the failure of city comedy tolled the death of theatre itself. Implicit in his revulsion at clowning had been his lifelong rejection of a theatre whose authority inhered in the body. Whereas the true poet attempts to "make all an even, and proportion'd body," only "the wretcheder" use disproportion, "presuming on their own *Naturals*," and for this "are esteemed of the *multitude*."⁵⁴ As a result, poets end up judged on the same terms as those clowns, "for they [playgoers] commend Writers, as they doe Fencers, or Wrastlers; who if they come in robustuously, and put for it with a great deale of violence, are receiu'd for the brauer fellows."⁵⁵ The poet loses all authority if he approaches theatre as a popularity contest, asking to be apprehended not as an artist but as a man, as himself. This is Jonson's very definition of the "theatrical," when in the *Discoveries* he affirms Aristotle's point that laughter – "a fowling for the peoples delight … a deformed vizard, or a rude Clowne" – is antithetical to comedy, for such *ad hominem* grossness merely panders to "the beast, the multitude" rather than ennobling it:

> What could have made them laugh, like to see *Socrates* presented … to have him hoisted up with a Pullie, and there play the Philosopher, in a basquet? Measure, how many foote a flea could skip *Geometrically*, by a just Scale, and edifie the people from the ingine? This was *Theatricall* wit, right Stage-jesting, and relishing a Play-house … what neede wee know any thing, that are nobly borne, more then a Horse-race, or a hunting-match, our day to breake with Citizens, and such innate mysteries? This is truly leaping from the Stage to the Tumbrell againe, reducing all witt to the originall Dungcart.⁵⁶

As much as he distrusted it, for Jonson theatre needed *more* mimesis, not less. It must have crushed him, then, to see that this quintessential "Playhouse" was all playhouses, and that even when he maximized the mimetic distance of drama, it was still collapsed – by its own audience – into a raw, shameless performativity of self. And thus, as we have it, he abjured the stage as his primary artistic medium, repairing to the static purity of his texts as the only stable vehicle through which dramatic authority could be secured.

There was another Jonson, however, who did not flee this theatre of embodiment, but rather embraced it – and who, despite all these austere pronouncements, had sought it all along.⁵⁷ It is the same Jonson, indeed, whose plays relentlessly incorporated the stool-sitters, the chief rivals of his desired monopoly over the audience's attention. Had merely holding their conduct up to ridicule been the sum total of his response, he doubtless – as others did – would have desisted from the futile tactic early on. But the stage gallants are not the ultimate object of Jonson's ridicule: Jonson himself is. No sooner had the didactic program of city comedy been overwhelmed in spectatorial insurgency than it improvised a new one – or, rather, repurposed an old one. At the precise moment that the clown becomes unavailable as an instrument of audience control, the playwright emerges as a dramatic character – or more accurately, an extradramatic one, a concrete and locatable individual in the playhouse, his body recruited onstage as both an agent and a site of performance.

More than any other dramatist, ironically, this is what Jonson materialized his stool-sitters to do: to materialize him, to commandeer the fractious conflict their real-life counterparts otherwise fomented between the audience and itself, and thereby redirect its energy at a new target, at another common, personified adversary – the author.[58] Insofar as he could never resist projecting himself onstage, indeed, these two strains of authority – the pedantic and the ludic – are deeply interwoven, his propensity toward egomaniacal domination always paired with a disarming capacity for self-abasement.[59] They are two halves of a single strategy. Habitually intimating his lurking presence behind the curtain, if Jonson could not make his audience "an even and proportion'd body," he made his own a disproportioned one, so as at least to concentrate their aggression – and their attention – on him. In the best clowning tradition, he picked a fight in order to lose it.

In contrast to the thinly veiled authorial doppelgangers of the Comical Satires, for instance, Jonson's onstage critics serve as mouthpieces as well, but the poet they describe is far more vulnerable: irascible, profligate, debauched, grotesque, impotent – in a word, clownish. The "author" of *Every Man Out* is on the one hand the cold, ascetic Asper, who vows "to strip the ragged follies of the time"; he is also, however, the volatile drunkard who subsists on "beanes and butter milke" and quaffs too much "*Castalian* liquor": "an honest pure Rogue," notes Buffone, "hee will take you off three, foure, fiue of these, one after another, and looke villanously when he has done, like a one-headed CERBERUS (he do'not heare me I hope)."[60] In *Cynthia's Revels* the boy actors are rather less fearful of him. Irked that he has sent out too many Prologues, and having drawn lots to proceed, the loser elects to "reuenge my selfe of the Author" by divulging – and savaging – the play's argument: its setting is "some Fustian Countrey," its characters cliché, its plot trite.[61] Like the stage-sitter he goes on to mimic, "plai[ing] the ignorant critique with euerie thing," he points out in advance the author's weaknesses to a predatory audience; Jonson performs from the outset his powerlessness over the play, his inability to control the bodies of his actors carnivalizing a more basic inability to regulate his own. Eventually this became his standard mode of self-presentation in the playhouse. In *Bartholomew Fair* he is again the backstage bully, and the clumsy oaf: the Stagekeeper worries that "the *Poet* heare me, or his man, Master *Broome*, behind the Arras," yet still confesses the defects of the play and the "absurd courses" of "these Master *Poets*" – who, despite tolerating no slapstick, "has (*sirreuerence*) kick'd me three, or foure times about the Tyring-house."[62] Though the contract stipulates his having "departed with his right," his lingering presence is implicit in its threats of physical enforcement: should anyone "ambitiously, play the foole by his place aforesaid, to challenge the Author," "the *Author* knowes where to finde him."[63] For all its obscurantist legalese, the contract ultimately seeks to make theatrical patronage an interpersonal relationship, a transaction occurring directly between author and audience.

By *The Staple of News*, Jonson is relying exclusively on his scripted stage-sitters to conduct this operation for him. "Yonder he is within (I was i' the Tiring-house a while to see the *Actors* drest)," observes Gossip Mirth,

> rowling himselfe vp and downe like a tun, i' the midst of 'hem, and spurges, neuer did vessel of wort, or wine worke so! His sweating put me in minde of a good Shrouing dish ... a stew'd *Poet*! He doth sit like an vnbrac'd Drum with one of his heads beaten out: For, that you must note, a *Poet* hath two heads, as a Drum has, one for making, the other repeating, and his repeating head is all to pieces: they may gather it vp i' the tiring house; for he hath torne the booke in a *Poeticall* fury, and put himselfe to silence in dead *Sacke* ... (Aa2v)

Knowing he no longer cuts the same lean figure, Jonson makes a meal of his corpulence, his rotundity again offered as a deflating counterpoint to his arrogant perfectionism, a Rabelaisian monstrosity of self-inflicted violence. Suddenly, the funniest thing onstage is backstage: and there, along with the stool-sitters', our eye remains fixed. In a playhouse where both titles were reopened to contest, only by playing the clown could Jonson play the author, making himself the central agent of theatre by becoming the object of constant attack. Wishing to "see the *Foole* ... [who] can commit ... errour, absurdity, as the toy takes him, and no man say, blacke is his eye, but laugh at him," Gossip Tattle is told that "they ha' no *Foole* i' this *Play*" – yet he has been replaced by the playwright, every indictment of the play's "scuruiness" ending in his execration.[64] For overtaxing the actors, he "has abused himselfe, like an Asse"; for his portrayal of Pecunia, they want to "sow him in a sack, and send him by sea to his *Princesse*"; the denouement they deem "worst of all," suspecting Pennyboy Sr. "a kin to the *Poet*" – "like enough, for hee had the chiefest part in his play ... Absurdity on him, for a huge ouergrowne *Play-maker*!"[65] They demand his humiliation: he must beg his characters forgiveness, "And vs too … In two large *sheetes* of paper … Or to stand in a *skin* of *parchment* … And those fill'd with newes! … dedicated to the sustaining of the *Staple*! … Which their *Poet* hath let fall, most abruptly! … let a *protest* go out against him."[66] In their own "protest," they fulfill their design: conflating poet and play, they organize performance as the emanation of a single personality.

"Spreading [his] body on the stage," indeed, Jonson came so to depend upon this orphic strategy that, palsied by a stroke in 1629 and left with no real body to spread, he could never find an alternative. *The New Inn* cannot resist materializing him, but in doing so only confirms his absence – that he is *not* peeping through the curtain, capable at any instant of a "robustuous" entrance to defy molestation: "If you expect more then you had to night," the Epilogue apologizes, "The maker is sick, and sad."[67] In *The Magnetic Lady* Damplay repeatedly asks, "where's one of your Masters, Sirrah, the Poet? … wee would speake with the Poet," but is told "hee is not here."[68] Jonson is now the removed genius whose agency ends where performance begins: "how hee will speed in it, we cannot tell, and hee himselfe (it seems) lesse cares."[69] "Hee shall not give me the Law," Damplay rages, "I will censure, and be witty, and take my Tobacco, and enjoy my *Magna Charta* of reprehension" – but there is really no one preventing him, no figure to give or embody "the law"; throughout, in fact, Damplay clamors not so much at as *for* an opponent, trying to provoke a feud that is unforthcoming.[70] He is met only with "the *Authors* … *Dictamen*," second-hand maxims about proper spectation – "sit still, and expect" – that reduce the poet to a sealed book of literary beatitude, and the play to a purely textual event: "Wee come here to behold *Playes*, and censure them, as they are made, and fitted for us; not to beslave[r] our owne thoughts, with censorious spittle tempering the *Poets* clay."[71] Plays, like poets, exist independently of their materiality and reception; yet play and poet have also become disidentical things. Eighteen years after his *Workes* appeared in print, only now does Jonson apply his textual model of authorship to performance – and only now, perhaps, because he had no other choice.

By the fifth act, Damplay too has vanished. He has not been tamed, however, or sublimed into the represented action of the play, so much as given up on it: with no one to insult, and nothing to do but watch, he simply fades away. We have thus returned to the image of the disappearing audience, but with a difference. If it takes Jonson decades longer to enact this coup of possessive, textual authorship than it did the clowns, his idea of authorship was surprisingly retrograde to theirs – indeed, it *was* theirs. For Damplay, as for the real stage-sitters he emulated, as well as for the whole private playhouse culture they epitomized, "the play" continued to have meaning only as the symbolic extension of a contest for social space. They needed a visible opponent to fulfill that function, and the author needed them to fulfill it – to the point of doing it for them: for thereby, crucially, the author becomes visible as such. Institutional agency can be more easily imagined only when it does not have to be imagined, but made bodily – and made so only in the process of its continuous and mutual unmaking. This the clown knew, and Jonson too. Only when he could no longer materialize himself enough to dichotomize performance between author and audience – between audience and stage, rather than audience onstage – did he try to rewrite the "Magna Charta" of playgoing to obtain merely between audience and play. This is how textuality enters his conception of theatrical experience: as an excuse, a retirement from the corporeal poetics that had hitherto brought his authority into being.

For most of this study, we have seen clowns become authors; as this final chapter suggests, there may be no final chapter to the story of how dramatic authorship emerges as an early modern discursive formation. Their relationship was reciprocal, ongoing, and dialectical: the author had to become the clown in turn, insofar as the authority of theatre – though it would end as a text – always originated in, and was conditioned by, performance. For Jonson, bibliographic encasement was a refuge from commercial and critical failure, but to the degree that he set himself up to fail, his plays can almost be counted successes; they realize a mode of self-publication exclusive to the playhouse, and attuned to its organic processes. His verse betrays none of the self-consolation in literary eternity found in the sonnets of his milder contemporary, Shakespeare, for whom writing and playwriting seem distinct pursuits requiring no reconciliation. To the poet who more than anyone advanced the literary legitimacy of theatre, ironically, dramatic authorship remained an irreducibly hybrid category, established not for all time but from moment to moment, in continuous rhetorical presence. Each foray into the playhouse came freighted with the same insecure need to make a name and a public body for himself, to possess the stage: authorship had to be won not just on title pages, but *in* the theatre itself, forged in the furnace of the theatrical event. If spectatorship had always been authorial, Jonson performed the author as spectator, his particularity exposed to the same laughter as any other self-resembled exhibitionist. The clown's erasure thus proved merely a prelude to his doubling. What he had been to the public playhouse, the playwright now became to the private, a transfer of identites brokered by the audience's bid to fill that void itself.

In these kaleidoscopic relations, finally, may lie a reason for the split course of dramatic authorship in early modern English culture – divided, paradoxically, between a textual culture of accelerating collection, connoisseurship, and encomiastic veneration, and a theatrical one of stubborn hostility and insubordination. These are the privileges, and penalties, of a personal, dysfunctional bond with the audience, just as the playgoer who "gape[d] to bite" Tarlton and impinge on his performance could also idolize him, and beg to see him in print. To defy a play was not to deny its playwright, if those objects were made the same. The obnoxious playgoers that Wycherley's Sparkish typifies in *The Country Wife* may look and act the same in 1675 as ones in 1585, but their barbarous dissonance is now governed by an overriding theme:

> Gad, I go to a play as to a Country-treat, I carry my own wine to one, and my own wit to t'other, or else I'm sure I would not be merry at either; and the reason why we are so often lowder, than the Players, is, because we think we speak more wit, and so become the Poet's Rivals in his audience: For to tell you the truth, we hate the silly rogues; nay, so much that we find fault even with their bawdy upon the stage, whilst we talk nothing else in the Pit as lowd. (F3v)

Far from oblivious of the poet, Wycherley's playgoers actually fashion their narcissistic practice around him, staging a contrapuntal entertainment that is explicitly imitative and "Rivalrous." It is rather the players' "silly rogues" whom Sparkish has come to look past, as negligible factors of the playwright – their wit really his wit, their "bawdy upon the stage" an extension of the one, totalized stage body that the voices from the pit really strive to displace. On playbooks, authorship inertly signified ownership of a property, but in the playhouse it remained alive, a way of opening such ownership to contest, making theatre a property only across many performances. Outside the building, authorship was a noun. Inside, it continued to be – as it had always been – the principal verb.

Notes

Introduction: The play is not the thing

1 On the post-Restoration history of the clown in England, see R. J. Broadbent, *A History of Pantomime* (New York: Benjamin Blom, 1901); Maurice Wilson Disher, *Clowns and Pantomimes* (London: Constable, 1925); John O'Brien, *Harlequin Britain: Pantomime and Entertainment, 1609–1760* (Baltimore: Johns Hopkins University Press, 2004); Jacky Bratton and Ann Featherstone, *The Victorian Clown* (Cambridge University Press, 2006); George Speaight discusses the survival of freestanding Shakespearean clown characters in Victorian circuses in "A Note on Shakespearean Clowns," *Nineteenth Century Theatre Research* 7 (1979), 93–98.

2 From, in no particular order, *Cambyses, Jack Straw, Locrine, The Old Wives Tale, The Famous Victories of Henry the Fifth, The Taming of the Shrew, Romeo and Juliet, James IV, Mucedorus, The Downfall of Robert Earl of Huntington, George a Greene the Pinner of Wakefield, A Match at Midnight, Swetnam the Woman-hater, Measure for Measure, The Fair Maid of the West, A Fine Companion, Thomas Lord Cromwell, The Fair Maid of the Exchange, Englishmen For My Money, The Variety, Greenes Tu Quoque,* and *The Triumph of Beauty.*

3 On Renaissance drama and "popular" culture, broadly conceived in terms of the drama's structural role as an organ of sociopolitical discourse, see Jeffrey S. Doty, "Shakespeare's *Richard II,* 'Popularity,' and the Early Modern Public Sphere," *Shakespeare Quarterly* 61.2 (2010), 183–205; Louis Montrose, *The Purpose of Playing: Shakespeare and the Cultural Politics of the Elizabethan Theatre* (University of Chicago Press, 1996); Jean E. Howard, *The Stage and Social Struggle in Early Modern England* (London and New York: Routledge, 1993); Stephen Greenblatt, *Shakespearean Negotiations: The Circulation of Social Energy in Renaissance England* (Berkeley: University of California Press, 1989); Steven Mullaney, *The Place of the Stage: License, Play and Power in Renaissance England* (University of Chicago Press, 1988); Jonathan Dollimore, *Radical Tragedy: Religion, Ideology and Power in the Drama of Shakespeare and His Contemporaries* (Raleigh, NC: Duke University Press, 1982). See also n. 9 below.

4 Sir Philip Sidney, *The Defence of Poesie* (London: William Ponsonby, 1595), K2r and K2v.

5 William Shakespeare, *The Tragicall Historie of Hamlet* (London: Nicholas Ling, 1604), G3r.
6 Thomas de Quincey, "On the Knocking at the Gate in *Macbeth*," in *The London Magazine*, Oct. 1823; for a contemporary variation, see Stephen Orgel, "Shakespeare and the Kinds of Drama," *Critical Inquiry* 6 (Autumn 1979), 107–23.
7 Being historically closer to those realities, Restoration and eighteenth-century critics like Rymer, Pope, and Johnson were perhaps also closer to the truth. For an overview, see Moody E. Prior, "The Elizabethan Audience and the Plays of Shakespeare," *Modern Philology* 49.2 (Nov. 1951), 101–23.
8 In addition to Barish (*Modern Philology* 51.2 (Nov. 1953), 83–92) and Levin (*Essays in Criticism* 16.1 (1966) 84–91), see Levin, "The Unity of Elizabethan Multiple-Plot Drama," *English Literary History* 34.4 (Dec. 1967), 425–46; Leonard Prager, "The Clown in *Othello*," *Shakespeare Quarterly* 11.1 (1960), 94–96. Needless to say, this reading strategy is a cornerstone of the New Criticism, and informs both monographs and articles on individual plays too numerous to catalogue. For an instance of its continued prosperity, see Bente Videbaek, "How to Teach a Moral Lesson: The Function of the Company Clown in *The Tragedy of Doctor Faustus* and *Love's Labour's Lost*," *Journal of the Wooden O Symposium* 5 (2005), 131–44.
9 See C. L. Barber, *Shakespeare's Festive Comedy* (Princeton University Press, 1959); Robert Weimann and Douglas Bruster, *Shakespeare and the Power of Performance: Stage and Page in the Elizabethan Theatre* (Cambridge University Press, 2008); Weimann, *Author's Pen and Actor's Voice: Playing and Writing in Shakespeare's Theatre*, ed. Helen Higbee and William N. West (Cambridge University Press, 2000); "Bifold Authority in Shakespeare's Theatre," *Shakespeare Quarterly* 39.4 (1998), 401–17; *Authority and Representation in Early Modern Discourse*, ed. David Hillman (Baltimore: Johns Hopkins University Press, 1996); *Shakespeare and the Popular Tradition in the Theater: Studies in the Social Dimension of Dramatic Form and Function*, ed. Robert Schwartz (Baltimore: Johns Hopkins University Press, 1978); Richard Helgerson, *Forms of Nationhood: The Elizabethan Writing of England* (University of Chicago Press, 1995); Erika T. Lin, "Popular Festivity and the Early Modern Stage: The Case of *George a Greene*," *Theatre Journal* 61.2 (May 2009), 271–97; Mary Ellen Lamb, *The Popular Culture of Shakespeare, Spenser and Jonson* (London and New York: Routledge, 2006); Michael Bristol, *Carnival and Theater: Plebeian Culture and the Structure of Authority in Renaissance England* (London and New York: Routledge, 1989); Annabel Patterson, *Shakespeare and the Popular Voice* (London: Blackwell, 1989); François Laroque, *Shakespeare's Festive World: Elizabethan Seasonal Entertainment and the Professional Stage* (Cambridge University Press, 1991).
10 See Eric Rasmussen, "Setting Down What the Clown Spoke: Improvisation, Hand B, and *The Book of Sir Thomas More*," *Library* 13.2 (June 1991), 126–36; Richard Preiss, "Natural Authorship," *Renaissance Drama* 34 (2005), 69–104; John Astington, "The London Stage in the 1580s," in A. L. Magnusson

and C. E. McGee, eds., *The Elizabethan Theatre XI* (Port Credit, ON: P. D. Meany, 1990), 1–18; Tiffany Stern, *Documents of Performance in Early Modern England* (Cambridge University Press, 2009), chapter 8. See also Chapter 2 of this study.

11 See Jean Baudrillard, *For a Critique of the Political Economy of the Sign*, trans. Charles Levin (St. Louis: Telos Press, 1981), which builds on Walter Benjamin's 1936 essay "The Work of Art in the Age of Mechanical Reproduction." The archetype of the mediatized figure – fittingly, a clown – might be said to be Ronald McDonald, who inhabits no particular medium but is a product of all of them. Philip Auslander describes the reciprocal effect of mediatization in contemporary mass entertainment to construct a value of "liveness," which still encodes within itself its status as reproduced: e.g. lip-synching, or jumbo-trons at stadium concerts, or "live" music performers wearing headset microphones. See *Liveness: Performance in a Mediatized Culture* (London and New York: Routledge, 1999).

12 Jean-Christophe Agnew, *Worlds Apart: The Market and the Theater in Anglo-American Thought, 1550–1750* (Cambridge University Press, 1986), 11.

13 Katharine Eisaman Maus, *Inwardness and Theater in the English Renaissance* (University of Chicago Press, 1995), 31.

14 Anne Barton (née Righter), *Shakespeare and the Idea of the Play* (London: Chatto & Windus, 1962), 21.

15 *Ibid.*

16 It is also the subject of Julie Stone Peters's magisterial *The Theatre of the Book*, which investigates how Renaissance theatre and print cultures "grew up together," and "how writing gets turned into action and how action gets recorded as writing" (1, 2). Peters, however, does not couple this account with an analysis of playhouse audience culture, which radically complicates how it became possible to have "a normative playtext" that "spelled out all the words to be spoken" (104). See *The Theatre of the Book, 1480–1880: Print, Text, and Performance in Europe* (London and New York: Oxford University Press, 2000); see also Elizabeth Eisenstein, *The Printing Press As an Agent of Change: Communications and Cultural Transformations in Early-Modern Europe* (Cambridge University Press, 1979).

17 Nora Johnson, *The Actor as Playwright in Early Modern Drama* (Cambridge University Press, 2003), 2. David Wiles' highly intelligent *Shakespeare's Clown: Actor and Text in the Elizabethan Playhouse* (Cambridge University Press, 1987) is another study to which mine is indebted. Wiles is less theoretical in orientation than Johnson, and more narrowly focused on Kemp. Both, however, see the published writings of clowns as straightforward extensions of their stage practice; I do not.

Chapter 1 What audiences did

1 See R. A. Foakes, ed., *Henslowe's Diary*, 2nd edn. (Cambridge University Press, 2002).

2 On such syndicates, see Heather Hirschfeld, *Joint Enterprises: Collaborative Drama and the Institutionalization of the English Renaissance Theater* (Amherst: University of Massachusetts Press, 2004).

3 On the statistical variation of authorial modes between amphitheatres and private halls, and on the King's Men's "reversion" to collaboration in the 1610s, see Hirschfeld, *Joint Enterprises*, as well as "Early Modern Collaboration and Theories of Authorship," *PMLA* 116.3 (May 2001), 609–22. For a dissenting view, see Jeffrey Knapp, *Shakespeare Only* (University of Chicago Press, 2009).

4 See Simon Palfrey and Tiffany Stern, *Shakespeare in Parts* (Oxford University Press, 2007), and Tiffany Stern, *Rehearsal from Shakespeare to Sheridan* (Oxford: Clarendon, 2000).

5 On benefits, see Tiffany Stern, "'A small-beer health to his second day': Playwrights, Prologues and First Performances in the Early Modern Theater," *Studies in Philology* 101.2 (2004), 172–99. On playbills, see Stern, *Rehearsal*, 84, and "'On each Wall and Corner Poast': Playbills, Title-pages and Advertising in Early Modern London," *ELR* 36.1 (2006), 57–89, esp. 83, which disputes Dryden's remark that Congreve's name on a bill for *The Double Dealer* is "a new manner of proceeding."

6 See William N. West, *Theatres and Encyclopedias in Early Modern Europe* (Cambridge University Press, 2002), and Maus, *Inwardness*.

7 Wendy Wall, for instance, notes the difficulty of "legitimating the authority of the theatrical book" because "the theatrical script was ... subject to multiple sites of production"; the audience is not one of those sites. *The Imprint of Gender: Authorship and Publication in the English Renaissance* (Ithaca: Cornell University Press, 1993), 89.

8 Stephen Orgel codifies this view: "[T]he text belonged to the company, and the authority represented by that text – I am talking now about the *performing* text – is that of the company, the owners" ("What is a Text?" *Research Opportunities in Renaissance Drama* 24 (1981), 3). Scott McMillin suggests "taking the companies as the organizing units of theatrical production," and reading plays "not as authorial texts but ... as collaborative endeavours which involve the writers and dozens of other theatre people" ("Reading the Elizabethan Acting Companies," *Early Theatre* 4 (2001), 111).

9 To be sure, the drawing – actually a copy of de Witt's sketch by Aernout van Buchel – attempts merely to delineate an amphitheatre's functional components rather than photographically to capture an event in progress; it is a diagram, and as Roy Strong notes, "the idea of a picture being direct reportage ... was utterly alien to the Elizabethan mind." See John B. Gleason, "The Dutch Humanist Origins of the De Witt drawing of the Swan Theatre," *Shakespeare Quarterly* 32.3 (Autumn 1981), 324–38, and Strong, *The Cult of Elizabeth: Elizabethan Portraiture and Pageantry* (London: Thames and Hudson, 1977), 46. What interests me about the drawing is not its likeness to any theatre, but the likeness of playbooks to *it* – how, in a sense, early modern printed playbooks become epistemologically equivalent to diagrams.

10 Richard Bonian and Henry Walley's preface to the second issue of Shakespeare's *Troylus and Cresseid* (1609), trumpeting "a new play, neuer stal'd with the Stage" (¶2r) is either the exception that confirms this rule, or simply a bogus claim, since they did not make it in the first issue.

11 Erika T. Lin, in *Shakespeare and the Materiality of Performance* (New York: Palgrave, 2012), uses this calculation to estimate that 97 percent of theatrical contact would have been with performance (13).

12 Robert Latham and William Matthews, eds., *The Diary of Samuel Pepys*, 11 vols. (Berkeley: University of California Press, 2000–2001).

13 Landmark studies of early modern playhouse demographics include Andrew Gurr, *Playgoing in Shakespeare's London* (Cambridge University Press, 1987); Ann Jennalie Cook, *The Privileged Playgoers of Shakespeare's London, 1576–1642* (Princeton University Press, 1981); Martin Butler, *Theatre and Crisis, 1632–1642* (Cambridge University Press, 1984).

14 Jeremy Lopez, *Theatrical Convention and Audience Response in Early Modern Drama* (Cambridge University Press, 2003), 7.

15 *Ibid.*, 34.

16 Dawson, "Performance and Participation," in Anthony B. Dawson and Paul Yachnin, *The Culture of Playgoing in Shakespeare's England: A Collaborative Debate* (Cambridge University Press, 2001), 11–37.

17 Dawson, "The Distracted Globe," in Dawson and Yachnin, *Culture*, 96 and 88–107.

18 Dawson and Yachnin, *Culture*, 35, 96.

19 Lopez, *Theatrical Convention*, 13.

20 Stephen Gosson, *Playes Confuted in Fiue Actions* (London: Thomas Gosson, 1582), G5r.

21 Jennifer A. Low and Nova Myhill, "Audience and Audiences," in Low and Myhill, eds., *Imagining the Audience in Early Modern Drama, 1558–1642* (London: Palgrave, 2011), 3.

22 *Ibid.*, 3, 5.

23 *Ibid.*, 5; see Keir Elam, *The Semiotics of Theatre and Drama* (London: Methuen, 1980).

24 *Ibid.*, 6.

25 *Ibid.*

26 *Ibid.*, 6, 7, 10.

27 See Forman's *Booke of Plaies and Notes therof per formans for Common Pollicie*, Bodleian Ashmole MS 208, fols. 201v–202r.

28 Charles Whitney, *Early Responses to Renaissance Drama* (Cambridge University Press, 2006), 1.

29 *Ibid.*, 9–10.

30 Sir Richard Baker, *Theatrum Redivivum, or Theatre Vindicated* (1662), 34.

31 "An excellent Actor," in Sir Thomas Overbury *et al.*, *New and Choise Characters* (1615), M5v.

32 See also Matthew Steggle's enormously useful *Laughing and Weeping in Early Modern Theatres* (Aldershot: Ashgate, 2007).

33 I use the word "inscription" here to prevent my analysis from falling into the familiar binary of "oral" vs. "literate" apprehensions of theatre. As will become clear, audience behavior frustrates any easy application of this binary: there were highly literate segments who performed that literacy quite obtrusively, as well as highly oral segments who demanded the textualization of their performance. What distinguishes my argument is that the *audience* is doing the performing; they are never apprehending theatre purely on one level or the other, because never just "apprehending" theatre. The difference between orality and literacy is less pertinent than the difference between improvised and scripted performance, on either side of the stage. See Walter J. Ong, *Orality & Literacy: The Technologizing of the Word* (London and New York: Routledge, 1982); Leah S. Marcus, *Unediting the Renaissance: Shakespeare, Marlowe, Milton* (London and New York: Routledge, 1996), esp. ch. 5; and Lukas Erne, *Shakespeare as Literary Dramatist* (Cambridge University Press, 2003).

34 Whitney, *Early Responses*, 125, and more generally 115–200.

35 Gosson, *Playes Confuted*, F1v.

36 Thomas Heywood, *The Apologie for Actors* (1616), G1v.

37 Thomas Nashe, *Pierce Penniless his Supplication to the Devil* (1592), F3r; George Chapman, *The Widowes Teares* (1612), G4r.

38 R. Gostelow, "On the death of Mr. Randolphe," in Thomas Randolph, *Poems* (1638) ***1v.

39 Thomas Palmer, "Master John Fletcher his dramaticall Works now at last printed," in Francis Beaumont and John Fletcher, *Comedies and Tragedies* (1647), *f*2v.

40 For a more detailed discussion of Jacobean and Caroline indoor hall behavior, see the Epilogue.

41 Quoted in David Masson, *The Life of Milton*, 2nd edn. (London: Macmillan, 1881), I.218.

42 Anon., *Pimlyco, or Runne Red-Cap* (1609), C1r.

43 Sir John Davies, "In Cosmum" and "In Rufum," in J[ohn]. D[avies]. and C(hristopher). M.(arlowe), *Epigrammes and Elegies* (n.d.), A4r and B2v–B3r.

44 Edmund Spenser, *The Faerie Queene* (1596) IV.3, C8r.

45 Michael Drayton, "Ode: The Sacrifice to Apollo," in *Poems* (1619), Pp1v; *Idea*, Sonnet #47, in *Poems* (1605), Cc4v.

46 Thomas Dekker, *If It Be Not Good The Diuel Is In It* (1612), Prologue, A4r–v (emphasis in original).

47 Thomas Carew, "To my worthy Friend, M. D'Avenant," in William Davenant, *The Just Italian* (1630), A3v–A4r.

48 See John N. Wall, "John Donne and the Practice of Priesthood," *Renaissance Papers* 2007, 1–16.

49 John Donne, *The Sermons of John Donne*, ed. G. R. Potter and Evelyn M. Simpson (Berkeley: University of California Press, 1953–62), X.132–33.

50 See John N. Wall *et al.*, *The Virtual Paul's Cross Project*, http://vpcp.chass.ncsu. edu/. My thanks to Sarah Wall-Randell for alerting me to this resource.

51 Donne, *Sermons*, X.134.

52 See Michael J. Hirrel, "Duration of Performances and Lengths of Plays: How Shall We Beguile the Lazy Time?" *Shakespeare Quarterly* 61.2 (Summer 2010), 159–82. In saying this, I do not contradict Hirrel's thesis that what filled the time not devoted to the play were "incidental entertainments" (176, 181). As will become clear in Chapter 2, those "incidental entertainments" were entirely about vocalizing the audience.

53 John Lyly, *Campaspe* (1584), A3v; *Midas* (1592), A2v; *Sapho and Phao* (1584), A2r.

54 Ev. B., "To the most understanding Poet," and Anon., "In SEIANVM BEN. IONSONI Et Musis, et sibi in Deliciis," in Ben Jonson, *Sejanus His Fall* (1605), A3v and ¶3r.

55 Such attitudes may inflect dramatic representations of crowds themselves: see Frederick Tupper Jr., "The Shakespearean Mob," *PMLA* 27 (1912), 486–523; Brents Stirling, *The Populace in Shakespeare* (New York: Columbia University Press, 1949); C. A. Patrides, "'The beast with many heads': Views on the Multitude," in *Premises and Motifs in Renaissance Thought and Literature* (Princeton University Press, 1982), 124–36; Ian Munro, *The Figure of the Crowd in Early Modern London: The City and Its Double* (New York and Hampshire, UK: Palgrave, 2005). For a compact survey of "Crowd Theory," see J. S. McClelland, *The Crowd and the Mob: From Plato to Canetti* (London: Unwin Hyman, 1989).

56 Leonard Digges, "Vpon Master William Shakespeare," in *Poems: Written by Wil. Shakespeare* (1640), *3v.

57 John Fletcher, "To His Worthy Friend Mr. Ben Jonson," in Jonson, *Catiline*, A3v.

58 John Fletcher, *The Faithfull Shepheardesse* (1610), "To The Reader," ¶2v.

59 John Webster, *The White Divel* (1612), "To The Reader," A2r–v.

60 John Marston, *What You Will* (1601), E2r.

61 Nathaniel Field, "To my lou'd friend M. John Fletcher," in *Faithfull Shepheardesse*, ¶3v.

62 John Davies of Hereford, *Wits Bedlam* (1617), Epigram 225, F7r.

63 William Fennor, "The Description of a Poet," in *Fennors Descriptions* (1616), B2r–v. Beaumont likewise says that "One company k[n]owing they iudgement lacke, / Ground their beliefe on the next man in blacke" ("To my friend Maister John Fletceher [*sic*]," in Fletcher, *Faithfull Shepheardesse*, ¶3v); Jonson's Scrivener warns the audience of *Bartholomew Fair* (pr. 1631) not to "censure by *Contagion*" (A5v).

64 Anthony Munday, *A second and third blast of retrait from plaies and Theaters* (London: Henrie Denham, 1580), 53, 89.

65 Thomas Dekker, *The Guls Horne-booke* (1609), E2v.

66 William Davenant, "Epilogue," *The Unfortunate Lovers* (London: R.H., 1643), G4v.

67 Henry Fitzgeffrey, *Satyres and Satyricall Epigrams* (London: Miles Partrich, 1617), E7v.

68 James Shirley, "Prologue," *The Example* (London: Andrew Crooke and William Cooke, 1637), A2r.

69 Henry Killigrew, *Pallantus and Eudora A Tragœdie* (London: John Hardesty, 1653), A2r.
70 Edward J. L. Scott, ed., *The Letter Book of Gabriel Harvey* (London: Camden Society, 1883–84), 67–68.
71 Edmund Gayton, *Pleasant Notes upon Don Quixot* (1654), Mm3r, p. 271.
72 John Tatham, *The Fancies Theater* (1640), H3r (emphasis in original).
73 *Ibid.*, Hh2v (emphasis in original).
74 Richard Lovelace, "A Prologue to The Scholars, a Comædy presented at the White-fryers," in *Lucasta* (London: Thomas Harper, 1649), 76 (emphasis in original).
75 Anon., *Tarltons Jests* (London: John Budge, 1613), B2r (emphasis in original).
76 *Ibid.*, B2v.
77 William Davenant, *News From Plymouth* (1635), in *The Works of William Davenant* (1673), Aaaa1r and Eeee1r.
78 Quoted in E. K. Chambers, *The Elizabethan Stage*, 4 vols. (Oxford: Clarendon, 1923) IV.280 and 282.
79 The Norwich incident is discussed in Scott McMillin and Sally-Beth MacLean, *The Queen's Men and Their Plays* (Cambridge University Press, 1998) 42–43.
80 Gurr, *Playgoing*, 56.
81 Quoted in Chambers, *Elizabethan Stage*. IV.297–98.
82 Public Records Office C115/8391, quoted in Herbert Berry, "The Stage and Boxes at Blackfriars," *Studies in Philology* 63 (1966), 163–86, p. 165.
83 *Stafforde's Letters* I.511, letter of 25 January 1636, quoted in Gurr, *Playgoing*, 244.
84 Henry Chettle, *Kind-Hartes Dreame* (London: William Wright, 1592), C4r; Richard Brathwait, *Whimzies: or a New Cast of Characters* (London: Felix Kingston, 1631), G5v–G6r.
85 Paul Menzer, "Crowd Control," in Low and Myhill, *Imagining the Audience*, 25.
86 Gerald Eades Bentley, *The Jacobean and Caroline Stage*, 7 vols. (Oxford: Clarendon, 1941–67), II.361.
87 T[homas]. M[ay]., *The Life of a Satyrical Puppy Called Nim* (1657), 101, H4r.
88 Quoted in W. W. Greg, ed., *Gesta Grayorum* (London: Malone Society, 1914), 22 (spelling modernized).
89 Norman E. McClure, ed., *Letters of John Chamberlain*, 2 vols. (Philadelphia, 1939), 1.328.
90 John Nichols, ed., *Progresses of King James the First*, 2 vols. (1828), II.72–73.
91 Gilbert Dugdale, *The Time Triumphant* (London: R.B., 1604), B1r–B2r.
92 *Ibid.*, B3r–v.
93 *Ibid.*, B3v.
94 *Miscellany*, Folger Shakespeare Library MS v.a.162, quoted in Stern, *Documents*, 250.
95 For a possible explanation of the play's notorious failure, see my Epilogue.
96 Palmer, "Fletcher," in Beaumont and Fletcher, *Comedies and Tragedies*, f2v.
97 Gayton, *Pleasant Notes*, B2r, p. 3.

98 Anon. (Thomas Gainsford?), "Player," in *The Rich Cabinet Furnished* (1616), Q5r–v (my emphasis).

99 Rastell's *Four Elements* (1520), for instance, suggests how much time to allot for performance, and how to abridge the text if needed: "yf ye hole matter be played [it] wyl conteyne the space of an hour and a halfe / but yf ye lyst ye ma leue out muche of the sad mater as the messengers perte / and some of naturys parte and some of experyens perte." Udall's *Jacob and Esau* (pr. 1568) lists separately "the partes and names of the Players who are to be consydered to be Hebrews and so should be apparailed with attire." Robert Wever's *Lusty Juventus* (*c.* 1550), amusingly, even reminds actors doubling roles to "tak of those partes that be not in place at once." See Greg Walker, *The Politics of Performance in Early Renaissance Drama* (Cambridge University Press, 1998) 6–50, and T. H. Howard-Hill, "The Evolution of the Form of Plays in English During the Renaissance," *Renaissance Quarterly* 43.1 (Spring 1990), 112–45.

100 Helgerson, *Forms of Nationhood*, 223ff., and more generally 195–245.

101 See Bristol, *Carnival and Theater*, 122–23 and 107–24.

102 Most of this catalogue is drawn from Erne, *Literary Dramatist*, supplemented by Douglas A. Brooks, *From Playhouse to Printing House: Drama and Authorship in Early Modern England* (Cambridge University Press, 2000), and Jeffrey Masten, *Textual Intercourse: Collaboration, Authorship and Sexualities in Renaissance Drama* (Cambridge University Press, 1997). Joseph Loewenstein, *The Author's Due: Printing and the Prehistory of Copyright* (University of Chicago Press, 2002) and James J. Marino's *Owning William Shakespeare* (Philadelphia: University of Pennsylvania Press, 2010) represent the commercially driven side of the legitimation narrative.

103 The development of the playbook's *mise en page* was of course a more drawn-out process, although most of the important breaks with earlier descriptive conventions seem to have occurred by the time late Elizabethan theatre began publishing itself in significant numbers. For a broader history, see Peters, *Theatre of the Book*, esp. chapters 1 and 4.

104 These are *The Fair Maid of the Exchange* (pr. 1607) and *Mucedorus* (pr. 1598).

105 Richard Edwards, *The excellent Comedie of two the moste faithfullest Freendes, Damon and Pithias* (London: Richard Jones, 1571), A1r (my emphasis).

106 John Marston, *The History of Antonio and Mellida, The First Part* (London: Mathewe Lownes and Thomas Fisher, 1602), B1v. Jonson also revised the ending to *Every Man Out of His Humour* (1600), which "many seem'd not to relish ... and therefore 'twas since alter'd" (R3r). For evidence of this practice throughout the seventeenth and eighteenth centuries, see Stern, *Documents*, 89–91.

107 I am sensitive to Stern's precaution that "playbooks [could not be] ever fully stripped of the theatre to become plays in an ideal literary form" (*Documents*, 254), but whatever traces of "theatre" we find in them tend to be accidental – artifacts of how playbooks were often patched together from

the scattered materials of performance – and are certainly not programmatic. See *Documents*, 160–67.

108 Erne, *Literary Dramatist*, 55, but see more generally 47ff.

109 The most notable exception to this convention is Heminges and Condell's "To the Great Variety of Readers" in Shakespeare's *Comedies, Histories and Tragedies* (1623).

110 This is not to say *exactly* the same people, in all cases. Many of these prefaces, epistles and verses *do* seek to foster a readership distinct from spectatorship, and scholars have begun attending to its formation in the specialized interpretive practices – recitation, commonplacing, marginalia, anthologization – that grew up around it. Rather than recuperate functions of the playbook *not* related to the playhouse, however, I wish to concentrate on the largest possible demographic, in order to call into question the duality of playgoing and playreading as a general principle.

111 See David Cressy, *Literacy and the Social Order: Reading and Writing in Tudor and Stuart England* (Cambridge University Press, 1980), esp. chapters 6 and 7, and my Epilogue.

112 See on this point Marta Straznicky, "The Red Bull Repertory in Print, 1605–60," *Early Theatre* 9.2 (2006), 144–56; see also my Epilogue.

113 On Bodley, see G. W. Wheeler, *The Letters of Sir Thomas Bodley to Thomas James* (Oxford: Clarendon, 1926), 219–22; on private aristocratic collections, see Heidi Brayman Hackel, "'Rowme' of Its Own: Printed Drama in Early Libraries," in John D. Cox and David Scott Kastan, eds., *A New History of Early English Drama* (Columbia University Press, 1997), 113–30; *Reading Material in Early Modern England: Print, Gender, and Literacy* (Cambridge University Press, 2005).

114 The case of Edward Dering furnishes an example not only of the migratory patterns of playbooks but also of amateur performance as an end-use of publication; see T. N. S. Lennam, "Sir Edward Dering's Collection of Playbooks, 1619–1624" (*Shakespeare Quarterly* 16 (1965), 145–53).

115 Richard Jones, "To the Gentlemen Readers," in Christopher Marlowe, *Tamburlaine the Great* (1590), A2r. This preface is routinely cited as fissioning spectatorship and readership: see Erne, *Literary Dramatist*, 47–51 (which thinks Jones is talking about "passages" rather than what he says, "Iestures").

116 Anon. [Valentine Simmes?], in Thomas Dekker, *The Shoemakers Holiday* (London: Valentine Simmes, 1600), A3r; Thomas Heywood, *The Four Prentices of London* (London: I[ohn]. W[right]., 1615), A2r.

117 Jonson, "To the Reader-in-Ordinarie," in *Catiline* (1611), A3r; Webster, "To the Reader," in *The White Divel* (1612), A2r.

118 Beaumont, "To my friend," in Fletcher, *Faithfull Shepheardesse*, ¶3v.

119 This synesthetic mixture would, in Romantic criticism, ultimately champion reading, but only insofar as reading realizes the immediacy of performance, without the distractions of materiality. See Charles Lamb, "On the Tragedies of Shakespeare" (*The Reflector*, 1811).

120 W[illiam]. B[asse]., "The *Authors* Friend to the Reader," in Philip Massinger, *The Bond-Man* (1624), A4r (emphasis in original).

121 James Shirley, "To the Reader," in Beaumont and Fletcher, *Comedies and Tragedies*, A3r.

122 Marta Straznicky asserts that "the early modern play could be play and book at one and the same time" (4). Since her concern is with practices specific to playbook reading, however, she really means at *different* times, not the *simultaneous* perception of theatre as both text and event needed to explain playbook consumption in general. See "Plays, Books, and the Public Sphere," in Straznicky, ed., *The Book of the Play: Playwrights, Stationers and Readers in Early Modern England* (Amherst: University of Massachusetts Press, 2006).

123 Alan B. Farmer and Zachary Lesser, "The Popularity of Playbooks Revisited," *Shakespeare Quarterly* 56.1 (2005), 1–32.

124 *Ibid.*, 10, 7–11.

125 Zachary Lesser, "Playbooks," in Joad Raymond, ed., *The Oxford History of Popular Print Culture*, vol. 1 (Oxford University Press, 2011), 521–535. I thank Lesser for sharing an early draft.

126 Tiffany Stern, "Watching as Reading: the Audience and Written Text in the Early Modern Playhouse," in Laurie Maguire, ed., *How to do Things with Shakespeare* (Oxford: Blackwell, 2008), 136–59.

127 Stern's emphasis is not mine, of course. Her claim is only that early modern performance environments were suffused with textual paraphernalia – not necessarily drama – that called on playgoers to be readers. Since the evidence for such reading usually involves their doing so *instead* of watching the play (in other words, still performing at its expense), my inquiry depends on deeper and more coordinated phenomena.

128 Stephen Orgel, "What is an Editor?" *Shakespeare Studies* 24 (1996), 23.

129 David Scott Kastan, *Shakespeare and the Book* (Cambridge University Press, 2001), 8–9.

130 See Peter W. M. Blayney, "The Publication of Playbooks," in Cox and Kastan, *A New History*, 383–422. The relation of advertisement to the thing advertised is here not only semiotically opaque, but competing; people are not generally asked to *buy* advertisements.

131 Middleton and Dekker, "To the Comicke, Play-readers," in *The Roaring Girl* (1611), A3r.

132 Thomas Heywood, *Pleasant Dialogues and Drammas* (1637), 248.

Chapter 2 Send in the clown

1 Douglas Bruster and Robert Weimann, *Prologues to Shakespeare's Theatre: Performance and Liminality in Early Modern Drama* (New York: Routledge, 2004), ix, 37.

2 *Ibid.*, 45.

3 Furthermore, see Stern, *Documents* 81–119, for the reminder that prologues were performed only once, at a play's premiere.

4 Humphrey Moseley, "The Stationer," in Beaumont and Fletcher, *Comedies and Tragedies*, g2r.

5 Trans. Peter Bietenholz, in Glynne Wickham, Herbert Berry, and William Ingram, eds., *English Professional Theatre, 1530–1660* (Cambridge University Press, 2000), 415–16.

6 Gayton, *Pleasant Notes*, 271.

7 *Ibid.*

8 For a diametrically opposed view – that what "deflects the centripedal gaze" of the audience is precisely "representation," the "distancing" effect of dramatic fiction itself – see Menzer, "Crowd Control," 25ff.

9 See Weimann, *Popular Tradition*.

10 Weimann, *Author's Pen*, 111.

11 *Ibid.*, 103.

12 *Ibid.*, 113–14.

13 See McMillin and MacLean, *Queen's Men*, 29. Archie Armstrong's *A Banquet of Jests* (1633) includes one jest where "In a Play time, hee that presented the Jester or Clowne" was "called to enter (for the Stage was emptie)" (E5r–v); see also the discussion of *The Pilgrimage to Parnassus* below.

14 The Vices' names in *Impacient Povertie* (1547), *Pacient Grissill* (1559), *Cambyses* (1561), *Apius and Virginia* (1564), *Like Will to Like* (1568), and *All For Money* (1577), respectively.

15 See Weimann, *Popular Tradition*.

16 That split already emerges within the corpus of Tudor morality in figures like Hob and Lob in *Cambyses*, Haunce in *Like Will to Like*, Hance in *Wealth and Health* (1557), Moros in *The Longer Thou Livest* (1559), Rusticus and Hodge in *Horestes* (1567), and Lomia in *Common Conditions* (1576). It is virtually complete by *Three Ladies of London* (1584), which juxtaposes its Vice, Dissimulation, with a miller called Simplicity.

17 *Mary Magdalene* (1567), l.1302; *The Tide Tarrieth No Man* (1576), E3r; *Like Will to Like*, l.894. Peter Happé provides a list of such directions in "'The Vice' and the Popular Theatre, 1547–80," in Antony Coleman and Antony Hammond, eds., *Poetry and Drama, 1570–1700: Essays in Honour of Harold F. Brooks* (London: Methuen, 1981), 13–31. After a visit by a troupe to Bungay in 1566, a payment was noted "To Kelsaye, the vyce, for his pastyme before the plaie, and after the playe" (quoted in E. K. Chambers, *The Medieval Stage* (London: Oxford University Press, 1903), II.343); during a production of Lyndsay's *Satyre of the Thrie Estaitis*, the vice Solace would "make mery, sing ballettes with his fellowes, and drinke at the interluydes of the play" (quoted in C. R. Baskervill, *The Elizabethan Jig and Related Song Drama* (University of Chicago Press, 1929), 85).

18 David Bevington examined this phenomenon in *From Mankind to Marlowe* (Cambridge MA: Harvard University Press, 1968). In *Mucedorus*, Mouse remains explicitly a part for one.

19 Wiles, *Shakespeare's Clown*, 23.

20 *Ibid.*

21 *Ibid.*, 20–22. Kemp's Launce does this in *Two Gentlemen of Verona*; during a court performance "Tarlton played the God Lutz with a flitch of bacon at his back, and the Queen bade them take away the knave for making her laugh so

excessively, as he fought against her little dog, Perrico de Faldas, with his sword and long staffe" (*Calendar of State Papers Domestic*, Eliz. Ccxv.89, quoted in Edwin Nungezer, *A Dictionary of Actors* (New Haven: Yale University Press, 1929), 351).

22 The custom is reconstructed in Frederick B. Jonassen, "The Meaning of Falstaff's Allusion to the Jack-a-Lent in *The Merry Wives of Windsor*," *Studies in Philology* 88.1 (Winter 1991), 46–68; see also E. K. Chambers, *The English Folk-Play* (Oxford: Clarendon, 1933), 157 and 153ff.

23 J. G. Nichols, ed., *The Diary of Henry Machyn* (London: Camden Society, 1848), 33.

24 Thomas Q. Couch, "The Folk Lore of a Cornish Village: Fasts and Festivals," *Notes and Queries* 12:297 (o.s.), 20 Oct. 1855; quoted in Jonassen, "Falstaff's," 53–54.

25 William Elderton, "Lenton Stuffe," in Thomas Wright, *Songs and Ballads* (London: J. B. Nichols, 1860), 188, from Ashmolean MS.48.

26 At a Norwich Shrovetide riding in 1443, "Lenten cladde in white with redde herrings and skinnes and his hors trapped with oyster shelles … in token that sadness and abstinence of merth shulde followe and an holy tyme; and so rode in diuerse stretes of the Cite with other peple with hym disgysed making merthe and disporte and pleyes." Quoted in Chambers, *Medieval Stage* I.262, and in Jonassen, "Falstaff's," 56 n.21.

27 Beaumont and Fletcher, *The Womans Prize, or the Tamer Tamed*, in *Comedies and Tragedies*, 116; Shakespeare, *The Merry Wives of Windsor*, in *Comedies, Histories and Tragedies*, E1v and E6r.

28 Ben Jonson, *A Tale of a Tub*, in *Workes* v.2 (1640), O1v.

29 John Taylor, *Jack-a-Lent His Beginning and Entertainment* (1620), A4v–B1r.

30 *Ibid.*, B1r.

31 Baskervill, *Jig*, 92–99. "English John" may be related, in one direction or the other, to the Italian "Gianni" that would become the *commedia* type of the *zanni*.

32 John Playford, *The English Dancing Master* (1651), I4r.

33 Robert Hornback, in *The English Clown Tradition from the Middle Ages to Shakespeare* (Suffolk: D. S. Brewer, 2009), illuminates the medieval roots of English comic performance in religious and political satire, and suggests their continuity with early modern clown practice.

34 John Foxe, *Actes and Monuments* (1563), 734–39; quoted in Baskervill, *Jig*, 46–47.

35 Edward Arber, ed., *A Transcript of the Registers of the Company of Stationers of London 1554–1640*, (London, 1875), I.205 and II.324; see Baskervill, *Jig*, 47.

36 Anon., "Jack of Lent's Ballat," in Anon., ed., *Choyce Drollery* (1656), C2v–C7v.

37 Variations on this persona would include Pasquil, No-body, Robin Goodfellow, Tom Tel-Troth, and Pierce Penniless.

38 Erasmus, *Apophthegmes*, trans. Nicholas Udall (1542), 245 and 34; quoted in Baskervill, *Jig*, 22.

39 Anon., *A Fooles Bolt is soone shot* (1636), A1r (broadside). See Baskervill, *Jig*, 22–23, and Leo Spitzer, "Ragamuffin, Ragman, Rigmarole and Rogue," *Modern Language Notes* 62.2 (February 1947), 85–93.

40 Foxe, *Actes and Monuments* (1583), II.2081.

41 Crypto-doctrinal vignettes of this type, in which clown personae feature prominently – such as *Rusticus and Sapyence* (1561) and the "knack to know a knave" genre – are discussed in Baskervill, *Jig*, 47–50.

42 Geffray Fenton, trans. *A Forme of Christian Pollicie* (1574), S4v; the passage is Fenton's addition.

43 Ulpian Fulwell, *The Arte of Flatterie* (1579), G4r (my emphasis).

44 Baskervill, *Jig*, 68 cites another Oxford ballad from the mid sixteenth century called "Ho, ho, John of Dogs, what news?" with the same opening stanza. *The Taming of the Shrew* replays the scenario between Curtis and Grumio, with Grumio replying "The devil is dead, for there I was."

45 Witnessing a performance of *The Winter's Tale*, Simon Forman describes Autolycus as "the Rog. that cam in all tottered like coll. pixci" (quoted in Baskervill, *Jig*, 93).

46 In *Grim the Collier of Croydon* (c. 1600), Robin Goodfellow appears as a very rustic sprite, while in *Wily Beguiled* (1606) he is fully a clown; Jonson's *The Devil Is An Ass* (1616) takes its premise from *Grim*, and Pug's cozening shares a great deal with clowning convention.

47 Donald Lupton, *London and the Countrey Carbonado'd* (1632), 93.

48 William Davenant, *The Wits* (1636) B2r; Richard Leigh, *The Transproser Rehears'd* (1673), 31. *Mercurius Democritus* for 22–29 December 1652 announces a "Tryal of Skill" between a fishwife and a kitchen-stuff woman, featuring "Tooth and Naile, Long tongue & Taile, Thou Whore, and thou Whore."

49 "A new Dialogue between Alice and Betrice, As they met at the Market one Morning early" (c. 1685–88), quoted in Baskervill, *Jig*, 70.

50 Mark C. Pilkinton, ed., *Records of Early English Drama: Bristol* (University of Toronto Press, 1997), 112.

51 Thomas Fuller, *The History of the Worthies of England* (1662), III.47.

52 Robert Wilson, *The three Lordes and three Ladies of London* (pr. 1590), C1v.

53 See variously Nungezer, *Actors*, 347–65; Mark Eccles, "Elizabethan Actors IV," *Notes and Queries* 40.2 (238), 1993, 165–76; *Dictionary of National Biography*, 369–71.

54 Misodiaboles [a.k.a. Sir John Harington], *Vlysses upon Aiax* (1596), F3v; Humphrey King, *An Halfe-Penny worth of Wit, in a Penny-worth of Paper* (1613), E1r.

55 Anon., *The Partiall Law*, ed. Bertram Dobell (London, 1908), 43. In *The Passions of the Minde* (1601) Thomas Wright recalls seeing "Tarleton play the clowne, and use no other breeches than such sloppes or slivings as now many gentlemen weare: they are almost capable of a bushel of wheate."

56 George Whetstone, *Promos and Cassandra* (1578), A2v; Sidney, *Defence*, K2r. William Rankins' *A Mirrour of Monsters* (1587), similarly, lists "Clownes cladde ... with Country condition, as in Ruffe russet" as a standard playhouse character (7), and Nicholas Breton warns "country Players, that old paltry

iests / Pronounced in a painted motley coate, / Fills all the world so full of Cuckoes nests, / That Nightingales can scarcely sing a note" (*Pasquils Mad-Cap* (1600), E2r).

57 The 1598 quarto of *Famous Victories* has the clown Derick enter already apprised of the report; he and the Justice furthermore share scenes, making such doubling difficult to envision.

58 Anon., *The Pilgrimage to Parnassus*, in J. B. Leishman, ed., *The Three Parnassus Plays, 1598–1601* (London: Ivor Nicholson & Watson, 1949), ll.670–74.

59 John Astington warns that both Scottowe's drawing and the woodcut from which it derives may be copies of an unrelated Dutch print of 1566; this pertains only to the figure's dress, however, not his stance and face. See "Tarlton and the Sanguine Temperament," *Theatre Notebook* 53.1 (1999), 2–7.

60 Thomas Bastard, *Chrestoleros: Seven bookes of Epigrames* (1598), VI.39 (155).

61 John Davies of Hereford, *Wits Bedlam* (1617), K6v.

62 Samuel Rowlands, *The Letting of Humours Blood to the Head* (1600), C2v and D8r.

63 Gabriel Harvey, *Foure Letters, and Certaine Sonnets* (1592), D4r, 29.

64 *Tarltons Jests*, B3r.

65 *Ibid.*, C2r–v; D1v; E2v.

66 *Ibid.*, C3v.

67 Martin Buzacott compares this to "Stockholm Syndrome" in *The Death of the Actor: Shakespeare on Stage and Page* (London: Routledge, 1991), 72–76. See also Peter Thomson, "The True Physiognomy of a Man: Richard Tarlton and his Legend," *Parergon* 14.2 (n.s.), January 1997, 29–50, and "Clowns, Fools and Knaves: Stages in the Evolution of Acting," in Jane Milling and Peter Thomson, eds., *The Cambridge History of British Theater, Vol. 1* (Cambridge University Press, 2004), 407–23.

68 *Tarltons Jests*, B4v and C3v.

69 *Ibid.*, D2v–D3r; B3r; C1v.

70 *Ibid.*, D1v–D2r.

71 As representatives, see Barber, *Festive*; Patterson, *Popular Voice*; Bristol, *Carnival*; Weimann, *Popular Tradition* and *Author's Pen*; Hornback, *English Clown*. Helgerson's argument in *Forms of Nationhood* is more complex and diachronic, and is dealt with directly in Chapter 5.

72 Wiles, *Shakespeare's Clown*, 2–3.

73 George Puttenham, *The Arte of English Poesie* (1589) I.11, E3r; Puttenham's description of classical drama here appears to borrow liberally from his experience of the Tudor morality.

74 William Watson, *A Decacordon of Ten Qvodlibeticall Questions* (1602), 156.

75 Anon., *Parnassus*, ll.664–67. Keir Elam suggests that the surprise with which characters often greet the clown, and the curiosity they express about his whereabouts, register his always having "arrived onstage from another place" (181). For Elam that place is the clown's "non-theatrical career"; for me, it may be as simple as his prior appearances elsewhere in that same day's theatrical program. See "'Enter Clowne': The Travels of the English Comic Performer,"

in Paola Pugliatti and Allesandro Serpieri, eds., *English Renaissance Scenes: From Canon to Margins* (Bern: Peter Lang, 2008), 179–202.

76 Even the space for the jig as a structural convention, it is worth noting, did not originate with the clown: musical codas are among the oldest features of recorded English drama. See Baskervill, *Jig*, 85–86.

77 F1r–v.

78 Thomas Nashe, *Strange Newes* (1592), E4r; in *Pierce Penniless* (1592) he imagines the enemies of the theater "brought vpon the Stage ... in a merriment of the Usurer and the Diuel" (F3v).

79 Quoted in Chambers, *Elizabethan Stage*, IV.274 (my emphasis).

80 *The Warres of Cyrus King of Persia* (London: William Blackwal, 1594), C3r.

81 On boys' plays and the absence of clowning from them, see my Epilogue.

82 Marlowe, *Tamburlaine* (pr. 1590), A3r.

83 On clowning's influence on Marlovian dramaturgy, see Kirk Melnikoff, "'[I]ygging vaines' and 'riming mother wits': Marlowe, Clowns and the Early Frameworks of Dramatic Authorship." *Early Modern Literary Studies* 16 (Oct. 2007) (Web).

84 Nashe, *Pierce Penniless*, D1v.

85 Richard Baker, *Theatrum Redivivum* (1662), 34.

86 Henry Peacham, *Thalia's Banquet* (1620), Epigram 94; on Reed, see below and also the Epilogue; Thomas Middleton, *The Mayor of Quinborough* (pr. 1661), 63.

87 In *Cynthia's Revels*, the aptly named Amorphus gives "the particular, and distinct face of euery your most noted *species* of persons" (D3v). *Greenes Tu Quoque* likewise calls for face-pulling from Bubble, who asks Staines to "set my face of any fashion" (G2r).

88 Thomas Goffe, *The Careles Shepherdess, a Tragicomedy* (pr. 1656), B2v–B3r.

89 John Davies of Hereford, *Wits Bedlam* (1617), K6v; Richard Brathwaite, *Remains After Death* (1618); Nungezer, *Actors*, 295. "Pickelherring" was the stage name of Robert Reynolds, who toured Germany and Holland with John Green; it was transplanted, however, into a native comic figure who appears in many German plays. For H. H. Furness, "There is nothing in the whole range of the old English drama ... that is not sweet and wholesome beside this Pickelherring's disgusting vileness" (qtd. in Ernest Brennecke, *Shakespeare in Germany, 1590–1700* (University of Chicago Press, 1964), 109). See William Schrickx, "'Pickleherring' and English actors in Germany," *Shakespeare Survey* 36 (1983), 134–47.

90 William Prynne, *Histrio-mastix* (1633), 877.

91 Munday, *Second and Third Blast*, 87–88.

92 Joseph Hall, *Virgidemiarum* (1597), B5v. Curiously, here the clown comes at the *end* of the play, after "frightfull showes of Fortunes fall, / And bloudy Tyrants rage"; Hall may thus be describing a jig.

93 I.H., *This Worlds Folly* (London: Nicholas Bourne, 1615), B2r.

94 Charles Fitzgeoffrey, "Richardo Tarltono," in *Cenotaphia* (1601), N2v (my translation).

95 Bruce R. Smith, *The Acoustic World of Early Modern England* (University of Chicago Press, 1999), 214.

96 John Oldham, *The Works of Mr. John Oldham, Together with his Remains* (1703), 108.
97 Anon., *The Famous Victories* (1598), A4r.
98 See David Mann, *The Elizabethan Player: Contemporary Stage Representations* (London: Routledge, 1991), and also Peter Thomson, "From Chanticlere to Richard Tarlton," in Sydney Higgins, ed., *European Medieval Drama I* (Turnhout, Belgium: Brepols, 1997), 33–42.
99 Anon. (Nicholas Breton?), *Machiuells Dogge* (1617), 17.
100 Goffe, *Careles Shepherdess*, B3r.
101 Anon., *Locrine* (1595), H1v.
102 It is unclear if "being meerie accting the part of the vize" means Kendall actually played a Vice in a morality – in 1620! – or refers to a customary postlude like "themes." In Mark C. Pilkinton, ed., *Records of Early English Drama: Bristol* (University of Toronto Press, 1997), 215; see also David N. Klausner, "The Improvising Vice in Renaissance England," in Timothy J. McGee, ed., *Improvisation in the Arts of the Middle Ages and Renaissance* (Kalamazoo: Western Michigan University Press, 2003), 273–85.
103 Anon., *The vnfortunate Gallant gull'd at London* (1623).
104 Munday, *Second and Third Blast*, 41.
105 Nashe, *Pierce Penniless*, I4v.
106 See Hirrel, "Duration," 176ff. Hirrel hypothesizes that the length of "incidental entertainments" could fluctuate to suit the length of the play; this seems entirely sound, since they are improvised and plays are not, but since it is also in the nature of improvisation to expand, one wonders if play length was really such a fixed parameter, and if plays did not still have to be cut on the fly – especially with so much improvisation occurring *before* they began.
107 William Vaughan, *The Golden Fleece* (1626), B2v.
108 Meres praises Robert Wilson, "who for learning and extemporall witte in this facultie is without compare or compeere, as … he manifested in his challenge at the *Swanne* on the Banke side" (*Palladis Tamia* (1598) Oo6r, 286).
109 William Fennor, *Fennors Defence* (1615), B3r–v. In *A Cast Ouer the Waters* (1615), Taylor disputes Fennor's extempol chops: "thou promist in thy Bill, / In rare Extemporie to show thy skill / When all thou spok'st, thou studied'st had before" – comparing him, incidentally, to "a Scar-crow or a Iack of lent" (B5v).
110 John Taylor, *Taylors Revenge* (1615), A8v–B2v.
111 *Tarltons Jests*, B4v; B3r–v; E3v; C2r.
112 *Ibid.*, A4v–B1r and B3r.
113 Quoted in Andrew Gurr, *The Shakespearian Playing Companies* (Oxford: Clarendon, 1996), 124. The apprentice mob was protesting the relocation of the Red Bull company to pricier environs; in a sense, if they could no longer destroy theatre from within, they destroyed it from without. See Mark Bayer, "Moving Upmarket: Queen Anne's Men at the Cockpit in Drury Lane, 1617," *Early Theatre* 4 (2001), 138–48.

114 John Stowe, *The Annales, or a Generall Chronicle of England* (1615), 697.
115 Lodge's compliment – "a peece surely worthy prayse, the practise of a good scholler" – occurs in *A Defence of Poetry, Music and Stage Plays* (1579), 43; on Wilson's life, see H. S. D. Mithal, "The Two-Wilsons Controversy," *Notes and Queries* 6 (n.s.) 1959, 106–9.
116 Henslowe, *Diary*, 208.
117 N. W. Bawcutt, ed., *The Control and Censorship of Caroline Drama: The Records of Sir Henry Herbert, Master of the Revels, 1623–73* (Oxford: Clarendon Press, 1996), 150; entry for 16 March 1624.
118 Everard Guilpin, *Skialetheia* (1598), Satire v.
119 Arber, *Register*, II.346. *Pigges Corantoe, or Newes from the North* (1642) says that the French "make good, old Tarltons song: / *The King of France with forty thousand men, / Went up a Hill, and so came downe agen*" (A2r).
120 Possibly "Willy" derived from a specific jig; Spenser seems to use it as a nickname for Tarlton himself, grieving in *The Teares of the Muses* (1591) that "he the man, whom Nature selfe had made / To mock her selfe, and Truth to imitate, / With kindly counter vnder Mimick shade, / Our pleasant *Willy*, ah is dead of late" (F2r). "*Peggy* and *Willy*" is one of the ballads Simplicity sells in *Three Lords and Three Ladies* (C1r); "Tarltons Willy" is preserved in Cambridge MS. Dd. IV.23 fol. 25. See Baskervill, *Jig*, 100–101.
121 Arber, *Register*, II.526.
122 ? Richard Tarlton, *Tarletons Tragical Treatises* (London: Henry Bynneman, 1578), *5r–v.
123 It is in the nature of theatre to mystify its labor. Every play-within-a-play that might dramatize that labor, indeed, either represents performance as already perfect (*Shrew, Tempest, Bartholomew Fair*) or offers such a perfunctory view of composition, study, and rehearsal (*Spanish Tragedy, Love's Labour's Lost, Dream, Hamlet, The Antipodes*), as well as such a disparity between preparation and execution, as to amount to the same thing. Early modern theatre invariably depicted its creative process as either magic or carelessness – *Histriomastix*'s Post-Haste, for example, would rather do everything "extempore" than write a word – with the result that, though the unified theatrical script may have been in practice an illusory document, it remained to audiences largely a fantastic document. See Paul Yachnin, *Stage-Wrights: Shakespeare, Jonson, Middleton, and the Making of Theatrical Value* (Philadelphia: University of Pennsylvania Press, 1997) and Tom Rutter, *Work and Play on the Shakespearean Stage* (Cambridge University Press, 2008).
124 William Shakespeare, *The Tragicall Historie of Hamlet Prince of Denmark* (1603), F2r–v; Barnabe Rich, *Faultes Faults, and nothing else but Faultes* (1606), B4v.
125 John Webster, "The Induction to the Malecontent," in John Marston, *The Malcontent* (QC, 1604), A3r.
126 John Heath, "In Momum," *Two Centvries of Epigrammes* (1610), II.E3v; Thomas Trescot, *The Zealous Magistrate* (1642), 14; Thomas Nabbes, "Prologue," *Hannibal and Scipio* (1635, pr. 1637), A3v.

127 John Marston, "Humours" (Satyre x), in *The Scourge of Villanie* (1598), H4r (emphasis in original).

128 Anon., *The Two Merry Milke-Maids* (1620), A4v.

129 Heywood, *Drammas*, 248.

130 Richard Levin, "Tarlton's Picture on the Elizabethan Stage," *Notes and Queries* 47.4 (245), Dec. 2000, 435–36.

Chapter 3   Wiring Richard Tarlton

1 C. H. Herford and Percy Simpson, eds., *Ben Jonson*, 11 vols (Oxford: Clarendon Press, 1925–52), VIII.582.

2 Robert Greene, *Greenes, Groats-worth of Witte Bought with a Million of Repentance* (London: William Wright, 1592), F1v.

3 *Ibid.*, F1v–F2r.

4 *Ibid.*, C3r.

5 *Ibid.*, D4r.

6 *Ibid.*, D4v.

7 *Ibid.*, E3r.

8 Ben Jonson, *Bartholomew Fair* (1631), B4v–C2v.

9 *Ibid.*, H3v.

10 *Ibid.*, L1v; emphasis in original.

11 Wright, *Passions*, 176 (my emphasis). Theories of acting that equate the actor's body to a machine, as discussed by Joseph Roach, are Enlightenment extensions of larger thought systems about the relation of human beings in general to machines; Jonson's specific eradication of the actor from theatrical production is thus qualitatively different and, depending on one's opinion of actors, ahead of its time. See *The Player's Passion: Studies in the Science of Acting* (Newark and London: University of Delaware Press, 1985).

12 Jonson, *Bartholomew Fair*, B4r.

13 Anonymous, "A Funerall Elegye on ye Death of the famous Actor Richard Burbedg," MS commonplace book (Huntington Library HM 198, 99–101), quoted in Nungezer, *Actors*, 74–76.

14 Richard Flecknoe, "A Short Discourse of the English Stage," in *Love's Kingdom, a Pastoral Trage-Comedy* (London: Richard Flecknoe, 1664), G6v–G7r. Flecknoe's play perhaps fittingly claims to be printed "not as it was acted at the theatre near Lincolns-Inn, but as it was written, and since corrected."

15 For a brilliant discussion of the parallels between stage acting, legal deposition, and demonic possession as modes of simultaneously present and "othered" performance, see Holger Schott Syme, *Theatre and Testimony: A Culture of Mediation* (Cambridge University Press, 2012), esp. ch. 3.

16 John Webster, *The Tragedy of the Dutchesse of Malfy* (London: Nicholas Okes and John Waterson, 1623), A2v.

17 *Ibid.*, C2v. Shortly after Cokes has his pocket picked in 2.6, he rides "pick-pack" on Wasp, thus putting him – as well as the memory of Tarlton with which he has been linked – in the puppet's spatial position.

18 Guildhall Library MS 7499/1, cited in Nungezer, *Actors*, 351.
19 Stowe, *Annales*, 698; Meres, *Palladis Tamia*, 632.
20 Patrick Collinson argues for the influence not only of Tarlton's grotesque, self-lampooning stage practice but of the theatrical *metier* itself on the writers of the Marprelate tracts: "without Tarleton," he writes, "there would have been no Martin Marprelate." See "Ecclesiastical Vitriol: Religious Satire in the 1590s and the Invention of Puritanism," in John Guy, ed., *The Reign of Elizabeth I: Court and Culture in the Last Decade* (Cambridge University Press, 1995), 150–70, esp. 158ff.
21 *Strange Newes*, 202, 201; Gabriel Harvey, *Pierces Supererogation* (1593), E3r, 35.
22 Wilson, *Three Lords and Three Ladies*, C1v.
23 Alexandra Halasz, "'So beloved that men use his picture for their signs': Richard Tarlton and the Uses of Sixteenth-Century Celebrity," *Shakespeare Studies 23* (London: Associated University Presses, 1995), 26.
24 *Ibid.*, 27.
25 *Ibid.*, 32.
26 Anon., *Tarltons Newes out of Purgatorie* (London: T. G. and T.N., 1590), B1v.
27 *Ibid.*, A2r.
28 *Ibid.*, B1v.
29 *Ibid.*
30 *Ibid.* B2r.
31 Besides playgoers, of course, the pamphlet courts another community – militant Protestants – implying that Purgatory exists only to punish those Catholics who believe in it. (What Tarlton is doing there he never explains.) For a reading of *Tarltons Newes* in this context, see Stephen Greenblatt, *Hamlet in Purgatory* (Princeton University Press, 2001), 36–40.
32 See Chapter 2's discussion of Tarlton's pictorial representation, and of "Tarlton's Jest of a Gridiron."
33 For a discussion of Tarlton's "themes," see Chapter 2.
34 Anon., *Tarltons Newes*, B1r.
35 *Ibid.*, B3r.
36 *Ibid.*, H2v.
37 *Ibid.*
38 To thicken the pamphlet's citational network further, the poem may be a parody of "Montanus's Sonnet" from Thomas Lodge's *Rosalynde* (1590) – somewhat belying (or perhaps ironizing) Tarlton's claim that it is a new style for English poets.
39 *Tarltons Newes*, H2v.
40 Anon., *The Cobler of Caunterburie, or an Invective Against Tarltons News out of Purgatorie* (London: R. Robinson, 1590), A2v.
41 *Ibid.*, B1v.
42 *Ibid.*, A4v.
43 *Ibid.*, A2r ff.
44 *Ibid.*, K4v.

45 Harvey, *Foure Letters*, B2r. Harvey later figures Greene's passing as his having "gone to Tarleton."

46 Chettle, *Kind-Harts Dreame*, A3v.

47 *Ibid.*, A4v, A4r.

48 See Harold Jenkins, "On the Authenticity of *Greene's Groatsworth of Wit* and *The Repentance of Robert Greene*," *Review of English Studies* 11 (41) (Jan. 1935), 28–41; Sidney Thomas, "The Printing of *Greenes Groatsworth of Witte* and *Kind-Harts Dreame*," *Studies in Bibliography* 19 (1966), 196–97; Louis Marder, "Chettle's Forgery of the *Groatsworth of Wit* and the 'Shake-scene' Passage," *Shakespeare Newsletter* 20 (1970), 42; D. Allen Carroll, "Who Wrote *Greenes Groatsworth of Wit?*," *Renaissance Papers* (1992), 69–77; John Jowett, "Johannes Factotum: Henry Chettle and *Greene's Groatsworth of Wit*," *Papers of the Bibliographical Society* of America 87.4 (Dec. 1993), 453–86; Lukas Erne, "Biography and Mythography: Rereading Chettle's Alleged Apology to Shakespeare," *English Studies* 79.5 (Sept. 1998), 430–40.

49 Chettle, *Kind-Harts Dreame*, B1r and B1v.

50 Among Chettle's collaborators were Anthony Munday, Thomas Dekker, William Haughton, John Webster, Thomas Heywood, Wentworth Smith, Michael Drayton, Robert Wilson, John Day, Ben Jonson, and Richard Hathway; the only playbook on which his name appears singly was *The Tragedy of Hoffman*, two decades after his death. He appears to have been in constant financial distress; Henslowe records loans to him nearly as often as payments, and in 1599 he was in Marshalsea prison for debt. See John Jowett, "Henry Chettle: 'Your old Compositor'" *Text* 15 (2002), 141–61; Neil Carson, "Collaborative Playwriting: the Chettle, Dekker, Heywood Syndicate," *Theatre Research International* 14.1 (Spring 1989), 13–23.

51 Alexandra Halasz, *The Marketplace of Print: Pamphlets and the Public Sphere in Early Modern England* (Cambridge University Press, 1997), 48.

52 *Kind-Harts Dreame*, E2v, G4v–H1r.

53 *Ibid.*, H1r.

54 *Ibid.*, C4r.

55 *Ibid.*, E3r–v.

56 *Ibid.*, B2v, B4r; my emphasis.

57 Thomas Dekker, *A Knights Conjuring* (London: T.C. for William Barley, 1607), L1v.

58 On Greene's career both living and dead, see Kirk Melnikoff and Edward Gieskes, eds., *Writing Robert Greene: Essays on England's First Notorious Professional Writer* (Aldershot: Ashgate, 2008).

59 This is what Tarlton gets in his last posthumous appearance on the stage, in William Percy's *The cuck-queanes and cuckolds errants* (c. 1600), preserved in manuscript. The play brings on "Tarltons Ghost" to speak the prologue, yet seemingly everywhere marks its decline. Not only is the prologue the most scripted of parts, but to complicate Tarlton's being played by another actor, the play is set at the fictitious "Tarlton Inn" in Colchester, for which a sign bearing Tarlton's image hangs over the stage. The truer representation of Tarlton,

therefore, is the inanimate one, which forces the ghost to spend an inordinate amount of time persuading the audience that he is, in fact, Tarlton – by his resemblance to the sign.

Chapter 4 Nobody's business

1 Thomas Nashe, *An Almond for a Parrat* (1590), A2r.
2 William N. West, in an important article, suggests an unnecessary bifurcation between Tarlton's postludes and Kemp's – namely, that Tarlton only engaged in "themes" (see Chapter 2), Kemp only in jigs. There is plentiful evidence of the jig's emergence under Tarlton, though none of Kemp's having sung "themes." See "When is the Jig Up – and What is it Up To?" in Helen Ostovich, Holger Syme, and Andrew Griffin, eds., *Locating the Queen's Men, 1583–1603* (London: Ashgate, 2009), 201–15.
3 The Lord Strange's Men were a brief amalgamation of the principal members of what would become the Admiral's and the Chamberlain's Men. For a discussion of this play in that context, see Marino, *Owning*, 25–27.
4 For a biography of Kemp, especially useful for the murky period in Holland and Denmark, see Wiles, *Shakespeare's Clown*, 31–42.
5 *Ibid.*, 53–56.
6 The effect is the same in *Dream*, if a dance is indeed implied after Theseus's "come, your Bergomask" – either the jig's pre-emption by another one, or its subsumption under the play entirely.
7 William Shakespeare, *The Second Part of Henrie the Fourth* (London: Andrew Wise and William Aspley, 1600), LIv. See Wiles, *Shakespeare's Clown*, 116ff.
8 Marston, *Scourge of Villanie*, H3v; Guilpin, *Skialetheia*, D5r–v.
9 Arber, *Register*, II.297, 298, 571, 600, 601, 669, 670, 671; III.49, 50 (emphasis in original). Since "the Thirde and last parte of *Kempes* Jigge" follows "the seconde parte of the gigge betweene Rowland and the Sexton," Kemp was almost certainly connected to the *Rowland* series as well, giving him as many as six printed jigs; a portion of the trilogy may be preserved in a German *singspiel* as *Roland genandt*, printed in Baskervill, *Jig*, 491–93. Furthermore, this list is one of entrance only, 1591–95; it is not an exhaustive catalogue of all jigs, or jigs that survive, or that survive in English (of which the only two here are "Sym," reprinted as "Singing Simpkin" by Robert Cox in *Actaeon and Diana* (1656), and "Frauncis," later attributed to George Attowell).
10 We are relying here, of course, on the terminology of the Register itself to define that genre. As the dual identity of "Cutting George" suggests – "a ballad … being a Jigge" – the scribe may not always have cared to discriminate between ballads and jigs (e.g. the 13 August 1591 entry for "a ballad of a new northerne Dialogue between Will, Sone, and the warriner, and how Reynold Peares gott faire Nannye to his Loue"). Likewise, "A newe Northerne Jigge" may be identical to the "merrye and plesant newe ballad. Intituled alas the poore Tynker" listed alongside it in the entry, for which only one fee was paid. Not only does this ambiguity increase manifold the number of jigs that

may have seen print, but it forces us to ask what exactly was the intended *use* of a printed jig, and whether it differed from that of a ballad.

11 Cox, *Actaeon*, includes adaptations of other, possibly Elizabethan jigs, like "Bumpkin the Huntsman," "Hobbinal the Shepherd," "John Swabber," and "Simpleton the Smith".

12 Intriguingly, the entry for "Frauncis" contains the note "A Transcript" – making it hard to guess whether the text of *every* printed jig was by default a transcript (and if so, how much it did or could transcribe), or whether "Frauncis" alone was such. The date, and relation to this entry, of the surviving pamphlet known as "Attowell's Jig" is uncertain.

13 See Frances K. Barasch, "'He's for a Iigge, or a tale of Baudry': Sixteenth-Century Images of the Stage-Jig," *Shakespeare Bulletin* 13:1 (Winter 1995), 24–28. See also Pamela Allen Brown, "'I care not, let naturals love nations': Cosmopolitan Clowning," *Shakespeare Studies* 35 (2007), 66–73, esp. 70ff.

14 Thus the satellite productions into which jigs themselves could spiral. The *Rowland* brand was evidently popular enough to spawn "Rowlands Godson" (reprinted in Baskervill, *Jig*, 437–43); Register entries of 18 and 29 April 1592, meanwhile, record two further ballads spun from this spinoff in turn, "the firste parte of *Rowland*es godson moralized" and "the Second parte of *Rowland*es god sonne moralised."

15 West, "When is the Jig Up," 214–15.

16 Anon., *The Returne From Parnassus, or the Scourge of Simony* (London: John Wright, 1606), G2v.

17 *Ibid.*, G2v, G3r. The joke is not present in the manuscript, suggesting the possibility that it was a later ad lib by the actor playing Kemp – which would be ironic in this context.

18 *Ibid.*, G2v.

19 *Ibid.*

20 The continuity of this domineering *ethos* with the fraternal vocabulary of modern stand-up comics – "He killed tonight," "I destroyed them," and so forth – suggests itself at this point.

21 Kemp was not even the only Chamberlain's Man to have had jigs printed, let alone to perform them: Attowell may have been with them in the early 1590s, and "Phillips his gigge of the slyppers" points to Augustine Phillips. To judge from the cast lists on which he appears, Phillips was hardly a comic specialist, yet the affixion of his name here implies he was also more than a dabbler in clown postludes. If it is facile to reduce the company's authorial interests to "Shakespeare," it is no more accurate to reduce its clowning faction to "Kemp."

22 "[Z]u endt der Comedien dantzeten sie ihrem gebrauch nach gar überausz zierlich, ye zwen in mannes undt 2 in weiber kleideren angethan, wunderbahrlich mitt einanderen." Quoted in Baskervill, *Jig*, 106.

23 In a 1604 letter, Dudley Carleton mentions another form of finale possibly introduced around this time, an early modern equivalent of the "curtain call": "all the actors being together on the stage – as use is at the end of a play." But

this may refer only to the dramatic denouement of plot convergence. Quoted in Gurr, *The Shakespeare Company, 1594–1642* (Cambridge University Press, 2004), 75 n. 54.

24 Shakespeare, *As You Like It*, in *Comedies, Histories, and Tragedies*, S2r, 207.

25 "Cinkapase" is an early modern spelling (or at least Q1's spelling) of "cinquepace," a dance – possibly any dance, possibly one related to the galliard – broken down into five steps.

26 If Hamlet's montage approximates Kemp's repertoire, indeed, then for any "gentlemen" in attendance it now takes the place of those "tables"; Hamlet speaks in inverted commas. On the portions of Q1 printed this way, see Zachary Lesser and Peter Stallybrass, "The First Literary *Hamlet* and the Commonplacing of Professional Plays," *Shakespeare Quarterly* 59.4 (2008), 371–420.

27 Shakespeare, *Hamlet* (Q1) E4r.

28 *Ibid.*, F3r. In Q2/F, his line occurs just after the dumbshow, which makes rather less sense.

29 *Ibid.*, C4v–D1r, F4r. Q2/F substitute terminology but retain the fivefold structure.

30 F (the only other text to contain a version of the clause) substitutes "tickled in the lungs" with "tickle o'th' sere," suggestively replacing a bodily organ with a machine part.

31 Shakespeare, *Hamlet* (Q1), E3v.

32 *Ibid.*, E4r.

33 *Ibid.*, F2r.

34 *Ibid.*, E3v. Both Q2 and F print "for the lawe of writ, and the liberty."

35 *Ibid.*, H4r.

36 Shakespeare, *Hamlet* (1604), H3r.

37 *Ibid.*, G1r.

38 For "pajock" as an Irish variant of "clown," I follow G. R. Hibbard, ed., *Hamlet* (London: Oxford University Press, 1987) 264–65.

39 Douglas Bruster argues that such denigration persisted in the jig-marked phrases "hey-day," "hoy-day," and "high-day" used by Thersites, Apemantus, and Caliban – the last of whom he reads as a belated caricature of Kemp. Thus, just as *Hamlet* wishes, Kemp remains "the improvising clown" who "resent[s] books" and "the economy of work in the Globe playhouse." See *Quoting Shakespeare: Form & Culture in Early Modern Drama* (Lincoln: University of Nebraska Press, 2000), 132–42.

40 To be sure, the gesture toward narrative recapitulation is a convention, but it begins to appear with such regularity in Shakespeare's later plays – *Measure, Othello, All's Well, Pericles, The Winter's Tale, The Tempest* – that its function, in playhouses devoid of jig postludes, may have been more than ceremonial.

41 *Hamlet*, M2v.

42 "Zu endt dantzeten sie auch auf Englisch undt Irlendisch gar zierlich," in Baskervill, *Jig*, 106–7. Bruce Boehrer discusses Jonson's allusion in "The Case

of Will Kemp's Shoes: *Every Man Out of His Humour* and the 'Bibliographic Ego'" (*Ben Jonson Journal* 7 (2000), 271–95).

43 Anon., *Returne from Parnassus*, G2v.

44 Brennecke, *Germany*, reprints an extract from Röshell's *Chronicles of the City of Münster* (trans. Albert Cohn): "On the 26. November, 1599, there arrived here eleven Englishmen, all young and lively fellows, with the exception of one, a rather elderly man, who had everything under his management. They acted on five successive days five different comedies in their own English tongue. They carried with them several musical instruments, such as lutes, citterns, viols, recorders and the like; they danced many new and foreign dances (not usual in this country) at the beginning and at the end of their comedies. They were accompanied by a clown who, when a new act had to begin and when they had to change their costumes, made many antics and pranks in German during the performance, by which he amused the audience … During those five days they took a great deal of money" (6).

45 Foakes, ed., *Henslowe's Diary*, 214, subscript #115 (May 1602).

46 Max W. Thomas reads Kemp's venture as a straightforward attempt to commercialize the morris, and thus detects no tension between the dance and its textual representation; Bart van Es, channeling the traditional interpretation of Kemp as populist hero, treats the pamphlet as equally transparent, suggesting that "Kemp's travelogue is filled with the spirit of health and festivity." See Thomas, "*Kemps Nine Daies Wonder*: Dancing Carnival into Market," *PMLA* 107:3 (May 1992), 511–23, and van Es, *Shakespeare in Company* (London: Oxford University Press, 2013), 163.

47 William Kemp, *Kemps Nine Daies Wonder* (1600), D2r. Ironically, such mischief was precisely the sort of thing expected from stage clowns; the same litany might be assembled from *Tarltons Jests*, where they form a celebration instead of a list of indictments.

48 R.J. [Richard Johnson?], *The Most Pleasant History of Tom-a-Lincoln, the Red-Rose Knight* (1600). It is unclear whether *Tom-a-Lincoln* actually parodies Kemp, or if other balladeers merely seized on their comic correspondences, since the pamphlet was entered in December 1599, before his morris began but probably after word of it became public.

49 Kemp, *Nine Daies Wonder*, A2r.

50 *Ibid.*

51 *Ibid.*, D2r.

52 *Ibid.*, A2r.

53 *Ibid.*

54 *Ibid.*, D2v, A2v.

55 *Ibid.*, A1r (title page). Kemp dedicates the pamphlet to Lady Anne Fitton, whom he still calls "Mayde of Honour to the most sacred Mayde Royall Queene *Elizabeth*," despite the fact that she was already married.

56 For an ethnography of the morris, see John Forrest, *The History of Morris Dancing, 1478–1750* (University of Toronto Press, 1999); also Jane Garry, "The Literary History of the English Morris Dance," *Folklore* 94 (1983): 219–28.

57 Kemp, *Nine Daies Wonder*, A3v–A4r.
58 *Ibid.*, A4r.
59 Quoted in Joseph Strutt, *Sports and Pastimes of the People of England*, 3rd edn. (London: William Tegg, 1867), 258.
60 Kemp, *Nine Daies Wonder*, A4r–v.
61 *Ibid.*, A4v–B1r.
62 *Ibid.*, B1r.
63 *Ibid.*, B1v.
64 *Ibid.*, B1v, C1r.
65 *Ibid.*, B2v–B3r.
66 *Ibid.*, B2r.
67 *Ibid.*, B1v.
68 *Ibid.*, B2v.
69 This moment may effect a verbal self-demarcation as well. Although recurrent in Elizabethan literature (appearing in *Love's Labour's Lost* too), the phrase "the hobby horse is forgot" may have had special reference to Kemp. Song xx of Thomas Weelkes' madrigal album *Ayeres or Phantasticke Spirites for three voices* (1608) relates how

> Since Roben Hood, maid Marian,
> and little Iohn are gone a,
> the hobby horse was quite forgot,
> when Kemp did daunce a lone a,
> he did labour
> after the tabour
> for to dance
> then into France,
> he tooke paines
> to skip it in hope of gaines
> he will trip it trip it trip it on the toe,
> diddle diddle diddle-doe. (D2v, lineation mine)

If this were indeed Kemp's catchphrase, Hamlet echoes it as well. Trying to rescue himself from citation, ironically, Kemp cites himself. See William Ringler, "The Hobby Horse is Forgot," *Shakespeare Quarterly* 4.4 (Oct. 1953), 485.
70 Kemp, *Nine Daies Wonder*, B4r (my emphasis).
71 *Ibid.*, C2r–v.
72 *Ibid.*, C4r–v.
73 West, "When is the Jig Up," 212.
74 Kemp, *Nine Daies Wonder*, C4v.
75 *Ibid.*, D1r.
76 *Ibid.*, D4r.
77 *Ibid.*, D3r.
78 Katherine Duncan-Jones, "Shakespeare's Dancing Fool: Did William Kemp Live on as 'Lady Hunsdon's Man'?", *Times Literary Supplement*, 11 August 2010.
79 Anon. [John Day, William Rowley, and George Wilkins], *The Trauails of the Three English Brothers* (London: John Wright, 1607), E4r–F1r.

80 On the figure of "Nobody," see Anston Bosman, "Renaissance Intertheater and the Staging of Nobody," *ELH* 71.3 (Fall 2004), 559–85; Luke Wilson, *Theaters of Intention: Drama and the Law in Early Modern England* (Stanford University Press, 2001); Gerta Calmann, "The Picture of Nobody: An Iconographical Study," *Journal of the Warburg and Courtauld Institutes* 23.1–2 (1960), 60–104.

Chapter 5 Private practice

1 Helgerson, *Forms of Nationhood*, 203–4.

2 *Ibid.*, 200–203.

3 *Ibid.*, 199–200. As argued in Chapter 2, however, *Tamburlaine*'s prologue may be read as announcing no such structural shift.

4 Alfred Harbage, *Shakespeare and the Rival Traditions* (New York: Macmillan, 1952); *Shakespeare's Audience* (New York: Columbia University Press, 1958); Walter Cohen, *Drama of a Nation: Public Theater in Renaissance England and Spain* (Ithaca: Cornell University Press, 1985); others cited above. See also Colin McCabe, "Abusing Self and Others: Puritan Accounts of the Shakespearean Stage," *Critical Quarterly* 30 (1988), 3–17.

5 Helgerson, *Forms of Nationhood*, 204.

6 See, in connection, Stephen Longstaffe, "'A Short Report and Not Otherwise': Jack Cade in *2 Henry VI*," in Ronald Knowles, ed., *Shakespeare and Carnival: After Bakhtin* (London and New York: Macmillan, 1988), 13–35; Maya Mathur, "An Attack of the Clowns: Comedy, Vagrancy, and the Elizabethan History Play," *Journal of Early Modern Cultural Studies* 7.1 (2007), 33–54.

7 Helgerson relies on Wiles's theory that Kemp played Falstaff in the first two *Henry IV* plays – a theory I find tempting enough to speculate with in Chapter 4, but not entirely convincing.

8 Helgerson, *Forms of Nationhood*, 204.

9 *Ibid.*, 227.

10 *Ibid.*, 199.

11 *Ibid.*, 226.

12 *Ibid.*, 223. Leslie Hotson's *Shakespeare's Motley* (London: Rupert Hart-Davis, 1952), 84–128 gives the most orthodox catalogue of these binaries. See also Enid Welsford, *The Fool: His Social and Literary History* (London: Farrar & Rinehart, 1935); Charles S. Felver, *Robert Armin, Shakespeare's Fool: A Biographical Essay* (Kent, OH: Kent State University Press, 1961); Olive M. Busby, *Studies in the Development of the Fool* (London: Oxford University Press, 1923); Austin K. Gray, "Robert Armine, The Foole," *PMLA* 42 (1927), 673–85; Nevill Coghill, "Wags, Clowns and Jesters," in John Garrett, ed., *More Talking of Shakespeare* (London: Longman, 1959), 1–16.

13 Wiles, *Shakespeare's Clown*, 159.

14 McCabe, "Abusing Self," 10.

15 Felver, *Armin*, 47.

16 George Wilkins, *The Miseries of Inforst Mariage* (London: George Vincent, 1611), A2v.

17 Wiles speculates that Nym was later added to *Henry V* for Armin, just as *Malcontent*'s Passarello was added upon the King's Men's acquisition of the play; see *Shakespeare's Clown*, 145–46 and 151–52.

18 In *The Italian Taylor and his Boy* (1609), Armin calls himself "writ downe for an Asse in his time … notwithstanding his Constableship and Office" (A3r) – which probably alludes to the role of Dogberry.

19 Helgerson, *Forms of Nationhood*, 226.

20 The epithet appears in the ballad "On the Time Poets," in Anon., *Choyce Drollery* (1656), B4r.

21 On the chronology of company clowns, see Gurr, *Companies*, 247 and 320.

22 Gurr discusses Shanke's transfer in *Shakespeare Company*, 72–73; on Greene, see Chapter 2. William Turner's reference in *Dish of Lentten Stuffe* (1612) to Shanke's having "l[eft] to sing his rimes" is often taken as evidence for the King's Men's continued abridgement of the jig, but more likely (given the date) implies some temporary efficacy to the Middlesex jig ban – and if anything actually furnishes a *reason* for Shanke's move to the Globe, outside the ban's jurisdiction. It was during his tenure there, indeed, that the jig *Shankes Ordinary* was entered for publication in 1624.

23 Thomas Middleton, *The Mayor of Quinborough* (London: Henry Herringman, 1661), I3r. Middleton's "country comedians" are grifters, who perform *The Cheater and the Clown* aided by an audience member, whose pocket they pick onstage – so "fribbling" is a necessary part of their craft.

24 For a compilation of eighteenth- and nineteenth-century anecdotes about actors "fribbling" – or, conversely, simply reading the script onstage – see Thornton S. Graves, "Some Aspects of Extemporal Acting," *Studies in Philology* 19.4 (October 1922), 429–56.

25 Robert Greene, *Orlando Furioso* (1594), F4v; Thomas Heywood, *2 Edward IV* (1600), L5r; Anon., *The Tryall of Chevalrie* (1605), G2 and E4; Jo[hn] Cooke, *Greenes Tu Quoque* (1614), J1r. See Mann, *Elizabethan Player*; Preiss, "Natural Authorship."

26 See Stern, *Rehearsal*; Rasmussen, "Setting Down"; Peter Davison, *Popular Appeal in English Drama to 1850* (Totowa, NJ: Barnes and Noble, 1982), 43ff.

27 John Stephens, *Essays and Characters*, 2nd edn. (London: Phillip Knight, 1615), 296–97.

28 Shakespeare, *Hamlet* (1604), G4r. William Prynne offers a similar analysis: "sometimes such who act the Clowne or amorous person, adde many obscene lascivious jests and passages of their owne … *to delight the auditors*, which were not in their parts before" (*Histriomastix*, 930, my emphasis).

29 John Marston, *Histrio-mastix* (London: Thomas Thorp, 1610), C4r.

30 James Shirley, *The Example* (London: Andrew Crooke and William Cooke, 1634), A1v.

31 Thomas Dekker, *A Strange Horse-Race* (London: Joseph Hunt, 1613), C4v.

32 Quoted in Baskervill, *Jig*, 116 (my emphasis).

33 Richard Brome, *The Antipodes* (London: Francis Constable, 1640), F1r.

34 Some familiar examples include *The Spanish Tragedy*, *The Taming of the Shrew*, *Love's Labour's Lost*, *A Midsummer Night's Dream*, *Hamlet*, *Histriomastix*, and *Bartholomew Fair*; even Prospero's masque in *The Tempest* is not without interference. For plays that depict fictitious audiences onstage for the sole purpose of disrupting the actual performance, see my Epilogue.

35 Anon., *Tarltons Jests* (1613), C2r.

36 Nashe, *Strange Newes*, D4v; Harvey, *Pierces Supererogation*, Aa2r.

37 See Chapter 3, n.20.

38 Van Es has persuasively argued for Armin's authorship of another pamphlet, *A Pil to Purge Melancholie* (1599) – which dates either just prior to Armin's joining the Chamberlain's, or to the exact moment he was replacing Kemp, since it ends with an invitation to "one pleasant conceit or other of *Mounsier de Kempe* on Monday next at the Globe, where I would gladly meete you" (B4v). *Pil* is a lunatic parody of the epistolary "cabinet," and seems in every way consistent with the mercurial, avant-garde performance practice Armin was preparing to launch: its title page features no fewer than three subtitles – "Or, a Preprative to a Purgation: / or, Topping, Copping, and Capping: take either or whether: / or, Mash them, and squash them, and dash them, and diddle come derrie come daw them, all together" – and offers no further information; its 'letters' are similar concatenations of alliterative, free-associative nonsense running to several pages, or copiously exaggerated salutations and valedictions with no content in between; its personae remain unidentified, and at various points change sexes; one of the letters is subscribed "Snuffe," which appears to have been both Armin's stage name and his *nom de plume*. See *In Company*, 165ff.

39 See F. P. Wilson, "The English Jest-books of the Sixteenth and Early Seventeenth Centuries," in Helen Gardner, ed., *Shakespearian and Other Studies* (Oxford: Clarendon Press, 1969), 285–324; H. F. Lippincott, "*King Lear* and the Fools of Robert Armin," *Shakespeare Quarterly* 26.3 (1975), 243–53.

40 [Robert Armin], *Foole Upon Foole, Or Six Sortes of Sottes* (London: William Ferbrand, 1600), A2r.

41 Johnson, *Actor as Playwright*, 40.

42 *Ibid.*, 39–40, and more generally 1–53. Johnson analyzes Armin as "carry[ing] over complex forms of theatrical subjectivity … into print", suggesting pluralistic "versions of authorship we have failed to consider" (6). Such versions are "extraordinary," however, only next to an absolutist model whose normativity in the period she overstates, and as I suggest, what look like the aspects of Armin's authorial strategy that resist proprietary authorship are actually the parts *making* it.

43 This page was excised from the second edition in 1605 – possibly to save space, or as superfluous to a second printing, but quite possibly because the new printer, William White, detected the insulting subtext.

44 Armin, *Foole*, A2r.

45 *Ibid.*, A4v, C4v, F2v–F3r.

46 Some examples of these intensives include "thus you haue heard" (A3v), "here you haue heard" (B2r), "ye shall quickly heare" (B3v), "you shall heare" (C4r), "I graunt" (C4r), "What should I say" (D3r), "as I speake of" (D4v), "I will let you understand in two wordes" (F1v), and "Well, to go forward in what I promised you" (F1v), as well as several "I saye"s.

47 *Ibid.*, D4v.

48 In an epistle to Lady Mary Chandos affixed to Gilbert Dugdale's *True Discourse of the Practises of Elizabeth Caldwell* (1604), Armin reminds her of "all my seruices to your Late deceased kind Lord" (D4v).

49 Armin, *Foole*, A4v–B2r, F4r.

50 John Davies of Hereford, *The Scourge of Folly* (London: Richard Redmer, 1611), 228–29. *The London Prodigal* (*c.* 1603), in which Armin may have played Matthew Flowerdale, has him pun on "armine"; in *As You Like It*, more famously, "Touchstone" may recall Armin's training as a goldsmith. For other allusions, see Nungezer, *Actors*, 19.

51 In the epistle to Lady Chandos in Dugdale's *True Discourse*, Armin claims (ironically) that "Your good Honour knowes *Pincks* poore hart, who in all my seruices … neuer sauoured of flatterie, or fixion" (D4v).

52 Anon. [Richard Tarlton?], *Tarletons Tragical Treatises*, *5r, discussed in Chapter 2.

53 Pompey, Elbow, and Froth in *Measure for Measure*, for example, or Nano, Castrone, and Hermaphroditus in *Volpone*; see Wiles, *Shakespeare's Clown*, 156, 161–62. On in-text allusions to Armin's size, see 147–48ff.

54 [Robert Armin], *Quips Vpon Questions* (London: William Ferbrand, 1600), A2r.

55 *Ibid.*, A2v.

56 *Ibid.*, A3r.

57 *Ibid.*, B1v.

58 *Ibid.*, D4r, C2r.

59 *Ibid.*, A4r–v.

60 *Ibid.*, B2v–B3r; C3r; F2v; C4v–D1r; D3r.

61 *Ibid.*, C4r–v; D4r–v.

62 *Ibid.*, B3v–B4r.

63 *Ibid.*, F3r–v; E3v–E4r; C1r.

64 Armin, *Quips*, F4r–v. In fact, the pronoun "I" emerges for the first time at the end of "He begins well, but endes ill," and seems to carry over into the final poem.

65 See Chapters 1 and 2.

66 Armin, *Quips*, D3r.

67 The effect is similar to that of the material which stand-up comics – especially of the borscht-belt variety, such as Don Rickles and Rodney Dangerfield – use to combat hecklers: seemingly off-the-cuff ("this is what happens when cousins marry," "I remember *my* first beer"), but widely applicable. Familiar

enough with such stock material, ironically, audiences will often try to elicit it, as if to experience the performer's "act" *as* artifice. Andy Kaufman would plant actors among the audience to heckle him, confusing what was and was not part of his act; Armin did the same, only by converting the *live* audience into those dummies.

68 On the theoretical intersection of acting and puppetry during the period (albeit hardly an exhaustive treatment), and its particular application to clowning, see Chapter 3.

69 Armin, *Quips*, C3r. In the same stanza, the speaker chastises his opponent for "set[ting] this Emblem in my sight," further recasting the verbal combat as an entirely mute exchange of slips of paper.

70 There is no instance of a poet's being onstage *in propria persona* in any play – that is, presented before the audience *as* both its author and a character in it; for verbal allusions to his presence in the playhouse, however, see the Epilogue. See also n.71 below, which may be the single exception.

71 This is the place to mention William Rowley (*c.* 1585–*c.* 1626), who would deserve lengthier treatment if he did not so aptly bear this claim out. Rowley was the clown of the Duke of York's/Prince Charles's Men (and of the King's Men late in his life), and specialized in fat comic characters; he played Plumporridge in Middleton's *Masque of Heroes* (1619) and the Black Bishop in *A Game at Chesse* (1625), and is likely the "fat foole of the Curtin" alluded to in Turner's *Dish* (1612). He was also a prolific playwright, collaborating with Middleton on *A Fair Quarrel* (*c.* 1615), *The World Tost at Tennis* (1620), *The Changeling* (*c.* 1622), and *The Spanish Gypsy* (*c.* 1623), as well as with Massinger and Middleton, with Ford and Dekker, and single-authoring *All's Lost By Lust* (*c.* 1619), among others. Yet his stage reputation, like Armin's, and like Robert Wilson's a generation earlier, seems to have attenuated in direct proportion to his writing pursuits. Aside from the one reference in 1612, there are no remembrances of him. To audiences, his clowning may have appeared entirely scripted and inauthentic: uniquely, the *dramatis personae* in the 1633 *All's Lost By Lust* specifies that the part of "*Iaques, a simple clownish gentleman*" was "*personated by the Poet*" (A1v). This is not to say he never performed solo postludes, just that no one especially cared for them. Authorship and clowning had now become divergent identities. Rowley seems to have written two plays that may have shed light on this choice – intriguingly titled *A Foole Without Booke* and *The Knaue in Print* – but both, perhaps fittingly, are now lost. See Bentley, *Jacobean*, II.555–58, V.1014–27.

72 Armin, *Quips*, D4v–E1r (my emphasis). "Asse" interpolates an account of a simple Collier who, thinking "the squint of *Tarletons* eie ... a sure mark that he would neuer die," goes to see him at the playhouse, and because "within the Play past, was his picture us'd," leaves convinced that he has seen him. This may refer to Wilson's *Three Lords and Three Ladies* (see Chapter 2), but given the decade separating that play from *Quips*, perhaps the use of Tarlton's picture onstage was a more pervasive custom.

73 *Ibid.*, B2r. See the discussion of this "theme" and its original setting in Chapter 2.

74 Jonson, *Every Man Out*, P3r; Shakespeare, *As You Like It*, 206; Shakespeare, *The Tempest*, 9.

75 Shakespeare, *Twelfth Night, Or What You Will*, in *Comedies, Histories and Tragedies*, Y3r–4r, Y6r, Z5v.

76 *Ibid.*, Z6r; the song recurs on the heath in *King Lear* (rr2v), sung by the Fool.

77 *Ibid.*, Z4r.

78 Shakespeare, *The Famous Historie of Troylus and Cresseid* (London: Bonian and Walley, 1609), G3v.

79 For a similar thesis applied to *King Lear*, see Van Es, *In Company*, 184ff.

80 Shakespeare, *Timon of Athens*, in *Comedies, Histories and Tragedies*, gg4v.

81 Robert Armin, *The History of the Two Maids of More-clacke* (London: Thomas Archer, 1609), A2v.

Epilogue: The principal verb

1 T.W., *Thorny-Abbey, or The London Maid*, in R.D., ed., *Gratiae Theatrales* (pr. 1662), B2r–v.

2 *Ibid.*, B2v.

3 According to Alfred Harbage, "[t]he coterie audience was an amalgam of fashionable and academic elements, socially and intellectually self-conscious … the most avant-garde, the most sophisticated, the most interested in art as art" (56); Michael Neill stresses this audience's "corporate sense of itself" as a "court of taste," wherein "the drama," for spectators and playwrights, became a field in which "one might emerge in virtuoso self-display" (344–45). My aim in linking this audience to the clowning culture of other theatres is to reveal both of these statements as more literally true than they realize. See Harbage, *Shakespeare and the Rival Traditions* (New York: Macmillan, 1952); Neill, "Wits Most Accomplish'd Senate: The Audience of the Caroline Private Theaters," *Studies in English Literature, 1500–1900* 18.2 (Spring 1978), 341–60.

4 James Shirley, *The Doubtful Heir* (1640), A3r; on John Shanke, see Chapters 2 and 5.

5 *Ibid.*, A3r; Lovelace, "The Epilogue" [to *The Scholars*], in *Lucasta*, 77.

6 See Gurr, *Playgoing*, 183–90, and *Companies*, 122–25; also Bayer, "Upmarket," and "The Curious Case of the Two Audiences: Thomas Dekker's *Match Me In London*," in Low and Myhill, *Imagining*, 55–70.

7 B[asse], "The Authors Friend," in Massinger, *Bond-Man*, A4r.

8 John Fletcher and Philip Massinger, *The Fair Maid of the Inn*, in Beaumont and Fletcher, *Comedies and Tragedies*, 6g4v.

9 Philip Massinger, *The Roman Actor* (1629), A2v.

10 Goffe, *Careles Shepherdess*, "Praeludium," B2v, B4v.

11 *Ibid.*, B3r.

12 Reed began with Queen Henrietta's Men at the Cock-pit; they moved to Salisbury Court in 1637, taking *The Changeling* with them. The company that

produced Goffe's revival was the King's Revels Men. See Bentley, *Jacobean*, I.239–45 and 283–96, II.540–41, IV.504.

13 *Careles Shepherdess*, B4r–v.

14 *Ibid.*, B4v.

15 James Shirley, *Changes, or Love in a Maze* (1632), A4r and H2r–H2v.

16 Nashe's *Summers Last Will and Testament* also has the ghost of Will Sommers declare, after reciting a lengthy and obviously scripted prologue, "I care not what I say now: for I play no more than you heare, & some of that you heard to (by your leaue) was extempore" (B2r).

17 There are other reasons for the emergence of city comedy, of course – the popularity of rogue literature; the French influx of *commedia dell'arte*, with its reliance on character types; the need for *some* new genre to develop to define the nascent market at the indoor theatres. My claim is simply an elaboration of this last reason, grounded in these theatres' new performance constraints. See Brian Gibbons, *Jacobean City Comedy*, 2nd edn. (London: Methuen, 1980).

18 Jonson, *Every Man Out*, K1r.

19 Ben Jonson, *The Alchemist* (pr. 1612), A4v.

20 Ben Jonson, *Bartholomew Fair* (pr. 1631), A5r–v (Jonson's emphasis).

21 See Stephen Orgel, *The Jonsonian Masque* (Cambridge, MA: Harvard University Press, 1965).

22 Of course, Buffone was played by Armin – who would have taken the Globe stage after the show, and whose postludic persona Buffone complemented. It is inconvenient for me that *Every Man Out* should be both one of the first city comedies and not written for boys. But perhaps, as Chapter 5 suggested, writing for a clownless company was not very different from writing for Armin.

23 Jonathan Haynes's insight that private hall audiences "lacked the organizing principle" of "performances at court … where it would be clear who was the patron of the occasion" becomes even more valuable when we remember that this was also the state of the amphitheatres. "The Elizabethan Audience Onstage," in James Redmond, ed., *The Theatrical Space* (Cambridge University Press, 1987), 63.

24 See Thelma N. Greenfield, *The Induction in Elizabethan Drama* (Eugene: University of Oregon Books, 1969), 67–95; Tiffany Stern, "Taking Part: Actors and Audience on the Stage at the Blackfriars," in Paul Menzer, ed., *Inside Shakespeare: Essays on the Blackfriars Stage* (Selinsgrove, PA: Susquehanna University Press, 2006); C. R. Baskervill, "The Custom of Sitting on the Elizabethan Stage," *Modern Philology* 8.4 (April 1911), 581–89.

25 Nova Myhill, "Taking the Stage: Spectators as Spectacle in the Caroline Private Theaters," in Low and Myhill, *Imagining*, 38, 42.

26 This seems an oversight of studies of unruliness in the private theatres: if the audience does not engage the play on a representational level, representational correctives are hopeless. See Haynes, "Onstage"; John G. Sweeney III, *Jonson and the Psychology of Public Theater* (Princeton University Press, 1985);

and Michael Shapiro, "Audience vs. Dramatist in Jonson's *Epicœne* and Other Plays of the Children's Troupes," *ELR* 3.3 (1973), 400–417.

27 Jonson, *Every Man Out*, C4r.

28 Jonson, *The Fovntaine of Selfe-Love, or Cynthias Revels* (1601), A3v; Webster, "Induction," A3r–A4r.

29 Heton's papers are reprinted in Bentley, *Jacobean*, II.684–87.

30 It resumed after the Restoration. A 17 January 1704 proclamation provided "that no person of what quality so ever presume to go behind the scenes or come upon the stage, either before or during the acting of a play"; ten years later, it was still being affixed to playbills. Quoted in Leo Hughes, *The Drama's Patrons: A Study of the Eighteenth-Century Audience* (Austin: University of Texas Press, 1971), 21–22.

31 Eighteenth-century stage-sitters are discussed in precisely these mixed terms. In 1708, Colley Cibber observes that "those gentlemen that thrust themselves forward upon the stage before a crowded audience, as if they resolv'd to play themselves, and save the actors the trouble of presenting them ... are above instruction so they scorn to be diverted by it"; in 1728, James Ralph calls them "the Hermaphrodites of the Theatre; being neither Auditors nor Actors perfectly, and imperfectly both ... so busy in neglecting the Entertainment, that they obstruct the View of the Audience." Quoted in Hughes, *Patrons*, 22.

32 George Chapman, *All Fools* (1605), A3v.

33 John Day, *The Isle of Gulls* (1606), A3r.

34 John Marston, *What You Will* (pr. 1607), A2r–A3r.

35 Webster, "Induction," A3r.

36 Francis Beaumont, *The Knight of the Burning Pestle* (pr. 1613), A2r.

37 Peter Happé's "Jonson's Onstage Audiences," *Ben Jonson Journal* 10 (2003), 23–41, is a useful resource.

38 Jonson, *Every Man Out*, B3v.

39 Jonson, *Cynthia's Revels*, A3v.

40 Ben Jonson, *Poetaster, or the Arraignment* (1602), A2r.

41 Jonson, *Bartholomew Fair*, Liv.

42 Ben Jonson, *The Devil Is An Ass* (pr. 1631), N2v, O4r.

43 Ben Jonson, *The Staple of News* (pr. 1631), Aa3r.

44 Ben Jonson, *The New Inne, or the Light Heart* (pr. 1631), *2r–v.

45 Ben Jonson, *The Magnetick Lady, or Humors Reconcil'd*, in *Workes*, 2nd edn. (1640), D3v.

46 *Ibid.*, F1v.

47 Dekker, *Horne-booke* (1609), E3r–v.

48 *Ibid.*, E4r–v.

49 *Ibid.*, E2v.

50 *Ibid.*, E3r.

51 Nor had it changed by 1745. Beau in Garrick's *Lethe* describes his stage-sitting: "I generally stand upon the Stage at a Play; talk a-loud, confound the Actors, and disturb the Audience; at which they hiss, and cry Off! Off! At which I take a pinch of Snuff, and smile ... upon which they attack us with

whole Vollies of suck'd Oranges, and chew'd Apples." Quoted in Hughes, *Patrons*, 23.

52 Dekker, *Horne-booke*, E2v.
53 Fitzgeffrey, *Satyres*, B7r–v.
54 Jonson, *Discoveries*, in Herford and Simpson, VIII.586–87 (Jonson's emphasis).
55 Jonson, *Alchemist*, A3r.
56 Jonson, *Discoveries*, in Herford and Simpson, VIII.643–44 (Jonson's emphasis).
57 In connection, see James D. Mardock, *Our Scene is London: Ben Jonson's City and the Space of the Author* (London and New York: Routledge, 2007); Holger Schott Syme, "Unediting the Margin: Jonson, Marston, and the Theatrical Page," *ELR* 38.1 (February 2008), 142–71.
58 Jonson was hardly the only playwright to adopt this strategy; I emphasize him simply because his case is the most ironic. Day's *The Isle of Gulls* depicts him backstage, "in his studie writing hard," confident of "certaine disgrace" from "the boundless hate / Of a confused Audience" (A2r–A3v); Marston's *Jack Drums Entertainment* (c. 1601) has him hijack the play, having "snatched [the book] from vs … and with violence keepes the boyes from coming on the Stage" (A2r); in *Wily Beguiled* (pr. 1606) the actors refuse to perform the author's intended play ("Spectrum"), tear down its sign, and replace it with "Wily Beguil'd," to "make him do penance" (A2r–v); Shakerly Marmion's *A Fine Companion* (pr. 1632) features a prologue in which "Critick" accuses "Author" of being a pompous gasbag, "Author" allocutes to the charges, and "Critick" then has him "Banisht the Stage" (A3r–v).
59 One is tempted to enlist into this argument Jonson's participation in the Poetomachia, in which he would be satirized onstage as Chrisogonus, Brabant Senior, and Lampatho Doria, and would return the favor to Marston and Dekker in kind. But while the episode supports the rise of a certain tabloid celebrity for playwrights of the indoor halls, the identities of these caricatures remain veiled, their valences partisan, and their animosities private. It is quite another matter to caricature *oneself*, unflatteringly, not under an allegorical mask but as the real-life author of the play the audience is watching.
60 Jonson, *Every Man Out*, C1v–C2r.
61 Jonson, *Cynthias Revels*, A2v–A3r.
62 Jonson, *Bartholomew Fair*, A4r–v.
63 *Ibid.*, A5r–A6r.
64 Jonson, *Staple of News*, C2v.
65 *Ibid.*, Aa2v, E2r, H3v.
66 *Ibid.*, H4r.
67 Jonson, *New Inne*, G7v. Jonson had known failure before, but never with such pitiful groveling, and we may read the fury of the Ode he appended as symptomatic of his shame at being no longer able to counter the "braue *plush*, and *veluet*-men" from within a body whose "nerues be shrunke, and blood be cold" (H1v–H2v). "Come Leave the Loath'd Stage" may thus express

Jonson's resolution to do just that: not to stop writing plays, but to quit starring in them.

68 Jonson, *Magnetick Lady*, A3r.
69 *Ibid.*, A4r.
70 *Ibid.*, F1v.
71 *Ibid.*, A4r, G2v.

Index

Lightning Source UK Ltd.
Milton Keynes UK
UKHW020133150622
404450UK00009B/84

9 781108 438773